THE
MEATLESS GOURMET

FAVORITE RECIPES
FROM AROUND THE WORLD

BOBBIE HINMAN

Illustrations by Vonnie Winslow Crist

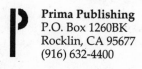
Prima Publishing
P.O. Box 1260BK
Rocklin, CA 95677
(916) 632-4400

Production by Tobi Giannone
Composition by Archetype Book Composition
Cover design by The Dunlavey Studio, Inc.
Cover photography by Kent Lacin
Food styling by Eréz

Recipes on pages 231, 408, 410, and 411 from *Burgers 'n Fries 'n Cinnamon Buns*, courtesy of The Book Publishing Co., Summertown, TN.

Library of Congress Cataloging-in-Publication Data

Hinman, Bobbie.
    The meatless gourmet : favorite recipes from around the world / Bobbie Hinman.
        p.   cm.
    Includes index.
    ISBN 1-55958-559-5
    1. Vegetarian cookery.   2. Cookery, International.   I. Title.
TX837.H56   1994
641.5´636—dc20   94-21794
                                                                  CIP

95 96 97 98 99 RRD 10 9 8 7 6 5 4

Printed in the United States of America

How to Order:
Single copies may be ordered from Prima Publishing, P.O. Box 1260BK, Rocklin, CA 95677; telephone (916) 632-4400. Quantity discounts are also available. On your letterhead, include information concerning the intended use of the books and the number of books you wish to purchase.

This book is dedicated to the love of my life, my soul mate, Harry. Thanks for testing, tasting, loving, supporting, and always being my number-one sous chef!

Special Thanks

To Reed Mangels, Ph.D., R.D., for being a good friend and my expert nutritional advisor.

To Pat Tabibian for being a good friend, a great cook, and an excellent resource person, who always knows where to find the answers.

To my invaluable recipe testers, lovingly known as the BAMMFS:

Betty Mihm
Anne Atkins
Marge Mather
Mary Whiting
Francoise Hirschberg
Sue Barbieri

To Carmen and Pedro Rivera and to Peg and Gaurang Munshi for their valuable help in reviewing recipes.

To the many friends and relatives who contributed ideas and recipe suggestions.

To my wonderful kids for putting up with me when I was stressed!

To my mom, Min Greenberg, for always believing I could do it!

To Harry, for eating, eating, eating . . .

About the Nutritional Information

Nutritional information is provided for each recipe in this book. When there is a choice between two ingredients, such as "salt-free" or "regular" tomato sauce, the breakdown is based on the first one mentioned. It is important to note that the nutritional analysis may vary slightly depending on the brands of food that are used. If a recipe contains a "trace" of a particular item (less than $1/2$ gram of protein, total fat, saturated fat, or carbohydrate or less than $1/2$ milligram of sodium or cholesterol) the number will be listed as zero.

Important

This book is not intended as a promotion or recommendation for any specific diet, nor as a substitute for your physician's advice. Its purpose is to show you how you can enjoy a balanced diet, which is low in fat and rich in fruits, vegetables, grains, and legumes.

Bobbie Hinman
"The Meatless Gourmet"

Bobbie Hinman is a pioneer in the field of lowfat cooking. She has been preparing healthy meals since she discovered, over twenty years ago, that her family has a hereditary cholesterol problem. She jokes about the fact that the rest of the world is "finally catching up to her." Determined to raise her family on a healthy lowfat diet, and aware of the fact that there were few, if any, teaching cookbooks available when she began, Bobbie set out to find ways to prepare healthy meals that are also tasty meals. She describes her transition to a vegetarian diet as a "natural progression" in her quest to master the art of healthy cooking and provide delicious meals for herself and her family. She is called "The Meatless Gourmet" because of her amazing ability to transform high-fat, meat-laden meals into healthy, meatless meals.

Bobbie is constantly in demand as a speaker and cooking teacher and has been a guest on numerous television and radio shows, including *The Regis Philbin Show* and *The Low Cholesterol Gourmet*. She also completed a media tour for General Mills, where she discussed the benefits of eating a lowfat, high-fiber diet. She is a consultant at Coolfont Resort and Spa in Berkeley Springs, West Virginia, where she teaches regular cooking classes. Bobbie is co-author of the *Lean and Luscious* series, bestselling books of easy lowfat recipes. She is the author of *Oat Cuisine,* a unique book of tasty high-fiber recipes, and *Burgers 'n Fries 'n Cinnamon Buns,* a collection of lowfat, meatless recipes for fast-food favorites. In addition to writing cooking columns for several monthly publications, Bobbie is a frequent contributor to *The Vegetarian Journal*. She also travels extensively, teaching classes and speaking to hospital groups, at cardiac centers, weight management centers, colleges, and private organizations.

Even with her busy schedule, Bobbie finds time to read as many health publications as possible and to consult with doctors, dietitians, and other health professionals. Her goal is to keep abreast of the latest advances in food and health issues so that she can continue to help people enjoy the benefits of healthful eating.

Bobbie resides in Delaware with her husband, Harry. They have four grown children.

Contents

Introduction

I believe this book is being published at an ideal time. More and more health professionals are encouraging consumers to cut back on fat, and meatless meals are finding a welcome place in the lives of more Americans. This does not mean that all Americans are becoming vegetarians, but many are now eating meatless meals at least several times a week.

More than ever, American shoppers are motivated by health concerns, especially about fats and cholesterol, and are turning *away* from meats and *toward* meals that are based on whole grains, fruits, and vegetables. American attitudes about the need to eat meat every day are changing, and with health experts agreeing that a diet with little or no meat *can* be a balanced diet, shoppers are reacting. Concerned about fats and cholesterol, and looking to add more fiber to their meals, they are choosing more vegetable-based meals and cutting back on the saturated fat found in meat and dairy products.

Surprisingly, some people seem to be leery of meatless meals, afraid that these meals will leave them feeling hungry and deprived. I have found just the opposite to be true. Because meatless meals can be made to contain less fat and fewer calories, they can be eaten in large quantities without the negative side effects associated with large amounts of fat and cholesterol. You can eat a huge amount of pasta (in a meatless sauce), for example, and never come close to consuming the amount of fat you would consume if you ate a small piece of meat.

Ethnic meals are becoming more popular, especially meals that de-emphasize meat. Many people regularly enjoy ethnic favorites without actually realizing that these foods are meatless. Bean burritos, pizza, and chop suey, for example, are extremely popular meatless foods. Other cultures have already figured out how to make satisfying meals that are not dependent on meat, and it's not surprising to learn that many of their people have a lower incidence of the diseases that are believed to be diet-related. It's a known fact that lower rates of chronic disease exist in countries where diet focuses on fresh fruits, vegetables, grains, breads, and beans. The Chinese and Japanese, for example, use very small amounts of meat and fish and round out their meals with lots of vegetables and rice. As a result, people in these countries consume a lot more fiber and a lot less fat than most Americans.

One of the challenges in writing this book has been to create meatless meals that are not only low in fat and high in fiber, but are also easy to prepare, filling, and most of all, appealing to the meat-eating majority. I have adapted the recipes and flavor principles from other countries, substituting familiar ingredients for the less familiar, and at the same time, accommodating today's needs for quick and easy recipes. In many cases I felt I had to substitute authenticity for ease, to keep you (and me!) from running all over town looking for a specific ingredient or type of cooking utensil. Now you can enjoy the diverse flavors of the world in your own home.

Another challenge was to classify each country's cuisine. There is such a cross-over of cultures today, that no matter how I tried to "corral" the foods into different countries, they kept "jumping the fence." The world truly is a melting pot of flavors.

I have enjoyed this culinary journey immensely and I have learned so much about other cultures and their traditions. I sincerely hope this book will inspire you to make many new and different vegetable-based meals and to always remember that your mother was right—"Vegetables are good for you!"

Enjoy your travels!

Basics of Meatless Meals

Whenever I tell people that I am a vegetarian, I invariably get lots of questions (and sometimes strange looks!). Following are the most frequently asked questions. In answering them, I have tried to take today's complicated health concerns and make them easy to understand and to apply.

What Are the Health Benefits of Meatless Meals?

Scientific studies have consistently shown that the higher the consumption of meat and high-fat dairy products, the higher the risk of heart disease, certain types of cancer, and possibly other diseases as well. On the other hand, studies have shown that the frequency of heart disease and cancer *decrease* as the consumption of fruits and vegetables *increase*.

Meatless meals are also a good source of carbohydrates, the "fuel" that gives our bodies energy. In countries where high-carbohydrate diets, based on fruits, vegetables, grains, and beans are the norm, there are lower incidences of the diseases that appear to be linked to high-fat foods. The old way of thinking was that foods such as pasta and potatoes were "fattening." Now we know that pasta and potatoes are high in energy-producing carbohydrates, and the only fattening part is what we put on them!

What Are the Main Components of Meatless Meals?

The main components of meatless meals are fruits, vegetables, grains, and beans (legumes). Like any other meals, meatless meals should be balanced and consist of a wide variety of foods. Simply eliminating the meat from your diet is not enough. The rest of your food should be fresh and wholesome, with as few packaged or processed ingredients as possible. In other words, if you give up the steak, but the rest of the meal consists of fried potatoes, iceberg lettuce, pastries, and beer, you are definitely on the wrong track!

Consume ample portions each day of:

Fruits   all types, preferably fresh
Vegetables   green, such as broccoli, kale, spinach, cabbage, and romaine lettuce, and yellow, such as carrots, squash, sweet potatoes, and pumpkin
Grains   whole, such as brown rice, corn, millet, oats, bulgur, barley, buckwheat, and wheat (including breads, pasta, and cereals)
Legumes   lentils, split peas, soy beans (including tofu), navy, kidney, pinto, lima, black, etc.

But Will I Get Enough Protein?

Most people are unaware that there is high-quality protein in vegetables, grains, nuts, seeds, and legumes. You can get protein and fiber without all the fat and cholesterol that comes from meat. Also, contrary to what we once believed, it is not necessary to combine proteins at each meal. The answer is to eat a balanced diet and include a variety of protein-rich foods each day. For instance, the protein from oatmeal for breakfast, peanut butter on whole wheat bread for lunch, and lentil casserole and broccoli for dinner, will all "find each other" and combine so that your body can utilize them.

Fat and Cholesterol

The subject of fat and cholesterol can be very confusing. Many people do not realize that fat and cholesterol are *not* the same thing.

What Is the Difference Between Fat and Cholesterol?

Cholesterol is a substance that is produced by the body and is used in the production of body tissues. We also get cholesterol from consuming foods that contain cholesterol. When faced with more cholesterol than the body can handle, the response is to "store" the excess cholesterol in the arteries. Health professionals feel that this is a major factor in the development of heart disease.

No plant contains cholesterol; it is only found in animal foods. However, some plant foods are relatively high in fat, so, while large amounts of them do not actually contain cholesterol, they still contribute too much fat to the diet and may raise cholesterol levels in the blood. These high-fat foods should be consumed in moderation. They include nuts, nut butters, coconut, olives, avocados, margarine, and vegetable oils. Be sure to read labels carefully and be aware that some advertisers may tout the advantages of their products as being *cholesterol-free*, but fail to mention the possible *high-fat* content of the ingredients.

Which Foods Contain Cholesterol?

Remember that *only animal products contain cholesterol.* This includes meat, poultry, seafood, dairy products, egg yolks (the egg white contains no cholesterol), and animal fats such as butter, chicken fat, suet, and lard. However, remember that any fat with a high percentage of saturated fat can also potentially raise your blood-cholesterol level. Vegetable sources with a high percentage of saturated fat include palm kernel oil, coconut, and coconut oil.

What Is the Difference Between Saturated and Unsaturated Fat?

Different fats affect the body in different ways. Saturated fats are thicker fats that are solid at room temperature. They tend to elevate blood-cholesterol levels. Unsaturated fats are liquid at room temperature and it is believed that they generally do not raise blood-cholesterol levels. Many health professionals recommend that we use the fats that contain the lowest amounts of *saturated* fat and the highest amount of *monounsaturated* fat. The better choices include olive oil and canola oil. (In all of my recipes that call for vegetable oil, I have used canola oil.) But remember that these are still all fat and should be consumed in moderation.

How Much Fat Should I Eat?

Many health professionals recommend that we get less than 30 percent of our total daily calories from fat. Still others feel that we should go as low as 10 percent. Most however, are somewhere in the middle. Of the total amount, most should come from unsaturated fat. No one is suggesting that you keep a calculator nearby whenever you eat. However, it is a good idea to keep track of your fat grams for a few days to see what you are actually consuming. You may be surprised. Many unsuspected foods contain hidden fats that can really add up if you are not careful. (See page 6.)

To figure your own daily-fat allowance, multiply your daily calorie intake by .3 to find 30 percent of calories, or by .2 to find 20 percent of calories. Then divide your answer by 9 for the number of fat grams that you would be allowed each day.

For example: 1500 calories x .30 = 450 ÷ 9 = 50 grams of fat daily

Total Daily Calories	Number of Fat Grams Daily 30% of Calories From Fat	Number of Fat Grams Daily 20% of Calories From Fat
1200	40	27
1500	50	33
2000	67	44
2500	83	56

Remember that fat grams are figured *by the day*, not by the individual food. If you eat a little more fat at one meal you can compensate by eating less fat at other meals. Ideally, the formula should be used to evaluate your daily or weekly diet, rather than single foods.

Are Some Fats Better Than Others?

A tablespoon of any oil contains 120 calories and 14 grams of fat. However, many researchers feel that the use of oils that are mostly monounsaturated, such as olive oil and canola oil, may contribute to lower rates of heart disease. Remember that these oils are still fat, and should be used in moderation.

What Is Hydrogenated Fat?

Hydrogenated fat is formed when hydrogen is added to liquid oil, a process used by many dessert manufacturers and fast food companies to add both texture and shelf life to their products. Hydrogenated fat is also found in margarine and peanut butter (except in "natural" peanut butter.) Hydrogenation changes an oil by making it more saturated, thereby giving it the potential to raise blood-cholesterol levels. If a manufacturer brags about the vegetable shortening used in a product, but the ingredient list indicates that this is a hydrogenated fat, be aware that the product contains saturated fat.

Which Foods Contain the Most Fat?

The foods that are highest in saturated fat are butter, whole milk dairy products, meat, poultry, eggs, and also the recipes and products that contain them. This includes mayonnaise, cheese, puddings, and chocolate products.

Where Are the Hidden Fats?

Many people are surprised to learn that foods such as crackers may contain very high amounts of (often saturated) fat. Other potential sources of hidden fats are some cereals (usually the granola types), non-dairy coffee creamers, whipped toppings, snack foods, and even the seemingly innocent foods such as packaged popcorn and dry bread crumbs. The answer here is to *always read the labels and ingredients carefully.*

Which Is Better, Butter or Margarine?

A tablespoon of butter or regular margarine contains 12 grams of fat. Butter however, is comprised mostly of saturated fat. Margarine that lists a liquid oil as its first ingredient would be a better choice. Many tub-style margarines are whipped with water (diet margarine), so water appears as the first ingredient and the liquid oil appears as the second ingredient. The good news about this type of margarine is that the fat has been "diluted" with water, so each serving has a lower overall fat content. Whether you choose butter or margarine, remember that moderation is the key.

What About Dairy Products?

When choosing dairy products, always choose those that are lowest in fat and cholesterol. Choose skim milk, nonfat yogurt, evaporated skim milk, buttermilk, nonfat dry milk, and nonfat or reduced-fat cheeses. If you want "meltability," the reduced-fat cheeses generally melt better than the nonfat ones.

Many people either are unable to, or choose not to, eat dairy products for a variety of reasons. Fortunately there are many new reduced-fat soy and rice-based substitutes on the market today, including milk and cheese. I have found these to work in any recipe that calls for dairy products.

What About Eggs?

In recipes that call for eggs, two egg whites can be substituted for each whole egg, thereby eliminating the cholesterol (found only in the yolk), and lowering the fat content. Commercial egg substitutes will also work. These are made from egg whites and you may want to compare the price to that of regular egg whites. If you want to eliminate the eggs completely, a three-ounce piece of tofu, blended until smooth, can be substituted for one whole egg (or two egg whites) in baked goods. There are also several completely egg-free egg substitutes available in health food stores.

What About Sugar?

Whatever your choice of sweetener, whether it's sugar, honey, molasses, or maple syrup, the nutritional values are about the same. When our well-meaning mothers told us that foods such as chocolate, cake, and pastry were "fattening," we all assumed that the sugar was causing the bulges. Now we know that the fat in these products is the culprit. The main goal is to reduce the total amount of fat called for in a recipe, and to remember that moderation is the key.

What About Calories?

It's a difficult concept to "swallow," but counting calories is out! It's the fat that's clogging our arteries, not the calories! No one is saying that you can eat everything in sight without regard to calories, but pay attention to the amount of fat in foods and make sure that in your daily diet you consume no more than 20 to 30 percent of your calories from fat. If you do this and plan your diet around fresh fruits, vegetables, whole grains, and beans, you will automatically eat fewer calories. Isn't it nice that most of the *foods that are low in fat are also low in calories?*

Fiber

Fiber is the flip-side of the coin. We always think of cutting back on things, but fiber is something that we actually need more of. Isn't it convenient that most of the *foods that are low in fat are also high in fiber?!*

What Is Fiber?

The word fiber refers to the indigestible parts of plant food, such as pectin, cellulose, and bran. In recent years there has been quite a lot of publicity about fiber. The reason for this is that studies have shown that a high-fiber diet may be our first line of defense against heart disease and several forms of cancer. One particular type of fiber—water-soluble fiber—may significantly lower blood-cholesterol levels. This type of fiber is abundant in many plant foods including oats, apples, figs, prunes, carrots, plums, squash, barley, kidney beans, split peas, and chick peas. The other type of fiber—insoluble fiber—is found in whole grains such as cornmeal and whole wheat flour (especially wheat bran), and in fruits and vegetables such as broccoli, cabbage, raspberries, and strawberries. This type of fiber seems to improve intestinal function and many researchers feel that it may help in preventing some types of cancer. It is important to have both types of fiber in our diet. Our grandmothers were right about fiber. They called it roughage and *knew* it was good for us.

Remember that *fiber is only found in plant foods*. No animal food contains this important nutrient.

How Much Fiber Do I Need?

Many health professionals recommend that we boost our intake of fiber-rich foods, preferably to between 25 and 30 grams a day. Remember that fresh fruits and vegetables, as well as whole grains and legumes are our main sources of fiber and we need to have several servings of each of these foods every day. *Meat and dairy products contain no fiber.*

How Can I Add More Fiber to My Meals?

Here are some quick and easy ways to add fiber to your meals:

- Choose whole-grain breads, crackers, and pasta.
- Choose breakfast cereals made from whole grains.
- Make your own bread crumbs from toasted whole-grain bread.
- Add peas, beans, and lentils to soups, stews, and salads.
- Leave the skin on fruits and vegetables whenever possible.
- Add grated vegetables to sauces and casseroles.
- Use puréed vegetables to thicken soups and stews.
- Make tossed salads using vegetables of all colors.
- Eat fresh or dried fruit for snacks and desserts.
- Use brown rice in place of white rice and try other whole grains, such as oats, millet, barley, and wheat.
- Add cooked grains to soups and casseroles.
- Replace at least half the flour in baked goods with whole wheat flour.

Sodium

We hear a lot about sodium. Here are some frequently asked questions.

What Is Sodium?

Sodium is a mineral that occurs naturally in many foods. Most of the sodium in the American diet however, comes from table salt and from sodium that is added to processed foods and beverages. It is added for flavor and as a preservative and sometimes appears under different names, such as sodium citrate, sodium nitrate, and sodium phosphate.

The problem is that too much sodium can contribute to high blood pressure. Although some sodium is essential to our health, the recommendation from many health professionals is that we limit our daily sodium intake to between 2,400 and 3,000 milligrams, or about 1 to 1¹/₂ teaspoons of salt. (Sounds easy until you read the ingredients and labels on packaged foods!) *Most plant foods are relatively low in sodium,* making them especially helpful in controlling high blood pressure.

Here are some helpful hints for reducing sodium in your diet:

- Use herbs and spices in place of salt.
- Always taste food before adding salt.
- Choose reduced-sodium or salt-free canned foods whenever available.
- Rinse canned foods, such as beans, to remove salt.
- Choose reduced-sodium soy sauce and other condiments.
- Don't add salt to boiling water when cooking pasta.
- Read labels carefully.

Basic Substitutions

Instead of:	Try:
Whole eggs	Two egg whites in place of each egg, or egg substitutes (In cakes and muffins, a 3-ounce piece of tofu will also work in place of 1 egg.)
Whole milk	Skim milk or reduced-fat soy or other non-dairy milk
Cream	Evaporated skim milk or plain nonfat yogurt
Sour cream	Plain nonfat yogurt (For a cooked sauce, blend 1 tablespoon of cornstarch into each cup of yogurt before heating. Do not boil.)
Ice cream	Ice milk or reduced-fat soy-based or other non-dairy frozen desserts
Whipped cream (as a dessert topping)	Vanilla nonfat yogurt
Chicken or beef broth	*Vegetable Broth* or water mixed with *Vegetable Broth Mix* (See pages 26–27.)
Mayonnaise	Half reduced-calorie mayonnaise and half plain nonfat yogurt
Butter	Margarine that lists a liquid oil as the first ingredient, or vegetable oil (However, all are high in fat and should be used sparingly.)

Vegetable oil	An oil with a high amount of monounsaturated fat such as olive oil or canola oil
Salad dressings with lots of oil	Replace half the oil with water or fruit juice
Cheese	Reduced-fat cheese or reduced-fat soy or other non-dairy cheese (Many reduced-fat cheeses are still relatively high in fat and sodium and should be used sparingly. Many are also loaded with chemicals and don't melt or even taste like cheese.)
Sugar	Use *half* the amount called for (This works in most recipes, except cookies.)
White rice	Brown rice or other whole grains
All-purpose flour	Replace half with whole wheat flour
French fries	Baked potatoes (with a lowfat topping such as nonfat yogurt and chopped chives)
Frying	Grilling, baking, roasting, or broiling

Bean Basics

Legumes are the dried seeds of certain pod-bearing plants. We call them simply "beans." They have long been a major part of the diets in India, Asia, Central and South America, and the Middle East. They have recently gained popularity in Europe and America due to their nutritional value and also their very low cost. Dried beans come in many shapes, colors, flavors, and textures.

Nutritional Information

Legumes contain high levels of protein, complex carbohydrates, and fiber, along with minerals and B vitamins. They are low in fat and sodium and contain no cholesterol.

What to Look For

Legumes are available year round and are usually sold in clear plastic bags. Choose beans with a uniform size and color, without a lot of cracking or holes. One pound of dried beans equals about two cups and will yield approximately six cups of cooked beans.

How to Store Beans

Stored in tightly-covered containers in a cool, dry place, legumes can be kept for six to nine months. Cooked beans can be refrigerated for up to one week and they can also be frozen for four to six months. They thaw quickly and are ready for use.

About Canned Beans

Canned beans are already cooked and ready to use. However, they usually contain salt and should be rinsed well and drained before using. In most of the recipes I refer to one-pound cans. Can sizes do vary, but as long as they are close to one pound, the recipes will not be affected. A one-pound can contains approximately two cups of beans.

Avoid Stomach Upset

Often people complain of gastric distress after eating beans. Sometimes the problem is not as much from the beans as it is from simply eating too much fiber, without allowing time for your body to become accustomed to a new type of diet. The good news is that with most people, the distress is temporary and disappears as their bodies become used to a high-fiber diet. Here are a few other hints to help you:

- Start by eating small portions of beans and gradually increase the serving size as your body becomes accustomed to them.
- Always chew your food thoroughly.
- Try different varieties of beans to see if some types affect you less than others.
- Start with canned beans which are cooked longer and tend to cause fewer stomach problems.
- Try lentils, which also tend to be less problematic.

Preparation Tips

- Always sort through the beans first to remove any stones, dirt, or discolored beans.
- Beans should be rinsed before using.
- With the exception of split peas and lentils, all dried beans need to be soaked before cooking.
- Legumes should always be simmered; rapid boiling will break them apart.

- Keep the lid of the pot partially open to keep the beans from boiling over.
- Stir beans occasionally while cooking and add additional water if necessary.

Cooking Legumes

Before cooking, beans need to be soaked in order to restore the water lost in drying. (This does not hold true for split peas and lentils, which do not require soaking.) Soak the beans, using either of the two following methods. Then, using 2 to 3 cups of water for each cup of beans, bring the water to a boil and add the beans. Reduce heat to low, cover partially, and simmer for the amount of time specified, or until beans are tender. Cooking times may vary depending on size, quality, and freshness of the legumes.

Quick soaking method   Place beans in a pot and add enough water to cover beans by three inches. Bring to a boil over medium heat. Boil two minutes. Remove from heat, cover, and let stand two hours. Drain and cook as directed.

Overnight soaking method   Place beans in a bowl and add enough water to cover beans by three inches. Soak overnight. Drain and cook as directed.

Cooking Times for Legumes

Black beans	1 to 2 hours
Black-eyed peas	30 to 45 minutes
Garbanzo beans	2 to 3 hours
Great Northern beans	1 to $1^1/_2$ hours
Kidney beans	$1^1/_2$ to 2 hours
Lentils	30 to 45 minutes
Lima beans	1 to $1^1/_2$ hours
Navy beans	$1^1/_2$ to 2 hours
Pinto beans	$1^1/_2$ to 2 hours
Soy beans	2 to 3 hours
Split peas	30 to 45 minutes

Cooking times are for soaked beans, except for split peas and lentils, which do not require soaking.

Grain Basics

Grains add different tastes and textures, as well as fiber and important nutrients to the diet. A variety of grains are used all over the world and we are lucky that virtually all of them are available to us in this country. Occasionally, you may have to visit a specialty store to find a particular grain, but large grocery stores are meeting the demand, and more and more of them are stocking large varieties of grains. Remember that grains are not just for dinner. Leftover grains topped with cinnamon and raisins, with added milk or orange juice, make a tasty, nutritious breakfast.

Nutritional Information

Grains are actually the seed kernels of certain plants. *Whole grains* have the bran and germ still intact and therefore contain more fiber and B vitamins than grains that have been *milled* or *polished*. (For example, brown rice, which is more nutritious than white rice, has had the bran and germ removed by milling.)

Grains are also an important source of carbohydrates, which provide fuel and energy to our bodies. The fiber in whole grains is also believed by health professionals to help protect us from heart disease and possibly some forms of cancer. (See *What Is Fiber?* on page 8.)

An ideal goal would be to add a variety of grains to the diet, supplying different nutrients and an assortment of flavors and textures.

What to Look For

Grains are available year round and are usually found packaged or in bulk in health food stores and most large grocery stores. Health food stores also carry many unusual grains, such as triticale, teff, quinoa, spelt, and job's tears. (I hope this will peak your interest and you will seek them out!)

Forms of Grains

Grains are available in several forms:

Whole grains   Called groats, these are the entire kernel with the bran and germ intact. Examples are brown rice, wheat berries, barley, and millet.

Cracked grains The entire kernel is cracked into small pieces, allowing the grains to cook more quickly. They are minimally processed
and contain most of their original vitamins. Examples are cracked
wheat and steel-cut oats.

Flakes The entire kernel is flattened and steamed allowing it to cook
quickly. An example is rolled oats, however, wheat and barley are
also available as flakes and make delicious breakfast cereals. The
"quick" or "instant" varieties are further processed, which reduces
their nutritional value.

Flour Most grains can be ground into flour. Whole wheat flour is
made from the entire kernel, unlike all-purpose flour that is made
from wheat and has been milled. *Stone-ground whole wheat flour* is
the best nutritionally because it is actually ground between heavy
stones using water power, and no artificial enrichment is added.
However, it is a little heavier than commercial whole wheat flour.
Unbleached flour is all-purpose flour that has been allowed to
whiten naturally, rather than chemically bleached like all-purpose
flour. It has a slightly higher protein content than all-purpose flour
and contains more vitamin E, which is lost during chemical
whitening. Unbleached flour is available in health food stores and
most large grocery stores and can be used wherever all-purpose
flour is called for.

How to Store Grains

Whole grains contain the germ that is rich in oil, making them
more susceptible to rancidity than milled grains. Cracked grains also
become rancid quickly because the oily germ is exposed. Therefore, it
is best to buy both of these types of grains in small quantities and
store them in airtight containers in the refrigerator, where they will
keep for several months. It is also wise to buy from a store that you
know has a rapid turnover.

Milled grains have a longer shelf life and can be stored in a cool,
dry place in airtight containers for up to one year.

Cooking Grains

Most packaged grains are clean, however, if you buy grains in
bulk, you may find bits of chaff or weeds among the grains, so it is
wise to pick over the grains before cooking.

Following are cooking times for a selection of the most popular grains. Generally, unless otherwise stated, they are stirred into boiling water, covered, the heat is reduced, and they are simmered until the grains are tender and most of the liquid has been absorbed. If the grain is not soft enough, add a small amount of hot liquid and cook a little longer. Grains can be cooked in water *or* broth.

It is important to remember that cooking times are approximate and may vary slightly depending on the size and quality of the grains. Grains with similar cooking times can be combined and cooked together.

Grain	Amount	Water	Cooking Method	Cooking Time	Yield
Barley	1 cup	4 cups	Add to boiling water	45 min	3$^1/_2$ cups
Kasha	1 cup	3 cups	Toast in pan and add boiling water	15 min	3$^1/_2$ cups
Bulgur	1 cup	2 cups	Add to boiling water	15 min	3 cups
Cornmeal	1 cup	3 cups	Add to boiling water	25 min	4 cups
Millet	1 cup	2 cups	Add to boiling water	20 min	3 cups
Rolled oats	1 cup	2 cups	Add to boiling water	5 to 8 min	1$^3/_4$ cups
Oats, steel-cut	1 cup	3$^1/_2$ cups	Add to boiling water	20 min	3 cups
Rice, brown	1 cup	2$^1/_2$ cups	Add to boiling water	45 min	3$^1/_2$ cups
Wheat berries	1 cup	3$^1/_2$ cups	Add to boiling water	40 to 60 min	3 cups

Cooking Brown Rice in a Microwave

It may not save a lot of time, but it is easy to cook brown rice in a microwave. Be sure to use an extra-large microwaveable casserole to prevent overflow (a 1³/₄-quart bowl or casserole is ideal for 1 cup of uncooked rice) and *do not* cover the casserole.

Place 1 cup of uncooked brown rice in the casserole and add 2¹/₂ cups of water or broth. Microwave on 100 percent power for 10 minutes, then 60 percent power for 20 minutes. Cover rice and let stand 5 minutes. Fluff with a fork before serving.

Note: Cooking times may vary according to the power and type of microwave used and you may have to make adjustments to fit your particular oven.

What Is Tofu?

When adapting recipes to make them meatless and lower in fat I often replace the meat with tofu. Probably few products are less understood than this versatile food. Many people have told me they have bought tofu, brought it home, unwrapped it, taken a big bite, and can't for the life of them understand how I can call it delicious! Well, by itself it isn't. It's actually rather bland and almost tasteless. The secret lies in how it is prepared.

Tofu, also known as bean curd (both unfortunate names!), is a protein food produced from soybeans. The process is similar to that of making cheese in that a coagulating agent is added to soy milk, causing the milk to separate into curds and whey.

Nutritional Information

Tofu is a superior source of protein and essential minerals and vitamins. Tofu is entirely free of cholesterol, very low in saturated fat, and also low in calories. Tofu is a good source of calcium, iron, phosphorus, potassium, sodium, essential B vitamins, and vitamin E. Clearly it is a nutritious alternative protein source that contributes to a healthy diet.

Types of Tofu

Tofu is available in a variety of forms that can be used in countless ways:

- *Regular or medium tofu* It has a soft texture resembling that of cheesecake and can be used in casseroles and in tofu "cheese-cakes."
- *Firm tofu* It is more solid and dense and is ideal for stir-frying.
- *Silken tofu* It has a smooth, custardy texture and is ideal for dips and sauces. Many large grocery stores carry 10-ounce aseptic packages of silken tofu (Mori-Nu® brand).

Note: Reduced-fat tofu is now available in all forms.

How to Store Tofu

Pre-packaged tofu is available in the produce section of most large grocery stores. Fresh tofu is also widely available in many health food stores. When buying packaged tofu, always check the date on the container to be sure it is fresh. When you get home, open the package, drain the water, add fresh water, cover, and refrigerate. The water should be changed every one to two days, and the tofu can be kept up to ten days. (This is not true of the tofu in aseptic packages, which can be stored at room temperature and opened just before using. Once opened it should be refrigerated, but not in water.)

Freezing Tofu

Tofu can easily be frozen, but the texture will change dramatically. Frozen tofu becomes slightly yellow in color and the texture becomes somewhat chewy and more meat-like. It can still be used in most recipes (except desserts), although the results will be different. To freeze tofu, remove it from the water and wrap it securely. To thaw, place the tofu in a heat-proof bowl and cover it with boiling water. Drain after 10 minutes and if tofu is still frozen repeat the process. Gently press the tofu between the palms of both hands to squeeze out the water before using. Tofu can also be thawed overnight in the refrigerator.

Is Tofu Expensive?

Along with tofu's high nutritional profile, here's an added bonus—it's very inexpensive. An entire meal consisting of tofu, vegetables, and whole grains can usually be prepared for a fraction of the cost of a meat-based meal.

Fruit and Vegetable Basics

Eat Your Fruits and Vegetables

Health experts recommend that we eat at least five servings of fruits and vegetables each day. And think of it—they contain vitamins, minerals, fiber, and almost *no fat at all*. Most fruits can be eaten raw and most vegetables can be eaten either raw or cooked. Generally, the longer vegetables are cooked, the more nutrients are lost. So remember one of my cardinal rules that says to "cook vegetables only until they are tender-crisp." Ideally, they should be steamed rather than boiled. Texture is an important factor when cooking vegetables. Nothing is less appealing than a plate of soggy veggies!

Wash Fruits and Vegetables

Always wash fruits and vegetables just before preparing. Do not soak them in water unless necessary because this may draw out some of the valuable vitamins. Vegetables such as leeks, romaine lettuce, and spinach are usually very sandy and should be washed well under running water to remove grit.

Leave the Skin On

Whenever possible, do not peel fruits or vegetables. There are valuable nutrients and fiber both in and under the skin that are lost in peeling. However, if you buy produce that has been waxed, such as apples or cucumbers, you *should* peel them.

Storage

In an ideal world, it would be nutritionally best to buy and eat freshly picked fruits and vegetables each day. However, for most of us this is quite impossible. It is best to use fruits and vegetables as soon as possible and to always store them in the refrigerator, preferably in the vegetable crisper. In addition, most vegetables will keep better if they are stored unwashed and then washed before preparing.

How to Select and Store Fruits and Vegetables

When shopping for vegetables, try to choose those that are bright in color and firm in texture. The healthy-looking vegetables that have deep, rich colors will contain more vitamins than the limp, pale ones.

Basic Steaming Directions for Vegetables

Steaming vegetables preserves much of their flavor and texture and keeps vitamin loss to a minimum. (There *are* some vegetables that are usually boiled or baked, such as beets and potatoes.) If you do choose to boil a vegetable, add just enough water to cover the vegetable, and be sure to save the cooking liquid to add to soups and sauces.

Always wash and trim vegetables before using. Place a steamer basket or rack in the bottom of a saucepan and add water almost up to, but not touching, the rack. Bring the water to a boil and add the vegetables. Cover and cook just until vegetables are tender-crisp. Cooking times will depend on the freshness and variety of the vegetables.

A word of caution: When removing the cover from a steaming pot, always open it *away* from you so as not to burn yourself.

Spices of the World

It has been said that "variety is the spice of life," but for food lovers, spice is the variety of life! Probably no other ingredients have changed the shape of world history and helped to define cultures as much as spices. Some cuisines depend heavily on the use of spices, and others hardly at all. But it is rare to find a dish anywhere in the world that has not been enhanced by spices in some way.

Herbs and spices are vital to cooking, especially when we are trying to reduce fat in our food and still keep the flavor. With the move toward *removing* so much from our food, let's concentrate instead on *adding* flavor. Herbs and spices enhance the flavor of food, without adding fat, sodium, or unwanted calories.

Most of the recipes in this book call for dried herbs and spices, which are readily available and easy to store and use. However, if you wish to substitute fresh herbs and spices, you will need to use two to three times the amount called for. Always keep dried herbs and spices in airtight containers away from heat and light. Buy packaged spices in small quantities because they will lose quality if stored for long periods of time. Be sure to buy from stores that have a fast turnover. Try not to keep dried spices for longer than six months to one year. If you are lucky enough to find a store that carries spices in bulk, you can buy small amounts at a time, giving you the added benefit of trying new flavors without investing a lot of money.

Note: We often use the terms spices and herbs interchangeably, but spices are actually derived from the seeds, bark, roots, flowers, and fruits of certain plants, and herbs are the aromatic leaves.

People's tastes differ greatly and therefore it is difficult to give exact amounts for seasoning. The recipes in this book contain suggested amounts. One important rule to remember is that when using an herb or spice for the first time, go easy. Remember—you can always add more!

Following is a list of some of the most commonly used herbs and spices, along with a few suggested uses for each one:

Allspice   This reddish-brown berry tastes somewhat like a blend of cloves, cinnamon, and nutmeg. Although it is native to the Western hemisphere, it is popular all over Europe. Ground allspice is used in stews, vegetables such as sweet potatoes and squash, and desserts such as spice cake and apple pie. Whole allspice is often added to the liquid when poaching fruit.

Aniseed   These tiny oval seeds, grown in the Mediterranean, have a delicate licorice-like flavor. They are often used in Italian cookies and cakes, and also in Oriental and Eastern European salads and vegetable dishes.

Basil   This aromatic herb is available fresh or dried and is a popular addition to Mexican, Italian, Indian, Greek, and Middle Eastern dishes. It goes well with almost any tomato dish and is also delicious with any type of cheese. To store fresh basil, wrap it in damp paper towels, then place in a plastic bag in the refrigerator for up to a few days. Pluck off the leaves just before using them.

Bay Leaf   This aromatic herb originated in Turkey and is used most often in soups, stews, and tomato sauces throughout the Mediterranean region and Europe. Always remove and discard the bay leaf before serving a dish.

Caraway Seed   A popular Eastern European ingredient, these seeds are especially good in rye bread and also in cabbage, cheese, and noodle dishes.

Cardamom   This pungent spice has a mildly fragrant, slightly lemon-like flavor and is available in pod, seed, or powdered form. It is native to India, is often used in Indian and Middle Eastern dishes, and is an important ingredient in curries. The pods can be added to beverages, such as punch or coffee, and the ground seeds are often added to fruit dishes and cakes.

Cayenne   This is the ground, dried pod of hot red peppers (chilies). It is used in many Mexican and Indian dishes, and will add "heat" to entrees and vegetables.

Celery Seed   The seed of the celery plant is used in many Indian and Mediterranean dishes. It is used in soups and stews and is also good in salads, such as slaws and potato salads.

Chili Powder   This is a seasoning blend that usually consists of chili peppers, oregano, cumin, garlic, and salt. The spiciness will vary with the blend, and authentic Mexican cooks always blend their own seasonings. It is used in Mexican dishes such as chili, tacos, and enchiladas, and also in guacamole and other dips and sauces.

Chives   These small, hollow green stems have a mild onion flavor. They are available fresh or dried and make an ideal garnish for vegetables and cheese dishes.

Cilantro   See *Coriander*.

Cinnamom   Available in stick or powder form, cinnamon originated in China and is the bark of a tree. It is probably the most important baking spice and is used as a flavoring for entrees, as well as desserts, in many parts of the world. Whole cinnamon sticks can be used to stir hot drinks such as coffee, tea, and cocoa. Ground cinnamon is used in all types of baked goods and also in vegetables such as squash and sweet potatoes.

Clove   This dark-colored spice originated in China and is available both whole and in powdered form. It has a strong, pungent flavor and is often used in combination with cinnamon to flavor breads and cakes. It can also be added to vegetables such as squash and sweet potatoes. Whole cloves are often used in pickling fruits and vegetables.

Coriander   This plant yields both aromatic coriander leaves (cilantro, or Chinese parsley), which are often used in Asian and Latin American cooking, and seeds that are used whole or ground into powder. The seeds and the leaves have two entirely different flavors. The seeds are an ingredient in most commercial curry powders and are also good in soups and in some desserts, such as apple dishes and bread pudding. The leaves have a somewhat musty flavor and are almost always used fresh. Often they are added just before a dish is served.

Cream of Tartar   This white powder is used when beating egg whites to stabilize them.

Cumin These small, yellowish seeds are used whole or ground into powder. Mexican, Middle Eastern, and Indian dishes rely heavily on its flavor and it is a mainstay in both chili powder and curry powder. It adds an earthy flavor to chili, tacos, enchiladas, and corn chips.

Curry Powder This is actually a blend of spices, rather than one spice. It is used to flavor Indian dishes, and authentic Indian cooks always prepare their own blends, which may vary. A typical blend consists of coriander, chili peppers, cumin, mustard seeds, peppercorns, fenugreek seeds, and turmeric. Curry powder is used to flavor entrees as well as vegetable dishes and fruit compotes.

Dill Seed A native of Europe, dill seed has a stronger, slightly different flavor than dill weed. It is used in making pickles and also in salads such as slaws and potato salads.

Dill Weed This green herb comes from the feathery green leaves of the dill plant. It can be purchased dried or fresh. It is very popular in both Middle Eastern and Eastern European cooking and adds an almost evergreen flavor to vegetables, cheese dishes, and grains. It also makes a nice garnish.

Fennel Seed These small, yellowish-brown seeds have a sweet, licorice-like flavor, and are popular in Indian, Italian, and Oriental cooking. They are used in tomato-based sauces, pickles, breads and pastries.

Garlic This edible bulb of the garlic plant, with its strong, pungent flavor is popular worldwide and has been used in cooking since recorded history. Fresh garlic is preferable, but garlic powder may also be used, with $1/8$ teaspoon powder equal to one medium clove. Its uses are endless—in salads, soups, entrees, breads, vegetables, etc.

Ginger Fresh ginger root is not actually a root, but a pungent plant that is used extensively in Oriental and Indian cooking. Whole ginger can be chopped or grated and used in vegetable dishes, marinades, and stir-fries. (It isn't necessary to peel fresh ginger.) Dried, ground ginger is essential to gingerbread and is also used in cookies and apple pie, and in vegetables such as carrots and sweet potatoes.

Mace Mace is the outer covering of the nutmeg fruit, and the spice known as nutmeg is the seed. Mace is orange in color and has a sweet flavor similar to nutmeg or cardamom. It is often used in Indian and Moroccan cakes, cookies, and fruit dishes.

Marjoram This herb is native to the Mediterranean and has a flavor similar to oregano. It is used in soups and stews, and goes especially well with tomato dishes.

Mint This herb is used in many Indian, Thai, Vietnamese, and Mediterranean dishes, from entrees to desserts. It can also be added to beverages, such as tea and fruit punch. Dried mint, sometimes called peppermint, is readily available and can be found in most large grocery stores.

Mustard The seeds of the mustard plant are used whole or ground into powder. They a have a pungent flavor and are used in whole form in pickles and relishes. The ground seeds are used to make prepared mustard and can be cooked with vegetables such as carrots, potatoes, or cauliflower, or added to cream sauces.

Nutmeg This is a seed that is grated into powder form. It has a warm, spicy flavor and is often used in combination with cinnamon in cookies, cakes, and custards. It is also added to cheese sauces and used with vegetables such as corn and spinach. The best flavor is obtained when the seeds are purchased whole and grated as needed.

Oregano This popular herb is used in many European and Mexican dishes, especially those with tomatoes such as pasta sauces, pizza, chili, and tacos. It blends very well with the flavors of basil and garlic and also makes a delicious addition to salad dressings.

Paprika Available in powdered form, this mild-tasting red powder is actually the mildest member of the pepper family. It is a popular spice in Eastern European and Indian dishes and is often sprinkled on vegetables, such as potatoes and cauliflower, as a garnish. In Hungary it is often the predominant flavor in soups and stews.

Parsley Native to the Mediterranean, this mild-flavored herb is used in soups, sauces, noodles, salads, and cheese dishes. It is widely available fresh or dried and also makes a nice garnish.

Pepper Black pepper is available as whole peppercorns or in powdered form and is one of the world's most-used spices. Whole pepper is often added to marinades and pickles. Ground pepper tastes best when ground just before using. White pepper, which is black pepper with the outer skin removed, tastes slightly milder than black pepper.

Poppy Seed These tiny black seeds have a slightly sweet, nutty flavor and are used in many Eastern European breads, muffins, cakes, pastries, and noodle dishes.

Rosemary This Mediterranean herb, with its evergreen flavor, is used in many Italian and Greek dishes, especially in tomato-based soups, sauces, and stews. It has thin, needle-like leaves and is available fresh or dried. The dried herb should be crumbled before using.

Saffron The most expensive spice in the world, this yellow treasure comes from Spain and is actually the dried stigmas from a certain type of crocus flower. It is a popular ingredient in Indian, Mediterranean, and Middle Eastern dishes and adds an orange color and a distinctive flavor to rice, soups, sauces, and baked goods. It is always used sparingly.

Sage This herb has gray-green, slightly furry leaves and a slightly musky taste. It is available dried or ground (rubbed) and is a popular Italian seasoning, adding flavor to broths and vegetable dishes. It is especially good with eggplant and tomatoes and is also a popular addition to bread stuffing.

Savory This green herb is available fresh or dried and adds a somewhat grassy flavor to Mediterranean stews, egg dishes, and vegetables. It is especially good with eggplant and in vegetable soup.

Sesame Seed One of the earliest recorded seasonings, this seed is a valued cooking ingredient in China, Japan, India, and the Middle East. It is added to all types of dishes from stir-fries and salads to chutneys and desserts, and is also ground into a paste (tahini).

Tarragon An herb with a slightly anise flavor, tarragon is delicious in salad dressings and in cream sauces, as well as on vegetables such as peas and tomatoes. It is a popular ingredient in French cooking.

Thyme This pungent herb is popular throughout the Mediterranean and is widely used in soups, tomato sauces, and stews. It also adds flavor to chowders, beans, and cheese dishes and is frequently used in bread stuffings. It is available fresh or dried and one particular variety, lemon thyme, has a slight citrus flavor.

Turmeric This yellow spice from India is used in curry powder and adds both color and a pungent, musty flavor to Indian dishes. It is also used in pickles and relishes.

Vanilla Vanilla beans come from an orchid that originated in Central America. Vanilla is prized for the sweet flavor it imparts to foods, especially desserts. The whole beans can be cooked in puddings and then discarded, and they can also be stored in your sugar bowl to add a subtle flavor. Pure vanilla extract is made from the bean. (Imitation vanilla extract does not have the strong, vanilla flavor of the real thing.)

Vegetable Broth

Vegetable broth is available in cans (in the soup section of most large grocery stores), in dry form (see Vegetable Broth Mix on page 27), or by simmering vegetables and herbs in water. Following is just one suggestion for home-made broth. You can create your own by using any combination of vegetables or vegetable trimmings. Vegetables that I consider a "must" in a good broth include onions (or leeks), carrots, potatoes, garlic, and celery. Other possibilities include winter squash, Swiss chard, tomatoes, shiitake mushrooms, eggplant, corn cobs, and tomatoes. Some vegetables may overpower a stock, so I avoid using them unless I want their particular flavor to be dominant. These include green peppers, broccoli, turnips, fennel bulbs, cauliflower, asparagus, and Brussels sprouts. Broth can be strained and used in other recipes, or the vegetables can be puréed and it can be served as a thick soup. Broths will keep well in the refrigerator for several days or may be frozen.

Makes 10 to 12 cups

1	large onion, chopped
1	large potato, unpeeled, cut into 1-inch pieces
2	leeks, cut into 1-inch pieces (white and green parts)
2	large carrots, cut into 1-inch pieces
2	stalks celery, with leaves, cut into 1-inch pieces
2	tomatoes, chopped
4	cloves garlic, coarsely chopped
1/4	cup chopped parsley
1	teaspoon dried basil
2	bay leaves
8	whole peppercorns
1/2	teaspoon *each* dried thyme and salt
1/4	teaspoon ground sage
12	cups cold water (3 quarts)

Combine all ingredients in a large soup pot. Bring to a boil over medium heat. Reduce heat to medium-low, cover, and simmer 1 hour. Strain and use as needed.

Each cup provides:

18	Calories	4 g	Carbohydrate
0 g	Protein	109 mg	Sodium
0 g	Total fat (0 g Sat. fat)	0 mg	Cholesterol

Vegetable Broth Mix

When soup recipes call for vegetable broth mix, you can either buy the ready-made mix in jars or packets or you can make your own. This is a basic mix, but don't be afraid to alter it by adding your own favorite herbs and spices. If you wish to reduce the amount of sodium, you can replace the celery salt with celery seed. This recipe can easily be doubled or tripled and will keep for several months if stored in a jar with a tightly fitting lid.

Makes 12 servings
(1 teaspoon each serving)

1	tablespoon onion powder
1	tablespoon dried parsley flakes
1¹/₂	teaspoons garlic powder
1¹/₂	teaspoons celery salt
¹/₂	teaspoon ground sage
¹/₂	teaspoon dried marjoram
¹/₂	teaspoon dried thyme
¹/₂	teaspoon dried basil
¹/₂	teaspoon dried oregano
¹/₄	teaspoon pepper
¹/₄	teaspoon dill weed

Combine all ingredients and mix well. Store in a jar with a tightly fitting lid. Stir before each use.

Use 1 rounded teaspoonful to each cup of water.

Each serving provides:

4	Calories	1 g	Carbohydrate
0 g	Protein	81 mg	Sodium
0 g	Total fat (0 g Sat. fat)	0 mg	Cholesterol

Flavors of Mexico

Colorful and exciting, Mexican cuisine is far more than just tortillas. This culinary art form boasts many textures and flavors.

The foods of Mexico are very much influenced by the early conquerors. The Spanish conquistadores made a dramatic contribution by bringing herbs and spices from the Mediterranean, the Orient, and the near East. Combining these flavors with those of the native Indians, these "newcomers" helped shape what we know today as Mexican cuisine. In addition to foreign influences, Mexican food revolves around whatever the land will yield. As with most ethnic foods, geography and climate play an important role in the formation of the Mexican diet.

The most abundant vegetables in Mexico are corn, onions, pumpkins, sweet potatoes, tomatoes, zucchini, tomatillos (a variety of green tomatoes), jicama (a sweet root vegetable), and peppers—including the ever-popular chili peppers. There is also the lesser known (to us) chayote squash, and the (yes!) cactus, which is popular dipped in batter and fried.

The fruits most commonly grown in Mexico are avocados, bananas, mangos, oranges, papayas, pineapples, lemons, and limes. Fruits are often blended with vegetables in unusual combinations to make colorful salads.

The herbs and spices used in Mexican cuisine add an intensity of flavor unique to this region. They include cilantro (also known as Chinese parsley), oregano, cumin, garlic, and cinnamon. Chili powder is also very common. Unlike commercial powder, which is actually a blend of chilies and other spices, the authentic version is made by grinding dried chili peppers. (See *About Chilies* on page 30.) In Mexican households the chilies are ground fresh daily, using a somewhat flattened version of a mortar and pestle. Vanilla extract is also a popular ingredient in Mexican food, and appears in many desserts.

The abundance and popularity of corn and its ability to thrive in Mexico, has made cornmeal an important part of the Mexican diet. From tortillas to corn bread, cornmeal is one of the most commonly used grains in Mexico and one that we have come to associate with "typical" Mexican food. Flour tortillas are also frequently used to prepare burritos. (Be sure to read labels carefully when buying flour tortillas and avoid those made with lard.)

Cheese is frequently added to Mexican dishes, but unfortunately it adds a lot of fat. To avoid the fat and still maintain the character, I have used reduced-fat cheeses in recipes as substitutes for the higher-fat cheeses. I have also replaced sour cream with nonfat yogurt.

No Mexican meal is complete without a salsa (sauce) of some kind. Salsas are usually red (made with tomatoes) or green (made with tomatillos or cilantro), but they may also be made from different combinations of chopped fruits, vegetables, and beans. Salsas may be served as dips or spooned over any entrée.

Adapting Mexican recipes to meatless meals is relatively easy because beans are one of the mainstays of the Mexican diet. Kidney beans, pinto beans, black beans, black-eyed peas, garbanzos, and lentils abound. They appear in everything from salads and sandwiches to desserts. Of course, I have deleted lard—the most commonly used cooking fat—from the recipes and added small amounts of canola oil in its place.

Tacos, burritos, and enchiladas are fast becoming part of the American diet. You will find lowfat, meatless versions of these popular dishes in this section, along with many other authentic recipes that have been adapted to fit a healthy, busy lifestyle.

Enjoy your tour of Mexico!

About Chilies

An authentic Mexican kitchen is never without chilies. Chilies are used in most Mexican dishes in varying strengths, from mild to very hot, and in various forms, either dried, fresh, or canned. Dried chilies are available whole or crushed. In order to adapt the Mexican recipes in this book to American tastes, and to make the foods easy to prepare, and the ingredients easy to find, I have called for canned chilies in the recipes. When a recipe calls for chopped chilies, I buy canned whole chilies and chop them myself, rather than using the ones that are already chopped, because in most cases I have found the quality of the whole chilies to be better.

If you wish to substitute fresh chilies for canned in any of the recipes, or to add chilies to any recipe, the following list will help you decide which chilies are best suited to your tastes. There are many types of chilies, and I have chosen the ones that are most likely to be available in local supermarkets. Remember that chilies—even mild ones—need to be handled with caution. Be sure not to touch your eyes, nose, or mouth while handling chilies, and always wash your hands well with soap and water after handling them. In fact, wearing rubber gloves is advisable. The hottest part of the chili is the inner membrane, and it should be removed and discarded.

Dried chilies can easily be ground into powder in a coffee or spice grinder. Mexican cooks usually use a type of mortar and pestle made from stone, and wouldn't think of using a commercially prepared chili powder. If you wish to use ground chilies in place of commercial chili powder, or vice versa, a good rule of thumb is to use one ground ancho chili in place of one tablespoon of chili powder. When buying dried chilies, choose ones that are slightly flexible, rather than brittle, and store them in an airtight container. They will keep for up to six months.

Chilies are added to recipes according to taste and you often have to taste as you go. However, a word of caution—if you are making a dish that is going to sit overnight—add the peppers the next day. The "heat" develops as the dish sits.

Anaheim   This is a long green chili that is *relatively mild*. Often recipes call for these to be roasted and peeled.* They are available fresh or canned.

Ancho   This dried chili is reddish-brown, about five inches long, and is considered to be *mildly hot*. It can be ground and used in sauces. To reconstitute, remove seeds and inner membrane, place chili in a saucepan, cover with water, and simmer over low heat until tender.

Cayenne   This medium-green chili measures about three inches long and is *quite hot*. It is generally roasted before using to enhance the flavor.* The dried form is often ground.

Chipotle   This is actually a jalapeño pepper that has been smoked and dried. It is *very hot* and is often soaked in warm water to soften before adding it to recipes.

Jalapeño   A chili with a well-known reputation, this *very hot* chili is dark green and about two inches long. It is available fresh or canned and can be added to any recipe in this chapter to increase "heat."

Poblano   (Also known as Anaheim) Available fresh or canned, this chili is very dark green and about five inches long. It ranges from *mild to mildly hot*. This is an ideal chili for stuffing with cheese or layering in casseroles. To prepare fresh poblano chilies for cooking, they should be roasted.*

Serrano   This *very hot* chili is one and a half inches long and ranges in color from dark green to orange or red when ripe. It is generally used fresh and roasted before using.* Serrano chilies often used interchangeably with jalapeño peppers.

*To roast chilies, place them on a hot griddle, under a broiler, or over the flame of an open burner until the skin blisters on all sides. Place them in a plastic bag to steam for about 15 minutes, then peel off and discard the skin.

Flavors of Mexico
Recipes

Suggested Menus

Lunch

Orange-Jicama Salad (49)
on a Bed of Lettuce
Bean Quesadillas (56)

Lentil Vegetable Soup (43)
Tortilla-Cheese Foldovers (53)
Layered Fruit Salad (46)

Tossed Salad
Sweet Potato Chili (73)
Apple-Cheddar Skillet Corn Bread (86)

Dinner

Fresh Vegetables with
Creamy Picante Dip (38)
Spinach and Black Bean
Burritos (69)
Kahlua® Surprise Brownies (91)
Fresh Fruit Cup

Tomato Vegetable Soup (45)
Mexi-Mac and Cheese (65)
Mexicana Green Beans (82)
Apple Tortillas (96)

Tomato Noodle Soup (44)
Tossed Salad
Cheese Enchiladas (68)
Corn and Zucchini
Mexi-Medley (84)
Tortilla Dessert Cups (98)
Filled with Fresh Berries

Tossed Salad
Black Bean Chili (62)
Peppered Corn Muffins (87)
Melon Half
Honey Crisps (97)

Recipe page numbers appear in parentheses.

Onion-Flavored Tortilla Crackers

It's so easy to make your own crackers out of tortillas. Pile them in a basket and use them for dipping, eat them as a snack, or serve them alongside any Mexican meal. They're crispy, crunchy, and just plain delicious.

*Makes 4 servings
(6 crackers each serving)*

4   6-inch flour tortillas
      Nonstick cooking spray
      Onion powder
      Salt

Preheat oven to 400°.
Have an ungreased baking sheet ready.
Cut each tortilla into 6 pie-shaped wedges. Place them on a flat dish or a sheet of wax paper.
Spray wedges lightly with nonstick cooking spray. Sprinkle them lightly and evenly with onion powder and salt. Place on baking sheet.
Bake 8 to10 minutes until crisp.
Place crackers on a wire rack to cool. Store in a loosely covered container. (Crackers will keep for 2 or 3 days.)
Variation: In place of onion powder, sprinkle lightly with garlic powder, chili powder, and ground cumin.

Each serving provides:

72	Calories	11 g	Carbohydrate
2 g	Protein	96 mg	Sodium
2 g	Total fat (0 g Sat. fat)	0 mg	Cholesterol

Cheese Empanadas

Instead of rolling dough, make these delicious, cheese-filled turnovers with refrigerator biscuits. Served with salsa they make a quick and easy appetizer. They can also be served as a side dish with lunch or dinner and they make a great accompaniment to Black Bean Chili *(page 62).*

Makes 10 turnovers

1/2   cup part-skim Mozzarella cheese (2 ounces)
1/2   cup reduced-fat Cheddar cheese (2 ounces)
3   tablespoons thinly sliced green onion (green part only)
1   jalapeño pepper (optional), finely minced, seeds and membrane discarded
1   10-ounce container refrigerator biscuits
      Salsa (hot or mild)

Preheat oven to 400°.

Have an ungreased baking sheet ready.

In a small bowl, combine both types of cheese. Mix well. Set aside, along with green onion and jalapeño pepper.

Separate biscuits and place between two sheets of wax paper, several inches apart. With a rolling pin, roll biscuits into 4-inch circles. Carefully remove the top sheet of wax paper.

Place cheese on one half of each circle, using about 2 rounded teaspoonfuls of cheese on each biscuit. Top each biscuit with a scant teaspoonful of green onion and a little bit of the jalapeño.

Carefully fold biscuits over, making a half-circle and stretching the dough gently over the filling. Crimp the edges together with a fork. Place turnovers on baking sheet.

Bake 8 to 10 minutes until golden.

Serve hot. Use the salsa as a dipping sauce or spoon it over the hot turnovers.

Each turnover provides:

113	Calories	12 g	Carbohydrate
5 g	Protein	367 mg	Sodium
6 g	Total fat (2 g Sat. fat)	7 mg	Cholesterol

Colorful Corn Bread Squares

These little squares of corn bread, topped with a creamy sauce and "deco-rated" with lettuce and salsa, make a wonderful appetizer. They're also great as a side dish with chili or soup. The bread can be baked early in the day or even a day ahead and topped just before serving.

Makes 12 servings
(3 squares each serving)

Corn Bread:

1	cup yellow cornmeal
2/3	cup all-purpose flour
1/3	cup whole wheat flour
1	tablespoon sugar
2	teaspoons baking powder
1/2	teaspoon chili powder
1/4	teaspoon salt
2	egg whites
1	cup plain nonfat yogurt
1/2	cup skim milk

Topping:

1	cup plain nonfat yogurt
1/2	teaspoon chili powder
1	cup finely chopped or shredded lettuce
1	cup salsa (mild or hot)

Preheat oven to 400°.

Lightly oil a 10 x 15-inch jelly-roll pan or spray with a nonstick cooking spray.

In a large bowl, combine cornmeal, both types of flour, sugar, baking powder, chili powder, and salt. Mix well.

In a small bowl, combine remaining corn bread ingredients. Beat with a fork or wire whisk until blended. Add to cornmeal mixture, mixing until all ingredients are moistened. Place mixture in prepared pan and spread evenly.

Bake 10 minutes, until a toothpick inserted in the center of the bread comes out clean. Cool completely in pan on a wire rack before topping it.

While bread is cooling, combine yogurt and chili powder. Chill.

To serve, spread yogurt mixture evenly over the corn bread, cut into 2-inch squares, and top each square with a heaping teaspoon each of lettuce and salsa.

Serve right away.

Each serving provides:

109	Calories	20 g	Carbohydrate
5 g	Protein	263 mg	Sodium
1 g	Total fat (0 g Sat. fat)	1 mg	Cholesterol

Creamy Picante Dip

For a delicious snack, this dip can't be beat and it's almost too easy for words! It can be whipped up in a few minutes and can be made up to several days ahead and refrigerated until needed. Serve it with tortilla chips or vegetable dippers, or thin it with a little skim milk for a delicious salad dressing.

Makes 10 servings
(2 tablespoons each serving)

1	cup lowfat (1%) cottage cheese
1/4	cup bottled picante sauce (hot or mild)
1/4	teaspoon chili powder

Combine all ingredients in a blender container. Blend just until smooth.

Chill several hours.

Each serving provides:

18	Calories	1 g	Carbohydrate
3 g	Protein	131 mg	Sodium
0 g	Total fat (0 g Sat. fat)	1 mg	Cholesterol

Spicy Black Bean Dip

For an unbelievable sandwich treat, spread this dip on a crusty roll and add a slice of ripe, juicy tomato. Or open a bag of tortilla chips (baked ones, of course), cut some veggies for dipping, and you have a perfect football game accompaniment!

Makes 12 servings
(2 tablespoons each serving)

1/2	cup chopped onion
1/2	cup chopped red or yellow bell pepper
1	to 2 cloves garlic, coarsely chopped
1	1-pound can black beans, rinsed and drained (or 2 cups of cooked beans)
1	teaspoon vinegar
1	teaspoon lime juice
1	teaspoon chili powder
1/2	teaspoon ground cumin
1/4	teaspoon ground coriander
1/4	teaspoon dried oregano
1/4	teaspoon salt

Place onion, bell pepper, and garlic in a food processor. Process with a steel blade until finely chopped. Add remaining ingredients and process until smooth. (A blender can be used, but you will need to blend the mixture in small batches and be careful not to let the mixture get soupy.)

Chill several hours or overnight to blend flavors.

Each serving provides:

26	Calories	5 g	Carbohydrate
2 g	Protein	109 mg	Sodium
0 g	Total fat (0 g Sat. fat)	0 mg	Cholesterol

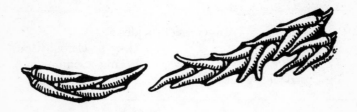

Bean Spirals

A perfect example of the Mexicans' artistic flair, these spiral-shaped appetizers will really make a hit at your next party. But don't wait for a party to try them. The whole family will love them and they provide a great way to get the kids to snack on healthy food.

Makes 8 servings
(4 spirals each serving)

1/4	cup chopped onion
1	to 2 cloves garlic, coarsely chopped
1	1-pound can kidney beans, rinsed and drained (or 2 cups of cooked beans)
1	teaspoon vinegar
1	teaspoon chili powder
1/2	teaspoon ground cumin
1/2	teaspoon dried oregano
1/4	cup *each* finely chopped red and yellow bell pepper
4	6-inch flour tortillas
	Salsa (optional)

Place onion and garlic in a food processor. Process with a steel blade until finely chopped. Add beans, vinegar, and spices. Process until smooth. (A blender can be used, but you will need to blend the mixture in small batches and be careful not to let the mixture get soupy.) Spoon mixture into a bowl and add chopped peppers. Mix well.

Divide mixture evenly and spread on tortillas, covering the entire tortilla.

Roll tortillas tightly. Wrap rolls tightly in aluminum foil or plastic wrap. Chill several hours or overnight.

To serve, slice tortillas crosswise into 1/2 -inch slices using a sharp serrated knife. (The end slices don't hold their shape well, so the kids can eat them on the spot!) Arrange slices on a platter and serve with salsa, if desired.

Each serving provides:

79	Calories	13 g	Carbohydrate
4 g	Protein	122 mg	Sodium
1 g	Total fat (0 g Sat. fat)	0 mg	Cholesterol

Creamy Potato Soup

This mellow soup is often served as a soothing accompaniment to an otherwise spicy meal. Or, turn up the "heat" by adding chopped chiles.

Makes 6 servings
(1 cup each serving)

1¹/₂ pounds potatoes, peeled and cut into small cubes (3 medium potatoes)
2¹/₂ cups *Vegetable Broth*, or 2¹/₂ cups of water plus 2¹/₂ teaspoons *Vegetable Broth Mix* (See pages 26–27.)
1   teaspoon vegetable oil
1   cup chopped onion
¹/₄   cup chopped celery
2   cloves garlic, crushed
3   cups skim milk
¹/₂   teaspoon ground cumin
¹/₈   teaspoon pepper
      Salt to taste
2   tablespoons grated Parmesan cheese
¹/₄   cup thinly sliced green onion (green part only)

In a large saucepan, combine potatoes and broth. Bring to a boil over medium heat. Reduce heat to medium-low, cover, and simmer until potatoes are very tender, about 20 minutes.

Heat oil in a medium nonstick skillet over medium heat. Add onion, celery, and garlic. Cook, stirring frequently, until onion is tender and begins to brown, 5 to 10 minutes. Remove skillet from heat.

Remove saucepan from heat and mash potatoes (right in the pot) using a fork or potato masher. (Potatoes should remain slightly lumpy.) Add onion mixture, milk, cumin, and pepper. Return saucepan to heat and heat through, but do not boil. Add salt to taste.

To serve, spoon soup into individual bowls and sprinkle with Parmesan cheese and green onion.

Each serving provides:

141	Calories	25 g	Carbohydrate
7 g	Protein	133 mg	Sodium
2 g	Total fat (1 g Sat. fat)	4 mg	Cholesterol

Mexicali Corn Soup

Almost every Mexican cookbook has a recipe for corn soup. I've come up with a version that uses cream-style corn and skim milk instead of the heavy cream that's usually called for. I've also added cilantro and the result is mellow and very tasty.

Makes 6 servings
(1 cup each serving)

1	teaspoon vegetable oil
1/2	cup chopped onion
3	cloves garlic, crushed
1	1-pound can salt-free (or regular) tomatoes, chopped, undrained
1	1-pound can salt-free (or regular) cream-style corn
2	cups *Vegetable Broth*, or 2 cups of water plus 2 teaspoons *Vegetable Broth Mix* (See pages 26–27.)
1/2	teaspoon dried oregano
1/8	to 1/4 teaspoon pepper
1/4	cup finely chopped fresh cilantro
1	cup skim milk
	Salt to taste

Heat oil in a medium saucepan over medium heat. Add onion and garlic. Cook, stirring frequently, 2 to 3 minutes, until onion is slightly tender. Add remaining ingredients, *except* milk and salt. Bring mixture to a boil. Reduce heat to medium-low, cover, and simmer 30 minutes.

Stir in milk and add salt, if desired. Heat through, but do not boil.

Each serving provides:

105	Calories	22 g	Carbohydrate
4 g	Protein	71 mg	Sodium
1 g	Total fat (0 g Sat. fat)	1 mg	Cholesterol

Lentil Vegetable Soup

In Mexico, thick soups—such as this one—are often served with crisp tortillas as the mainstay of the midday meal. This one is loaded with cabbage and lots of other vegetables and is really a meal-in-one. For a spicy addition, a few chopped jalapeño peppers will definitely do the trick.

Makes 10 servings
(1 1/3 cups per serving)

2	teaspoons vegetable oil
1	cup chopped onion
1	cup chopped celery
1	cup carrots, cut crosswise into 1/2-inch slices
4	cloves garlic, crushed
4	cups shredded cabbage
1 1/2	pounds potatoes, peeled and cut into small cubes (3 medium potatoes)
6 1/2	cups water
1	15-ounce can salt-free (or regular) tomato sauce
1	cup lentils, uncooked
1/2	cup chopped fresh cilantro
1	bay leaf
	Salt and pepper to taste

Heat oil in a large soup pot over medium heat. Add onion, celery, carrots, and garlic. Cook, stirring frequently, 10 minutes. Add small amounts of water as necessary, about a tablespoon at a time, to prevent sticking.

Add remaining ingredients, *except* salt and pepper. Bring mixture to a boil. Reduce heat to medium-low, cover, and simmer 1 hour or until vegetables are tender. Add salt and pepper to taste.

Remove and discard bay leaf before serving.

Each serving provides:			
150	Calories	28 g	Carbohydrate
8 g	Protein	34 mg	Sodium
1 g	Total fat (0 g Sat. fat)	0 mg	Cholesterol

Tomato Noodle Soup

*This popular Mexican soup consists of broken pieces of spaghetti simmered in
a rich tomato base. Sometimes hot peppers are added and often the soup is
spooned into bowls and then topped with cheese.*

*Makes 4 servings
(1¹/4 cups each serving)*

2   teaspoons vegetable oil
¹/2   cup thin spaghetti, uncooked, broken into 1-inch pieces
¹/2   cup finely chopped onion
3   cloves garlic, crushed
1   28-ounce can Italian plum tomatoes, chopped, undrained
2   cups *Vegetable Broth,* or 2 cups of water plus 2 teaspoons
       Vegetable Broth Mix (See pages 26–27.)
1   teaspoon *each* dried basil and dried oregano
1   teaspoon sugar
1   bay leaf
       Salt and pepper to taste
       Grated Parmesan cheese (optional)

Heat oil in a large nonstick skillet over medium heat. Add
spaghetti pieces, onion, and garlic. Cook, stirring constantly, until
spaghetti pieces are golden. Remove from heat.

Place tomatoes, spaghetti mixture, and remaining ingredients, *except* salt, pepper, and Parmesan cheese in a medium saucepan. Bring
to a boil over medium heat. Reduce heat to medium-low, cover, and
simmer 10 to 12 minutes, until spaghetti is tender.

Remove and discard bay leaf before serving.

Spoon soup into serving bowls, add salt and pepper to taste, and
sprinkle lightly with Parmesan cheese, if desired.

Each serving provides:

139	Calories	25 g	Carbohydrate
4 g	Protein	380 mg	Sodium
3 g	Total fat (0 g Sat. fat)	0 mg	Cholesterol

Tomato Vegetable Soup

This is one of the richest, "tomatoey-est" soups around, loaded with onions, peppers, corn, and beans. It's a great soup to serve as a light meal, along with a chunk of Apple-Cheddar Skillet Corn Bread *(page 86).*

Makes 8 servings
(1 cup each serving)

2	teaspoons vegetable oil
1	cup chopped onion
1	cup chopped green bell pepper
1/2	cup chopped celery
3	cloves garlic, finely chopped
1	1-pound can stewed tomatoes, undrained
4	cups tomato juice
1	1-pound can salt-free (or regular) corn, drained
1	1-pound can black-eyed peas, rinsed and drained (or 2 cups of cooked beans)
2	teaspoons chili powder
1	teaspoon *each* dried oregano and dried basil
1/2	teaspoon salt
1/4	teaspoon pepper
2	bay leaves
1	cup shredded fresh spinach

Heat oil in a large saucepan over medium heat. Add onion, bell pepper, celery, and garlic. Cook, stirring frequently, 5 minutes. Add small amounts of water if necessary, about a tablespoon at a time, to prevent sticking.

Add remaining ingredients, *except* spinach. Bring mixture to a boil, then reduce heat to medium-low, cover, and simmer 20 minutes.

Add spinach and continue to cook, covered, 10 minutes more.

Remove and discard bay leaves before serving.

Each serving provides:

149	Calories	30 g	Carbohydrate
7 g	Protein	744 mg	Sodium
2 g	Total fat (0 g Sat. fat)	0 mg	Cholesterol

Layered Fruit Salad

For a festive look, layer this salad in a straight-sided, clear glass bowl. If you like, you can vary the fruit combinations and add any other fruits you wish. The authentic Mexican version uses cream and a sprinkling of pomegranate seeds. I prefer yogurt, coconut, and walnuts for color and crunch.

Makes 6 servings

1	large, sweet apple, unpeeled, cut into small cubes
1	ripe papaya, peeled and cut into small cubes, seeds discarded
1	large, ripe banana, cut into small cubes
1	cup ripe pineapple, cut into small cubes, or 1 can of crushed pineapple (packed in juice), drained
1	cup vanilla nonfat yogurt
1	teaspoon shredded unsweetened coconut
1	tablespoon chopped walnuts or pecans
1	tablespoon honey

Chill all fruit before preparing the salad. Cut the fruit and assemble the salad just before serving.

Layer the fruits in the order listed. Spread the yogurt over the top of the salad. Sprinkle evenly with coconut and nuts. Drizzle with honey.

Serve right away. (The leftovers can be chilled for later servings, but the salad is best when served fresh.)

Each serving provides:

123	Calories	27 g	Carbohydrate
3 g	Protein	29 mg	Sodium
1 g	Total fat (0 g Sat. fat)	1 mg	Cholesterol

Chili-Corn Salad

For a brilliant Mexican salad, just open a few cans and chop a few vegetables. Serve it on a bed of lettuce alongside Tortilla-Cheese Foldovers (page 53) for a delicious south-of-the-border lunch.

Makes 8 servings

1	1-pound can salt-free (or regular) corn, drained
1	4-ounce can green chilies (hot or mild), chopped and drained
1/2	cup chopped tomato
1/2	cup finely chopped green bell pepper
1/2	cup chopped cucumber (Peel cucumber if the skin has been waxed.)
1/3	cup finely chopped onion
1	tablespoon dried parsley flakes
1/2	teaspoon dried oregano
2	tablespoons vegetable oil
1	tablespoon vinegar
1	tablespoon water
3	cloves garlic, crushed
1/2	teaspoon ground cumin
1/4	teaspoon pepper

In a large bowl, combine corn, chilies, tomato, bell pepper, cucumber, and onion. Sprinkle with parsley and oregano and mix well.

In a small bowl, combine remaining ingredients. Mix until blended and pour over corn mixture. Mix well, cover, and chill several hours or overnight. Stir before serving.

Each serving provides:

79	Calories	12 g	Carbohydrate
2 g	Protein	90 mg	Sodium
4 g	Total fat (0 g Sat. fat)	0 mg	Cholesterol

Grilled Vegetable Salad

This is my interpretation of a unique, warm salad that Harry and I enjoyed at a Mexican restaurant in Texas. The vegetables can be grilled or broiled, but grilling imparts a wonderful flavor that only the fiery coals can provide.

Makes 4 servings

1	medium zucchini, sliced crosswise into 1-inch slices
2	medium onions, sliced crosswise into 1/2-inch slices
1	large red bell pepper, cut into 1 1/2-inch squares
1	large yellow bell pepper, cut into 1 1/2-inch squares
8	large mushrooms, cut in half
2	plum tomatoes, cut lengthwise into quarters

Sauce:

1/2	cup bottled picante sauce (hot or mild)
2	teaspoons lemon juice
1/2	teaspoon ground cumin
1/4	teaspoon garlic powder

Place all vegetables, *except* tomatoes, on a hot grill that has been lightly oiled. (If broiling vegetables, place them in a broiler pan that has been sprayed with a nonstick cooking spray.) Cook until the edges of the vegetables are crisp.

Turn vegetables, add tomato wedges, and continue to grill until both sides of the vegetables are crisp. (Do not turn the tomatoes.)

While vegetables are cooking, prepare sauce by combining all sauce ingredients in a small bowl and mixing well.

Place grilled vegetables in a large bowl. Spoon sauce over vegetables and toss gently.

Serve right away.

Each serving provides:

82	Calories	18 g	Carbohydrate
3 g	Protein	202 mg	Sodium
1 g	Total fat (0 g Sat. fat)	0 mg	Cholesterol

Orange-Jicama Salad

Jicama (pronounced HEE-kah-mah) is a crisp, sweet, root vegetable shaped like a turnip, with brown skin. Once available only in specialty stores, jicama can now be found in the produce section of many large grocery stores. It is eaten raw and makes a wonderful "dipper." This unusual salad is sweet, crunchy, and very refreshing.

Makes 8 servings

1	medium jicama (1 pound), peeled and cut into matchstick-size strips (3 cups)
4	large oranges, peeled and sectioned (Discard white membrane.)
1	cup red onion, cut vertically into small, thin slivers
1	cup orange juice
1/4	cup lime juice
1	tablespoon sugar
1/4	teaspoon salt

In a large bowl, combine jicama strips, orange sections, and onion.

In a small bowl, combine remaining ingredients, mixing well. Pour over jicama. Mix well, then cover and chill several hours or overnight. Mix several times while chilling.

Stir before serving.

Each serving provides:

95	Calories	23 g	Carbohydrate
2 g	Protein	74 mg	Sodium
0 g	Total fat (0 g Sat. fat)	0 mg	Cholesterol

Zucchini and Tomato Salad

*Bright and colorful in the Mexican tradition, this delicious salad will add an
exciting touch to any meal. It's a typical south-of-the-border medley of vegetables and spices, with just a hint of lime.*

Makes 8 servings

3	cups (1 pound) small zucchini, sliced crosswise into 1/4-inch slices (If zucchini are large, cut each slice into quarters.)
2	large, ripe tomatoes, chopped (2 cups)
1/2	cup red onion, cut vertically into thin slivers
3	tablespoons water
2	tablespoons vegetable oil
1 1/2	tablespoons vinegar
1	tablespoon lime juice
1	teaspoon dried oregano
1/4	teaspoon garlic powder
1/8	teaspoon salt
1/8	teaspoon pepper

In a large bowl, combine zucchini, tomatoes, and onion.

In a small bowl, combine remaining ingredients, mixing well. Pour
over tomato mixture. Mix gently, until dressing is evenly distributed.
Chill several hours or overnight. Mix several times while chilling.
Stir before serving.

Each serving provides:			
53	Calories	5 g	Carbohydrate
1 g	Protein	42 mg	Sodium
4 g	Total fat (0 g Sat. fat)	0 mg	Cholesterol

Salad in a Tortilla

Almost anything can be rolled up in a tortilla and Mexican cooks often create exciting new dishes with something as simple as chopped vegetables. Here's a prize-winning example. Serve it as an appetizer, salad, or a delicious light lunch.

Makes 6 servings

1	large, ripe tomato, chopped (1 cup)
1/2	cup chopped cucumber (Peel cucumber if the skin has been waxed.)
1/4	cup finely chopped red onion
1/4	cup finely chopped red bell pepper
1/4	cup finely chopped fresh cilantro
2	teaspoons lemon juice
1	teaspoon red wine vinegar
1/8	teaspoon *each* garlic powder, chili powder, and dried oregano
1	ripe avocado, peeled and chopped
6	6-inch flour tortillas
2/3	cup plain nonfat yogurt
	Salsa (hot or mild)

In a large bowl, combine tomato, cucumber, onion, bell pepper, and cilantro. Add lemon juice, vinegar, and spices. Mix well. Add avocado and mix gently.

Chill for one to two hours. (It can be chilled overnight, but the salad is fresher if served the same day.)

To serve, stack tortillas and wrap them tightly in aluminum foil. Place in a preheated 350° oven for 10 minutes.

Divide salad evenly onto warm tortillas, using 1/3 cup on each tortilla. Top each salad with a heaping tablespoon of yogurt, and wrap tortilla around filling. Top with salsa and serve right away.

Each serving provides:

145	Calories	18 g	Carbohydrate
4 g	Protein	123 mg	Sodium
7 g	Total fat (1 g Sat. fat)	1 mg	Cholesterol

Avocado and Greens with Warm Orange Dressing

Being an avocado lover, I adore this salad. Nothing interferes with the buttery, mellow flavor of the avocado; it is simply enhanced by the warm orange dressing.

Makes 6 servings

Dressing:

1/4	cup plus 2 tablespoons orange juice
1 1/2	tablespoons vegetable oil
1 1/2	tablespoons lime juice
1 1/2	tablespoons honey
1 1/2	tablespoons red wine vinegar
2 1/4	teaspoons cornstarch

Salad:

6	cups torn greens (Choose a combination of the "tender" ones, such as red and green leaf lettuce and fresh spinach.)
1	medium, ripe avocado, peeled and thinly sliced

In a very small saucepan, combine all dressing ingredients. Stir to dissolve cornstarch. Cook over medium heat, stirring constantly, until mixture comes to a boil. Continue to cook and stir for 1 minute more. Remove from heat and let stand 5 minutes.

Divide greens evenly onto six salad plates. Arrange avocado slices over greens. Stir dressing and spoon over salads, allowing 2 tablespoons for each serving.

Note: If you are not using all of the dressing, refrigerate the leftovers. To serve, stir in a teaspoon or two of water and heat dressing in the microwave until hot. Do not boil.

Each serving provides:

123	Calories	12 g	Carbohydrate
2 g	Protein	29 mg	Sodium
9 g	Total fat (1 g Sat. fat)	0 mg	Cholesterol

Tortilla-Cheese Foldovers

Known as Quesadillas (KAY-sa-DEE-yahs), this is the Mexican answer to grilled cheese sandwiches. If you like, you can place a teaspoonful of chopped tomato, green onion, or green chilies on top of the cheese before you fold the tortillas. Served with salsa, this makes a great appetizer or light lunch.

Makes 4 foldovers

4   6-inch flour tortillas
1/2   cup shredded reduced-fat Cheddar or Monterey Jack cheese
       Salsa (hot or mild)

Preheat a large nonstick griddle over medium heat. Spray with a nonstick cooking spray.

Place tortillas on griddle. Divide cheese evenly and place on one half of each tortilla. Add additional toppings, if desired. Fold tortillas in half and press down gently. Heat tortillas, flipping them back and forth, until cheese is melted and tortillas are hot and crispy on both sides.

Top with salsa and serve right away.

Each foldover provides:			
112	Calories	12 g	Carbohydrate
6 g	Protein	196 mg	Sodium
4 g	Total fat (2 g Sat. fat)	10 mg	Cholesterol

Black Bean Tostadas

These tostadas (actually Mexican open-faced sandwiches) are made by top-ping crisp corn tortillas with refried black beans, cheese, and shredded vegeta-bles that are laced with cumin and lime. Serve them with plenty of salsa and top each tostada with a dollop of yogurt, if desired. You're in for a treat!

Makes 6 tostadas

Lime Dressing:

1	tablespoon lime juice
$1/2$	teaspoon sugar
$1/4$	teaspoon ground cumin

Refried Black Beans:

1	teaspoon vegetable oil
1	cup chopped onion
3	large cloves garlic, crushed
1	19-ounce can black beans, rinsed and drained (or $2^1/4$ cups of cooked beans)
2	tablespoons water
$1/2$	teaspoon dried oregano
$1/2$	teaspoon ground cumin
	Salt and pepper to taste

Also:

6	6-inch corn tortillas
1	cup shredded, reduced-fat Cheddar or Monterey Jack cheese (4 ounces)
4	cups shredded lettuce
$1/2$	cup coarsely shredded carrots
	Salsa (hot or mild)
	Plain nonfat yogurt (optional)

Combine dressing ingredients in a custard cup and set aside. Preheat oven to 400°.

Heat oil in a large nonstick skillet over medium heat. Add onion and garlic. Cook, stirring frequently, until onion begins to brown, about 5 minutes. Reduce heat to medium-low and add beans and water. Sprinkle with spices. Cook until hot, mixing well and mashing the beans with a fork or potato masher.

While the bean mixture is cooking, place tortillas on a large baking sheet. Spray both sides of the tortillas lightly with nonstick cooking spray. Bake 8 to10 minutes, until crisp.

To assemble: divide bean mixture evenly and spread on each tortilla. Top with cheese. Combine lettuce and carrots in a small bowl and add lime dressing. Toss and divide evenly onto each tortilla.

Serve right away.

Pass the salsa (and the yogurt, if desired.)

Each tostada provides:			
206	Calories	26 g	Carbohydrate
11 g	Protein	327 mg	Sodium
6 g	Total fat (2 g Sat. fat)	13 mg	Cholesterol

Bean Quesadillas

Pronounced KAY-sa-DEE-yahs, these hot tortilla sandwiches can also be cut into smaller wedges and served as an appetizer. If you don't want to make all of the sandwiches at once, you can refrigerate the bean filling and simply heat and use as needed. Or, you can make all of the sandwiches and either reheat them as needed or serve them cold.

Makes 8 sandwiches

1	teaspoon vegetable oil
1	cup chopped onion
3	cloves garlic, crushed
1	1-pound can salt-free (or regular) tomatoes, chopped and drained
1	8-ounce can salt-free (or regular) tomato sauce
2	jalapeño peppers (optional), finely minced, seeds and membranes discarded
1	teaspoon vinegar
2	teaspoons ground cumin
2	teaspoons chili powder
1	teaspoon dried oregano
1/4	teaspoon ground cinnamon
2	1-pound cans pinto beans, rinsed and drained (or 4 cups of cooked beans)
16	6-inch flour tortillas
2	cups shredded reduced-fat Cheddar or Monterey Jack cheese (8 ounces)
	Salsa *or* shredded lettuce and chopped tomato

Heat oil in a large nonstick skillet over medium heat. Add onion and garlic. Cook, stirring frequently, until onion is tender, about 5 minutes. Add tomatoes, tomato sauce, jalapeños, vinegar, and spices. Stir in beans. Cook, stirring frequently, until mixture is heated through.

Preheat oven to 400°. Lightly oil a large baking sheet or spray with a nonstick cooking spray. (You will need more than one baking sheet if you are making all of the sandwiches.)

Place half of the tortillas on prepared baking sheets. Top each with 1/2 cup of the bean mixture, spreading it almost to the edges of the tortillas. Top each with another tortilla and press the top tortillas down slightly. Sprinkle 1 ounce (1/4 cup) of cheese evenly over each tortilla.

Bake 7 or 8 minutes, until cheese is melted and edges of tortillas are lightly browned. Remove from pan and cut into wedges. (Kitchen shears work well.)

Serve with salsa or open each sandwich, tuck in some lettuce and tomato, and close it up.

Each sandwich provides:			
323	Calories	41 g	Carbohydrate
17 g	Protein	596 mg	Sodium
9 g	Total fat (4 g Sat. fat)	20 mg	Cholesterol

Mexican Dipping Sandwich

In Mexico, lots of different fillings are served in small, crusty rolls, with salsa as a dipping sauce. This bean mixture is one filling, but you can also use almost any bean dish, dip, or salad, and it's a great way to use leftovers. This filling is also good cold.

Makes 10 sandwiches

1	teaspoon vegetable oil
1/2	cup chopped onion
1/2	cup chopped red bell pepper
3	cloves garlic, finely chopped
1	1-pound can pinto beans, rinsed and drained (or 2 cups of cooked beans)
2	large tomatoes, chopped (2 cups)
1/4	cup raisins
2	tablespoons slivered almonds
1/2	teaspoon ground cumin
	Salt and pepper to taste
6	small, crusty rolls, about 1 1/2 ounces each
	Salsa (hot or mild)

Heat oil in a large nonstick skillet over medium heat. Add onion, bell pepper, and garlic. Cook, stirring frequently, until onion is tender, about 3 minutes.

Add beans, tomatoes, raisins, almonds, cumin, salt, and pepper. Cook, stirring frequently, until mixture is hot and bubbly, about 3 minutes.

To serve, slice a thin piece off the end of each roll and scoop out the center. (Save it for bread pudding or stuffing, or give the birds a treat!) Fill each roll with bean mixture (about 1/3 cup each) and serve with salsa for dipping. If you prefer, the filling can be chilled and served cold.

Each sandwich provides:

138	Calories	24 g	Carbohydrate
5 g	Protein	217 mg	Sodium
3 g	Total fat (0 g Sat. fat)	0 mg	Cholesterol

Chunky Tomato Salsa

If you're out of commercial salsa, or just want to try your hand at a home-made variety, here's one of my favorites. Make it at least several hours ahead so the flavors will have a chance to blend. Use it as a topping for burritos, as a dip for chips, or in any recipe that calls for salsa. It's important to choose a good brand of tomatoes for this recipe. Some of the less expensive brands have too few tomatoes and too much water.

Makes 12 servings
(3 tablespoons each serving)

1	1-pound can salt-free (or regular) tomatoes, chopped, undrained
1/3	cup finely chopped onion
1/4	cup finely chopped celery
1	4-ounce can green chilies (hot or mild), chopped and drained
1	small clove garlic, crushed
1	teaspoon lime juice
1	teaspoon sugar
1/2	teaspoon dried oregano
1/2	teaspoon ground coriander
1/4	teaspoon salt
	Pepper to taste

Optional Ingredients:

1	finely chopped jalapeño pepper
1/4	cup very finely chopped green bell pepper
2	tablespoons chopped fresh cilantro

Combine all ingredients in a medium bowl. Mix well. Spoon into a jar and chill several hours or overnight. (This salsa will keep in the refrigerator for 5 or 6 days.)

Each serving provides:

14	Calories	3 g	Carbohydrate
1 g	Protein	167 mg	Sodium
0 g	Total fat (0 g Sat. fat)	0 mg	Cholesterol

Mango Salsa

Spicy Mexican meals often include the cool, refreshing touch of a fruit-based salsa. If you prefer, add the optional jalapeño pepper and add a little "heat" to your meal! Either way, it's a perfect accompaniment to dishes such as Tortilla-Cheese Foldovers *(page 53) or* Pinto-Cheese Casserole *(page 75).*

Makes 4 servings
(about 1/3 cup each serving)

1	large, ripe mango, peeled and cut into 1/4-inch pieces, center seed discarded (1 cup)
1/4	cup red bell pepper, chopped into 1/4-inch pieces
1 1/2	tablespoons finely chopped fresh basil (Fresh basil adds a distinctive flavor that just can't be duplicated with dried basil.)
1 1/2	teaspoons red wine vinegar
2	teaspoons lime juice
1/2	teaspoon sugar
1	jalapeño pepper (optional), finely minced, seeds and membrane discarded

In a medium bowl, combine all ingredients. Mix well.

Let stand at room temperature a half hour before serving or refrigerate for up to 24 hours. (Because of the delicate nature of fresh mangoes, this salsa, unlike most others, does not hold up well after a day or two.)

Each serving provides:

32	Calories	8 g	Carbohydrate
0 g	Protein	1 mg	Sodium
0 g	Total fat (0 g Sat. fat)	0 mg	Cholesterol

Black Bean and Corn Salsa

Scoop up this chunky salsa with tortilla chips for an irresistible appetizer or snack, or serve it alongside any entrée. Two Mexican favorites are combined—black beans and corn. It is especially tasty spooned over Tortilla-Cheese Foldovers *(page 53) or* Cheddar-Topped Rice Casserole *(page 78). I've also served it as a Sunday TV football accompaniment and everyone raved!*

Makes 12 servings
(1/3 cup per serving)

2	1-pound cans salt-free (or regular) tomatoes, chopped and drained
1	1-pound can black beans, rinsed and drained (or 2 cups of cooked beans)
1	cup salt-free (or regular) canned corn, drained
1/4	cup *each* finely chopped onion and chopped celery
1	4-ounce can green chilies (mild or hot), chopped and drained
1	tablespoon red wine vinegar
2	teaspoons honey
1	teaspoon *each* ground coriander and ground cumin
1/4	teaspoon *each* garlic powder and salt
	Pepper to taste *or* chopped jalapeños

In a medium bowl, combine all ingredients, mixing well. Chill several hours or overnight to blend flavors.

Stir before serving.

Serve cold with tortilla chips or vegetable dippers. (If using chips, choose those that are baked rather than fried.)

Each serving provides:

58	Calories	12 g	Carbohydrate
3 g	Protein	337 mg	Sodium
0 g	Total fat (0 g Sat. fat)	0 mg	Cholesterol

Black Bean Chili

A classic Mexican combination of black beans and spices, this wonderful chili makes a great Sunday afternoon meal. It takes a few hours to cook, but it makes enough to last all week!

Makes 10 servings
(1¹/4 cups each serving)

1	pound dried black beans, uncooked
2	teaspoons vegetable oil
2	cups chopped onion
2	cups chopped green bell pepper
5	cloves garlic, crushed
5	medium, ripe tomatoes, peeled and chopped (5 cups)
1	tablespoon dried oregano
2	tablespoons chili powder (or more, if you like)
1	tablespoon ground cumin
2	teaspoons paprika
1	teaspoon ground coriander
1	bay leaf
¹/2	teaspoon salt
3¹/2	cups water
1	6-ounce can tomato paste
1	tablespoon red wine vinegar

Garnishes: (optional)
Grated Parmesan cheese
Plain nonfat yogurt
Chopped tomato
Chopped fresh cilantro

Place black beans in a large saucepan and add enough water to cover beans by 3 inches. Bring to a boil over medium heat. Boil 2 minutes. Cover, remove from heat, and let stand 1 to 2 hours. Drain.

Heat oil in a large soup pot over medium heat. Add onion, bell pepper, and garlic. Cook, stirring frequently, 5 minutes. Add tomatoes and spices. Cook, stirring occasionally, 10 minutes. Add water, tomato paste, vinegar, and soaked beans. Bring mixture to a boil. Reduce heat to medium-low, cover, and simmer 2 hours or until beans are tender. Stir occasionally while cooking.

Remove and discard bay leaf.

Spoon chili into bowls, and if desired, garnish with any (or all!) of the optional garnishes.

Each serving provides:			
226	Calories	42 g	Carbohydrate
12 g	Protein	272 mg	Sodium
3 g	Total fat (0 g Sat. fat)	0 mg	Cholesterol

Apricot Picante Tofu

The sweetness of apricot jam provides an unusual flavor backdrop for the pi-cante sauce and spices in this easy entrée. It's my version of a Mexican-in-spired barbecue sauce. You can make it hot or mild, depending on the picante sauce you choose. Serve it with brown rice, add a green vegetable, and dinner is complete.

Makes 4 servings

1	8-ounce jar picante sauce (hot or mild)
1/4	cup fruit-only apricot (or peach) jam
1/2	teaspoon chili powder
1/2	teaspoon onion powder
1/2	teaspoon ground cumin
1/4	teaspoon garlic powder
1/4	teaspoon dried oregano
1	teaspoon vegetable oil
1	pound firm tofu, cut into 3/4- to 1-inch cubes, drained slightly on layers of towels

In a small bowl, combine picante sauce, jam, and spices. Mix well. Set aside.

Heat oil in a large nonstick skillet over medium heat. Add tofu. Cook, stirring gently, until tofu is lightly browned on all sides. Add picante mixture. Reduce heat to medium-low, cover, and simmer 20 minutes.

Each serving provides:			
240	Calories	20 g	Carbohydrate
18 g	Protein	403 mg	Sodium
11 g	Total fat (2 g Sat. fat)	0 mg	Cholesterol

Mexi-Mac and Cheese

Cilantro and tomatoes give this traditional American favorite a whole new twist. Once available only in gourmet or import stores, cilantro can now be found in most large grocery stores.

Makes 4 servings

8	ounces elbow macaroni, uncooked (about 1 1/2 cups)
1	cup skim milk
1	cup lowfat (1%) cottage cheese
3	tablespoons all-purpose flour
3	cloves garlic, coarsely chopped
1/2	teaspoon ground cumin
1/2	teaspoon dried oregano
1/4	teaspoon *each* salt and pepper
1	cup reduced-fat Cheddar cheese (4 ounces)
1 1/2	cups chopped ripe tomatoes, drained well between layers of towels
1/4	cup finely chopped fresh cilantro

Preheat oven to 375°.

Lightly oil a shallow 2-quart casserole or spray with a nonstick cooking spray.

Cook macaroni according to package directions. Drain.

While macaroni is cooking, combine milk, cottage cheese, flour, garlic, and spices in a blender container. Blend until smooth. Pour into a medium saucepan. Cook over medium heat, stirring constantly, until mixture comes to a boil. Continue to cook and stir for 2 minutes more. Remove from heat and stir in Cheddar cheese. Mix until cheese is completely melted. Stir in tomatoes and cilantro, then add macaroni. Mix well. Spoon mixture into prepared casserole.

Bake uncovered, until hot and bubbly, 20 minutes.

Each serving provides:

413	Calories	57 g	Carbohydrate
26 g	Protein	608 mg	Sodium
8 g	Total fat (4 g Sat. fat)	23 mg	Cholesterol

Tamale Corn and Bean Casserole

Instead of the usual method of shaping individual tamales and baking them in corn husks, this casserole provides a much easier variation. Two layers of cornmeal mixture are filled with cheese, beans, and chilies, then baked and topped with the easiest of sauces.

Makes 6 servings

1	1-pound can salt-free (or regular) cream-style corn
1/2	cup skim milk
1	tablespoon vegetable oil
1	cup yellow cornmeal
1	teaspoon sugar
1	teaspoon baking powder
1/2	teaspoon dried oregano
1/4	teaspoon salt
1	4-ounce can whole green chilies (hot or mild), rinsed and drained, and cut lengthwise into 1/2-inch strips
3/4	cup reduced-fat Cheddar cheese (3 ounces)
1	1-pound can pinto beans, rinsed and drained (or 2 cups of cooked beans)
2	1-pound cans salt-free (or regular) stewed tomatoes

Preheat oven to 350°.

Lightly oil a 1-quart casserole or spray with a nonstick cooking spray. In a large bowl, combine corn, milk, and oil. Mix well.

In a small bowl, combine cornmeal, sugar, baking powder, oregano, and salt. Mix well. Add to corn mixture, mixing until all ingredients are moistened.

Place *half* of the corn mixture into prepared casserole. Arrange chilies over corn mixture. Spread cheese evenly over chilies and top with beans. Top with remaining corn mixture. Bake uncovered, 1 hour.

While casserole is baking, heat stewed tomatoes. To serve, top each casserole serving with a generous helping of stewed tomatoes.

Each serving provides:

299	Calories	49 g	Carbohydrate
12 g	Protein	549 mg	Sodium
7 g	Total fat (2 g Sat. fat)	10 mg	Cholesterol

Pinto Picante Pasta

Whew! Say that name three times fast! (It seemed a fitting, fun name for family-pleasing fare.) If you like, you can sprinkle some chopped cilantro over the casserole along with the cheese.

Makes 6 servings

8	ounces elbow macaroni, uncooked (about 1 1/2 cups)
1	8-ounce jar picante sauce (hot or mild)
1	15-ounce can salt-free (or regular) tomato sauce
1	1-pound can pinto beans, rinsed and drained (or 2 cups of cooked beans)
1	cup salt-free (or regular) canned or frozen corn
1	teaspoon chili powder
1/2	teaspoon ground cumin
1/4	teaspoon garlic powder
1	jalapeño pepper (optional), finely minced, seeds and membrane discarded
1	cup shredded reduced-fat Cheddar cheese (4 ounces)

Cook macaroni according to package directions. Drain.

In a large nonstick skillet, combine remaining ingredients, *except* cheese. Bring to a boil over medium heat, stirring frequently. Add cooked pasta, mixing well. Cook and stir until heated through.

Sprinkle cheese evenly over pasta. Turn off heat, cover skillet, and let stand 5 minutes before serving.

Each serving provides:

309	Calories	50 g	Carbohydrate
15 g	Protein	535 mg	Sodium
5 g	Total fat (2 g Sat. fat)	13 mg	Cholesterol

Cheese Enchiladas

In this popular Mexican dish, corn tortillas are filled with two kinds of cheese and then topped with your choice of hot or mild picante sauce.

Makes 4 servings
(2 enchiladas each serving)

8	corn tortillas
1	cup bottled picante sauce (hot or mild)
2	cups lowfat (1%) cottage cheese
1	cup shredded reduced-fat Cheddar cheese (4 ounces)
$1/2$	cup thinly sliced green onions (green and white parts)
$1/2$	teaspoon dried oregano
$1/2$	teaspoon ground cumin
$1/4$	teaspoon garlic powder
$1/8$	teaspoon pepper
	Salt to taste

Preheat oven to 350°.

Lightly oil a 6 x 10-inch baking pan or spray with a nonstick cooking spray.

Stack tortillas and wrap them tightly in aluminum foil. Heat in oven for 10 minutes.

While tortillas are heating, spread $1/3$ cup of the picante sauce in the bottom of prepared pan.

In a large bowl, combine cottage cheese, $3/4$ cup of the Cheddar cheese, and remaining ingredients. Mix well.

Spoon $1/3$ cup of the cheese mixture across the center of each tortilla. Roll up tightly into cylinder-shaped rolls and place seam side down on top of sauce in pan. Spoon remaining picante sauce over tortillas. Cover tightly and bake 30 minutes.

Uncover, sprinkle with remaining cheese, and return to oven for 5 minutes.

Let stand 5 minutes before serving.

Each serving provides:

319	Calories		33 g	Carbohydrate
25 g	Protein		1127 mg	Sodium
9 g	Total fat (4 g Sat. fat)		25 mg	Cholesterol

Spinach and Black Bean Burritos

From Southern Mexico, these unusual burritos can't be beat. I first tasted them at one of my favorite Mexican restaurants and rushed home to make my own version. They're so quick and easy, you can whip them up in no time.

Makes 12 burritos

12	8-inch flour tortillas
1	1-pound can black beans, rinsed and drained (or 2 cups of cooked beans)
1	10-ounce package frozen chopped spinach, thawed and drained well
1	16-ounce jar picante sauce (hot or mild)
1	cup salt-free (or regular) canned corn, drained
1	teaspoon ground cumin
1¹/2	cups shredded reduced-fat Cheddar cheese (6 ounces)

Preheat oven to 350°.

Stack tortillas and wrap them tightly in aluminum foil. Heat in oven for 10 minutes.

While tortillas are heating, combine beans, spinach, and picante sauce in a large nonstick skillet over medium heat. Mix well, mashing about half of the beans with a fork. Add corn and cumin. Cook over medium heat, stirring frequently, about 5 minutes or until mixture is hot and bubbly.

Prepare a few burritos at a time, leaving remaining tortillas wrapped to keep them from drying out. Divide cheese evenly onto the centers of the heated tortillas. Top with 1/3 cup of bean mixture. Fold in tops and bottoms of tortillas, then fold in the sides so that filling is enclosed. Turn burritos over and place on a serving plate.

Serve topped with salsa, if desired.

―❀―

Each burrito provides:			
213	Calories	30 g	Carbohydrate
10 g	Protein	649 mg	Sodium
5 g	Total fat (2 g Sat. fat)	10 mg	Cholesterol

Pinto-Chili Burritos

Burritos are made by wrapping a filling (usually cheese, beans, or meat) in a flour tortilla. These scrumptious bean and cheese burritos are topped with both salsa and a creamy yogurt sauce and served on a bed of lettuce and tomatoes. This is a quick and easy last minute dish in the true Mexican style.

Makes 10 burritos

Sauce:

1	cup plain nonfat yogurt
1	teaspoon chili powder
1/4	teaspoon ground cumin
1/4	teaspoon garlic powder

Tortillas:

10	8-inch flour tortillas
2	teaspoons vegetable oil
1	cup chopped onion
3	cloves garlic, crushed
1	teaspoon ground cumin
1/2	teaspoon chili powder
2	1-pound cans pinto beans, rinsed and drained (or 4 cups of cooked beans)
1	4-ounce can green chilies (mild or hot), chopped and drained
1	cup shredded reduced-fat Cheddar cheese (4 ounces)

Also:

1	16-ounce jar salsa (mild or hot)

In a small bowl, combine all sauce ingredients, mixing well. Set aside.

Preheat oven to 350°.

Stack tortillas and wrap them tightly in aluminum foil. Heat in oven for 10 minutes.

While tortillas are heating, heat oil in a large nonstick skillet over medium heat. Add onion, garlic, cumin, and chili powder. Cook, stirring frequently, until onion is tender and begins to brown. Reduce heat to medium-low and add beans, mashing them with a fork or potato masher. Cook just until beans are heated through. Stir in chilies and cheese. Remove from heat. (If beans seem too dry, stir in a little water.)

Prepare a few burritos at a time, leaving remaining tortillas wrapped to keep them from drying out. Divide bean mixture evenly onto the centers of the heated tortillas, using 1/3 cup for each burrito. Fold in tops and bottoms of tortillas, then fold in the sides so that filling is enclosed. Turn burritos over and place on a serving plate.

To serve, place each burrito on a bed of shredded lettuce and tomato. Pass the salsa and yogurt sauce.

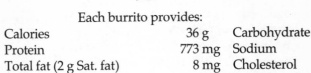

Each burrito provides:			
246	Calories	36 g	Carbohydrate
11 g	Protein	773 mg	Sodium
6 g	Total fat (2 g Sat. fat)	8 mg	Cholesterol

Hot Butter Beans

In a typical Mexican home, a pot of beans is almost always on the stove. Called frijoles en la olla *—which means "cooked beans"—this dish can be made with whatever type of bean is available. I prefer butter beans because I love their tender texture, but pinto beans are the most popular. Serve this easy, spicy, one-pot dish over brown rice, add a green vegetable, and dinner is complete.*

Makes 4 servings

2	teaspoons vegetable oil
1	cup finely chopped onion
1/2	cup finely chopped green bell pepper
2	cloves garlic, finely chopped
1	1-pound can butter beans, rinsed and drained
1	1-pound can salt-free (or regular) tomatoes, chopped, undrained
3	tablespoons molasses
2	teaspoons chili powder
1/16	teaspoon ground allspice
1/16	teaspoon ground cloves
	Salt to taste

Heat oil in a large nonstick skillet over medium heat. Add onion, bell pepper, and garlic. Cook, stirring frequently, 5 minutes or until onion is lightly browned.

Add remaining ingredients and when mixture boils reduce heat to medium-low, cover, and simmer 15 minutes. Stir occasionally while cooking.

Serve over brown rice.

Each serving provides:

183	Calories	35 g	Carbohydrate
6 g	Protein	217 mg	Sodium
3 g	Total fat (0 g Sat. fat)	0 mg	Cholesterol

Sweet Potato Chili

Based on an interesting Mayan stew, this recipe used the unlikely combination of meat and fruit. I replaced the meat with sweet potatoes and the result is incredibly delicious. If you like, you can make this dish hotter by adding more chili powder or a chopped jalapeño pepper.

Makes 8 servings

2	teaspoons vegetable oil
1	cup chopped onion
1	cup chopped green bell pepper
1	15-ounce can salt-free (or regular) tomato sauce
1	cup canned pineapple chunks (packed in juice), drained
1	cup water
1 1/2	pounds sweet potatoes, peeled and cut into 1-inch chunks
2	large Granny Smith apples, unpeeled, cut into 1-inch chunks
2	1-pound cans kidney beans, rinsed and drained (or 4 cups of cooked beans)
2	teaspoons chili powder
1	teaspoon ground cumin
1/2	teaspoon *each* salt and ground cinnamon

Heat oil in a large saucepan over medium heat. Add onion and bell pepper. Cook, stirring frequently, until onion begins to brown, about 5 minutes.

Add remaining ingredients and bring mixture to a boil. Cover, reduce heat to medium-low, and simmer, stirring occasionally, 45 minutes or until sweet potatoes are tender.

Serve in bowls or spoon over brown rice.

Each serving provides:

232	Calories	46 g	Carbohydrate
8 g	Protein	305 mg	Sodium
3 g	Total fat (0 g Sat. fat)	0 mg	Cholesterol

Chili Beans and Cheese

This is a reduced-fat (but not reduced-flavor) version of a popular Mexican bean dish called Frijoles Especiales, *which means "Special Beans." One reason that it's so special is because it's so easy. Spoon it over rice or a baked potato and your dinner is complete.*

Makes 4 servings

2	teaspoons vegetable oil
1	cup chopped green bell pepper
1/2	cup chopped onion
2	cloves garlic, finely chopped
1	1-pound can salt-free (or regular) tomatoes, chopped, undrained
1	1-pound can kidney beans, rinsed and drained (or 2 cups of cooked beans)
1	jalapeño pepper (optional), finely minced, seeds and membrane discarded
1 1/2	teaspoons chili powder (or more, to taste)
1	teaspoon ground cumin
1/2	teaspoon dried oregano
	Salt to taste
1	cup shredded reduced-fat Cheddar cheese (4 ounces)

Heat oil in a large nonstick skillet over medium heat. Add bell pepper, onion, and garlic. Cook, stirring frequently, 5 minutes.

Add remaining ingredients, *except* cheese. Cover and cook, stirring occasionally, 5 minutes.

Sprinkle with cheese, cover, and remove from heat. Let stand 5 minutes in order for cheese to melt.

Spoon over rice or baked potatoes.

Each serving provides:

235	Calories	23 g	Carbohydrate
16 g	Protein	367 mg	Sodium
9 g	Total fat (3 g Sat. fat)	20 mg	Cholesterol

Pinto-Cheese Casserole

Beans and rice are usually served separately in Mexico, but, occasionally the two are combined in delicious casseroles. If you're in a hurry and looking for something to do with leftover rice, this is the quick and easy answer. While it bakes, just toss a salad, steam a green vegetable, and your meal is complete. For extra "zip" add a finely chopped jalapeño or serrano chili.

Makes 4 servings

1¹/₂	cups cooked brown rice
1	1-pound can pinto beans, rinsed and drained (or 2 cups of cooked beans)
1	cup shredded reduced-fat Cheddar cheese (4 ounces)
³/₄	cup skim milk
3	egg whites
1¹/₂	teaspoons chili powder
1	teaspoon ground cumin
¹/₂	teaspoon garlic powder
¹/₂	teaspoon onion powder
¹/₄	teaspoon salt

Preheat oven to 350°.

Lightly oil a 1-quart casserole or spray with a nonstick cooking spray.

In a large bowl, combine rice, beans, and cheese. Mix well.

In another bowl, combine remaining ingredients. Beat with a fork or wire whisk until well blended. Add to rice mixture, mixing until thoroughly combined. Place in prepared casserole. Press mixture down gently with the back of a spoon.

Bake uncovered, 35 minutes or until set.

Let stand 5 minutes before serving.

Each serving provides:

280	Calories	32 g	Carbohydrate
19 g	Protein	597 mg	Sodium
8 g	Total fat (3 g Sat. fat)	21 mg	Cholesterol

South-of-the-Border Pizza

This is my own cross-cultural version of an Italian pizza gone Mexican! A quick and easy crust is topped with favorite Mexican spices, creating an exciting new taste combo that's very festive looking, as well as delicious. In fact, a Spanish friend, Carmen Collazo, who tested this recipe said it was one of her favorites. She also added chopped cilantro to the sauce and loved the results.

Makes 4 servings

Crust:
3/4   cup whole wheat flour
3/4   cup all-purpose flour
1   teaspoon baking powder
1/4   teaspoon salt
3/4   cup plus 1 tablespoon water

Sauce:
1   8-ounce can salt-free (or regular) tomato sauce
1/3   cup salsa (hot or mild)
1   teaspoon ground cumin
1   teaspoon chili powder
1   teaspoon dried oregano
1/8   teaspoon garlic powder

Topping:
1 1/2   cups shredded part-skim Mozzarella cheese (6 ounces)
3/4   cup thinly sliced onion
3/4   cup thinly sliced green bell pepper
1/2   cup salt-free (or regular) canned corn, drained
3   tablespoons sliced, pitted black olives

Preheat oven to 400°.

Lightly oil a 12-inch pizza pan or spray with a nonstick cooking spray.

In a large bowl, combine both types of flour, baking powder, and salt. Mix well. Add water, mixing until all ingredients are moistened. With your hands, work dough into a ball. Place dough in prepared pan and press to form a crust, flouring your hands slightly to avoid sticking.

Bake 10 minutes. Remove pan from oven.

Combine tomato sauce, salsa, and spices, mixing well. Spread evenly over baked crust, staying 1/2 inch away from edge of crust.

Sprinkle cheese and then remaining topping ingredients evenly over sauce.

Bake 10 to 15 minutes, until cheese is melted.

Each serving provides:

354	Calories	51 g	Carbohydrate
18 g	Protein	653 mg	Sodium
10 g	Total fat (5 g Sat. fat)	25 mg	Cholesterol

Cheddar-Topped Rice Casserole

No Mexican meal is complete without rice. Combined with cheese and chilies, it's a mainstay of the Mexican diet. Usually long grain white rice is used, however, I prefer brown rice because of its nutty flavor and higher fiber content. This dish is perfect for using up that leftover cup of rice. In fact, it's so tasty, you'll probably plan to have leftover rice more often.

Makes 4 servings

1	teaspoon vegetable oil
1	cup chopped onion
3	cloves garlic, finely chopped
1	cup cooked brown rice
1	1-pound can salt-free (or regular) stewed tomatoes
1	cup salt-free (or regular) canned corn, drained
1	jalapeño pepper (optional), finely minced, seeds and membrane discarded
1	teaspoon chili powder
1/2	teaspoon ground cumin
1	cup shredded reduced-fat Cheddar cheese (4 ounces)

Preheat oven to 350°.

Lightly oil a 1-quart baking dish or spray with a nonstick cooking spray.

Heat oil in a small nonstick skillet over medium heat. Add onion and garlic. Cook, stirring frequently, 5 minutes, until onion is tender and begins to brown.

While onion mixture is cooking, combine remaining ingredients, *except* Cheddar cheese, in a large bowl. Add onion mixture and mix well. Spoon into prepared baking dish.

Sprinkle cheese evenly over casserole.

Bake uncovered, 30 minutes.

Each serving provides:

254	Calories	34 g	Carbohydrate
12 g	Protein	233 mg	Sodium
8 g	Total fat (3 g Sat. fat)	20 mg	Cholesterol

Taco Rice

You can turn this side dish into an easy one-pot entrée by simply adding a can of pinto beans along with the rice. My kids enjoyed it with a light sprinkling of Parmesan cheese (Mexican cooks would never use a commercial seasoning mix, but it's so easy and tasty, I just had to give in.)

Makes 6 servings

2   cups water
1   8-ounce can salt-free (or regular) tomato sauce
1   package taco seasoning mix (1 1/4 ounces)
1   cup salt-free (or regular) canned corn, drained (or frozen corn)
1/2 cup finely chopped red or green bell pepper
1/2 teaspoon dried oregano
1/8 teaspoon garlic powder
1   cup brown rice, uncooked

In a medium saucepan, combine all ingredients, *except* rice. Bring mixture to a boil over medium heat. Stir in rice. When mixture boils again, stir, then reduce heat to medium-low, cover, and simmer, until most of the liquid has cooked out, 45 minutes to 1 hour. Remove from heat and set aside covered, for 5 minutes.

Mix well before serving.

Each serving provides:

176	Calories	37 g	Carbohydrate
4 g	Protein	472 mg	Sodium
1 g	Total fat (0 g Sat. fat)	0 mg	Cholesterol

Baked Eggplant Olé

Spoon this dish onto your plate like a typical casserole or serve it Mexican style, piled onto heated flour tortillas and rolled like a burrito. It works well either way and makes a perfect accompaniment to any Mexican entrée.

Makes 6 servings

1	teaspoon vegetable oil
1/2	cup chopped onion
1/2	cup chopped green bell pepper
3	cloves garlic, crushed
1	medium eggplant, peeled and cut into 1/2-inch pieces (3 cups)
2	medium, ripe tomatoes, peeled and chopped (2 cups)
1	4-ounce can green chilies (mild or hot), chopped and drained
1/2	cup shredded reduced-fat Cheddar cheese (2 ounces)
1/2	cup shredded part-skim Mozzarella cheese (2 ounces)
2	1-ounce slices whole wheat bread, cut into very small cubes
1/2	teaspoon ground cumin
1/2	teaspoon chili powder
1/2	teaspoon dried oregano
1/4	teaspoon salt
1/8	teaspoon pepper

Preheat oven to 375°.

Lightly oil a 1 1/2-quart casserole or spray with a nonstick cooking spray.

Heat oil in a large nonstick skillet over medium heat. Add onion, bell pepper, garlic, and eggplant. Cook, stirring frequently, 10 minutes. Remove from heat.

Add remaining ingredients. Mix well. Spoon mixture into prepared casserole.

Bake covered, 30 minutes.

Each serving provides:			
130	Calories	14 g	Carbohydrate
7 g	Protein	376 mg	Sodium
5 g	Total fat (2 g Sat. fat)	12 mg	Cholesterol

Chili Potatoes

In a hurry? Here's a Mexican-inspired idea for a quick and easy potato topper. Add a bowl of soup and a salad, and what could make a better Sunday supper?

Makes 4 servings

4	medium baking potatoes, about 8 ounces each
2	medium, ripe tomatoes, chopped (about 1¼ cups)
1	4-ounce can green chilies (mild or hot), chopped and drained
1	teaspoon chili powder
¹/8	teaspoon salt
¹/2	cup shredded reduced-fat Cheddar cheese (4 ounces)

Preheat oven to 375°.

Pierce potatoes several times with a sharp knife and bake until tender, about 50 minutes.

While potatoes are baking, in a medium bowl, combine tomatoes, chilies, chili powder, salt, and *half* of the cheese. Mix well.

Make a lengthwise slit in each baked potato. Squeeze the ends of the potatoes, making an opening in the top of each one. Divide tomato mixture evenly and pile into each potato. Divide remaining cheese and sprinkle on top of each potato.

Place potatoes on a baking sheet and bake 15 minutes, until topping is hot and cheese has melted.

Each serving provides:

276	Calories	44 g	Carbohydrate
12 g	Protein	466 mg	Sodium
5 g	Total fat (3 g Sat. fat)	20 mg	Cholesterol

Mexicana Green Beans

This bean medley has a pleasant flavor and is milder than many Mexican dishes. If you like, you can dust it lightly with grated Parmesan cheese just before serving.

Makes 4 servings

1	10-ounce package frozen French-style green beans
2	cups sliced mushrooms
1	cup onion, sliced vertically into thin slivers
3	cloves garlic, crushed
3	tablespoons slivered almonds
1	2-ounce jar sliced pimientos, drained
	Salt and freshly ground pepper to taste
	Grated Parmesan cheese (optional)

Cook green beans according to package directions. Drain.

While beans are cooking, combine mushrooms, onion, garlic, and almonds in a large nonstick skillet over medium heat. Cook, stirring frequently, 5 to 8 minutes or until onion is tender. Add pimientos and green beans to skillet. Mix well and heat through.

Add salt and lots of freshly ground pepper.

Spoon mixture into a serving bowl and sprinkle lightly with Parmesan cheese, if desired.

Each serving provides:

91	Calories	13 g	Carbohydrate
4 g	Protein	8 mg	Sodium
4 g	Total fat (0 g Sat. fat)	0 mg	Cholesterol

South-of-the-Border Zucchini

Squash is very popular in Mexico and the versatile zucchini makes its way into many dishes. This one is especially tasty when served with a bean dish, such as Hot Butter Beans *(page 72).*

Makes 6 servings

8	ounces zucchini, sliced into 1/8-inch slices (about 2 cups)
2	cups cooked brown rice
1	cup plain nonfat yogurt
1	4-ounce can green chilies, chopped and drained (I prefer the mild chilies for this dish because the blandness of the yogurt and the zucchini seems to magnify the heat of the chilies and the chili powder.)
1	teaspoon chili powder
1/4	teaspoon garlic powder
1/4	teaspoon salt
3/4	cup shredded reduced-fat Cheddar cheese (3 ounces)
	Salsa (hot or mild)

Preheat oven to 350°.

Lightly oil a 6 x 10-inch baking pan or spray with a nonstick cooking spray.

Layer *half* of the zucchini in the bottom of the pan. Spoon the rice evenly over the zucchini.

In a small bowl, combine the yogurt, chilies, chili powder, garlic powder, and salt. Mix well. Spoon evenly over rice. Top with remaining zucchini. Sprinkle cheese evenly over the top.

Bake uncovered, 30 minutes.

Top each serving with salsa.

Each serving provides:

157	Calories	21 g	Carbohydrate
8 g	Protein	343 mg	Sodium
4 g	Total fat (2 g Sat. fat)	11 mg	Cholesterol

Corn and Zucchini Mexi-Medley

Squash and corn are often combined in Mexican cooking, and if you are look-ing for a colorful, spicy dish to spark up a buffet, this is it. The variety of col-ors, and zesty flavors, makes this a perfect dish. This recipe makes a lot, but the leftovers can easily be reheated or even served cold as a delicious salad.

Makes 8 servings

1	teaspoon vegetable oil
1	cup chopped onion
1	cup chopped green bell pepper
3	cloves garlic, finely chopped
3	cups zucchini, unpeeled, cut into 1/2- to 3/4-inch pieces
1	1-pound can salt-free (or regular) corn, drained
2	1-pound cans salt-free (or regular) tomatoes, drained slightly, then chopped
1	4-ounce can green chilies (mild or hot), chopped and drained
2	teaspoons vinegar
1	teaspoon dried oregano
1/2	teaspoon ground cumin
	Salt to taste

Heat oil in a large nonstick skillet over medium heat. Add onion, bell pepper, and garlic. Cook, stirring frequently, 2 minutes. Add zuc-chini and corn. Cook, stirring frequently, 5 minutes.

Add remaining ingredients. Mix until thoroughly combined.

Cover and simmer, 5 minutes or until zucchini is tender-crisp.

Each serving provides:

87	Calories	19 g	Carbohydrate
3 g	Protein	106 mg	Sodium
1 g	Total fat (0 g Sat. fat)	0 mg	Cholesterol

Baked Tomatoes with Cilantro-Corn Stuffing

In Mexico, peppers and tomatoes are often filled with other vegetables creating a colorful presentation. If you prefer a little extra "zing," add a chopped fresh chili pepper.

Makes 4 servings

4	medium, ripe (yet firm) tomatoes
1	teaspoon vegetable oil
1/4	cup finely chopped onion
2	cloves garlic, finely minced
1	cup salt-free (or regular) canned corn, drained (or frozen corn)
1/2	cup shredded reduced-fat Cheddar cheese (2 ounces)
1	tablespoon finely chopped fresh cilantro
1/8	teaspoon *each* salt and pepper

Preheat oven to 375°.

Lightly oil a baking pan that is just large enough to hold the four tomatoes, or spray with a nonstick cooking spray. (If the pan is too large for the tomatoes to fit snugly, slice a *tiny* piece off the bottoms of the tomatoes to keep them from rolling around while baking.)

Slice off the top of each tomato, and using a teaspoon, scoop out the pulp, leaving a 1/4-inch shell. Chop the pulp and place in a strainer to drain. Turn the tomato shells upside-down on towels to drain.

Heat oil in a medium nonstick skillet over medium heat. Add onion and garlic. Cook, stirring frequently, until onion is tender, 3 to 4 minutes. Add tomato pulp, along with corn. Cook, stirring frequently, 5 minutes. Remove from heat and stir in remaining ingredients, using only *half* of the cheese.

Divide mixture evenly into tomatoes, top with remaining cheese, and place in prepared pan.

Bake uncovered, 15 minutes, just until tomatoes are hot and steamy and cheese is melted.

Each serving provides:

151	Calories	20 g	Carbohydrate
7 g	Protein	329 mg	Sodium
6 g	Total fat (2 g Sat. fat)	10 mg	Cholesterol

Apple-Cheddar Skillet Corn Bread

While corn tortillas are by far the most popular bread in Mexico, cornmeal is used in other breads as well. Apples are added to this one, lending a sweetness and texture that is very appealing.

Makes 12 servings

2	cups yellow cornmeal
2	teaspoons baking powder
1/2	teaspoon baking soda
1/4	teaspoon salt
1 1/4	cups skim milk
1	teaspoon vinegar
1	1-pound can salt-free (or regular) cream-style corn
3	egg whites
1/4	cup honey
2	tablespoons vegetable oil
1	cup shredded reduced-fat Cheddar cheese (4 ounces)
2	medium Granny Smith apples, unpeeled, diced into 1/8- to 1/4-inch pieces (1 1/2 cups)

Preheat oven to 400°.

Lightly oil a 10-inch cast iron skillet or spray with a nonstick cooking spray.

In a large bowl, combine cornmeal, baking powder, baking soda, and salt. Mix well. Place milk in a small bowl. Add vinegar and set aside.

In another bowl, combine corn, egg whites, honey, and oil. Beat with a fork or wire whisk until blended. Gradually whisk in milk. Stir in cheese and apples. Add to cornmeal mixture, mixing until all ingredients are moistened.

Heat skillet in oven for 3 minutes. Remove hot skillet from oven and pour in batter. Bake 30 to 35 minutes, until a toothpick inserted in the center of the bread comes out clean. Place on a wire rack to cool slightly. To serve, cut into pie-shaped wedges while still warm.

Each serving provides:

204	Calories		33 g	Carbohydrate
7 g	Protein		274 mg	Sodium
5 g	Total fat (1 g Sat. fat)		7 mg	Cholesterol

Peppered Corn Muffins

I couldn't resist converting a colorful Mexican bread into tender muffins. Lots of little bits of red and yellow peppers add flavor, crunch, and a touch of color. They're at their best served hot and steamy, right out of the oven.

Makes 12 muffins

1	cup yellow cornmeal
2/3	cup all-purpose flour
1/3	cup whole wheat flour
2	teaspoons baking powder
1/4	cup sugar
1/2	teaspoon salt
2	egg whites
2	tablespoons vegetable oil
1 1/2	cups skim milk
1/3	cup *each* very finely chopped red and yellow bell pepper
1/3	cup very finely chopped onion

Preheat oven to 450°.

Lightly oil 12 muffin cups or spray with a nonstick cooking spray.

In a large bowl, combine cornmeal, both types of flour, baking powder, sugar, and salt. Mix well.

In a small bowl, combine egg whites, oil, and milk. Beat with a fork or wire whisk until blended. Add to dry mixture, along with peppers and onion. Mix until all ingredients are moistened. Divide mixture evenly into prepared muffin cups.

Bake 12 to 15 minutes, until muffins are golden and a toothpick inserted in the center of a muffin comes out clean. Remove muffins to a wire rack.

Each muffin provides:

139	Calories	23 g	Carbohydrate
4 g	Protein	199 mg	Sodium
3 g	Total fat (0 g Sat. fat)	1 mg	Cholesterol

Pumpkin Torte with Rum Creme Filling

This delectable dessert is the Mexican answer to Boston Cream Pie! The spicy, moist cake is filled with a creamy, rum-flavored filling that is usually made with eggs and cream. When my recipe testers tasted this one, their only reaction was, "wow!" (If you're using canned pumpkin and don't know what to do with the leftovers, be sure to try Yellow Split Pea and Pumpkin Soup *on page 114).*

Makes 12 servings

Cake:
3/4   cup all-purpose flour
3/4   cup whole wheat flour
1   teaspoon baking soda
1/2   teaspoon baking powder
1/8   teaspoon salt
1   tablespoon cocoa
1   teaspoon ground cinnamon
1   teaspoon ground nutmeg
1/2   teaspoon ground cloves
1/4   teaspoon ground ginger
2/3   cup sugar
3 1/2 tablespoons orange juice
2   tablespoons vegetable oil
4   egg whites
1   cup canned pumpkin (or cooked and mashed fresh pumpkin)

Rum Creme Filling:
1 1/2 cups part-skim ricotta cheese (1 15-ounce container)
1/4   cup confectioners sugar
2   teaspoons vanilla extract
1   teaspoon rum extract

Preheat oven to 325°.

Lightly oil a 9-inch cake pan or spray with a nonstick cooking spray. Line the bottom of the pan with wax paper and spray again.

In a medium bowl, combine both types of flour, baking soda, baking powder, salt, cocoa, and spices. Mix well.

In a large bowl, beat sugar, orange juice, and oil on medium speed of an electric mixer for 3 minutes. Add egg whites and beat 2 minutes more. Reduce speed to low and alternately beat in flour mixture and pumpkin. Beat until all ingredients are blended. Spoon batter into prepared pan.

Bake 35 minutes, until a toothpick inserted in the center of the cake comes out clean.

Cool in pan on a wire rack for 10 minutes. Then remove cake from pan, carefully remove wax paper, and let cool completely on wire rack.

To prepare filling: combine all filling ingredients in a small bowl. Mix well.

To assemble: split cooled cake horizontally into 2 layers. Spread filling on bottom half, staying 1/2 -inch away from the edge of the cake. Replace top layer.

Cover cake and chill thoroughly.

Each serving provides:			
201	Calories	30 g	Carbohydrate
7 g	Protein	213 mg	Sodium
6 g	Total fat (2 g Sat. fat)	11 mg	Cholesterol

Cinnamon Creamy Corn Cake

Very tender and moist, moist, moist! There's no other way to describe this unusual cake. The original Mexican version is made with a lot of butter and eggs, which I replaced with my secret ingredient, cream-style corn!

Makes 12 servings

Topping:

2	teaspoons sugar
1/4	teaspoon ground cinnamon

Cake:

3/4	cup yellow cornmeal
3/4	cup all-purpose flour
1	teaspoon baking powder
1/2	teaspoon ground cinnamon
1/8	teaspoon salt
1	1-pound can salt-free (or regular) cream-style corn
2/3	cup sugar
3	egg whites
1	tablespoon vanilla extract

Preheat oven to 350°.

Lightly oil an 8-inch square baking pan or spray with a nonstick cooking spray.

Combine topping ingredients in a small bowl or custard cup. Set aside.

In a large bowl, sift together cornmeal, flour, baking powder, cinnamon, and salt.

In a blender container, combine remaining cake ingredients. Blend until almost smooth. (It's all right for some pieces of corn to remain.) Add to dry mixture. Mix until all ingredients are moistened. Spoon into prepared pan. Sprinkle topping evenly over cake.

Bake 35 minutes, until a toothpick inserted in the center of the cake comes out clean. Cool in pan on a wire rack.

Cut into squares to serve. Refrigerate leftovers.

Each serving provides:

141	Calories	31 g	Carbohydrate
3 g	Protein	79 mg	Sodium
1 g	Total fat (0 g Sat. fat)	0 mg	Cholesterol

Kahlua® Surprise Brownies

Kahlua® is a coffee-flavored Mexican liqueur that adds a deep, rich flavor to many Mexican desserts. The surprise in these brownies is the wonderful moistness that comes from the zucchini. (Now, be honest—if I had named them Kahlua® Zucchini Brownies, would you have read this far?)

Makes 16 servings

3/4   cup all-purpose flour
1/2   cup whole wheat flour
1/4   cup cocoa (unsweetened)
1/2   teaspoon *each* baking powder and baking soda
1/2   teaspoon ground cinnamon
1/4   cup Kahlua® (or other coffee-flavored liqueur)
2   tablespoons skim milk
2   tablespoons vegetable oil
2   egg whites
2   teaspoons vanilla extract
2/3   cup sugar
1   cup (packed) finely shredded zucchini, unpeeled

Preheat oven to 350°.

Lightly oil an 8-inch square baking pan or spray with a nonstick cooking spray.

In a large bowl, combine both types of flour, cocoa, baking powder, baking soda, and cinnamon.

In another bowl, combine Kahlua®, milk, oil, egg whites, vanilla, and sugar. Beat with a fork or wire whisk until blended. Add to dry mixture, along with zucchini. Mix until all ingredients are moistened. Spoon into prepared pan.

Bake 25 minutes, until a toothpick inserted in the center of the brownies comes out clean. Cool in pan on a wire rack.

Cut into squares to serve. Refrigerate leftovers.

Each serving provides:			
104	Calories	18 g	Carbohydrate
2 g	Protein	63 mg	Sodium
2 g	Total fat (0 g Sat. fat)	0 mg	Cholesterol

Garbanzo-Raisin Cake

*Each bite of this moist and airy cake is filled with the sweetness of raisins.
And, best of all, there's no oil in the recipe at all!*

Makes 12 servings

1	1-pound can garbanzo beans (chick peas), rinsed and drained (or 2 cups of cooked beans)
3	egg whites
1/4	cup skim milk
2	teaspoons vanilla extract
1/2	cup sugar
1/2	teaspoon baking powder
1/2	teaspoon ground cinnamon
1	teaspoon grated fresh lemon peel
1/2	cup raisins
1/4	teaspoon cream of tartar

Topping:

2	teaspoons sugar
1/4	teaspoon ground cinnamon

Preheat oven to 350°.

Lightly oil an 8-inch square baking pan or spray with a nonstick cooking spray.

In a blender container, combine beans, *one* of the egg whites, milk, vanilla, sugar, baking powder, cinnamon, and lemon peel. Blend until smooth. Spoon into a large bowl. Add raisins.

Place remaining 2 egg whites and cream of tartar in a deep bowl. Beat on medium speed of an electric mixer until foamy. Beat on high speed until egg whites are stiff. Gently fold into bean mixture. Spoon into prepared pan. Combine sugar and cinnamon and sprinkle evenly over cake.

Bake 35 minutes, until a toothpick inserted in the center of the cake comes out clean. Cool in pan on a wire rack.

Cut into squares to serve. Refrigerate leftovers.

Each serving provides:			
91	Calories	18 g	Carbohydrate
3 g	Protein	79 mg	Sodium
1 g	Total fat (0 g Sat. fat)	0 mg	Cholesterol

Pumpkin-Almond Custard

Puddings and custards are among the most popular Mexican desserts. This one, flavored with some of the country's favorite spices, is smooth and creamy and downright delicious. (One of my recipe testers served this dessert for Thanksgiving and everyone wanted the recipe.)

Makes 6 servings

Custard:

1	1-pound can pumpkin
3	egg whites
1/2	cup skim milk
1/2	cup firmly packed brown sugar
1	tablespoon molasses
1	teaspoon almond extract
1	teaspoon ground cinnamon
1/4	teaspoon ground cloves

Topping:

2	teaspoons firmly packed brown sugar
1/4	teaspoon ground cinnamon
2	tablespoons slivered almonds

Preheat oven to 350°.

Lightly oil a 1-quart baking dish or spray with a nonstick cooking spray.

In a large bowl, combine pumpkin with remaining custard ingredients. Beat on low speed of an electric mixer until blended. Continue to beat 1 minute more. Place in prepared baking pan.

Combine brown sugar and cinnamon in a small bowl. Sprinkle almonds over pudding, then top with brown sugar mixture.

Bake uncovered, 1 hour.

Let custard cool a half hour before serving. Refrigerate leftovers and enjoy them cold.

Each serving provides:

152	Calories	30 g	Carbohydrate
4 g	Protein	51 mg	Sodium
2 g	Total fat (0 g Sat. fat)	0 mg	Cholesterol

Fiesta Coffee Cake

You'll love the taste and sweet aroma of this delicately spiced cake. It combines the flavors of lemon, banana, and coriander and tops them with a sweet glaze of chocolate and cinnamon. This cake definitely reflects the native Mexican artistry and love of sweets.

Makes 12 servings

1	cup whole wheat flour
1	cup all-purpose flour
1	teaspoon baking powder
1	teaspoon baking soda
1³/₄	teaspoons ground coriander
¹/₄	teaspoon ground cinnamon
³/₄	cup vanilla nonfat yogurt
1	medium, very ripe banana, mashed (¹/₂ cup)
2	tablespoons vegetable oil
1	teaspoon grated fresh lemon peel
1	teaspoon vanilla extract
2	egg whites
²/₃	cup sugar

Glaze:

2	tablespoons cocoa (unsweetened)
¹/₈	teaspoon ground cinnamon
1	tablespoon skim milk
2	tablespoons honey

Preheat oven to 350°.

Lightly oil an 8-inch square baking pan or spray with a nonstick cooking spray.

In a large bowl, combine both types of flour, baking powder, baking soda, coriander, and cinnamon. Mix well.

In another bowl, combine remaining cake ingredients. Beat with a fork or wire whisk until blended. Add to dry mixture, mixing until all ingredients are moistened. Place in prepared pan.

Bake 30 to 35 minutes, until a toothpick inserted in the center of the cake comes out clean.

Cool in pan on a wire rack.

When cake is completely cool, combine glaze ingredients in a small bowl or custard cup. Mix until smooth. Spread over cake.

Cut into squares to serve.

Each serving provides:			
172	Calories	33 g	Carbohydrate
4 g	Protein	166 mg	Sodium
3 g	Total fat (0 g Sat. fat)	0 mg	Cholesterol

Apple Tortillas

Tortillas make wonderful "packages" for fruits, as well as beans. Mexican cooks often use combinations of fruits and cheese is sometimes rolled up with the hot fruit. This apple filling, laced with the flavors of lime and apricot, is really delectable.

Makes 6 servings

6	6-inch flour tortillas
2	large Golden Delicious apples, unpeeled, coarsely shredded (2 cups)
1/4	cup raisins
1/2	cup orange juice
2	teaspoons lime juice
1/2	teaspoon ground cinnamon
2	tablespoons fruit-only apricot jam
1	teaspoon confectioners sugar

Preheat oven to 350°.

Stack tortillas and wrap them tightly in aluminum foil. Heat in oven for 10 minutes.

While tortillas are heating, combine apples, raisins, orange juice, lime juice, and cinnamon in a small saucepan. Cook over medium heat, stirring frequently, 5 to 7 minutes or until apples are tender.

To assemble, spread 1 teaspoon of jam on each of the heated tortillas. Divide apple mixture evenly and spoon it along the center of each tortilla. Roll each tortilla up tightly into a cylinder and place them seam-side down on a serving plate. Sprinkle with confectioners sugar and serve right away. (Place sugar in a small strainer and shake it over the tortillas.)

Each serving provides:

131	Calories	28 g	Carbohydrate
2 g	Protein	97 mg	Sodium
2 g	Total fat (0 g Sat. fat)	0 mg	Cholesterol

Honey Crisps

My close friend Pat Tabibian came up with this delicious baked version of Sopapillas (SOH-peh-PEE-yahs); popular Mexican pastries that are normally deep-fried and topped with honey or syrup. You'll love them!

Makes 36 crisps

6	6-inch flour tortillas
1	tablespoon confectioners sugar
1/4	teaspoon ground cinnamon
3	tablespoons honey

Preheat oven to 400°.

Cut each tortilla into 6 pie-shaped wedges. (Kitchen shears work well.) Place on an ungreased baking sheet. Bake 8 to 10 minutes, until crisp. Remove tortillas from baking sheet and place on a sheet of wax paper or a serving plate.

While crisps are baking, combine confectioners sugar and cinnamon in a small bowl or custard cup. Mix well.

Drizzle 1/4 teaspoon of honey over each hot crisp. Sprinkle with sugar mixture. (An easy way to do this is to place sugar and cinnamon in a small strainer and shake it over the crisps.)

Serve warm.

Each crisp provides:

17	Calories	4 g	Carbohydrate
0 g	Protein	16 mg	Sodium
0 g	Total fat (0 g Sat. fat)	0 mg	Cholesterol

Tortilla Dessert Cups

These crispy, crunchy cups can be used for many different desserts. Let your imagination be your guide! You can fill them with ice milk, sherbet, fruit; the possibilities are endless. After enjoying the filling, you can devour the bowl! For more servings, while these are cooling, simply repeat the process.

Makes 4 cups

2¹/₂   teaspoons sugar
¹/₄   teaspoon ground cinnamon
4   6-inch flour tortillas
       Nonstick cooking spray

Preheat oven to 400°.

Place 4 custard cups (6-ounce size) upside-down on an ungreased baking sheet, leaving as much room as possible between the cups.

Combine sugar and cinnamon in a small bowl. Mix well.

Place tortillas on a plate or a sheet of wax paper. Spray both sides lightly with nonstick cooking spray. Sprinkle both sides of tortillas evenly with sugar mixture, using a rounded quarter-teaspoonful on each side.

Place 1 tortilla on each custard cup. (Tortillas will soften as they bake and form loosely-shaped cups.)

Bake 8 to 10 minutes, until lightly browned. (Open the oven once, about halfway through baking and carefully press each tortilla down around the cups. If any of the tortillas have puffed up, poke a hole in the tortilla with a toothpick.)

Remove tortillas to a wire rack to cool, then store in a loosely covered container until serving time. (Cups will keep 2 to 3 days.)

To serve, fill with any of the following fillings or be creative and design your own original dessert. Fill just before serving.

Suggested Fillings:
- Vanilla ice milk topped with a few teaspoons of coffee-flavored liqueur
- Chocolate ice milk topped with a few teaspoons of almond-flavored liqueur and a few toasted almonds
- Orange sherbet topped with fresh orange sections
- Pineapple sherbet topped with vanilla nonfat yogurt that has been mixed with a few drops of coconut extract
- Fresh fruit salad made with tropical fruits such as mango, kiwi, banana, and papaya

- Warm baked apples topped with vanilla nonfat yogurt
- Fresh berries topped with vanilla nonfat yogurt and grated orange peel

---

Each crisp provides:

82	Calories	14 g	Carbohydrate
2 g	Protein	96 mg	Sodium
3 g	Total fat (0 g Sat. fat)	0 mg	Cholesterol

Flavors of the Caribbean

Stretching from the coast of Florida to the tip of Venezuela, the Caribbean Islands are truly a cultural melting pot. From the popular islands of Barbados, Jamaica, and St. Thomas, to the less familiar Montserrat and Saint Kitts–Nevis, island cuisine exhibits a diverse blend of tastes and textures.

The cuisine of the Caribbean Islands is influenced by many traditions and cultures. People who live on the islands come from all over the world and have brought with them a great variety of tastes and styles.

Island cuisine has been greatly influenced and enriched by the culinary traits of "newcomers" to the islands, many of whom arrived several hundred years ago. These travelers arrived mainly from Spain, Great Britain, France, Holland, Portugal, India, China, and Africa. There is a more recent American influence on the food, brought about both by tourism and the influx of former United States residents to the beautiful islands that many now call home. The immigrants to the Caribbean brought with them their tastes in food and adapted their own traditional dishes to the local foods of the islands. However, we can still see, for example, a definite Spanish influence on the islands of Cuba, Puerto Rico, and the Dominican Republic; a Dutch influence on the islands of Curaçao, Aruba, and Bonaire; and an undeniable French influence on the cuisine of Martinique, Haiti, and Guadeloupe. The result is a delicate blend of foods and tradition, leading to the development of a new Caribbean cuisine. Many times the origins of the dishes are unclear, dominated by the unquestionable modern-day Caribbean influences.

Among the most popular Caribbean fruits are the mango, pineapple, banana, avocado, coconut, papaya, lemon, orange, and lime. Some of the island fruits that are generally less familiar to us are the plantain, star apple, jackfruit, tamarind, and soursop.

The most abundant vegetables on the islands include the potato, sweet potato, yam, red and green bell pepper, tomato, corn, peas, pumpkin, and okra. The less familiar ones include the christophene (a type of squash), taro root, cassava root, and callaloo (a spinach-like green). Also frequently used are legumes, such as kidney beans, split peas, black-eyed peas, and black beans, in addition to the less familiar pigeon peas.

Popular herbs and spices found in Caribbean cuisine include allspice, bay leaves, cloves, cinnamon, garlic, ginger, nutmeg, oregano, thyme, pepper, and curry. In addition, foods are often flavored with hot chilies. They can be chopped and added to almost any recipe in this chapter to add more authentic "heat," if desired. Vanilla extract and rum are frequently used in Caribbean recipes, as are the grated peels of oranges, lemons, and limes.

A familiar grain that appears in Caribbean food is rice. Cornmeal is also very widely used, with corn bread appearing in the cuisine of many of the islands.

It is interesting to note, that while many of the foods used in authentic island dishes may sound familiar, many of them, such as pumpkin and chilies, are usually varieties that are somewhat different from the ones with which we are familiar.

Adapting Caribbean cuisine to meatless, lot fat meals was quite a challenge, due mostly to the large amounts of seafood, the heavy use of coconut, and the scarcity and expense of true Caribbean fruits and vegetables in most parts of the United States. To make the foods compatible with our lifestyle—combining popular island flavors with more familiar and more readily available ingredients, often substituting health and availability for some of the authenticity—I have come up with new and innovative ways to enjoy the flavors of the Caribbean.

Enjoy your island tour!

Flavors of the Caribbean
Recipes

Suggested Menus

Lunch

Cold Melon Soup *(115)*
Orange Bean Salad Sandwich *(135)*
Tossed Salad
Pineapple-Banana Parfaits *(150)*

Tropical Fruit Soup *(116)*
Sweet Sunshine Pasta Salad *(124)*
Lettuce and Sliced Tomatoes
Sweet Potato Biscuits *(148)*

Orange-Basil Tomato Soup *(113)*
Stuffed Papaya Boats *(120)*
Raisin-Pecan-Ginger Muffins *(147)*

Dinner

Green Bean Salad with Honey-Lime
Dressing *(122)*
Calypso Pineapple Bean Pot *(126)*
Tomato Rice *(144)*
Coconut Custards with Coffee-Rum
Sauce *(152)*

Pineapple Wedding Boats with
Creamy Orange Sauce *(119)*
Caribbean Baked Tofu Cutlets *(131)*
Curried Apple Rice *(143)*
Steamed Green Beans
Caribbean Ginger Cake *(158)*

Orange-Basil Tomato Soup *(113)*
Fresh Vegetables
Creamy Avocado Dip *(109)*
Sweet Pineapple-Bean Salad *(123)*
Calypso Sweet Potato–Fruit
Salad *(121)*
Cornmeal Raisin Cake with Rum
Sauce *(156)*

Black Bean Soup *(111)*
Tossed Salad
Creole Potato Stew *(134)*
Brown Rice
Pineapple Crisp *(155)*

Recipe page numbers appear in parentheses.

Paradise Fruit Kabobs with
Creamy Coconut Dip

The cornucopia of fruits available on the islands provides inspiration for fantastic fruit dishes. This is one of the most attractive ways to serve fruit! The creamy dip can be used both as a delectable topping for other fruits or for a slice of warm cake.

Makes 4 servings
(2 kabobs and 1/4 cup dip each serving)

Creamy Coconut Dip:

1	cup lowfat (1%) cottage cheese
3	tablespoons firmly packed brown sugar
2	tablespoons skim milk
1	teaspoon vanilla extract
1/2	teaspoon coconut extract

Fruit Kabobs:

16	cantaloupe balls or 1-inch cubes
16	honeydew balls or 1-inch cubes
16	pineapple chunks, canned (packed in juice) or fresh
16	seedless red grapes
8	8-inch bamboo skewers

To prepare dip: in a blender container, combine all dip ingredients. Blend until smooth. Spoon into a bowl and chill several hours or overnight.

To prepare kabobs: have fruit well chilled. Alternate fruit on skewers, placing 2 pieces of each fruit on each skewer. (These can be made 1 to 2 hours ahead and chilled until serving time.)

Serve with dipping sauce.

(If you wish, instead of using skewers, fruit can be placed in a bowl and served with fancy toothpicks.)

Each serving provides:

168	Calories	33 g	Carbohydrate
9 g	Protein	255 mg	Sodium
1 g	Total fat (0 g Sat. fat)	2 mg	Cholesterol

Pineapple Mini-Fritters with
Pineapple-Poppy Seed Dipping Sauce

Antigua's sweet pineapples are usually the star ingredient in these delicious miniature fritters. However, for ease, I've substituted crushed pineapple. These sweet, little pancakes are often served as an appetizer, but they also make a family-pleasing breakfast that's tasty and fun.

Makes 6 servings
(6 mini-fritters and
2 tablespoons sauce each serving)

Pineapple-Poppy Seed Dipping Sauce:
1 cup pineapple juice
1¹/2 tablespoons firmly packed brown sugar
¹/2 teaspoon poppy seeds
1 tablespoon plus 1 teaspoon cornstarch

Pineapple Mini-Fritters:
¹/3 cup all-purpose flour
¹/3 cup whole wheat flour
1 teaspoon baking powder
¹/2 teaspoon ground cinnamon
1 egg white
¹/2 cup skim milk
2 tablespoons firmly packed brown sugar
¹/2 teaspoon vanilla extract
¹/4 teaspoon lemon extract
1 8-ounce can crushed pineapple (packed in juice), drained

To prepare sauce: in a small saucepan, combine all sauce ingredients. Stir to dissolve cornstarch. Bring to a boil over medium heat, stirring constantly. Continue to cook and stir for 1 to 2 minutes. Remove from heat, cover, and set aside.

To prepare fritters: in a large bowl, combine both types of flour, baking powder, and cinnamon. Mix well.

In a small bowl, combine remaining ingredients. Beat with a fork or wire whisk until blended. Add to dry mixture, mixing until all ingredients are moistened.

Preheat a large nonstick griddle or skillet over medium heat. Oil it lightly or spray with a nonstick cooking spray.

Drop mixture by rounded teaspoonfuls onto skillet. Turn fritters once, when edges appear dry and bottoms are lightly browned. Cook until golden brown on both sides. As fritters are cooked, place them on a serving plate and cover tightly with aluminum foil to keep warm.

Stir sauce and place in a small bowl. Serve alongside fritters for dipping.

Each serving provides:

223	Calories	32 g	Carbohydrate
3 g	Protein	106 mg	Sodium
9 g	Total fat (1 g Sat. fat)	0 mg	Cholesterol

Sunset Mango Dip

Variations of this cool, creamy dip are served on many of the Caribbean islands, where mangos are a way of life. It's perfect for dipping fresh fruits and can also be spooned over other fruits, or over pancakes or waffles to make a very special breakfast. I've replaced the more typical sweet cream with vanilla yogurt and the taste is still creamy and sweet.

Makes 8 servings
(2 tablespoons each serving)

1	ripe mango, peeled and cut into chunks, seed discarded
1 1/2	teaspoons firmly packed brown sugar
1/2	teaspoon lime juice (or lemon juice)
1/2	cup vanilla nonfat yogurt
	Dash nutmeg

Place mango chunks in a blender container with brown sugar and lime juice. Blend until smooth. Spoon into a bowl.

Stir yogurt into mango purée, stirring until blended.

Chill thoroughly.

Just before serving, sprinkle very lightly with nutmeg (preferably freshly grated).

Each serving provides:

33	Calories	8 g	Carbohydrate
1 g	Protein	11 mg	Sodium
0 g	Total fat (0 g Sat. fat)	0 mg	Cholesterol

Creamy Avocado Dip

This creamy dip blends a unique combination of flavors, resulting in a delicious treat. It's from a recipe that originated in the French Caribbean, on the beautiful island of Martinique. I like to garnish the dip with red bell pepper rings and sliced olives and serve it with vegetable dippers or crackers. The leftovers make a great sandwich spread.

Makes 16 servings
(2 tablespoons each serving)

1	cup lowfat (1%) cottage cheese
1	teaspoon lemon juice
1/4	cup ketchup
1/4	teaspoon ground allspice
1/8	teaspoon pepper
	Dash salt
1	ripe avocado, peeled and mashed
12	small, stuffed green olives, finely chopped
1	tablespoon sweet pickle relish

In a blender container, combine cottage cheese, lemon juice, ketchup, and spices. Blend until smooth. Place in a bowl and add remaining ingredients. Mix well.

Cover tightly and chill several hours or overnight.

Each serving provides:

39	Calories	3 g	Carbohydrate
2 g	Protein	171 mg	Sodium
2 g	Total fat (0 g Sat. fat)	1 mg	Cholesterol

Plantain Chips

Plantains are a member of the banana family. They look like bananas, but they must be cooked before eating and they have a mildly sweet flavor similar to squash. Harry and I fell in love with this popular Caribbean snack while honeymooning on Barbados. Unfortunately, the island version was fried (and might account for some of the weight we gained!), so I was determined to create a lowfat version. You can easily double or triple the recipe if you wish.

Makes 2 servings

1   green plantain (The ripe, yellow ones are too soft to slice thin.)
        Salt to taste
        Garlic powder

Preheat oven to 350°.
Lightly oil a large baking sheet or spray with a nonstick cooking spray.
Peel the plantain. Using a vegetable peeler, thinly slice the plantain into uniform slices. Place on prepared baking sheet. Sprinkle lightly with salt and a very light dusting of garlic powder.
Bake 12 to 15 minutes, until light brown. Remove to a wire rack to cool. (Baking time may vary according to thickness of plantain slices. They need to be light brown all over, or they will become soggy when cooled.)
Enjoy right away or store in an airtight container.

Each serving provides:

129	Calories	29 g	Carbohydrate
1 g	Protein	4 mg	Sodium
3 g	Total fat (0 g Sat. fat)	0 mg	Cholesterol

Black Bean Soup

This delicious soup is popular in Cuba and Puerto Rico, and has a delicate flavor all its own. The combination of cumin and wine vinegar is often found in the cuisine of these two islands.

Makes 4 servings
(1¹/4 cups each serving)

2	teaspoons vegetable oil
1	cup finely chopped onion
¹/2	cup finely chopped green bell pepper
4	large cloves garlic, finely minced
2	medium, ripe tomatoes, peeled and chopped (1¹/2 cups)
1	tablespoon red wine vinegar
1	teaspoon paprika
¹/2	teaspoon *each* ground cumin, dried oregano, and pepper
1	bay leaf
1	1-pound can black beans, rinsed and drained (or 2 cups of cooked beans)
3	cups *Vegetable Broth*, or 3 cups of water plus 3 teaspoons *Vegetable Broth Mix* (See pages 26–27.)
	Salt to taste

Heat oil in a medium saucepan over medium heat. Add onion, bell pepper, and garlic. Cook, stirring frequently, 5 minutes.

Add tomatoes, vinegar, and spices. Reduce heat to low and cook, stirring occasionally, 15 minutes.

Place 1 cup of the beans in a bowl and mash with a fork. Add to saucepan, along with remaining beans, water, and broth mix.

Simmer uncovered, stirring occasionally, 40 minutes.

Add salt to taste.

Remove and discard bay leaf before serving.

Each serving provides:

130	Calories	21 g	Carbohydrate
6 g	Protein	253 mg	Sodium
3 g	Total fat (0 g Sat. fat)	0 mg	Cholesterol

Creamy Sweet Potato Soup

Sweet potatoes and yams thrive on many of the Caribbean islands. They show up in everything from soups to desserts. This soup is creamy, sweet, and very tasty!

Makes 4 servings
(1 cup each serving)

3	medium sweet potatoes (1 3/4 pounds)
1	teaspoon vegetable oil
1/2	cup finely chopped onion
1/2	cup finely chopped celery
1	clove garlic, crushed
1	teaspoon dried basil
2	cups skim milk
1/2	teaspoon salt
1/4	teaspoon pepper
1/8	teaspoon ground allspice

Pierce sweet potatoes several times with a sharp knife and bake in a 350° oven 1 hour or until tender. When cool enough to handle, peel, place in a large bowl, and mash with a fork or potato masher.

Heat oil in a medium saucepan over medium heat. Add onion, celery, garlic, and basil. Cook, stirring frequently, 10 minutes or until vegetables are tender. Add small amounts of water as necessary, about a tablespoon at a time, to prevent sticking.

Gradually stir milk into saucepan. Add mashed sweet potatoes, salt, pepper, and allspice. Cook, stirring frequently, until soup just begins to boil. Serve right away or remove from heat and cover until serving time.

Each serving provides:

216	Calories	44 g	Carbohydrate
7 g	Protein	370 mg	Sodium
2 g	Total fat (0 g Sat. fat)	2 mg	Cholesterol

Orange-Basil Tomato Soup

I adapted this sweet, rich soup from a Trinidad seafood recipe. It's slightly sweet and can easily be "heated up" island-style by adding a chopped chili, such as a jalapeño.

Makes 4 servings
(1 cup each serving)

1	teaspoon vegetable oil
1	cup chopped onion
2	cloves garlic, crushed
6	medium, ripe tomatoes, peeled and chopped (5 cups)*
2	teaspoons dried basil
1	cup orange juice
2¹/₂	teaspoons sugar
¹/₂	teaspoon salt
¹/₈	teaspoon pepper

Heat oil in a medium saucepan over medium heat. Add onion and garlic. Cook, stirring frequently, until onion is tender, about 5 minutes. Add tomatoes and basil. Bring mixture to a boil. Reduce heat to medium-low, cover, and simmer 30 minutes.

Place soup in a blender container and blend until smooth. Pour soup, a little at a time, through a sieve or strainer, back into saucepan. Press the pulp through the strainer using the back of a spoon. Only the seeds should remain in the strainer, to be discarded.

Stir orange juice, sugar, salt, and pepper into soup. Heat through. Taste soup and add additional sugar or salt, if desired.

Serve hot or refrigerate and serve cold.

To peel tomatoes: With a sharp knife, cut an x in the skin at the stem end of each tomato, place in boiling water for 1 minute, then place immediately in a bowl of ice water.

Each serving provides:

116	Calories	25 g	Carbohydrate
3 g	Protein	297 mg	Sodium
2 g	Total fat (0 g Sat. fat)	0 mg	Cholesterol

Yellow Split Pea and Pumpkin Soup

In Haiti, this rich, stew-like soup is made from calabaza, a type of West Indian pumpkin, and native beans called pigeon peas. It's so thick and hearty, it can be served as an entrée. Add a salad and a chunk of crusty bread and dinner is complete. (If you use canned pumpkin and have leftovers, try the Pumpkin Torte with Rum Creme Filling *on page 88.)*

Makes 4 servings
(1¹/2 cups each serving)

2	teaspoons vegetable oil
1¹/2	cups onion, cut vertically into thin slivers
1	large clove garlic, crushed
4	cups water
1	cup yellow split peas, uncooked (Look for them near the dried beans in most grocery stores.)
1	cup canned pumpkin (or fresh pumpkin, cooked and mashed)
1	tablespoon *Vegetable Broth Mix* (See page 27.)
¹/2	teaspoon dried basil
¹/4	teaspoon dried thyme
¹/2	teaspoon salt
¹/4	teaspoon pepper
1	bay leaf

Heat oil in a large saucepan over medium heat. Add onion and garlic. Cook, stirring frequently, until onion is tender, about 5 minutes. Add small amounts of water if necessary, about a tablespoon at a time, to prevent sticking.

Add remaining ingredients and bring mixture to a boil. Reduce heat to medium-low, cover, and simmer 45 to 50 minutes.

Remove and discard bay leaf before serving.

Each serving provides:

238	Calories	41 g	Carbohydrate
14 g	Protein	346 mg	Sodium
3 g	Total fat (0 g Sat. fat)	0 mg	Cholesterol

Cold Melon Soup

Many different types of melons can be used in this cool, fresh soup, however, honeydew melons definitely get my vote! I'm not sure what made the Barbados version so creamy, but I have duplicated it by using vanilla yogurt. For a wonderful island touch, serve the soup in hollowed-out pineapple halves. Your family and guests will rave!

Makes 4 servings
(1 cup each serving)

4   cups ripe honeydew, cut into small balls or cubes
4   teaspoons lime juice (preferably fresh)
2   teaspoons honey
1   cup vanilla nonfat yogurt
1/2   cup honeydew balls for garnish

In a blender container, combine honeydew, lime juice, and honey. Blend until smooth. Pour into a bowl and add yogurt. Beat with a fork or wire whisk until blended.

Chill several hours.

Serve cold. Whisk before serving and garnish each bowl with a few melon balls.

Each serving provides:

129	Calories	30 g	Carbohydrate
4 g	Protein	60 mg	Sodium
0 g	Total fat (0 g Sat. fat)	2 mg	Cholesterol

Tropical Fruit Soup

Tropical fruits are abundant in the Caribbean. So it's no surprise that Caribbean cooks use them in everything from soups to desserts. This refreshing cold soup blends a variety of island fruits and makes a perfect beginning to any meal, especially during hot summer months. For an attractive way to present it, float a thin slice of starfruit on top of each serving.

Makes 4 servings
(1 cup each serving)

1	ripe mango, peeled and cut into chunks, seed discarded
1	ripe papaya, peeled and cut into chunks, seeds discarded
1	cup very ripe pineapple, cut into small chunks (or canned, crushed pineapple, packed in juice)
1	large orange, peeled, and sectioned (Discard white membrane.)
1/4	cup orange juice
1	tablespoon honey
1	cup vanilla nonfat yogurt

In a blender container, combine all ingredients, *except* yogurt. Blend until smooth. Pour into a bowl and add yogurt. Beat with a fork or wire whisk until smooth.

Chill several hours.

Serve cold. Whisk before serving. (If a thinner consistency is desired, whisk a little more orange juice into soup before serving.)

Each serving provides:

177	Calories	42 g	Carbohydrate
4 g	Protein	44 mg	Sodium
0 g	Total fat (0 g Sat. fat)	2 mg	Cholesterol

Banana Waldorf Salad

The classic American salad and the tropical banana come together in this salad, which is actually a combination of several island recipes. Serve it on a bed of greens, or for a prettier presentation, piled into an apple that has been cut into wedges and opened like a flower.

Makes 4 servings

1/2	cup vanilla nonfat yogurt
1/4	teaspoon coconut extract
1/8	teaspoon ground cinnamon
1/2	cup finely chopped celery
1/4	cup raisins
2	tablespoons chopped walnuts or pecans
2	ripe (yet firm) bananas, cut into 1/2-inch pieces

In a medium bowl, combine yogurt, coconut extract, and cinnamon. Mix well. Add celery, raisins, and nuts. Mix until well blended.

Gently stir bananas into yogurt mixture.

Chill several hours. (This salad is best when made, chilled, and served on the same day. Otherwise the bananas may become mushy.)

Each serving provides:

132	Calories	27 g	Carbohydrate
3 g	Protein	35 mg	Sodium
3 g	Total fat (0 g Sat. fat)	1 mg	Cholesterol

Mango-Berry Delight

Cool as a tropical breeze, and popular on all of the islands, fruit cups make a delicious appetizer and double as a light, refreshing dessert. For special flair, serve in crisp Tortilla Dessert Cups *(page 98).*

Makes 4 servings

1	cold, ripe mango, peeled and cut into chunks, seed discarded
2	teaspoons orange juice
1	teaspoon honey
2	cups (total) fresh blueberries, strawberries, or raspberries (or any combination of berries)

Place mango chunks in a blender container with orange juice and honey. Blend until smooth.

Divide berries evenly into four serving bowls or sherbet glasses. Divide mango purée evenly and spoon over berries. Serve right away.

Note: Berries and mango purée can be refrigerated in *separate* bowls for up to 24 hours and assembled just before serving.

Each serving provides:

81	Calories	21 g	Carbohydrate
1 g	Protein	5 mg	Sodium
0 g	Total fat (0 g Sat. fat)	0 mg	Cholesterol

Pineapple Wedding Boats with Creamy Orange Sauce

Pineapples are abundant in the Caribbean. They make perfect fruit "boats" that are often served at weddings and other grand celebrations. The fruits vary but the presentation is the same.

Makes 8 servings

1	large, ripe pineapple
1	ripe papaya, peeled and cut into 1/2- to 1-inch pieces, seeds discarded
1	large orange, peeled, sectioned, and cut into 1-inch pieces (Discard white membrane.)
1/4	cup raisins
1	tablespoon honey
2	teaspoons lime juice

Creamy Orange Sauce:

3/4	cup vanilla nonfat yogurt
2	tablespoons *each* honey and orange juice
1/4	teaspoon orange extract

Cut pineapple in half lengthwise. Using a small, sharp knife, scoop out pineapple, leaving a 1/2-inch shell. (If you wish, you can cut off all but about 3 inches of the leaves.) Remove and discard center core and cut pineapple into 1/2- to 1-inch pieces. Place in a large bowl. Turn pineapple shells upside-down to drain.

Add papaya, orange, and raisins to pineapple in bowl. Toss to combine. Drizzle with honey and lime juice. Toss gently. Pile mixture into pineapple shells, cover, and chill thoroughly.

In a small bowl, combine all sauce ingredients. Mix well. Chill several hours.

To serve, use pineapples as the serving bowls and top each individual serving with 2 tablespoons of the sauce.

Each serving provides:			
125	Calories	31 g	Carbohydrate
2 g	Protein	18 mg	Sodium
0 g	Total fat (0 g Sat. fat)	1 mg	Cholesterol

Stuffed Papaya Boats

*Papayas are native to the Caribbean and usually appear on the table at break-
fast or for dessert, often accompanied by a wedge of lemon or lime. This tanta-
lizing papaya salad can be served as an appetizer, salad, light luncheon dish,
or a deliciously different breakfast. Close your eyes when you bite into this
luscious salad and you'll think you're on a tropical island.*

Makes 4 servings

1	cup lowfat (1%) cottage cheese
1/3	cup canned crushed pineapple (packed in juice), drained
3	tablespoons honey
1	tablespoon lime juice (preferably fresh)
	Dash ground cinnamon
	Dash ground allspice
2	cold, ripe papayas

In a small bowl, combine all ingredients *except* papayas. Mix well.
Chill several hours.

At serving time, peel papayas and cut them in half lengthwise.
Scoop out and discard seeds. Cut a very thin slice off the bottom of
each half so they will remain stable on the plate. Stir the cottage
cheese mixture and mound it into the papaya shells.

Sprinkle lightly with additional cinnamon.

Serve right away.

Each serving provides:			
162	Calories	33 g	Carbohydrate
8 g	Protein	235 mg	Sodium
1 g	Total fat (0 g Sat. fat)	2 mg	Cholesterol

Calypso Sweet Potato–Fruit Salad

This enticing vegetable-fruit salad combines the ever-popular and abundant sweet potato and pineapple. I have replaced the coconut cream in the original version with yogurt and coconut extract, recreating a dish that can be served as a side dish, or alongside a mound of cottage cheese as a filling lunch.

Makes 8 servings

2   large sweet potatoes (1 1/2 pounds)
1   cup fresh or canned pineapple chunks (packed in juice), drained
2   large oranges, peeled and sectioned (Discard white membranes.)
1/2   cup vanilla nonfat yogurt
1   tablespoon honey
1/2   teaspoon grated fresh orange peel
1/2   teaspoon coconut extract
2   teaspoons shredded unsweetened coconut (optional)

Preheat oven to 375°.

Pierce sweet potatoes several times with a sharp knife and bake 45 minutes or until just tender. (Do not overbake potatoes.)

When potatoes are cool enough to handle, peel them and cut into 1-inch cubes.

Place cubes in a large bowl and add pineapple and orange sections. (Before peeling oranges, grate enough peel to equal 1/2 teaspoon.)

In a small bowl, combine remaining ingredients, *except* shredded coconut. Mix well. Spoon over sweet potato mixture. Mix gently, until evenly coated.

Chill several hours or overnight. Just before serving, mix well and sprinkle with coconut, if desired.

Each serving provides:

117	Calories	27 g	Carbohydrate
2 g	Protein	18 mg	Sodium
0 g	Total fat (0 g Sat. fat)	0 mg	Cholesterol

Green Bean Salad with Honey-Lime Dressing

Caribbean limes are the basis for numerous island salads. This colorful example combines green beans, tomatoes, and onion in a sweet lime dressing. It tastes best when made ahead and chilled for a day or two before serving.

Makes 6 servings

1	10-ounce package frozen whole green beans (or fresh beans)
2	medium, ripe tomatoes, cut into small wedges
1/2	cup onion, cut vertically into thin slivers
2	tablespoons lime juice (preferably fresh)
2	tablespoons honey
1 1/2	teaspoons vegetable oil
3	cloves garlic, crushed
1 1/4	teaspoons dried basil
1/4	teaspoon salt
1/8	teaspoon pepper

Cook beans according to package directions until just tender-crisp. Rinse under cold water and drain.

In a medium bowl, combine beans with tomatoes and onion. Toss to combine.

In a small bowl or custard cup, combine remaining ingredients. Mix well. Add to bean mixture and mix until thoroughly combined.

Chill thoroughly, preferably at least overnight, mixing several times.

Mix again before serving.

Each serving provides:

66	Calories	14 g	Carbohydrate
2 g	Protein	97 mg	Sodium
1 g	Total fat (0 g Sat. fat)	0 mg	Cholesterol

Sweet Pineapple-Bean Salad

From the magnificent island of Antigua, this sweet salad makes a delicious side dish or light entrée. Serve it on a bed of lettuce garnished with slices of tomato and melon for a dish that's tropical, attractive, and tasty. It serves six as a side salad or four as an entrée.

Makes 6 servings

1	1-pound can kidney beans, rinsed and drained (or 2 cups of cooked beans)
1	cup canned crushed pineapple (packed in juice), drained
1/4	cup finely chopped celery
1/4	cup raisins
2	tablespoons chopped almonds or walnuts
2	tablespoons thinly sliced green onion
2	tablespoons reduced-calorie mayonnaise
2	tablespoons fruit-only apricot or peach jam
1	tablespoon red wine vinegar
1/4	teaspoon garlic powder
1/4	teaspoon ground ginger
1/8	teaspoon cayenne pepper

In a medium bowl, combine kidney beans, pineapple, celery, raisins, nuts, and green onion.

In a small bowl, combine remaining ingredients. Mix until well blended, add to bean mixture, and mix again.

Chill several hours or overnight. Stir before serving.

Each serving provides:

142	Calories	25 g	Carbohydrate
5 g	Protein	127 mg	Sodium
3 g	Total fat (0 g Sat. fat)	2 mg	Cholesterol

Sweet Sunshine Pasta Salad

While vacationing on the island of St. John, Harry and I enjoyed a pasta salad similar to this one. Although I think it was more to please the tourists than authentic island cuisine, I still consider it a Caribbean recipe.

Makes 12 servings

8	ounces spiral-shaped pasta, uncooked (about 2¹/₂ cups)
1	10-ounce package frozen peas and carrots
1	20-ounce can pineapple tidbits (packed in juice), drained, juice reserved
1	1-pound can black beans, rinsed and drained (or 2 cups of cooked beans)
1	cup red bell pepper, cut lengthwise into thin slices, then cut crosswise into thirds
¹/₂	cup thinly sliced green onions (green and white parts)
2	large oranges, peeled and sectioned, each section cut into 3 pieces (Discard white membranes.)
¹/₂	cup orange juice
2	tablespoons *each* vegetable oil and red wine vinegar
2	teaspoons honey
2	teaspoons dried basil
1	teaspoon grated fresh orange peel
¹/₂	teaspoon garlic powder
¹/₈	teaspoon *each* salt and pepper

Cook pasta according to package directions for the minimum cooking time. Place peas and carrots in a colander. When pasta is done, pour into the colander over peas and carrots. (The hot water will cook the vegetables slightly.) Drain and place in a large bowl. Add pineapple, beans, bell pepper, onions, and orange sections. Toss to combine.

Combine ¹/₂ cup of pineapple juice and remaining ingredients. Mix well. Pour over pasta mixture. Mix gently until well combined.

Chill thoroughly, preferably overnight. Mix several times while chilling.

Each serving provides:

180	Calories		35 g	Carbohydrate
5 g	Protein		106 mg	Sodium
3 g	Total fat (0 g Sat. fat)		0 mg	Cholesterol

Tomato and Avocado Salad à la Caribe

Tomatoes and avocados are abundant in the Caribbean and avocado lovers especially will be in heaven when they try this delicious island salad. It's usually served on a bed of greens for a colorful—and very tasty—salad. You can also pile it into a pita for a unique veggie sandwich.

Makes 4 servings

1	large, ripe tomato, finely chopped
1	ripe avocado, peeled, and cut into 1/2-inch pieces
1/4	cup thinly sliced green onions (green part only)
2	tablespoons orange juice
1 1/2	teaspoons red wine vinegar
1	large clove garlic, crushed
1/8	teaspoon salt
1/16	teaspoon pepper

In a medium bowl, combine tomato, avocado, and green onions. Toss gently.

In a small bowl or custard cup, combine remaining ingredients. Mix well and add to tomato mixture. Mix gently until thoroughly blended.

Chill several hours to blend flavors.

Each serving provides:			
98	Calories	7 g	Carbohydrate
2 g	Protein	80 mg	Sodium
8 g	Total fat (1 g Sat. fat)	0 mg	Cholesterol

Calypso Pineapple Bean Pot

Many types of beans are grown throughout the Caribbean and they appear in abundance in soups, stews, and side dishes. This intriguing recipe is based on a stew from Haitian, where kidney beans are popular. The unusual combination of beans and pineapple with oregano and lime juice gives a surprisingly delicious result. (The chick peas were my own addition, replacing the meat in the original dish.)

Makes 6 servings

2	cups finely chopped, ripe, fresh pineapple
1	cup chopped onion
4	cloves garlic, crushed
1	tablespoon firmly packed brown sugar
3	medium, ripe tomatoes, peeled and chopped ($2^1/2$ cups)
2	tablespoons lime juice (preferably fresh)
$1^1/2$	teaspoons dried oregano
1	teaspoon grated fresh lime peel
$1/8$	teaspoons cayenne pepper
	Salt to taste
1	1-pound can chick peas, rinsed and drained (or 2 cups of cooked chick peas)
1	1-pound can kidney beans, rinsed and drained (or 2 cups of cooked beans)

In a large nonstick skillet, combine pineapple, onion, garlic, and brown sugar. Cook over medium heat, stirring frequently, 15 minutes or until mixture becomes dry and onion begins to brown.

Add remaining ingredients, mixing well. Reduce heat to medium-low, cover, and cook 30 minutes. Stir several times while cooking.

Serve over brown rice or any other cooked grain.

Each serving provides:

170	Calories	32 g	Carbohydrate
8 g	Protein	188 mg	Sodium
2 g	Total fat (0 g Sat. fat)	0 mg	Cholesterol

Creole Beans

Often thought of as a strictly Indian spice blend, curry was actually brought to the Caribbean years ago by Indian travelers. The mixture of spices varies from island to island and from dish to dish, resulting in variations of this popular dish. It's usually made with small native beans called "pigeon peas," but can also be made with kidney beans, or almost any type of bean. Serve it as a side dish at your next cook-out or as a tasty entrée over hot brown rice.

Makes 8 servings

2	teaspoons vegetable oil
2	cups coarsely chopped onion
2	cups coarsely chopped green bell pepper
3	cloves garlic, crushed
1¹/₂	cups water
1	6-ounce can tomato paste
2	1-pound cans kidney beans, rinsed and drained (or 4 cups of cooked beans)
¹/₂	cup raisins
2	tablespoons firmly packed brown sugar
2	teaspoons curry powder
1	teaspoon *Vegetable Broth Mix* (See page 27.)
1	bay leaf

Preheat oven to 350°.

Lightly oil a 1³/₄-quart casserole or spray with a nonstick cooking spray.

Heat vegetable oil in a large nonstick skillet over medium heat. Add onion, bell pepper, and garlic. Cook, stirring frequently, 5 minutes.

Add remaining ingredients to skillet. Cook, stirring frequently, 5 minutes more. Spoon mixture into prepared casserole.

Cover tightly and bake 45 minutes.

Remove and discard bay leaf before serving.

Each serving provides:

179	Calories	33 g	Carbohydrate
8 g	Protein	324 mg	Sodium
3 g	Total fat (0 g Sat. fat)	0 mg	Cholesterol

Molasses-Pineapple Black-Eyed Peas

Molasses is often used in many traditional island recipes. These beans have a delicious sweet-and-sour taste created by combining the sweet flavors of molasses and pineapple with the tart flavor of vinegar. Garlic adds the crowning touch. Served over brown rice, this makes a distinctive meal.

Makes 4 servings

2	tablespoons molasses
2	tablespoons red wine vinegar
1	teaspoon prepared yellow mustard
1	teaspoon firmly packed brown sugar
1/2	teaspoon garlic powder
1	1-pound can black-eyed peas, rinsed and drained (or 2 cups of cooked black-eyed peas)
1	8-ounce can sliced pineapple rings (packed in juice), drained, juice reserved

Preheat oven to 350°.

Lightly oil a 1-quart casserole or spray with a nonstick cooking spray.

In a medium bowl, combine molasses, vinegar, mustard, brown sugar, garlic powder, and reserved pineapple juice. Mix well. Stir in beans.

Place mixture in prepared casserole. Arrange pineapple slices over beans.

Bake uncovered, 45 minutes.

Each serving provides:

178	Calories	35 g	Carbohydrate
7 g	Protein	25 mg	Sodium
2 g	Total fat (2 g Sat. fat)	0 mg	Cholesterol

Cuban Stew

This tangy stew, which is normally made with meat, combines unusual ingredients, such as tofu (my own addition), olives, and raisins, with delicious results. It can be served in a bowl like chili or spooned over hot brown rice.

Makes 4 servings

2	teaspoons vegetable oil
1	cup chopped onion
1	cup chopped green bell pepper
3	cloves garlic, crushed
1	15-ounce can salt-free (or regular) tomato sauce
1	tablespoon red wine vinegar
1	teaspoon ground cumin
2	bay leaves
8	stuffed green olives, thinly sliced
3	tablespoons raisins
	Salt and pepper to taste
1	pound firm tofu, cut into 1/2-inch cubes and drained between layers of towels

Heat oil in a medium saucepan over medium heat. Add onion, bell pepper, and garlic. Cook, stirring frequently, 5 minutes. Remove from heat.

Add remaining ingredients, *except* tofu. Mix well. Add tofu and stir gently. Return saucepan to heat. When mixture boils, reduce heat to medium-low, cover, and simmer 20 minutes. Stir gently several times while cooking.

Remove and discard bay leaves before serving

Each serving provides:

281	Calories	25 g	Carbohydrate
21 g	Protein	230 mg	Sodium
14 g	Total fat (2 g Sat. fat)	0 mg	Cholesterol

Island Beans and Rice

Almost all of the islands serve a version of this traditional dish. Some recipes use black beans, others use kidney beans, and others use the native pigeon peas. The beans and rice are either cooked together or separately and sometimes coconut milk is added to the rice while cooking. In this version I have combined several island flavors and techniques.

Makes 4 servings

2¹/₂	cups water
1	cup brown rice, uncooked
1	teaspoon vegetable oil
1	cup chopped onion
3	large cloves garlic, crushed
1	8-ounce can salt-free (or regular) tomato sauce
1	1-pound can kidney beans, rinsed and drained (or 2 cups of cooked beans)
1¹/₂	teaspoons red wine vinegar
1	2-ounce jar sliced pimientos, drained
¹/₄	teaspoon dried thyme
¹/₄	teaspoon dried oregano
¹/₈	teaspoon pepper

Bring water to a boil in a medium saucepan. Add rice. When water boils again, reduce heat to low, cover, and simmer 40 to 45 minutes, until water has been absorbed. Remove from heat and let stand covered, 5 minutes. Fluff rice with a fork before serving.

While rice is cooking, heat oil in a large nonstick skillet over medium heat. Add onion and garlic. Cook, stirring frequently, 5 minutes. Add remaining ingredients. When mixture boils, reduce heat to medium-low, cover, and simmer 15 minutes.

Serve over rice.

Each serving provides:

305	Calories	58 g	Carbohydrate
11 g	Protein	160 mg	Sodium
3 g	Total fat (0 g Sat. fat)	0 mg	Cholesterol

Caribbean Baked Tofu Cutlets

There are several ways to serve these cutlets. I like to serve them hot along-side a rice dish, such as Tomato Rice *(page 144), then I serve the cold left-overs in sandwiches or cut into cubes with a toothpick in each one as an appetizer.*

Makes 4 servings

1	pound firm tofu, sliced 1-inch thick
1	8-ounce can salt-free (or regular) tomato sauce
2	tablespoons lime juice (preferably fresh)
1	tablespoon grated onion
3/4	teaspoon dried oregano
1/4	teaspoon garlic powder
1/8	teaspoon *each* salt and pepper
1 1/4	teaspoons coconut extract

Press tofu slices between two pans for one to two hours to squeeze out the water and compress the tofu.*

While tofu is draining, combine remaining ingredients. Mix well and set aside.

Preheat oven to 350°.

Lightly oil a 7 x 11-inch baking pan or spray with a nonstick cooking spray.

Spoon about a third of the sauce into prepared pan. Place pressed tofu on sauce and top with remaining sauce. Bake uncovered, 45 minutes.

*Place slices between two baking sheets, top them with something heavy, such as a pile of books or about eight 1-pound cans of food. Place near the edge of the sink and prop up one end so the water can drain off the pans and into the sink. (Pressing the tofu first gives it a denser texture.)

Each serving provides:

200	Calories	11 g	Carbohydrate
19 g	Protein	99 mg	Sodium
11 g	Total fat (2 g Sat. fat)	0 mg	Cholesterol

Pineapple-Pepper Tofu

In Puerto Rico a dish resembling this is made with chicken, ginger, garlic, and thyme. This tasty dish is full of color and flavor.

Makes 4 servings

1	20-ounce can pineapple chunks (packed in juice), drained, juice reserved
2	tablespoons honey
1	tablespoon red wine vinegar
1	tablespoon cornstarch
1	teaspoon dry mustard
1/4	teaspoon ground ginger
1/8	teaspoon *each* salt and pepper
2	teaspoons vegetable oil
1	pound firm tofu, cut into 3/4- to 1-inch cubes, drained between layers of towels
1	cup onion, cut vertically into slices 1/4-inch thick
1	cup red bell pepper, cut into 1/4-inch strips
2	large cloves garlic, crushed
1/2	teaspoon dried thyme

In a small bowl, combine reserved pineapple juice with honey, vinegar, cornstarch, mustard, ginger, salt, and pepper. Stir to dissolve cornstarch. Set aside.

Heat 1 teaspoon of the oil in a large nonstick skillet over medium-high heat. Add tofu. Cook, stirring gently, until tofu is lightly browned on all sides. Remove tofu to a bowl and cover to keep warm. Reduce heat to medium and add remaining oil to skillet. Add onion, bell pepper, and garlic. Sprinkle with thyme. Cook, stirring constantly, 2 minutes. Add pineapple chunks. Cook, stirring frequently, 5 minutes.

Stir pineapple juice mixture and add to skillet, along with tofu. Cook, stirring gently, until sauce has thickened and turned clear.

Serve over brown rice.

	Each serving provides:		
338	Calories	44 g	Carbohydrate
19 g	Protein	89 mg	Sodium
13 g	Total fat (2 g Sat. fat)	0 mg	Cholesterol

Islander Black Beans and Pineapple

There is a Chinese influence in Caribbean cooking. In this easy dish, based on a stew from Trinidad, the flavors of the islands abound with a slight Oriental influence. This casserole serves six as an entrée—delicious over rice—or eight as a savory side dish.

Makes 6 servings

1	8-ounce can salt-free (or regular) tomato sauce
2	tablespoons reduced-sodium (or regular) soy sauce
1	tablespoon molasses
2	teaspoons prepared yellow mustard
2	teaspoons white vinegar
3/4	teaspoon onion powder
1/4	teaspoon garlic powder
1	1-pound can black beans, rinsed and drained (or 2 cups of cooked beans)
1	1-pound can crushed pineapple (packed in juice), drained

Preheat oven to 375°.

Lightly oil a 1 1/2-quart baking dish or spray with a nonstick cooking spray.

In a large bowl, combine all ingredients, *except* beans and pineapple. Mix well. Stir in beans and pineapple. Spoon into prepared pan.

Bake covered, 40 minutes.

Each serving provides:

122	Calories	25 g	Carbohydrate
4 g	Protein	354 mg	Sodium
1 g	Total fat (0 g Sat. fat)	0 mg	Cholesterol

Creole Potato Stew

This thick and hearty stew is based on a Cuban recipe and goes well with a salad and a piece of crusty bread.

Makes 6 servings
(1¹/4 cups each serving)

2	teaspoons vegetable oil
2	cups chopped green bell pepper
1¹/2	cups chopped onion
1	8-ounce can salt-free (or regular) tomato sauce
1	1-pound can salt-free (or regular) tomatoes, chopped, undrained
¹/2	cup water
¹/4	cup dry sherry
2	tablespoons red wine vinegar
3	large potatoes, unpeeled, cut into ¹/2-inch cubes (2 pounds)
1	1-pound can kidney beans, rinsed and drained (or 2 cups of cooked beans)
8	cloves garlic, crushed (yes, eight!)
12	stuffed green olives, cut crosswise in half
1	bay leaf
1	teaspoon sugar
	Salt and pepper to taste

Heat oil in a large saucepan over medium heat. Add bell pepper and onion. Cook, stirring frequently, 5 minutes. Add small amounts of water if necessary, about a tablespoon at a time, to prevent drying.

Add remaining ingredients. Bring mixture to a boil. Reduce heat to medium-low, cover, and simmer 1¹/2 hours or until potatoes are very tender. Stir several times while cooking. Taste stew and add salt and pepper, if desired. Remove and discard bay leaf before serving.

Each serving provides:

265	Calories	49 g	Carbohydrate
10 g	Protein	313 mg	Sodium
4 g	Total fat (0 g Sat. fat)	0 mg	Cholesterol

Orange Bean Salad Sandwich

The unlikely combination of oranges and onions really adds zest to this tasty island salad that I turned into a filling sandwich. Lined with fresh spinach and sliced tomatoes, it's a nutrition powerhouse as well as a colorful and delicious dish.

Makes 4 servings

1	tablespoon plus 1 teaspoon reduced-calorie mayonnaise
1/2	teaspoon grated fresh orange peel
1	large orange, peeled and sectioned, each section then cut into thirds (Discard white membrane.)
2	tablespoons thinly sliced green onion (green part only)
1/4	teaspoon salt
1/8	teaspoon pepper
1/8	teaspoon garlic powder
1	1-pound can Great Northern beans, rinsed and drained (or 2 cups of cooked beans)
2	2-ounce whole wheat pita breads, cut in half
	Fresh spinach leaves
	Sliced tomato

In a medium bowl, combine mayonnaise, orange peel, orange sections, onion, and spices. Mix well. Add beans and mix until well blended.

Chill several hours, or preferably overnight.

To serve, open up each pita half and line each one with spinach leaves. Add a few slices of tomato. Mix bean salad, divide evenly, and pile into pitas.

Each serving provides:

175	Calories	32 g	Carbohydrate
7 g	Protein	497 mg	Sodium
3 g	Total fat (0 g Sat. fat)	2 mg	Cholesterol

Sweet Potato Fritters with Fresh Pineapple Salsa

Fritters—little pancakes—are a very popular way to prepare vegetables on many of the Caribbean Islands. These are slightly sweet due to the inherent sweetness of the sweet potatoes, and they are further enhanced by the flavors of the tomatoes and fresh pineapple in the salsa. This recipe makes more salsa than needed, so be creative with the rest. Try it hot or cold, on sandwiches, over rice, or as a relish-type meal accompaniment.

Makes 4 servings
(4 fritters each serving)
Makes 3 cups salsa
(1/4 cup each serving with extra left over)

Fresh Pineapple Salsa:
1   teaspoon vegetable oil
1   cup chopped onion
4   cloves garlic, crushed
1 1/2   cups finely chopped fresh pineapple
2   medium tomatoes, chopped (2 cups)
1/4   teaspoon dried oregano
        Salt and pepper to taste

Sweet Potato Fritters:
2   medium sweet potatoes, peeled and finely shredded (1 pound)
2   tablespoons grated onion
2   egg whites
1/2   teaspoon salt
1/8   teaspoon pepper

To prepare salsa: heat oil in a small saucepan over medium heat. Add onion and garlic. Cook, stirring frequently, 5 minutes. Add small amounts of water if necessary a tablespoon or 2 at a time, to prevent sticking. Add pineapple, tomatoes, and oregano. Bring mixture to a boil. Reduce heat to medium-low and simmer uncovered, 30 minutes. Add salt and pepper, if desired.

To prepare fritters: in a medium bowl, combine all fritter ingredients. Mix well for several minutes until thoroughly combined.

Heat a large nonstick griddle or skillet over medium heat. Oil it lightly or spray with a nonstick cooking spray. Drop mixture by tablespoonfuls onto hot skillet. Using the back of a spoon, flatten fritters slightly and smooth the edges so fritters are not too "raggedy." Turn fritters when edges appear dry and bottoms are lightly browned. Cook until lightly browned on both sides.

To serve, spoon hot salsa over fritters.

Each serving provides:			
204	Calories	36 g	Carbohydrate
5 g	Protein	322 mg	Sodium
5 g	Total fat (1 g Sat. fat)	0 mg	Cholesterol

Sweet Basil–Corn Fritters

I've "eased up" and "slimmed down" the island version of these delicious little pancakes that Harry and I enjoyed on St. Thomas, replacing the cream and whole eggs with cream-style corn and egg whites. They're often served as an appetizer, but I like them as a side dish or even for breakfast.

Makes 6 servings
(4 fritters each serving)

1/2	cup whole wheat flour
1/2	cup all-purpose flour
2	teaspoons baking powder
1/4	cup sugar
1	teaspoon dried basil
1/4	teaspoon salt
1	1-pound can salt-free (or regular) cream-style corn
3	egg whites
2	tablespoons skim milk
2	teaspoons molasses

In a large bowl, combine both types of flour, baking powder, sugar, basil, and salt. Mix well.

In another bowl, combine corn, egg whites, milk, and molasses. Beat with a fork or wire whisk until well blended. Add to flour mixture, mixing until all ingredients are moistened.

Preheat a large nonstick griddle or skillet over medium heat. Oil it lightly or spray with a nonstick cooking spray. Drop batter by tablespoonfuls into skillet. Turn once when edges appear dry and bottoms are lightly browned. Cook until golden brown on both sides.

Each serving provides:

188	Calories	37 g	Carbohydrate
6 g	Protein	287 mg	Sodium
3 g	Total fat (0 g Sat. fat)	0 mg	Cholesterol

Baked Bananas and Sweet Potatoes

The delectable combination of bananas and sweet potatoes — two island favorites — is often found in Caribbean cooking. The two flavors complement each other beautifully and make a dish that is both attractive and very tasty.

Makes 6 servings

3	medium sweet potatoes (1 3/4 pounds)
4	medium bananas, sliced crosswise into 1/4-inch slices (Choose ones that have just ripened and are still firm.)
1/4	cup firmly packed brown sugar
	Ground cinnamon
1/2	cup orange juice

Pierce sweet potatoes several times with a sharp knife and bake in a 350° oven 30 to 40 minutes or until just barely tender. When cool enough to handle, peel potatoes and slice crosswise into 1/4-inch slices.

Preheat oven to 375°. Lightly oil an 8-inch square baking pan or spray with a nonstick cooking spray.

Arrange *half* of the sweet potatoes in prepared pan. Top with *half* of the banana slices. Sprinkle with *half* of the brown sugar and then sprinkle lightly with cinnamon.

Arrange remaining sweet potatoes over bananas, then add remaining bananas. Drizzle evenly with orange juice.

Top with remaining brown sugar and sprinkle again with cinnamon.

Bake uncovered, 30 minutes.

Serve hot.

Each serving provides:

221	Calories	52 g	Carbohydrate
2 g	Protein	17 mg	Sodium
1 g	Total fat (0 g Sat. fat)	0 mg	Cholesterol

Dominican Sweet Potatoes

This tasty recipe from the Dominican Republic is usually made with a type of island pumpkin called calabaza. I've adapted it for use with our American sweet potatoes. The unlikely combination of onion, thyme, and fruit juice gives this dish a unique flavor that's truly delicious.

Makes 6 servings

2	teaspoons vegetable oil
1	cup finely chopped onion
1/4	cup thinly sliced green onions (white part only)
3	medium sweet potatoes, peeled and cut into 1-inch cubes (2 pounds)
1	cup orange juice
1/4	cup lime juice (preferably fresh)
1/4	teaspoon dried thyme
1/4	teaspoon salt
1/4	teaspoon pepper

Heat oil in a large nonstick skillet over medium heat. Add both types of onion. Cook, stirring frequently, 5 minutes.

Add sweet potatoes, mixing with the onions.

Combine remaining ingredients and add to skillet. Mix well. Cover skillet, reduce heat to medium-low, and cook 40 minutes or until sweet potatoes are tender. Stir occasionally while cooking.

Uncover and continue to cook, stirring occasionally, 10 minutes.

Each serving provides:

160	Calories	34 g	Carbohydrate
2 g	Protein	108 mg	Sodium
2 g	Total fat (0 g Sat. fat)	0 mg	Cholesterol

Cabbage in Cheese Sauce

Several versions of this unusual cabbage dish are popular on the Spanish-speaking islands of Cuba and Puerto Rico. Creamy and rich, it can be made either mild or hot, depending on the amount of pepper used and whether or not you add a hot chili pepper. It can be served as is, but I like it best spooned over steaming brown rice.

Makes 8 servings

2	teaspoons vegetable oil
1	cup thinly sliced onion
5	cloves garlic, crushed
6	cups shredded cabbage
1	cup water
2	cups skim milk
3	tablespoons cornstarch
1/8	teaspoon cayenne pepper (or more, to taste)
3/4	cup shredded reduced-fat Swiss cheese (3 ounces)
1	jalapeño pepper, finely chopped (optional), seeds and inner membrane discarded
	Salt to taste

Heat oil in a large saucepan over medium heat. Add onion and garlic. Cook, stirring frequently, 5 minutes. Add cabbage and water. Cover and cook, stirring occasionally, 20 minutes or until cabbage is tender.

In a small bowl, combine milk, cornstarch, and pepper. Stir to dissolve cornstarch. Add to saucepan. Bring mixture to a boil, stirring constantly. Continue to cook and stir, 2 minutes. Reduce heat to medium-low, add cheese and jalapeño. Mix until cheese is melted. Add salt to taste.

Let stand covered, 5 minutes before serving.

Each serving provides:

100	Calories	11 g	Carbohydrate
7 g	Protein	59 mg	Sodium
3 g	Total fat (1 g Sat. fat)	9 mg	Cholesterol

Jamaican Cornmeal Pudding

Even though this is called a "pudding," in Jamaica it is usually served as a side dish or a hearty breakfast. Other versions of this dish are less sweet and appear throughout the Caribbean where cornmeal is a popular ingredient. In this recipe I've replaced the traditional high-fat coconut cream with skim milk and coconut extract, and the results are still smooth and sweet. Leftovers can either be reheated or sliced while cold and pan-fried in a nonstick skillet with a small amount of oil or a nonstick cooking spray.

Makes 6 servings

1	cup yellow cornmeal
1/3	cup firmly packed brown sugar
3/4	teaspoon ground cinnamon
1/4	teaspoon ground allspice
1	cup skim milk
2 1/2	cups water
2	teaspoons molasses
1/3	cup raisins
1	teaspoon vanilla extract
1	teaspoon coconut extract

In a medium saucepan, combine cornmeal, brown sugar, cinnamon, and allspice. Mix well. Gradually stir in milk, mixing until smooth.

Add remaining ingredients, *except* vanilla and coconut extracts. Bring mixture to a boil over medium heat, stirring frequently. Reduce heat to medium-low and simmer, stirring frequently, 15 to 20 minutes, until mixture is thick. Remove from heat and stir in extracts, mixing thoroughly.

Spoon pudding into a serving bowl and let stand 5 minutes before serving.

Each serving provides:			
178	Calories	40 g	Carbohydrate
4 g	Protein	29 mg	Sodium
0 g	Total fat (0 g Sat. fat)	1 mg	Cholesterol

Curried Apple Rice

Curry was brought to the islands from India and often appears in rice dishes throughout the Caribbean. In this recipe the rice is "sizzled" as in Chinese fried rice. I've substituted a Granny Smith apple for the slightly tart native variety that is usually used.

Makes 6 servings

2¹/2	cups water
1	cup brown rice, uncooked
2	teaspoons vegetable oil
1	cup chopped onion
1	large Granny Smith apple, peeled and chopped into ¹/2-inch pieces
2¹/2	teaspoons curry powder
	Salt to taste

Bring water to a boil in a medium saucepan. Add rice. When water boils again, reduce heat to low, cover, and simmer 40 to 45 minutes, until water has been absorbed. Remove from heat and keep covered.

Heat oil in a large nonstick skillet over medium heat. Add onion. Cook, stirring frequently, 3 to 5 minutes, until onion begins to brown. Add apple and curry powder. Cook, stirring frequently, 5 minutes. Add small amounts of water as necessary, about a tablespoon at a time, to prevent sticking.

Fluff rice with a fork and add to skillet. Cook, stirring constantly, 2 to 3 minutes, until rice is hot and sizzly.

Add salt to taste.

Each serving provides:

154	Calories	30 g	Carbohydrate
3 g	Protein	3 mg	Sodium
3 g	Total fat (0 g Sat. fat)	0 mg	Cholesterol

Tomato Rice

Rice dishes similar to this one are popular throughout the Caribbean Islands. This mild version makes a nice accompaniment to a spicier entrée. The Cuban and Puerto Rican versions are often topped with grated cheese, which I've added to this one.

Makes 6 servings

2	teaspoons vegetable oil
1/2	cup finely chopped onion
3	large cloves garlic, finely minced
2 1/2	cups *Vegetable Broth,* or 2 1/2 cups of water plus 2 1/2 teaspoons *Vegetable Broth Mix* (See pages 26–27.)
1	cup brown rice, uncooked
2	medium, ripe tomatoes, peeled and chopped (1 1/2 cups)
1/4	teaspoon salt
1/8	teaspoon pepper
1/8	teaspoon dried thyme
	Grated Parmesan cheese

Heat oil in a medium saucepan over medium heat. Add onion and garlic. Cook, stirring frequently, 5 minutes.

Add broth and bring to a boil.

Add remaining ingredients, *except* Parmesan cheese. Reduce heat to medium-low, cover, and simmer 45 minutes, until rice is tender and most of the liquid has been absorbed. Remove from heat and let stand covered, 5 minutes. Fluff rice with a fork before serving.

Top each serving with a sprinkling of Parmesan cheese.

Each serving provides:

147	Calories	28 g	Carbohydrate
3 g	Protein	124 mg	Sodium
3 g	Total fat (0 g Sat. fat)	0 mg	Cholesterol

Pumpkin Raisin Bread

Many variations of this spicy bread are found throughout the Caribbean, either with pumpkin, sweet potatoes, or squash, and often with added dried fruits or nuts. My version is delicious, oil-free, slices well, and is wonderful toasted.

Makes 14 servings

1¹/₄	cups whole wheat flour
1	cup all-purpose flour
2	teaspoons baking powder
1	teaspoon baking soda
¹/₂	teaspoon *each* ground cinnamon, nutmeg, and cloves
¹/₂	cup raisins
3	egg whites
¹/₂	cup plus 2 tablespoons firmly packed brown sugar
1	1-pound can pumpkin
2	tablespoons molasses
1¹/₂	teaspoons vanilla extract

Preheat oven to 350°.

Lightly oil a 5 x 9-inch loaf pan or spray with a nonstick cooking spray.

In a large bowl, combine both types of flour, baking powder, baking soda, and spices. Mix well. Add raisins.

In a small bowl, combine remaining ingredients. Beat with a fork or wire whisk until blended. Add to flour mixture. Mix until all ingredients are moistened. (Dough will be stiff.) Place dough in prepared pan, smooth the top with the back of a spoon and bake 40 to 45 minutes, until a toothpick inserted in the center of the bread comes out clean.

Cool in pan on a wire rack 5 minutes, then turn out onto rack to finish cooling.

Each serving provides:

149	Calories	33 g	Carbohydrate
4 g	Protein	180 mg	Sodium
1 g	Total fat (0 g Sat. fat)	0 mg	Cholesterol

Island Banana Bread

Banana bread seems to be popular wherever bananas are found, and bananas are plentiful in the Caribbean. The addition of lemon peel and hint of allspice make this sweet, moist Caribbean version unique.

Makes 10 servings

3/4	cup whole wheat flour
1/2	cup all-purpose flour
1/3	cup firmly packed brown sugar
1 1/2	teaspoons baking powder
1/2	teaspoon ground cinnamon
1/4	teaspoon ground allspice
1/2	cup skim milk
2	egg whites
1 1/2	tablespoons vegetable oil
1/2	cup mashed ripe banana (the riper, the better)
1	teaspoon *each* grated fresh lemon peel and vanilla extract

Preheat oven to 350°.

Lightly oil a 4 x 8-inch loaf pan or spray with a nonstick cooking spray.

In a large bowl, combine both types of flour, brown sugar, baking powder, and spices. Mix well.

In a small bowl, combine remaining ingredients. Beat with a fork or wire whisk until blended. Add to dry mixture, mixing until all ingredients are moistened.

Place mixture in prepared pan.

Bake 35 minutes, until a toothpick inserted in the center of the bread comes out clean.

Cool in pan on a wire rack 5 minutes, then turn out onto rack to finish cooling.

Each serving provides:

123	Calories	22 g	Carbohydrate
3 g	Protein	94 mg	Sodium
3 g	Total fat (0 g Sat. fat)	0 mg	Cholesterol

Raisin-Pecan-Ginger Muffins

I couldn't resist creating a muffin using the flavors of a sweet, griddle-fried bun that I fell in love with in Jamaica. You'll love the hint of orange, sweetness of raisins, and crunch of pecans, combined with the tropical flavor of ginger.

Makes 12 muffins

1 1/4	cups all-purpose flour
1	cup whole wheat flour
2 1/2	teaspoons baking powder
1/2	teaspoon baking soda
1 1/4	teaspoons ground ginger
2/3	cup raisins
1/4	cup chopped pecans
1 1/2	cups plain nonfat yogurt
1/3	cup firmly packed brown sugar
3	egg whites
2	tablespoons vegetable oil
1 1/2	teaspoons vanilla extract
1	teaspoon orange extract

Preheat oven to 400°.

Lightly oil 12 muffin cups or spray with a nonstick cooking spray.

In a large bowl, combine both types of flour, baking powder, baking soda, and ginger. Mix well. Stir in raisins and pecans.

In another bowl, combine remaining ingredients. Beat with a fork or wire whisk until well blended. Add to dry mixture, mixing just until all ingredients are moistened.

Divide mixture evenly into prepared muffin cups.

Bake 15 minutes, until a toothpick inserted in the center of a muffin comes out clean. Remove muffins to a wire rack to cool.

Each muffin provides:			
195	Calories	33 g	Carbohydrate
6 g	Protein	193 mg	Sodium
5 g	Total fat (1 g Sat. fat)	1 mg	Cholesterol

Sweet Potato Biscuits

Sweet potatoes add moistness and a sweet flavor to these "biscuits-gone-Caribbean." Island versions are often deep-fried, so I made a few adaptations, with delicious results. Try them piping hot, right out of the oven, for a breakfast, lunch, or dinner treat.

Makes 14 biscuits

1	cup all-purpose flour
3/4	cup whole wheat flour
1	tablespoon baking powder
1	tablespoon sugar
1/8	teaspoon salt
3/4	cup mashed cooked sweet potatoes (canned or baked)
3/4	cup skim milk
2	tablespoons vegetable oil

Preheat oven to 450°.

Lightly oil a baking sheet or spray with a nonstick cooking spray.

In a large bowl, combine both types of flour, baking powder, sugar, and salt. Mix well.

In another bowl, combine sweet potatoes, milk, and oil. Beat with a fork or wire whisk until blended. Add to flour mixture. Mix until dry ingredients are moistened.

Place dough on a floured surface and knead a few times until dough holds together in a ball. (If dough is sticky, you may need to add a bit more flour.) Roll or press dough to a thickness of 1/2-inch.

Using a 3-inch biscuit cutter or a glass, cut 14 biscuits. (Scraps can be put together and rolled again.) Place biscuits on prepared baking sheet.

Bake 10 to 12 minutes, until bottoms of biscuits are lightly browned. Remove to a wire rack.

Each biscuit provides:

101	Calories	18 g	Carbohydrate
3 g	Protein	134 mg	Sodium
3 g	Total fat (0 g Sat. fat)	0 mg	Cholesterol

Haitian Banana Fritters

Bananas are almost a way of life in the Caribbean. On Haiti, where this dish originated, bananas appear in all types of dishes, from breakfast to dessert. Enjoy these versatile, egg-free fritters for breakfast, drizzled with maple syrup, or for dessert, sprinkled with powdered sugar. They're also delicious topped with crushed pineapple.

Makes 4 servings
(Six 2¹/₂ -inch pancakes per serving)

¹/₂	cup whole wheat flour
¹/₂	cup all-purpose flour
2	teaspoons baking powder
1	teaspoon baking soda
¹/₄	teaspoon ground cinnamon
1	cup skim milk
¹/₂	cup mashed, very ripe banana (1 medium banana)
1¹/₂	teaspoons vanilla extract
1	medium, ripe banana, diced

Sift both types of flour, baking powder, baking soda, and cinnamon into a medium bowl.

In another bowl, combine milk, mashed banana, and vanilla. Beat with a fork or wire whisk until blended. Stir in diced banana. Add to dry mixture, stirring until all ingredients are moistened.

Preheat a nonstick skillet or griddle over medium heat. Oil it lightly or spray with a nonstick cooking spray.

Drop batter onto hot griddle, using 1 tablespoonful of batter for each pancake. Turn pancakes once, when tops are bubbly and edges appear dry. Cook until golden brown on both sides.

Each serving provides:

219	Calories	40 g	Carbohydrate
6 g	Protein	593 mg	Sodium
4 g	Total fat (1 g Sat. fat)	1 mg	Cholesterol

Pineapple-Banana Parfaits

Pineapples and bananas are a "natural" island combination. This is my lower-fat version of a sweet island parfait.

Makes 4 servings

Pineapple-Banana Layers:
1   cup pineapple juice
1   tablespoon lemon juice
3   tablespoons firmly packed brown sugar
1/2   teaspoon ground cinnamon
1   tablespoon plus 1 teaspoon cornstarch
4   medium, ripe bananas, cut lengthwise into quarters, then cut crosswise into 1/4-inch slices (3 1/2 cups)

Cream Filling:
1   cup lowfat (1%) cottage cheese with pineapple
1   teaspoon vanilla extract
1/8   teaspoon *each* lemon extract and coconut extract

Garnish:
2   teaspoons finely chopped walnuts (optional)

In a small saucepan, combine pineapple juice, lemon juice, brown sugar, cinnamon, and cornstarch. Stir to dissolve cornstarch. Cook over medium heat, stirring constantly, until mixture comes to a boil. Continue to cook and stir for 1 to 2 minutes. Remove from heat and cool for 10 minutes. Add bananas and mix gently. Chill several hours.

In a blender container, combine all filling ingredients. Blend until smooth. Chill.

Using *half* of the banana mixture, divide evenly into four 8-ounce parfait glasses. Top each one with 2 tablespoons of the cottage cheese mixture. Then spoon remaining banana mixture into the glasses, followed by the remaining cottage cheese. Top each parfait with 1/2 teaspoon chopped nuts, if desired.

Chill until serving time, at least 1 hour, but preferably *not* overnight.

	Each serving provides:		
247	Calories	55 g	Carbohydrate
7 g	Protein	172 mg	Sodium
1 g	Total fat (0 g Sat. fat)	3 mg	Cholesterol

Piña Colada Bread Pudding

The piña colada is probably the most popular Caribbean beverage, one that combines the cool, fresh flavors of the islands. This refreshing dessert makes a perfect, light ending to any meal.

Makes 8 servings

4	cups skim milk
1/4	cup cornstarch
1/3	cup firmly packed brown sugar
1	teaspoon vanilla extract
1	teaspoon coconut extract
8	slices whole wheat bread, cut into cubes (Stale bread is best.)
1	1-pound can crushed pineapple (packed in juice), drained
2	teaspoons shredded coconut (optional), unsweetened

Have an ungreased 8-inch square baking dish ready.

In a medium saucepan, combine milk, cornstarch, and brown sugar. Mix well to dissolve cornstarch. Cook over medium heat, stirring constantly, until mixture comes to a boil. Continue to cook and stir for 2 minutes. Remove from heat and stir in extracts.

Add bread cubes and pineapple. Mix gently and thoroughly.

Spoon mixture into baking dish. Sprinkle with coconut, if desired. Cover and chill.

Each serving provides:

199	Calories	41 g	Carbohydrate
7 g	Protein	218 mg	Sodium
1 g	Total fat (0 g Sat. fat)	2 mg	Cholesterol

Coconut Custards with Coffee-Rum Sauce

The unique sauce on this custard can also be used to top vanilla ice milk or any type of bread or rice pudding.

Makes 4 servings

Coconut Custards:

4	egg whites
2	cups evaporated skim milk
1	teaspoon *each* vanilla extract and coconut extract
2^1/$_2$	tablespoons firmly packed brown sugar

Coffee-Rum Sauce:

1	tablespoon plus 1 teaspoon cornstarch
1	tablespoon water
3	tablespoons firmly packed brown sugar
1	teaspoon rum extract
1	cup freshly brewed coffee (regular or decaffeinated)

Preheat oven to 325°.

Lightly oil four six-ounce custard cups or spray with a nonstick cooking spray.

Combine all custard ingredients in a medium bowl. Beat with a fork or wire whisk for 1 full minute. Pour into prepared cups. Place cups in a baking pan and pour enough hot water into the larger pan to come halfway up the sides of the cups. Bake 50 to 55 minutes, until custard is set. Remove cups from pan and place on a wire rack to cool slightly, then chill.

Just before serving, in a small saucepan, combine cornstarch, water, brown sugar, and rum extract. Stir until cornstarch is completely dissolved. Gradually stir in coffee. Cook over medium heat, stirring constantly, until mixture comes to a boil. Continue to cook and stir for two minutes. Remove from heat.

To serve, run a sharp knife around the sides of the custard and invert into four individual serving bowls. Divide hot sauce evenly and spoon over custard. Serve right away.

Each serving provides:

228	Calories	37 g	Carbohydrate
13 g	Protein	210 mg	Sodium
3 g	Total fat (0 g Sat. fat)	5 mg	Cholesterol

Mango Custard

Based on a rich dessert from the exotic island of St. John, this scrumptious custard is so smooth, refreshing, and fruity, you'll be tempted to eat it all! For the richest flavor, choose mangos that are very ripe.

Makes 6 servings

2	very ripe mangos, peeled and cut into chunks, center seed removed (2 cups)
1	teaspoon lemon juice
1	teaspoon coconut extract
1	cup skim milk
1/4	cup cornstarch
3	tablespoons firmly packed brown sugar

In a blender container, combine mango chunks, lemon juice, and coconut extract. Blend until smooth.

In a small saucepan, combine remaining ingredients. Mix until cornstarch is dissolved. Stir in mango mixture.

Cook over medium heat, stirring constantly, until mixture comes to a boil. Continue to cook and stir for 2 full minutes. Spoon into a 1-quart shallow bowl.

Chill thoroughly.

Each serving provides:

106	Calories	26 g	Carbohydrate
2 g	Protein	26 mg	Sodium
0 g	Total fat (0 g Sat. fat)	1 mg	Cholesterol

Tropical Tofu Treat

Soft tofu makes a wonderful, custardy pudding atop a layer of pineapple in this tropical treat. This is my own invention, a silken dish that reflects cool Caribbean flavors.

Makes 8 servings

10	2¹/₂-inch graham cracker squares
1	1-pound can crushed pineapple (packed in juice), drained
2	tablespoons (total) fruit-only peach, apricot, or pineapple jam
2	teaspoons shredded unsweetened coconut
¹/₄	teaspoon ground cinnamon
10	ounces soft tofu, drained (Health food stores and many large grocery stores carry 10-ounce packages of soft tofu in the produce department.)
1	cup skim milk
¹/₄	cup honey
1¹/₂	tablespoons cornstarch
1	teaspoon vanilla extract
¹/₂	teaspoon lemon extract
¹/₄	teaspoon *each* almond extract and coconut extract

Line the bottom of an 8-inch square baking pan with 9 of the graham crackers, setting the remaining one aside.

In a medium bowl, combine pineapple, jam, coconut, and cinnamon. Mix well. Spoon evenly over graham crackers.

In a blender container, combine tofu with remaining ingredients. Blend until smooth. Pour into a medium saucepan. Bring to a boil over medium heat, stirring frequently. Continue to cook, stirring constantly, 2 minutes. Spoon over pineapple.

Crush remaining graham cracker and sprinkle over tofu. Chill thoroughly.

Each serving provides:

159	Calories	31 g	Carbohydrate
5 g	Protein	72 mg	Sodium
2 g	Total fat (0 g Sat. fat)	1 mg	Cholesterol

Pineapple Crisp

With a Caribbean influence and an up-to-date American presentation, fresh pineapple gives this dessert a very refreshing flavor. Served alone or topped with a scoop of vanilla ice milk, it will remind you of cool island breezes!

Makes 8 servings

4	cups fresh very ripe pineapple, cut into 1/2-inch pieces, skin and center core removed
2	to 5 tablespoons firmly packed brown sugar (The amount of sugar will depend on the sweetness of the pineapple.)
1	teaspoon vanilla extract
1/2	cup water
2	teaspoons cornstarch

Topping:

1	cup rolled oats
2	tablespoons whole wheat flour
2	tablespoons firmly packed brown sugar
1	teaspoon ground cinnamon
1	tablespoon plus 1 teaspoon vegetable oil
3	tablespoons orange juice

Preheat oven to 350°.

Lightly oil a 9-inch pie pan or spray with a nonstick cooking spray.

In a medium saucepan, combine pineapple, brown sugar, vanilla, and 1/4 cup of the water. Bring to a boil over medium heat, stirring frequently. Continue to cook for 5 minutes more.

Dissolve cornstarch in remaining water and stir into pineapple mixture. Continue to cook and stir for 2 minutes. Remove from heat and spoon into prepared pan.

To prepare topping: in a medium bowl, combine oats, flour, brown sugar, and cinnamon, mixing well. Add oil and orange juice. Mix until all ingredients are moistened. Distribute topping evenly over pineapple.

Bake uncovered, 30 minutes, until topping is crisp.

Each serving provides:

152	Calories	29 g	Carbohydrate
2 g	Protein	5 mg	Sodium
4 g	Total fat (0 g Sat. fat)	0 mg	Cholesterol

Cornmeal Raisin Cake with Rum Sauce

Cornmeal breads and cakes are found on many of the islands. Most of the authentic versions are very high in fat, due to the addition of lots of coconut and butter. My recipe doesn't use any oil at all! What could be tastier than a thick, dense cake, loaded with plump raisins and topped with a creamy rum sauce?

Makes 12 servings

Cake:
4   cups skim milk
3/4   cup raisins
1/3   cup honey
1   cup yellow cornmeal
1 1/2   teaspoons vanilla extract
2   teaspoons rum extract

Topping:
2   teaspoons sugar
1/4   teaspoon ground cinnamon

Rum Sauce:
1 1/2   cups skim milk
3   tablespoons firmly packed brown sugar
2   tablespoons cornstarch
1/2   teaspoon rum extract

To prepare cake: lightly oil an 8-inch spring form pan or spray with a nonstick cooking spray.

Place 3 cups of the milk in a medium saucepan with raisins and honey. Place cornmeal in a small bowl and gradually add remaining milk. Set aside. Bring mixture in saucepan to a boil over medium heat, stirring constantly. Stir in cornmeal mixture. When milk returns to a boil, cook and stir 2 to 3 minutes, until mixture is thick and smooth. Remove from heat and stir in extracts. Spoon batter into prepared pan, smoothing the top with the back of a spoon.

To prepare topping: combine sugar and cinnamon and sprinkle evenly over top of cake.

Chill several hours, until firm. Remove cake from refrigerator a half hour before serving.

When ready to serve, prepare Rum Sauce: combine milk, brown sugar, and cornstarch in a small saucepan. Stir to dissolve cornstarch.

Bring to a boil over medium heat, stirring constantly. Continue to cook and stir for 2 minutes. Remove from heat and stir in rum extract.

To serve, cut cake into slices and place on individual serving plates. Spoon hot sauce over cake, using 2 tablespoons of sauce for each serving.

(Leftover sauce can be reheated briefly in a microwave or stirred and served cold.)

Each serving provides:

167	Calories	35 g	Carbohydrate
5 g	Protein	62 mg	Sodium
1 g	Total fat (0 g Sat. fat)	2 mg	Cholesterol

Caribbean Ginger Cake

Jamaiican ginger, known for its delicate taste, is shipped all over the world. In this cake, ginger is combined with allspice to create a sweet cake with a "bit of a bite." This cake is even better on the second or third day.

Makes 16 servings

Cake:

1	cup whole wheat flour
1	cup all-purpose flour
1¹/₄	teaspoons *each* baking soda and ground allspice
1	teaspoon ground ginger
1	cup skim milk
¹/₂	cup applesauce (unsweetened)
¹/₃	cup firmly packed brown sugar
¹/₄	cup molasses
2	egg whites
2	tablespoons vegetable oil
1¹/₂	teaspoons vanilla extract

Topping:

2¹/₂	tablespoons fruit-only peach or apricot jam
¹/₈	teaspoon ground allspice

Preheat oven to 350°.

Lightly oil an 8-inch square baking pan or spray with a nonstick cooking spray.

In a large bowl, combine both types of flour, baking soda, and spices. Mix well.

In another bowl, combine remaining cake ingredients. Beat with a fork or wire whisk until blended. Add to dry mixture, mixing until all ingredients are moistened.

Pour batter into prepared pan and bake 30 to 35 minutes, until a toothpick inserted in the center of the cake comes out clean.

Combine jam and allspice, mixing well. When cake is done, remove from oven and spread with jam mixture. Cool in pan on a wire rack.

Each serving provides:

122	Calories	23 g	Carbohydrate
3 g	Protein	117 mg	Sodium
2 g	Total fat (0 g Sat. fat)	0 mg	Cholesterol

Flavors of Italy

Italian cuisine is regional. Each region claims its own unique dishes, and to demonstrate the differences remember that Italy is shaped like a boot. At the top of the boot is the dairy zone of Italy. In this affluent part of the country the cooking fat is butter, rice and polenta are staples, and pasta is a relative newcomer to the area.

In the southern part of Italy the climate is warmer, the sauces more pungent, and the sweets much richer than in the northern sections. Olive trees abound, and as a result, olive oil is used abundantly. In fact, some of the best olive oil in the world comes from southern Italy.

The central region of Italy has characteristics of both the north and the south, with the main difference being the addition of beans to almost every part of the meal except dessert. Numerous varieties of kidney beans are grown commercially, with cannellini (white kidney beans) being one of the most common. Chick peas (called *ceci*) are also popular throughout the country.

Pasta also has its own regional characteristics, with flat egg noodles being predominant in the north, and eggless macaroni and spaghetti, in its multitude of shapes, predominant in the south.

A traditional Italian meal is often a complex affair. The meal usually begins with an antipasto, which translated means "before the meal." An antipasto platter is made up of many different vegetables, cheeses, and marinated or pickled salads. There is no main course as we know it. Instead there are actually two main courses, which are never brought to the table at the same time. The first course can be either pasta, risotto (a rice dish), or soup. The second course is the meat course, often accompanied by one or two vegetables. A light salad and dessert both come at the end of the meal. The dessert that ends an Italian meal is rarely a rich dessert, but rather a bowl of fresh, seasonal fruit and perhaps some cheese. (Rich pastries and pies are eaten more often as afternoon and evening snacks, served with strong coffee.)

The fruits grown in Italy are almost all familiar to us. Among them are apples, cherries, pears, oranges, grapefruit, lemons, bananas, peaches, plums, and grapes. Fruits are served either fresh or marinated in wine or liqueur.

Vegetables are one of the glories of Italian cuisine. Most people will shop daily at local markets and purchase vegetables to be cooked and eaten the same day. Among the vegetables most often seen in Italian cuisine are artichokes, asparagus, broccoli, cauliflower, eggplant, fennel, green beans, leeks, mushrooms, onions, peppers, potatoes, pumpkin, spinach, zucchini, and, of course, tomatoes.

Spices and herbs play a very important role in Italian cuisine and they are almost always used fresh. The most frequently used herbs are basil, bay leaf, fennel, oregano, parsley, rosemary, saffron, sage, and thyme. And what would Italian food be without the flavor of garlic?

Italian cuisine also features a wide variety of cheeses. Among the most familiar are Mozzarella, Parmesan, and Ricotta. Others include Gorgonzola, Bel Paese, Pecorino, and Fontina, all of which are also exported to America.

Adapting Italian cuisine to lowfat, meatless cuisine was relatively easy because of the already low fat content of many of the most commonly used foods. I eliminated the use of butter, reduced the amount of oil, used lowfat or nonfat dairy products, and lots of Italian herbs and spices.

I know you'll enjoy your tour of Italy!

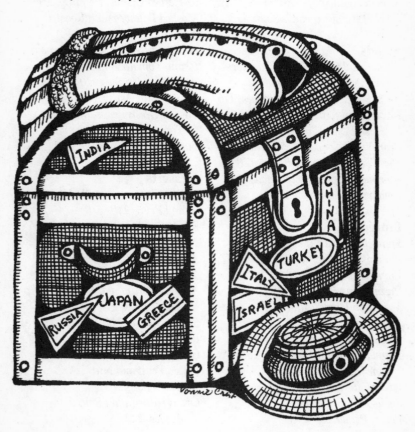

Flavors of Italy
Recipes

Suggested Menus

Lunch

Tomato and Basil Crostini (164)
Tossed Salad
Sicilian Lentil Soup with
Pasta (172)
Fresh Fruit

Bean-Filled Tomato Cups (177)
Marinated Cauliflower Salad (179)
Almond Cornmeal Coffee
Cake (215)

Pasta Salad with Cherry Tomatoes
and Pesto Vinaigrette (174)
on Bed of Lettuce
Sweet Fruit and Nut Bread (216)

Dinner

Cream of White Bean Soup (169)
Spinach and Ricotta Pie (181)
Wine-Glazed Tomatoes (199)
Steamed Green Beans
Melon Half Filled with
Vanilla Ice Milk

Tossed Salad
Stuffed Mushrooms (165)
Angel Hair Pasta with
Chunky Marinara Sauce (195)
Italian Bread
Berries with Apricot Creme (218)

Herb-Topped Tomato Slices (178)
on Bed of Lettuce
Tofu with Peppers and
Mushrooms (187)
Risotto with Asparagus (206)
Orange-Burgundy Spiced
Apples (222)

Fresh Vegetables with
Spinach Pesto Dip (167)
Veggie Pizza Subs (190)
Oranges in Amaretto (219)

Recipe page numbers appear in parentheses.

Tomato and Basil Crostini

*These simple, yet delicious, tomato-topped toasts are fast becoming the rage
in Italian restaurants across America. The secret to the sweet, pleasant flavor
is to use fresh plum tomatoes and fresh basil. Italians often remove the crust,
but I prefer to leave it on.*

*Makes 8 servings
(2 crostini each serving)*

8	ounces plum tomatoes, finely chopped (4 medium tomatoes)
1/4	cup fresh basil, finely chopped
3	large cloves garlic, very finely minced
	Salt to taste
16	1/2-inch thick slices Italian bread, cut on a slight diagonal (Use narrow Italian bread or a French baguette.)
	Freshly ground black pepper to taste
	Grated Parmesan cheese (optional)

In a medium bowl, combine tomatoes, basil, garlic, and salt. Mix
well. Let mixture stand at room temperature for 1 hour to give the flavors a chance to blend. (It doesn't hold up well if prepared much further ahead or refrigerated.)

To serve, lightly toast the bread slices either in a toaster oven or on
a baking sheet in a 400° oven, until lightly browned. Stir the tomato
mixture and pile 1 tablespoonful on each piece of toast. Top each with
a sprinkling of freshly ground pepper, and Parmesan cheese, if desired.

Serve right away.

Each serving provides:

38	Calories	7 g	Carbohydrate
1 g	Protein	65 mg	Sodium
0 g	Total fat (0 g sat. fat)	0 mg	Cholesterol

Stuffed Mushrooms

Look for large, white mushrooms, weighing about 1 ounce each, for this superb appetizer. It also works well as a side dish and makes a beautiful presentation when used to encircle a platter of pasta.

Makes 4 servings
(3 mushrooms each serving)

12	large mushrooms
1	teaspoon olive oil
1/4	cup finely chopped onion
2	cloves garlic, crushed
1/4	cup Italian seasoned bread crumbs
1	tablespoon grated Parmesan cheese
1/2	teaspoon dried basil
1/8	teaspoon pepper
1/4	cup water

Remove stems from mushrooms. (Hold each mushroom in the palm of your hand and gently work the stem loose by moving it back and forth. Remove the entire stem.) Finely chop the stems.

Preheat oven to 375°.

Lightly oil a large baking sheet or spray with a nonstick cooking spray.

Heat oil in a small nonstick skillet over medium heat. Add chopped mushroom stems, onion, and garlic. Cook, stirring frequently, 5 minutes, until onion is tender. Remove from heat and add remaining ingredients, mixing well.

Fill mushroom caps with stuffing. Place mushrooms on prepared baking sheet.

Bake 15 minutes.

Serve hot.

Each serving provides:

81	Calories	11 g	Carbohydrate
4 g	Protein	226 mg	Sodium
3 g	Total fat (1 g sat. fat)	1 mg	Cholesterol

White Bean and Basil Spread

Spreads such as this are usually served on slices of toasted Italian bread or on crisp vegetables, such as zucchini or cucumber rounds. You can also pile it into a crusty roll, add lettuce and tomato, and enjoy a delicious lunch.

Makes 12 servings
(2 tablespoons each serving)

1	1-pound can white beans (cannellini), rinsed and drained (or 2 cups of cooked beans)
2	cloves garlic, chopped
2	teaspoons dried basil
2	teaspoons red wine vinegar
1/8	teaspoon salt
1/8	teaspoon pepper

Combine all ingredients in a food processor. Process with a steel blade until smooth. (A blender can be used, but be careful not to let the mixture get too soupy.)

Chill several hours or overnight.

Each serving provides:

28	Calories	5 g	Carbohydrate
2 g	Protein	70 mg	Sodium
0 g	Total fat (0 g sat. fat)	0 mg	Cholesterol

Roasted Garlic

What a wonderful delicacy! Simply roast garlic in the oven, then spread it on crackers or toasted Italian bread for an easy, delicious appetizer. You can also use it to make the oh-so-tasty Mashed Potatoes with Roasted Garlic *on page 202.*

Makes 6 to 10 servings
(Depending on the size of the garlic.)

1   whole, unpeeled bulb of garlic (Choose one with large, firm cloves.)

Preheat oven to 350°.

Cut the top off of the garlic bulb, removing just a tiny bit of each clove. Wrap garlic tightly in foil, twisting the ends of the foil to seal.

Bake 40 minutes, until soft.

To serve, carefully peel garlic and separate the cloves. Squeeze the soft garlic onto bread or crackers. Spread with a knife.

Serve right away.

Store leftover garlic in the refrigerator. To reheat, wrap garlic in foil and heat in a conventional or toaster oven, or peel the cloves and heat in the microwave.

Each clove provides:			
4	Calories	1 g	Carbohydrate
0 g	Protein	1 mg	Sodium
0 g	Total fat (0 g sat. fat)	0 mg	Cholesterol

Spinach-Pesto Dip

Pesto is a pungent, aromatic sauce made with fresh basil. (Dried basil just will not do.) In this dish I've combined the flavor of pesto with lowfat cottage cheese to make a creamy dip that brings fresh veggies to life. I've also had delicious results using it as a salad dressing and as a sandwich spread.

*Makes 9 servings
(2 tablespoons each serving)*

1	cup lowfat (1%) cottage cheese
1/2	cup (packed) fresh spinach, torn into small pieces, stems removed and discarded
1/4	cup (loosely packed) fresh basil, torn into small pieces
1	clove garlic, chopped
1	tablespoon chopped onion
1	tablespoon grated Parmesan cheese
1/8	to 1/4 teaspoon pepper

In a blender container, combine all ingredients. Blend until smooth. Chill several hours or overnight to blend flavors.

Each serving provides:

24	Calories	1 g	Carbohydrate
4 g	Protein	117 mg	Sodium
0 g	Total fat (0 g sat. fat)	1 mg	Cholesterol

Cream of White Bean Soup

Cannellini (white kidney beans) are one of the most popular Italian beans. They have been a staple of the Italian diet for centuries. This creamy cannellini soup actually contains no cream. It has a wonderful texture created by blending the beans, and a subtle flavor from simmering the beans with bay leaves.

Makes 6 servings
(1 cup each serving)

2	teaspoons olive oil
3	large leeks, sliced (white part only)
1	cup chopped carrots (1/4 to 1/2-inch pieces)
1/2	cup chopped celery (1/4 to 1/2-inch pieces)
2	1-pound cans white beans (cannellini), rinsed and drained (or 4 cups of cooked beans)
4	cups water
1	tablespoon *Vegetable Broth Mix* (See page 27.)
4	large bay leaves
	Salt and pepper to taste

Heat oil in a large saucepan over medium heat. Add leeks, carrots, and celery. Cook, stirring frequently, 10 minutes. Add small amounts of water if necessary, about a tablespoon at a time, to prevent sticking.

Add beans, water, and broth mix. Bring mixture to a boil, then reduce heat to medium-low, cover, and simmer 30 minutes. Remove from heat and spoon soup into a heatproof bowl.

Place soup, a few cups at a time, in a blender container. Blend until smooth. Return to saucepan and add bay leaves, along with salt and pepper to taste. Simmer uncovered on low heat, 45 minutes.

Remove and discard bay leaves before serving.

Each serving provides:

166	Calories	28 g	Carbohydrate
9 g	Protein	254 mg	Sodium
3 g	Total fat (0 g sat. fat)	0 mg	Cholesterol

Tomato Soup with Fennel

Fennel is a unique vegetable that has been cultivated in Italy for centuries. It has a celery-like texture and a flavor similar to licorice that mellows when cooked. In this soup the combination of fennel and tomato, delicately laced with orange, provides one of the simplest ways to brighten a meal.

Makes 8 servings
(1¹/4 cups each serving)

2	teaspoons olive oil
3	medium leeks (white part only), chopped (1¹/2 cups)
4	cloves garlic, crushed
2	pounds fennel bulbs, sliced ¹/8- to ¹/4-inch thick, cores and green parts removed and discarded (3 bulbs)
¹/4	cup dry white wine
4	cups *Vegetable Broth,* or 4 cups of water plus 4 teaspoons *Vegetable Broth Mix* (See pages 26–27.)
1	28-ounce can tomato purée
2	3-inch strips orange peel
2	teaspoons dried basil
¹/2	teaspoon fennel seed
1	bay leaf
	Salt and pepper to taste

Heat oil in a large saucepan over medium heat. Add leeks and garlic. Cook, stirring frequently, 2 minutes.

Add fennel and wine. Cover and cook 5 minutes.

Add remaining ingredients, *except* salt and pepper. Bring to a boil, then cover, reduce heat to medium-low, and simmer 30 minutes.

Remove and discard bay leaf.

Add salt and pepper to taste.

Each serving provides:

84	Calories	17 g	Carbohydrate
3 g	Protein	522 mg	Sodium
1 g	Total fat (0 g sat. fat)	0 mg	Cholesterol

Mushroom-Burgundy Bisque

This hearty soup has an impressive, delicate flavor. If different varieties of mushrooms are available, do as the Italians do and use a combination of several types for an even more intriguing flavor.

Makes 6 servings
($1^1/3$ cups each serving)

1	teaspoon olive oil
1	pound mushrooms, sliced (4 cups)
2	cups chopped onion
2	medium potatoes, unpeeled, cut into $1/4$- to $1/2$-inch pieces (8 ounces each)
$1/2$	cup burgundy wine
$1^1/2$	cups *Vegetable Broth,* or $1^1/2$ cups of water plus $1^1/2$ teaspoons *Vegetable Broth Mix* (See pages 26–27.)
$1/2$	teaspoon ground nutmeg
$1^1/2$	cups evaporated skim milk
	Salt and freshly ground pepper to taste

Heat oil in a large saucepan over medium heat. Add mushrooms and onion. Cook, stirring frequently, 8 minutes or until tender. Add potatoes, wine, broth, and nutmeg. Bring to a boil, then reduce heat to medium-low, cover, and simmer 15 minutes.

Working in several batches, spoon soup into a blender container. Blend until smooth. Return puréed soup to saucepan and stir in milk. Add salt to taste. Heat through, but do not boil.

Spoon soup into individual serving bowls and top each serving with a generous sprinkling of freshly ground pepper.

Each serving provides:

171	Calories	29 g	Carbohydrate
9 g	Protein	112 mg	Sodium
1 g	Total fat (0 g sat. fat)	3 mg	Cholesterol

Sicilian Lentil Soup with Pasta

This is a rich, classic, yet simple, soup. It can be the main event of a hearty one-dish meal; just add a salad and a chunk of bread to make the meal complete.

Makes 6 servings
(1¹/₄ cups each serving)

2	teaspoons olive oil
¹/₂	cup *each* finely chopped onion, celery, and carrots
¹/₄	cup chopped celery leaves
3	cloves garlic, crushed
1	1-pound can salt-free (or regular) tomatoes, chopped, undrained
4	cups *Vegetable Broth*, or 4 cups of water plus 4 teaspoons *Vegetable Broth Mix* (See pages 26–27.)
1¹/₂	cups water
1	cup lentils, uncooked
1	bay leaf
1	teaspoon *each* dried oregano and dried basil
¹/₄	teaspoon pepper
³/₄	cup ditalini pasta (small tubes), uncooked
	Grated Parmesan cheese

Heat oil in a large saucepan over medium heat. Add onion, celery, carrots, celery leaves, and garlic. Cook, stirring frequently, 5 minutes.

Add remaining ingredients, *except* pasta and Parmesan cheese. Bring mixture to a boil, stirring occasionally. Reduce heat to medium-low, cover, and simmer 40 minutes or until vegetables are tender. Stir in pasta and continue to cook, covered, 10 minutes more. Remove and discard bay leaf before serving.

Top each serving with a sprinkling of Parmesan cheese.

Each serving provides:

213	Calories	37 g	Carbohydrate
12 g	Protein	100 mg	Sodium
2 g	Total fat (0 g sat. fat)	0 mg	Cholesterol

Chick Pea and Vegetable Soup

My version of this classic soup sacrifices a little authenticity for a lot of ease. You'll love the tasty results and you won't mind the fact that this recipe yields a lot of soup.

Makes 12 servings
(1¹/3 cups each serving)

3	cups shredded cabbage
2	cups *each* sliced carrots and celery (¹/4-inch thick)
2	cups chopped onion
2	cups chopped zucchini (¹/2-inch pieces)
1	10-ounce package frozen cut green beans
1	1-pound can chick peas (garbanzo beans), rinsed and drained (or 2 cups of cooked beans)
3	cloves garlic, crushed
1	tablespoon *each* dried parsley flakes and dried basil
1	teaspoon dried oregano
¹/2	teaspoon *each* dried thyme and crumbled, dried rosemary
2	bay leaves
1	46-ounce can V8 Juice®
5	cups water
1	cup elbow macaroni, uncooked (4 ounces)
	Salt and pepper to taste
	Grated Parmesan cheese

In a large soup pot, combine all ingredients, *except* macaroni, salt, pepper, and Parmesan cheese. Bring to a boil over medium heat, stirring occasionally. Reduce heat to low, cover, and simmer 45 minutes or until vegetables are just tender. Stir in macaroni, cover, and continue to cook 15 minutes more. Remove and discard bay leaves. Add salt and pepper to taste.

To serve, spoon soup into serving bowls and sprinkle lightly with Parmesan cheese.

Each serving provides:

124	Calories	25 g	Carbohydrate
5 g	Protein	434 mg	Sodium
1 g	Total fat (0 g sat. fat)	0 mg	Cholesterol

Pasta Salad with Cherry Tomatoes and Pesto Vinaigrette

Few flavors compare with the exquisite combination of garlic and basil. Based on the ever-popular pesto sauce, this salad can be made with flat fettucine noodles or with spirals. My testers were divided on their preference so the choice is yours.

Makes 8 servings

12	ounces pasta spirals or fettucine, uncooked
1	large clove garlic, cut in half
1/4	cup (packed) fresh basil leaves
1/4	cup (packed) fresh parsley
1/4	cup red wine vinegar
3	tablespoons vegetable oil (Or you can use a very light-flavored extra-virgin olive oil or half of each.)
2	tablespoons water
2	tablespoons grated Parmesan cheese
1/2	teaspoon sugar
12	cherry tomatoes, cut in half
	Freshly ground black pepper

Cook pasta according to package directions. Drain. Rinse under cold water and drain again.

In a blender container, combine remaining ingredients, *except* tomatoes and pepper. Blend until smooth. Pour over pasta and toss until all of the pasta is coated. Add cherry tomatoes and pepper to taste. Toss again.

Chill several hours to blend flavors.

Mix before serving.

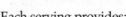

Each serving provides:			
208	Calories	32 g	Carbohydrate
7 g	Protein	36 mg	Sodium
6 g	Total fat (1 g sat. fat)	1 mg	Cholesterol

Pasta Salad with Two Tomatoes

Cold pasta salads were probably invented by busy Italians who were convinced that a lunch without pasta was no lunch at all! This one combines pasta, herbs, and lots of fresh and sun-dried tomatoes.

Makes 8 servings

1/2	cup sun-dried tomatoes, cut into 1/4-inch pieces (Choose the ones that are dry and not packed in oil.)
	Boiling water
1/4	cup vegetable oil (Or you can use a very light-flavored extra-virgin olive oil or half of each.)
1/3	cup red wine vinegar
1/2	cup water
2	teaspoons *each* dried oregano and dried basil
1	teaspoon dry mustard
3	cloves garlic, crushed
	Salt and pepper to taste
12	ounces pasta spirals, uncooked (4 cups)
4	large plum tomatoes, chopped into 1/2-inch pieces

Place sun-dried tomatoes in a small bowl or custard cup. Cover with boiling water and set aside for 10 minutes.

In a small bowl, combine oil, vinegar, water, oregano, basil, mustard, garlic, salt, and pepper. Set aside.

Cook pasta according to package directions. Drain. Rinse under cold water and drain again. Place in a large bowl.

Drain sun-dried tomatoes and add to pasta, along with herb mixture and chopped plum tomatoes. Mix well. Chill thoroughly, mixing several times. Serve cold. Mix before serving.

Each serving provides:

247	Calories	38 g	Carbohydrate
7 g	Protein	13 mg	Sodium
8 g	Total fat (1 g sat. fat)	0 mg	Cholesterol

Bread Salad with Tomatoes and Fresh Basil

The delectable flavor of fresh basil shines when combined with the tomatoes and toasted bread cubes in this refreshing salad from the Tuscan region of Italy. This recipe serves six, but I have to confess that the first time I made it, Harry and I ate the whole salad by ourselves!

Makes 6 servings

5	1/2-inch thick slices of Italian bread, cut into 1/2-inch cubes (3 cups)
3	cups plum tomatoes, chopped into 1/2-inch pieces (about 9 tomatoes)
1/4	cup very finely chopped onion
1/4	cup (packed) chopped fresh basil leaves
3	large cloves garlic, very finely minced
1/8	teaspoon *each* salt and pepper
2	tablespoons olive oil

Preheat oven to 300°.

Place bread cubes on an ungreased baking sheet in a single layer. Bake 10 minutes, until very lightly toasted. Set aside to cool.

In a large bowl, combine tomatoes, onion, basil, garlic, salt, and pepper. Toss to combine. Drizzle with oil and toss again.

Add bread cubes, half at a time, to tomato mixture, mixing well. Chill several hours.

Stir before serving. (The bread cubes will become softer if the salad is chilled longer, but that's okay; in some versions the bread is actually soaked in water before it's added to the salad.)

Each serving provides:

115	Calories	15 g	Carbohydrate
3 g	Protein	157 mg	Sodium
5 g	Total fat (1 g sat. fat)	0 mg	Cholesterol

Bean-Filled Tomato Cups

These colorful tomato cups can be served the Italian way—as part of an antipasto, or they can stand alone as a delicious light entrée.

Makes 4 servings

4	large, ripe (yet firm) tomatoes
1	1-pound can white beans (cannellini), rinsed and drained (or 2 cups of cooked beans)
1/4	cup red onion, cut into thin slivers
2	teaspoons olive oil
1 1/2	teaspoons red wine vinegar
1	teaspoon dried parsley flakes
1/2	teaspoon dried basil
1/8	teaspoon salt
1/8	teaspoon pepper

Slice the top off of each tomato. Using a melon ball scoop or a teaspoon, scoop out the pulp and seeds. (Since they are not needed in the recipe, I save the pulp and add it to a soup or casserole.) Turn tomatoes over and drain on layers of towels for about 10 minutes.

Place beans in a large bowl. Add remaining ingredients and mix well. Fill tomatoes with bean mixture.

Serve right away or chill for later serving. (If you are not serving this until the next day, you can prepare and chill the bean mixture ahead, but prepare and fill the tomatoes within several hours of serving time.)

Each serving provides:

129	Calories	19 g	Carbohydrate
7 g	Protein	222 mg	Sodium
3 g	Total fat (0 g sat. fat)	0 mg	Cholesterol

Herb-Topped Tomato Slices

Quick and easy, and with the unrivaled flavor of fresh basil, this creative salad can be used as part of an antipasto or as an attractive garnish alongside any Italian or Middle Eastern entrée. (It can also turn a simple cheese sandwich into an elegant affair!)

Makes 6 servings

4	large, ripe tomatoes, sliced 1/4-inch thick
1/2	cup finely chopped red onion
1/2	cup finely chopped cucumber, peeled
2	cloves garlic, very finely chopped
1/2	cup finely chopped fresh basil, loosely packed (Dried basil will not do here.)
1	tablespoon red wine vinegar
1	tablespoon plus 1 teaspoon olive oil
1	teaspoon sugar
	Salt and pepper to taste

Arrange tomato slices in a single layer on a large platter.

Combine onion, cucumber, garlic, and basil in a medium bowl. Combine remaining ingredients and mix well. Add to vegetables, mix well, and let stand 10 minutes.

Stir onion mixture and divide evenly, spooning it onto each tomato slice. If there is any dressing left in the bowl, drizzle it over the tomatoes.

Let stand at room temperature for 20 to 30 minutes before serving. (The leftovers can be chilled and served later, but this dish is at its best when served fresh.)

Each serving provides:

63	Calories	8 g	Carbohydrate
1 g	Protein	12 mg	Sodium
3 g	Total fat (0 g sat. fat)	0 mg	Cholesterol

Marinated Cauliflower Salad

Salads such as this one are typically served as part of an antipasto or appetizer course. A meatless antipasto would consist of several types of marinated salads, along with raw vegetables, bread sticks, olives, and cheeses. To me it's a whole meal!

Makes 10 servings

1	cup celery, cut into 1-inch pieces
1	cup carrots, cut into 1-inch pieces (If carrots are very thick, cut in half lengthwise first.)
4	cups cauliflower, cut into small flowerets
1	medium, red bell pepper, cut into 1-inch squares
8	medium, stuffed green olives, very thinly sliced
3$^1/_2$	tablespoons red wine vinegar
1$^1/_2$	tablespoons olive oil
2	tablespoons water
3	cloves garlic, crushed
1	teaspoon dried basil
$^1/_2$	teaspoon sugar
$^1/_4$	teaspoon *each* salt and pepper

Place a steamer basket in the bottom of a large saucepan. Fill with water almost up to the bottom of the basket and bring to a boil over medium heat.

Place celery in the basket, cover the saucepan, and steam 5 minutes. Add carrots, cover, and steam 3 minutes more. Add cauliflower and bell pepper. Cover and continue to steam 7 minutes more. Place vegetables in a colander and run under cold water. Drain and place in a large bowl. Add olives.

In a small bowl or custard cup, combine remaining ingredients. Spoon over vegetables. Toss until vegetables are evenly coated. Chill several hours or overnight.

Mix before serving.

Each serving provides:

43	Calories	5 g	Carbohydrate
1 g	Protein	150 mg	Sodium
3 g	Total fat (0 g sat. fat)	0 mg	Cholesterol

Roman Zucchini Salad

This dish really turns the humble squash into something special. In Rome I tried several different versions of this delicious salad and in one restaurant I was given some "inside information" about the ingredients and the unusual use of the shredded vegetables and wine.

Makes 8 servings

3	medium zucchini, unpeeled, sliced 1/8-inch thick (1 1/4 pounds)
1/2	cup coarsely shredded green bell pepper
1/2	cup coarsely shredded onion
1/2	cup coarsely shredded celery
1/2	cup cider vinegar
1/3	cup sugar
3	tablespoons burgundy wine
2	tablespoons vegetable oil (or a very light-flavored extra-virgin olive oil)
1	tablespoon red wine vinegar
1/2	teaspoon salt
1/2	teaspoon pepper

In a large bowl, combine zucchini, bell pepper, onion, and celery.

In another bowl, combine remaining ingredients. Stir until most of the sugar is dissolved. Pour over vegetables. Mix well.

Chill several hours or overnight to blend flavors.

Mix before serving.

Each serving provides:

85	Calories	13 g	Carbohydrate
1 g	Protein	146 mg	Sodium
4 g	Total fat (0 g sat. fat)	0 mg	Cholesterol

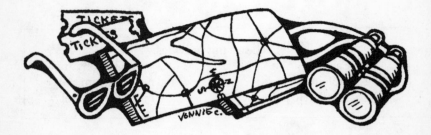

Spinach and Ricotta Pie

Italian vegetable puddings and pies are often made with lots of butter and eggs. This lighter version is similar to lasagne, but without noodles. It's an easy main dish pie that also makes a lovely luncheon dish.

Makes 6 servings

2   tablespoons dry bread crumbs, or Italian seasoned bread crumbs
1   cup part-skim ricotta cheese
2   egg whites
1/2 cup plain nonfat yogurt
1/2 cup all-purpose flour
2   teaspoons dried basil
1/4 teaspoon *each* salt and pepper
1/16 teaspoon ground nutmeg
1   10-ounce package frozen chopped spinach, thawed and drained well
1/2 cup meatless spaghetti sauce
1   cup shredded part-skim Mozzarella cheese (4 ounces)
1   tablespoon grated Parmesan cheese

Preheat oven to 375°.

Lightly oil a 9-inch pie pan or spray with a nonstick cooking spray.

Sprinkle bread crumbs in pan and tilt pan to coat the bottom and sides with crumbs.

In a large bowl, combine ricotta cheese, egg whites, yogurt, flour, and spices. Mix well. Stir spinach into cheese mixture. Spoon into prepared pan and spread evenly. Spread sauce over mixture. Top with Mozzarella cheese and then sprinkle with Parmesan cheese.

Bake uncovered, 35 minutes, until cheese is melted and begins to brown.

Let stand 5 minutes before serving.

Each serving provides:

207	Calories	19 g	Carbohydrate
15 g	Protein	435 mg	Sodium
8 g	Total fat (4 g sat. fat)	25 mg	Cholesterol

Italian Garden Lasagne

In Italy, lasagne is usually eaten as the first course, but we all know how substantial it can be. My version is so full of veggies that it's virtually a "garden in a pan." Don't worry about the long list of ingredients. The only time-consuming part is chopping the vegetables. After that it's a breeze!

Makes 8 servings

1	8-ounce package lasagne noodles, uncooked
1	30-ounce jar meatless spaghetti sauce
1 1/2	cups water

Vegetables:

2	teaspoons olive oil
1	cup chopped onion
1	cup chopped yellow or red bell pepper
1	cup coarsely shredded carrots
4	cloves garlic, crushed
2	cups sliced mushrooms
1	cup finely chopped zucchini
1	cup finely chopped broccoli flowerets
1	teaspoon *each* dried basil and dried oregano
1/2	teaspoon salt
1/4	teaspoon pepper
1	10-ounch package frozen chopped spinach, thawed and drained well

Cheese Filling:

1	15-ounce container part-skim ricotta cheese
1 1/4	cups part-skim Mozzarella cheese (5 ounces)
1	tablespoon grated Parmesan cheese

Preheat oven to 350°.

Lightly oil a 9 x 13-inch baking pan or spray with a nonstick cooking spray.

In a large bowl, combine sauce and water. Set aside.

To prepare vegetables: heat oil in a large nonstick skillet over medium heat. Add onion, bell pepper, carrots, and garlic. Cook, stirring frequently, 3 minutes. Add remaining vegetables, *except* spinach. Sprinkle with spices. Cook, stirring frequently, 5 minutes. Remove from heat and stir in spinach. Set aside 1 cup of the vegetables.

To prepare cheese filling: set aside 1/2 cup of the Mozzarella cheese. In a medium bowl, combine remaining Mozzarella cheese with ricotta and Parmesan. Mix well.

To assemble: spread 1 cup of the sauce in the bottom of prepared pan. Top with a third of the noodles, then 1/2 cup of the sauce. Next, spoon half of the cheese mixture over the noodles. Top with half of the vegetables, pressing them down into the cheese. Top with another 1/2 cup of the sauce.

Top with another third of the noodles. Press them down firmly onto the filling. Repeat layers, adding 1/2 cup sauce, remaining cheese, remaining vegetables, 1/2 cup sauce, and remaining noodles. Again, press noodles down firmly.

Spoon reserved vegetables over noodles. Top with remaining sauce, making sure noodles are entirely covered with sauce.

Cover and bake 40 minutes. Uncover and spoon sauce from sides of pan over noodles. Sprinkle with reserved Mozzarella cheese and continue to bake uncovered, 30 minutes more.

Let stand 5 minutes before serving.

Each serving provides:			
398	Calories	50 g	Carbohydrate
19 g	Protein	864 mg	Sodium
15 g	Total fat (6 g sat. fat)	27 mg	Cholesterol

Roman Dumplings

Gnocchi *is the Italian name for these heavenly baked dumplings. I first tasted them in Italy and then found them in many Italian cookbooks, unfortunately loaded with butter, eggs, and cheese. So I set about to create my own version that has proven to be a knock-out. In Italy gnocchi are served like pasta, as a first course, but can actually be served as an appetizer, side dish, or an entrée. I prefer to serve them as an entrée, accompanied by a salad, a green vegetable and* Wine-Glazed Tomatoes *(page 199).*

Makes 6 servings
(9 dumplings each serving)

1	tablespoon vegetable oil
2	egg whites
1/4	cup plus 1 tablespoon grated Parmesan cheese
3	cups skim milk
1/2	teaspoon salt
1/8	teaspoon pepper
3/4	cup Quick Cream of Wheat®
	Freshly ground black pepper to taste

Lightly oil a 10 x 15-inch jelly roll pan or spray with a nonstick cooking spray.

In a small bowl, combine oil, egg whites, and 1/4 cup of the cheese. Beat with a fork or wire whisk until blended. Set aside.

In a medium saucepan, combine milk, salt, and pepper. Bring to a boil over medium heat, stirring frequently. Add the Cream of Wheat® gradually, beating briskly with a fork or wire whisk to prevent lumps. Reduce heat to medium-low and cook, stirring constantly, until mixture is very thick and comes away from the sides of the pan, about 5 minutes. Remove from heat and add egg white mixture, beating it in quickly. (This is to keep the egg whites from starting to cook when they touch the hot mixture.)

Spoon mixture into prepared pan. Using a metal spatula, and dipping it in hot water as you work, spread the mixture 1/4-inch thick and smooth the top. (It will not fill the entire pan.)

Chill until firm, at least 1 hour, or overnight if desired.

To cook: Preheat oven to 450°.

Lightly oil a 9 x 13-inch baking pan or spray with a nonstick cooking spray.

Using a 2-inch round biscuit cutter or a glass, cut the dough into circles. Press the scraps together tightly into a ball and roll or press flat, then cut into more circles. Lay dumplings on a sheet of wax paper and spray them lightly with nonstick cooking spray. Place them in slightly overlapping rows in prepared pan. Sprinkle with remaining tablespoon of cheese and freshly ground black pepper.

Place oven rack on the top position and bake dumplings 15 minutes. Then turn on the broiler and continue to cook a few minutes, until dumplings are lightly browned and crisp. (Watch them carefully to prevent burning.)

Each serving provides:			
174	Calories	24 g	Carbohydrate
9 g	Protein	406 mg	Sodium
4 g	Total fat (1 g sat. fat)	6 mg	Cholesterol

Pizza Beans

Here's a quick Italian idea for those nights when you're really in a hurry! Serve it plain, spoon it over rice or a baked potato, or put it in a roll and make a "pizza bean sub."

Makes 4 servings

1   19-ounce can kidney beans, rinsed and drained (or 2¹/₄ cups of cooked beans)
1   cup meatless pizza sauce or spaghetti sauce
1   cup shredded part-skim Mozzarella cheese (4 ounces)
1   tablespoon grated Parmesan cheese
     Thinly sliced onions and/or green bell pepper (optional)

Preheat oven to 375°.
Lightly oil a 9-inch pie pan or spray with a nonstick cooking spray.
Spread beans evenly in pan. Spoon sauce over beans. Top with Mozzarella cheese and sprinkle with Parmesan cheese. Spread onions and/or bell pepper over the top, if desired.
Bake uncovered, 20 minutes or until cheese is melted and sauce is hot and bubbly.

Each serving provides:

216	Calories	20 g	Carbohydrate
16 g	Protein	577 mg	Sodium
8 g	Total fat (3 g sat. fat)	17 mg	Cholesterol

Tofu with Peppers and Mushrooms

Based on a recipe from Milan, this hearty stew uses tofu in place of meat and is simmered with tomato paste, herbs, and wine. It can be served with rice as in Milan, or if you prefer, over any shape pasta.

Makes 4 servings

2	teaspoons olive oil
8	ounces mushrooms, thinly sliced (2 1/2 cups)
2	large, green bell peppers, sliced 1/4-inch thick
1	cup chopped onion
3	large cloves garlic, chopped
1	6-ounce can tomato paste
1/2	cup dry white wine
1/2	cup *Vegetable Broth*, or 1/2 cup of water plus 1 teaspoon *Vegetable Broth Mix* (See pages 26–27.)
1	teaspoon dried oregano
1 1/2	teaspoons dried basil
1/4	teaspoon dried thyme
1/8	teaspoon pepper
1	pound firm tofu, cut into 1/2- to 3/4-inch cubes, drained between layers of towels
	Salt and pepper to taste

Heat oil in a large nonstick skillet over medium heat. Add mushrooms, bell peppers, onion, and garlic. Cook, stirring occasionally, 7 minutes.

In a small bowl, combine tomato paste, wine, broth, and spices. Add to skillet and mix well. Gently stir in tofu. Cover, reduce heat to medium-low, and simmer 25 minutes.

Add salt and additional pepper to taste.

Each serving provides:

293	Calories	25 g	Carbohydrate
22 g	Protein	372 mg	Sodium
13 g	Total fat (2 g sat. fat)	0 mg	Cholesterol

Polenta-Filled Red Peppers

Once a staple dish of the early Romans, polenta *still plays a large part in the Italian diet. Similar to American cornmeal mush, it makes a wonderful filling for sweet red peppers.*

Makes 4 servings

2¼   cups water
¾   cup yellow cornmeal
1   teaspoon *each* dried basil and dried oregano
¼   teaspoon salt
⅛   teaspoon *each* pepper and garlic powder
1   tablespoon grated Parmesan cheese
2   large red bell peppers (8 ounces each), cut in half lengthwise through the stems, seeds removed
1   15-ounce jar meatless spaghetti sauce (or 1¾ cups sauce)
2   ounces shredded part-skim Mozzarella cheese (½ cup)

Place 1¼ cups of the water in a small saucepan and bring to a boil over medium heat.

Place cornmeal in a small bowl with basil, oregano, salt, pepper, and garlic powder. Gradually add remaining water. Mix well and stir into boiling water. When water boils again, reduce heat to low and cook, stirring constantly, 20 minutes. (Italian cooks stir with a wooden stick or paddle.) Remove from heat. Stir in Parmesan cheese.

Preheat oven to 375°.

Lightly oil an 8-inch square baking pan or spray with a nonstick cooking spray.

Reserve ½ cup of sauce and set aside. Spoon remaining sauce into prepared pan. Divide polenta and pile into pepper halves. Place in pan. Bake, covered, 40 minutes.

Uncover and spoon reserved sauce over polenta. Top with Mozzarella cheese. Return to oven uncovered, for 5 minutes, until cheese is melted.

Each serving provides:

282	Calories	43 g	Carbohydrate
9 g	Protein	719 mg	Sodium
9 g	Total fat (3 g sat. fat)	9 mg	Cholesterol

Eggplant-Noodle Casserole

Alive with the flavors of Italy, this layered casserole is simple enough for a family dinner, and yet elegant enough for a party.

Makes 6 servings

1	large eggplant, peeled and sliced 1/2-inch thick (about 1 1/2 pounds)
4	ounces medium (yolk-free) noodles, uncooked (about 2 1/2 cups)
1	1-pound can crushed tomatoes
1	6-ounce can tomato paste
1/2	cup water
3	cloves garlic, crushed
2	teaspoons dried basil
1/4	teaspoon *each* salt and pepper
3	tablespoons grated Parmesan cheese (1 ounce)
1	cup shredded part-skim Mozzarella cheese

Lightly oil a 7 x 11-inch baking pan or spray with a nonstick cooking spray.

Place eggplant slices in a lightly oiled broiler pan. Broil 6 to 7 minutes on each side, until lightly browned, turning once. Remove from oven and reduce temperature to 375°. While eggplant is browning, cook noodles according to package directions. Drain.

In a large bowl, combine tomatoes, tomato paste, water, garlic, basil, salt, and pepper. Mix well.

Arrange half of the eggplant slices in the bottom of prepared pan. Top with a third of the tomato sauce. Sprinkle a third of each cheese over the sauce. Spread all of the noodles evenly on top. Top with another third of the sauce and another third of the cheeses. Make a top layer with the remaining eggplant. Top with remaining sauce and then remaining cheeses. Cover with aluminum foil and bake 40 minutes.

Each serving provides:

209	Calories	29 g	Carbohydrate
12 g	Protein	622 mg	Sodium
6 g	Total fat (3 g sat. fat)	15 mg	Cholesterol

Veggie Pizza Subs

This is one of the simplest ways to enjoy the taste of pizza without a lot of fuss. Add any veggies you like and pile them high.

Makes 4 servings

4	6-inch submarine rolls
1	8-ounce can salt-free (or regular) tomato sauce
1/4	teaspoon dried oregano
1/4	teaspoon dried basil
1/8	teaspoon garlic powder
	Pepper to taste
1 1/2	cups shredded part-skim Mozzarella cheese (6 ounces)
1/2	cup thinly sliced onion
1/2	cup thinly sliced green bell pepper
1/2	cup thinly sliced mushrooms
12	black olives, sliced

Preheat oven to 425°.

Cut rolls in half lengthwise and open them up. *Do not cut all the way through.* Place rolls cut-side up on an ungreased baking sheet.

In a small bowl, combine tomato sauce, oregano, basil, garlic powder, and pepper. Mix well. Divide evenly and spread on cut sides of rolls. Sprinkle evenly with cheese.

In another bowl, toss together onion, bell pepper, mushrooms, and olives. Divide mixture evenly and pile on top of cheese.

Bake 12 minutes or until cheese is melted and vegetables begin to brown.

Serve like a pizza or fold them up and enjoy as a sandwich.

Each serving provides:

407	Calories	56 g	Carbohydrate
20 g	Protein	854 mg	Sodium
12 g	Total fat (5 g sat. fat)	25 mg	Cholesterol

Baked Ziti

Always a favorite, this easy macaroni casserole originated in the region around Naples, an area known for its simple dishes and peasant-style cooking. It can be made with any leftover pasta sauce, or you can use a jar of prepared sauce.

Makes 6 servings

8	ounces ziti, uncooked (2 cups)
3/4	cup part-skim ricotta cheese
1	cup shredded part-skim Mozzarella cheese (4 ounces)
1	15-ounce jar meatless spaghetti sauce (or 1 3/4 cups sauce)
1/2	teaspoon dried basil
1/8	teaspoon pepper
1	tablespoon grated Parmesan cheese

Cook pasta according to package directions, using the minimum amount of cooking time given. Drain.

Preheat oven to 375°.

Lightly oil a 1 1/2-quart casserole or spray with a nonstick cooking spray.

In a large bowl, combine ricotta cheese with *half* of the Mozzarella. Stir in *half* of the sauce, along with the basil and pepper. Add the cooked ziti and mix well. Spoon into prepared casserole.

Spread remaining sauce over top of casserole, then sprinkle with remaining Mozzarella cheese and then the Parmesan cheese.

Cover and bake 20 minutes. Uncover and continue to bake 15 minutes more.

Each serving provides:

319	Calories	42 g	Carbohydrate
15 g	Protein	496 mg	Sodium
10 g	Total fat (4 g sat. fat)	21 mg	Cholesterol

Shells Florentine

This quick and easy recipe was given to me by my good friend, Lee. Her Italian grandmother used to make this for her grandchildren and it became known as her "specialty." The beauty of this dish is that you can personalize it in so many ways. You can add sauteed onions and/or green bell peppers, cooked beans, steamed vegetables such as broccoli or carrots, or whatever else your imagination can devise. Or, enjoy it as is!

Makes 6 servings

12   ounces macaroni shells, uncooked (4 cups)
1   26-ounce jar meatless spaghetti sauce
1   10-ounce package frozen chopped spinach, drained well
1   cup shredded part-skim Mozzarella cheese (4 ounces)
       Grated Parmesan cheese

Cook macaroni according to package directions, using the minimum cooking time given. Drain, then return pasta to saucepan.

Add sauce and spinach, mixing well. Cook over medium-low heat until heated through. Remove from heat and stir in Mozzarella cheese.

Top each serving with a light sprinkling of Parmesan cheese.

Each serving provides:

343	Calories	58 g	Carbohydrate
16 g	Protein	778 mg	Sodium
6 g	Total fat (2 g sat. fat)	11 mg	Cholesterol

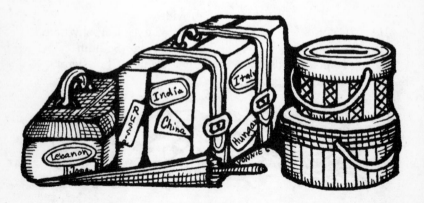

Penne Primavera

Penne, a tube shaped pasta, lends itself nicely to this delicious recipe. Chock full of vegetables, this is a dish they'll really love. Add a salad and a slice of crusty Italian bread and that's all you need for an Italian feast.

Makes 6 servings

2	teaspoons olive oil
4	cloves garlic, finely chopped
1	large red bell pepper, cut into thin strips
1 1/2	cups chopped onion
1 1/2	cups green beans, cut into 1 1/2-inch pieces (about 6 ounces)
1 1/2	cups sliced mushrooms
1	cup carrots, cut crosswise into 1/4-inch slices
1/4	cup water
1	28-ounce can Italian plum tomatoes, chopped, undrained
1	6-ounce can tomato paste
2 1/2	teaspoons dried basil
1/2	teaspoon dried oregano
	Salt and pepper to taste
8	ounces penne, uncooked

Heat oil in a large saucepan over medium heat. Add garlic and vegetables. Cook, stirring frequently, 5 minutes. Add water, cover, and cook 5 minutes more.

Add tomatoes, tomato paste, and spices, mixing well. Bring mixture to a boil. Reduce heat to medium-low, cover, and simmer 30 minutes or until vegetables are almost tender, stirring several times.

While sauce is cooking, prepare pasta according to package directions. Drain.

Add pasta to sauce, cover, and cook 5 minutes.

Each serving provides:

249	Calories	49 g	Carbohydrate
9 g	Protein	453 mg	Sodium
3 g	Total fat (0 g sat. fat)	0 mg	Cholesterol

Cacciatora Pasta Sauce

This rich, full-bodied sauce is one of my family's favorites. It's delicious and aromatic, and makes a superb topping for any size or shape of pasta.

Makes 6 servings
($1/2$ cup each serving)

2	teaspoons olive oil
2	cups sliced onion
3	cloves garlic, crushed
1	1-pound can salt-free (or regular) tomatoes, chopped, undrained
1	8-ounce can salt-free (or regular) tomato sauce
1	tablespoon tomato paste
1	teaspoon dried oregano
$1/2$	teaspoon dried rosemary, crumbled
$1/8$	teaspoon dried thyme
$1/4$	teaspoon pepper
	Salt to taste
$1/4$	cup dry red wine

Heat oil in a medium saucepan over medium heat. Add onion and garlic. Cook, stirring frequently, 5 minutes.

Add remaining ingredients, *except* wine, to saucepan, mixing well. Reduce heat to medium-low, cover, and simmer, stirring occasionally, 35 to 40 minutes. Add wine and cook covered, 15 minutes more.

Serve over your favorite pasta.

Each serving provides:

75	Calories	12 g	Carbohydrate
2 g	Protein	156 mg	Sodium
2 g	Total fat (0 g sat. fat)	0 mg	Cholesterol

Chunky Marinara Sauce

Vegetables are often added to pasta sauces, creating dense, richly-flavored sauces that contain the essence of the vegetables. I added carrots to a basic tomato sauce, creating a chunky sauce that goes well with any type of pasta or cooked grain.

Makes 6 servings
(1/2 cup each serving)

2	teaspoons olive oil
3	cloves garlic, crushed
1 1/2	cups chopped onion
1	cup chopped carrots (1/4- to 1/2-inch pieces)
1	28-ounce can Italian plum tomatoes, chopped and drained (Reserve 3/4 cup of the liquid.)
1	tablespoon dried basil
1/4	teaspoon dried oregano
1/2	teaspoon sugar
	Salt and pepper to taste

Heat oil in a medium saucepan over medium heat. Add garlic, onion, and carrots. Cook, stirring frequently, until vegetables are tender, about 10 minutes. Add small amounts of water if necessary, about a tablespoon at a time, to keep vegetables from sticking.

Add remaining ingredients, along with the reserved tomato liquid. Bring mixture to a boil, reduce heat to low, and simmer, stirring occasionally, 30 minutes or until carrots and onion are tender.

Serve over pasta, rice, or polenta.

Each serving provides:

72	Calories	13 g	Carbohydrate
2 g	Protein	255 mg	Sodium
2 g	Total fat (0 g sat. fat)	0 mg	Cholesterol

Tomato "Cream" Sauce

Cream sauces in Italy are made with cream. No one would ever guess that mine uses tofu instead to create a velvety texture and thick, creamy taste. If you're in a hurry, serve this sauce over angel hair pasta. The total preparation time will be about 10 minutes!

Makes 6 servings
(2/3 cup each serving)

1	10-ounce package soft or silken tofu (Look for silken tofu in 10-ounce aseptic packages in the produce section of most large grocery stores.)
1	30-ounce jar meatless spaghetti sauce

In a blender container, combine tofu with enough sauce to enable it to blend well. Blend until smooth. Mix with remaining sauce and heat in a saucepan or microwave until hot and bubbly.

Serve over pasta.

Optional: add any leftover cooked vegetables or reconstituted sundried tomatoes.

Each serving provides:

184	Calories	24 g	Carbohydrate
7 g	Protein	735 mg	Sodium
8 g	Total fat (1 g sat. fat)	0 mg	Cholesterol

Orange-Basil Tomato Sauce

The intriguing combination of orange and basil enhances this sauce, giving it a gourmet flavor without a lot of fuss. This sauce has a distinctive character that adds a delectable flavor to pasta, rice, or even vegetables.

Makes 6 servings
($1/2$ cup each serving)

2	teaspoons vegetable oil
$1/2$	cup chopped onion
$1/2$	cup coarsely shredded carrots
3	cloves garlic, crushed
2	pounds plum tomatoes, unpeeled, cored, and chopped into $1/2$-inch pieces (8 to 10 tomatoes)
1	tablespoon plus 1 teaspoon dried basil
$1/2$	teaspoon sugar
$1/4$	teaspoon salt
$1/8$	teaspoon pepper
1	tablespoon grated fresh orange peel
	Salt and pepper to taste

Heat oil in a medium saucepan over medium heat. Add onion, carrots, and garlic. Cook, stirring frequently, 5 minutes. Add small amounts of water as necessary, about a tablespoon at a time, to prevent sticking.

Add tomatoes, basil, sugar, salt, and pepper. Bring to a boil, then reduce heat to medium-low, cover, and simmer 15 minutes.

Uncover and add orange peel. Simmer gently, uncovered, 30 minutes or until desired thickness is reached.

Add additional salt and pepper to taste.

Each serving provides:

59	Calories	10 g	Carbohydrate
2 g	Protein	107 mg	Sodium
2 g	Total fat (0 g sat. fat)	0 mg	Cholesterol

Herb-Stuffed Tomatoes

Fresh vine-ripened tomatoes filled with a mixture of herbs make a delicious light side dish. This is an ideal midsummer dish when tomatoes are at their best.

Makes 4 servings

4	large, ripe tomatoes
1	tablespoon dried parsley flakes
2	teaspoons dried basil
3	cloves garlic, crushed
1/8	teaspoon salt
1/8	teaspoon pepper
1/3	cup Italian seasoned bread crumbs

Preheat oven to 375°.

Lightly oil a 1-quart baking pan or spray with a nonstick cooking spray.

Slice the top off of each tomato. Using a melon ball scoop or a teaspoon, scoop out the pulp. Chop the pulp and place in a small bowl. Slice a very thin sliver off the bottom of each tomato to keep them from rolling over in the pan. Turn the tomatoes over and drain on paper towels for 10 minutes.

Add the remaining ingredients to the tomato pulp. Mix well. Spoon into tomato shells and place in prepared baking pan.

Cover and bake 30 minutes.

For a crisp top, place the baked tomatoes under the broiler for a few minutes.

Each serving provides:

100	Calories	19 g	Carbohydrate
4 g	Protein	353 mg	Sodium
2 g	Total fat (0 g sat. fat)	0 mg	Cholesterol

Wine-Glazed Tomatoes

This delicious side dish makes a tasty accompaniment to many Italian entrées and also goes well with dishes from other countries. It's scrumptious served with Roman Dumplings *(page 184) or* Lentil and Potato Special *(page 250).*

Makes 4 servings

2	teaspoons vegetable oil
2	tablespoons firmly packed brown sugar
1/4	teaspoon salt
1 1/4	pounds plum tomatoes, sliced crosswise into 1/4-inch slices (5 or 6 tomatoes)
1/3	cup dry white wine
3/4	teaspoon dried basil
	Freshly ground black pepper to taste

In a large nonstick skillet, combine oil, brown sugar, and salt. Heat over medium heat until sugar melts. Place tomato slices in skillet in a single layer, spreading the brown sugar mixture evenly under them. Cook 2 minutes, then turn tomatoes and cook 2 minutes more.

Drizzle wine over tomatoes. Sprinkle evenly with basil. Increase heat to high and cook until most of the liquid has cooked out, 1 to 2 minutes. Be careful not to let the tomatoes burn.

Transfer tomatoes carefully to a serving plate and sprinkle with freshly ground black pepper.

Each serving provides:

90	Calories	14 g	Carbohydrate
1 g	Protein	152 mg	Sodium
3 g	Total fat (0 g sat. fat)	0 mg	Cholesterol

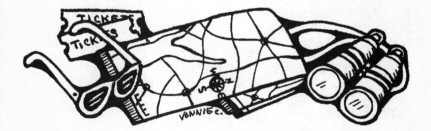

Broccoli with Lemon and Garlic

Broccoli is a popular Italian vegetable often served at dinner. This is an easy and delicious version of a favorite Italian way to dress up steamed broccoli. Try the tasty sauce over other vegetables too, such as asparagus or cauliflower.

Makes 4 servings

4	cups broccoli flowerets
3	cloves garlic, crushed
1	tablespoon plus 1 teaspoon lemon juice (preferably fresh)
1	teaspoon olive oil
1/2	teaspoon dry mustard
1/2	teaspoon dried basil
1 1/2	teaspoons grated Parmesan cheese
	Freshly ground black pepper

Place a steamer rack in the bottom of a medium saucepan. Add enough water to come almost up to the bottom of the rack. Place saucepan over medium heat. When water boils, add broccoli, cover saucepan, and cook 8 to 10 minutes or until broccoli is tender-crisp. (Length of cooking time will depend on the size of the flowerets.) Drain.

While broccoli is cooking, in a small bowl combine remaining ingredients, *except* Parmesan cheese and pepper. Mix well.

Place cooked broccoli in a serving bowl. Drizzle with garlic mixture. Sprinkle with Parmesan cheese and freshly ground black pepper to taste.

Serve right away.

Each serving provides:

59	Calories	9 g	Carbohydrate
5 g	Protein	43 mg	Sodium
2 g	Total fat (0 g sat. fat)	0 mg	Cholesterol

Zucchini and Tomato Casserole with Herbed Crumb Topping

The delicate flavor of the zucchini is really enhanced by the tomatoes and herbs in this enticing dish. It makes a beautiful addition to any buffet.

Makes 6 servings

1	teaspoon olive oil
2	medium zucchini, unpeeled, sliced crosswise into 1/8-inch slices (1 pound total)
	Salt and pepper to taste
2	1-pound cans salt-free (or regular) tomatoes, chopped (Drain one can and leave the other can undrained.)
2	teaspoons dried basil
2	cloves garlic, crushed
1/3	cup Italian seasoned bread crumbs
1	tablespoon grated Parmesan cheese
	Nonstick cooking spray

Heat oil in a large nonstick skillet over medium heat. Add zucchini. Sprinkle with salt and pepper to taste. Cook, stirring frequently, 7 or 8 minutes, until tender. Remove from heat and place zucchini in a bowl.

Return skillet to heat and add tomatoes, basil, and garlic. Bring mixture to a boil, then reduce heat slightly and simmer 15 minutes or until most of the liquid has cooked out. Remove from heat and stir in zucchini.

Preheat oven to 450°.

Lightly oil a 1 1/2-quart shallow casserole.

Spoon zucchini mixture into prepared casserole.

Combine bread crumbs and Parmesan cheese in a small bowl. Mix well. Spoon evenly over zucchini. Spray the top lightly with nonstick cooking spray.

Bake 10 minutes or until lightly browned.

Each serving provides:

85	Calories	14 g	Carbohydrate
4 g	Protein	213 mg	Sodium
2 g	Total fat (0 g sat. fat)	1 mg	Cholesterol

Mashed Potatoes with Roasted Garlic

Roasting garlic gives it an extraordinary, mellow flavor that turns ordinary mashed potatoes into an Italian culinary delight. This pleasing, unpretentious dish is perfect for family dinners.

Makes 6 servings

5	to 6 cloves roasted garlic, peeled (See page 167.)
1 1/2	pounds potatoes, unpeeled, cut into large cubes (3 medium potatoes)
1/2	cup skim milk
1/4	teaspoon salt
1/8	teaspoon pepper
2	teaspoons grated Parmesan cheese
	Nonstick cooking spray

Roast the garlic. Peel the cloves when cool enough to handle.

Place potatoes in 2 inches of boiling water, cover, and cook over medium heat 15 to 20 minutes or until potatoes are tender. Drain potatoes and remove skin.

Preheat oven to 375°.

Lightly oil a 1-quart casserole or spray with a nonstick cooking spray.

Place cooked potatoes in a large bowl and add garlic, milk, salt, and pepper. Mash with a fork or potato masher. Taste the potatoes and add more garlic, if desired. Beat on medium speed of an electric mixer until smooth. Add a little more milk if potatoes are too dry.

Spoon potatoes into prepared casserole. Sprinkle with Parmesan cheese. Lightly spray the potatoes with nonstick cooking spray.

Bake uncovered, 10 to 15 minutes, until heated through.

Each serving provides:

88	Calories	17 g	Carbohydrate
3 g	Protein	117 mg	Sodium
1 g	Total fat (0 g sat. fat)	1 mg	Cholesterol

Potato Casserole
with Mushrooms and Tomatoes

This delicious Italian specialty makes a marvelous side dish or luncheon entrée.

Makes 8 servings

1	teaspoon olive oil
8	ounces mushrooms, sliced 1/4-inch thick (2 1/2 cups)
1	large onion, thinly sliced, separated into rings
2	large cloves garlic, finely chopped
2	teaspoons dried oregano
1	large potato, unpeeled, sliced crosswise into paper-thin slices (12 ounces)
2/3	cup *Vegetable Broth,* or 2/3 cup of water plus 1 teaspoon *Vegetable Broth Mix* (See pages 26–27.)
	Freshly ground black pepper to taste
1	pound plum tomatoes, sliced into 1/4-inch slices (4 to 5 tomatoes)
1/4	teaspoon salt
1 1/2	cups shredded part-skim Mozzarella cheese (6 ounces)

Heat oil in a large nonstick skillet over medium heat. Add mushrooms, onion, garlic, and oregano. Cook, stirring frequently, until onion is tender, about 8 minutes. Remove from heat.

Preheat oven to 400°.

Lightly oil a 7 x 11-inch baking pan or spray with a nonstick cooking spray.

Arrange potato slices in overlapping layers in prepared pan. Pour broth over potatoes and sprinkle with freshly ground black pepper to taste. Spoon mushroom mixture evenly over potatoes. Arrange tomato slices in overlapping layers over mushrooms. Sprinkle with salt and additional pepper to taste.

Bake uncovered, 25 to 30 minutes, until potatoes are tender. Remove pan from oven and sprinkle cheese evenly over tomatoes. Bake 10 minutes more.

Each serving provides:			
129	Calories	15 g	Carbohydrate
8 g	Protein	186 mg	Sodium
5 g	Total fat (2 g sat. fat)	12 mg	Cholesterol

Italian Garden Bake

This layered side-dish casserole consists of layers of tomatoes, zucchini, and cheese, sprinkled with herbs and baked until golden. It makes a beautiful buffet dish, as well as a real family pleaser. If you are lucky enough to have leftovers, you can reheat them or enjoy them cold.

Makes 8 servings

1	teaspoon olive oil
1	cup finely chopped onion
3	tablespoons dry bread crumbs (plain or Italian seasoned)
4	medium zucchini, unpeeled, sliced crosswise into 1/4-inch slices (about 2 pounds)
	Salt and pepper to taste
1/8	teaspoon garlic powder
4	large tomatoes, sliced into 1/4-inch slices
1	teaspoon dried basil
1	cup shredded part-skim Mozzarella cheese (4 ounces)
1	tablespoon grated Parmesan cheese

Preheat oven to 375°.

Lightly oil a 7 x 11-inch baking dish or spray with a nonstick cooking spray.

Heat oil in a small nonstick skillet over medium heat. Add onion and cook, stirring frequently, 6 to 8 minutes, until onion just begins to brown. Remove from heat.

Sprinkle bread crumbs evenly in prepared baking dish. Arrange *half* of the zucchini slices, in slightly overlapping rows on top of crumbs. Sprinkle lightly with salt and pepper and *half* of the garlic powder. Sprinkle with *half* of the onion.

Arrange *half* of the tomato slices, in slightly overlapping rows, over the onion. Sprinkle lightly with salt and pepper and *half* of the basil. Top with *half* of the Mozzarella cheese.

Next, repeat with remaining zucchini, sprinkled with salt and pepper and remaining garlic powder, followed by remaining onion, then remaining tomatoes, sprinkled with salt and pepper and remaining basil. (Don't worry if it all piles up a little higher than the sides of the pan. It will sink while cooking.)

Cover tightly with foil and bake 35 minutes or until zucchini is tender-crisp. (If the vegetables are cold when you start, they may take a little longer to cook, but don't let them get soggy. This dish tastes best when the zucchini retains a slight crispness.) Uncover and sprinkle with remaining Mozzarella and Parmesan cheese. Continue to bake 25 minutes more, until cheese is nicely browned.

Each serving provides:

107	Calories	13 g	Carbohydrate
7 g	Protein	114 mg	Sodium
4 g	Total fat (2 g sat. fat)	9 mg	Cholesterol

Risotto with Asparagus

A variety of fresh vegetables and herbs add color and flavor to this delicious medley. The arborio rice, with its unique, creamy texture, is essential to the dish. This Italian specialty is served as a first course and is often used to stuff tomatoes. Look for arborio rice in specialty stores and many large grocery stores.

Makes 6 servings

5	cups *Vegetable Broth,* or 5 cups of water plus 5 teaspoons *Vegetable Broth Mix* (See pages 26–27.)
2	teaspoons olive oil
1/2	cup finely chopped onion
1/2	cup coarsely shredded carrots
2	cloves garlic, finely minced
11/2	cups arborio rice, uncooked (The dish doesn't work well with other types of rice.)
1/2	cup dry white wine
1/2	pound fresh asparagus, cut diagonally into 1/2-inch pieces
2	large plum tomatoes, chopped
1/2	teaspoon dried basil
1/4	teaspoon *each* dried oregano and dried thyme
11/2	tablespoons grated Parmesan cheese
	Freshly ground black pepper to taste

Bring the broth to a simmer in a medium saucepan over medium heat. Reduce heat to low and keep broth warm.

Heat oil in a large nonstick skillet over medium heat. Add onion, carrots, and garlic. Cook, stirring frequently, 3 to 4 minutes, until onion is tender. Add rice. Cook and stir, 1 minute. Add the wine and cook until most of it is evaporated. Then add 1/2 cup of broth and continue cooking, stirring constantly, until the rice has absorbed the liquid. Add another 1/2 cup of broth, along with asparagus, tomatoes, and herbs. Stir until broth is absorbed.

Continue to add broth, 1/2 cup at a time, stirring constantly. Continue to cook and stir for 1 minute after the last addition of broth. The finished consistency should be creamy, yet the texture of the rice should still be firm. (The whole process will take about 20 minutes.)

Remove from heat and stir in Parmesan cheese. Spoon into a serving bowl and top with lots of freshly ground pepper.

Serve right away. (If you can't serve it right away, undercook the dish by 5 minutes and just before serving complete the cooking process.)

Each serving provides:			
253	Calories	47 g	Carbohydrate
5 g	Protein	875 mg	Sodium
3 g	Total fat (1 g sat. fat)	1 mg	Cholesterol

Tuscan Green Beans and Tomatoes

If fresh beans are not available, frozen cut green beans can be substituted in this tasty bean and tomato combo from the Tuscan region of Italy. Cook the beans first according to package directions and add them to the hot, herbed tomato sauce.

Makes 4 servings

12	ounces green beans, cut into 2-inch pieces
1	teaspoon olive oil
1/4	cup finely chopped onion
3	cloves garlic, sliced lengthwise into paper-thin slivers
1	1-pound can salt-free (or regular) tomatoes, chopped, undrained
1	teaspoon dried basil
1/4	teaspoon dried oregano
1/4	teaspoon *each* salt and pepper
1/4	teaspoon sugar
1/16	teaspoon ground nutmeg

Place a steamer rack in the bottom of a medium saucepan. Add enough water to come almost up to the bottom of the rack. Place saucepan over medium heat. When water boils, add green beans, cover saucepan, and cook 12 to 15 minutes or until beans are tender. Drain.

Heat oil in a large nonstick skillet over medium heat. Add onion and garlic. Cook, stirring frequently, until onion is tender, about 3 minutes. Add tomatoes and spices, mixing well. When mixture boils, reduce heat to medium-low and simmer uncovered, stirring occasionally, 10 minutes.

Add green beans to skillet. Mix well and cook until heated through.

Each serving provides:

69	Calories	13 g	Carbohydrate
33 g	Protein	156 mg	Sodium
2 g	Total fat (0 g sat. fat)	0 mg	Cholesterol

Tuscan Bread Casserole

Italians eat a great deal of bread, not only serving it with every meal, but using it in soups, salads, and even desserts. I decided to turn it into a casserole. Looking for an easy, inexpensive side dish to "throw together?" This take-off on lasagna may be just the thing.

Makes 8 servings

2	cups chopped mushrooms
2	cups broccoli, cut into very small flowerets
1	cup chopped onion
1	32-ounce jar meatless spaghetti sauce
6	slices whole wheat bread (1 ounce slices), cut into cubes, or Italian bread (Slightly stale bread or dense, heavy bread work best.)
1	cup shredded part-skim Mozzarella cheese (4 ounces)
3	tablespoons grated Parmesan cheese (1 ounce)

Preheat oven to 350°.

Lightly oil a 7 x 11-inch baking pan or spray with a nonstick cooking spray.

Heat a large nonstick skillet over medium heat. Add mushrooms, broccoli, and onion. Cook, stirring frequently, 5 minutes. Remove from heat.

To assemble casserole: spread *half* of the bread cubes in prepared pan. Spoon 1 cup of the sauce evenly over bread. Top with *half* of the vegetables, another cup of the sauce, and *half* of each type of cheese. Repeat layers using remaining ingredients.

Cover tightly and bake 1 hour.

Each serving provides:

255	Calories	33 g	Carbohydrate
11 g	Protein	816 mg	Sodium
10 g	Total fat (3 g sat. fat)	11 mg	Cholesterol

Ricotta Cheesecake with
Almonds and Fruit

You'll find hints of orange, lemon, and rum in this "lightened" version of a classic Italian favorite. Most authentic versions use butter pastry for the crust, however, using a graham cracker crust really helped reduce the amount of fat. The result is still scrumptious!

Makes 12 servings

Crust:
1/2   cup graham cracker crumbs
1   tablespoon margarine, melted
1   tablespoon honey

Filling:
2   15-ounce containers ricotta cheese (I use one container of non-fat ricotta and one of part-skim ricotta. The result is a creamier texture than if both were nonfat cheese and less total fat than if both were part-skim cheese.)
4   egg whites
1/2   cup sugar
1   tablespoon all-purpose flour
1   teaspoon grated fresh lemon peel
1/2   teaspoon grated fresh orange peel
1 1/4   teaspoons rum extract

Topping:
2   tablespoons sliced almonds
3   tablespoons chopped mixed dried fruit (or you can use all apricots or all raisins)

Preheat oven to 350°.

Lightly oil the sides of a 9-inch spring form pan or spray with a nonstick cooking spray.

Combine graham cracker crumbs, margarine, and honey in the bottom of prepared pan. Mix well, until crumbs are moistened. Press crumbs onto the bottom of the pan.

Bake 8 minutes.

Place ricotta cheese in a large bowl. Beat on medium speed of an electric mixer 2 minutes. Add remaining filling ingredients. Beat on low speed until blended, then beat on medium speed 1 minute. Spoon filling over crust.

Sprinkle evenly with almonds and chopped fruit.

Bake 1 hour, until set.

Cool slightly, then chill.

	Each serving provides:		
171	Calories	19 g	Carbohydrate
11 g	Protein	148 mg	Sodium
5 g	Total fat (2 g sat. fat)	11 mg	Cholesterol

Ricotta Torte with Apricots and Nuts

This spectacular cake comes from Sicily. It's a big, special occasion dessert that serves 16. There's no baking, and even though it looks like a lot of ingredients, it's easy to assemble. I especially like the fact that it's made a day ahead, leaving lots of time for last minute dinner preparations.

Makes 16 servings

1   large angel food cake sliced into ¹/₂-inch slices

Syrup:
¹/₃   cup honey
1   tablespoon orange juice
1   teaspoon rum extract

Ricotta Filling:
2   15-ounce containers ricotta cheese (I use one container of non-fat ricotta and one of part-skim ricotta. The result is a creamier texture than if both were nonfat cheese and less total fat than if both were part-skim cheese.)
³/₄   cup confectioners sugar
2   teaspoons vanilla extract
1¹/₄   teaspoons rum extract
¹/₂   teaspoon grated fresh orange peel
¹/₄   teaspoon ground cinnamon
2   tablespoons chocolate chips, or carob chips
2   tablespoons chopped pistachio nuts, or almonds
¹/₄   cup finely chopped dried apricots

Apricot Glaze:
¹/₂   cup apricot jam
1   tablespoon water

Line a 9-inch spring form pan with plastic wrap.

To prepare syrup: combine syrup ingredients in a small saucepan and heat over medium-low heat for 5 minutes, then reduce heat to low to keep syrup warm.

To prepare ricotta filling: in a large bowl, combine ricotta cheese, sugar, extracts, orange peel, and cinnamon. Beat on low speed of an electric mixer until combined. Beat on high speed 1 minute. Stir in remaining filling ingredients.

To assemble: arrange a third of the cake slices in the bottom of the pan. (Arrange them attractively as this will become the top of the cake.) Using a pastry brush and a third of the syrup, paint the cake with the syrup. Spread half of the cheese mixture over the cake.

Arrange half of the remaining cake slices over the cheese, then paint with half of the remaining syrup and top with remaining cheese.

Top with remaining cake slices and paint them with remaining syrup.

Cover and chill overnight or up to two days.

A few hours before serving, invert cake onto a platter and remove the pan and plastic wrap.

To glaze: combine apricot jam and water in a small saucepan. Heat over medium heat, stirring until jam is melted. Remove from heat and brush jam all over the outside of the cake. (The sides of the cake are mostly ricotta and will just take a small amount of glaze. The top will take most of it.)

Chill until serving time.

Each serving provides:			
204	Calories	35 g	Carbohydrate
8 g	Protein	230 mg	Sodium
3 g	Total fat (2 g sat. fat)	8 mg	Cholesterol

Almond Bread Pudding with Apricot Glaze

This bread pudding is truly Italian, from the golden apricots to the rich almond flavor and sweet fruity glaze. It's traditionally served at room temperature, but it's just as good cold.

Makes 12 servings

8	1-ounce slices Italian bread (preferably slightly stale), torn into 1-inch pieces (5 1/2 cups)
2	cups skim milk
1/2	cup sugar
3	egg whites
2 1/2	teaspoons almond extract
1/3	cup dried apricots, cut into 1/4-inch pieces (or golden raisins)
1/4	cup sliced almonds

Glaze:

1/2	cup water
2	teaspoons cornstarch
1/4	cup apricot jam

Preheat oven to 325°.

Lightly oil a 9-inch square baking pan or spray with a nonstick cooking spray.

Place bread pieces in a large bowl. Pour milk over bread and let stand 10 minutes, mixing several times.

In a small bowl, combine sugar, egg whites, and almond extract. Beat with a fork or wire whisk until blended. Stir into bread mixture. Gently fold in apricots and almonds. Spoon into prepared pan, pressing mixture down lightly with the back of a spoon.

Bake uncovered, 45 minutes. Let cool 1 hour.

Combine water and cornstarch in a small saucepan, stirring until cornstarch is dissolved. Add apricot jam. Bring to a boil over medium heat, stirring constantly. Continue to boil and stir, 1 minute. Spoon evenly over cooled bread pudding.

Each serving provides:

146	Calories	27 g	Carbohydrate
4 g	Protein	149 mg	Sodium
2 g	Total fat (0 g sat. fat)	1 mg	Cholesterol

Almond Cornmeal Coffee Cake

From Northern Italy where cornmeal is most popular comes this mouth-watering cake, which contains no eggs or shortening. The cake can be served by itself or topped with any type of cooked or marinated fruit. Or, for a really festive presentation, split the cooled cake into two layers and fill the center with raspberry jam.

Makes 8 servings

1	cup sifted all-purpose flour (Sift before measuring.)
1	cup yellow cornmeal (plus a little extra for dusting the pan)
3/4	cup sugar
2	teaspoons baking powder
1	cup skim milk
1/4	cup unsweetened applesauce
1	teaspoon *each* vanilla extract and almond extract

Topping:

2	tablespoons chopped or slivered almonds
2	teaspoons sugar
1/4	teaspoon ground cinnamon

Preheat oven to 375°.

Lightly oil a 9-inch cake pan or spray with a nonstick cooking spray. Dust pan lightly with cornmeal, shaking out any excess.

Into a large bowl, sift together sifted flour, cornmeal, sugar, and baking powder.

In a small bowl, combine milk, applesauce, and extracts. Add to dry mixture, mixing until all ingredients are moistened. Place batter in prepared pan. Sprinkle top of cake with almonds. Then combine sugar and cinnamon and sprinkle evenly over cake.

Bake 25 to 30 minutes, until a toothpick inserted in the center of the cake comes out clean.

Place pan on a wire rack to cool. Serve warm and refrigerate leftovers.

Each serving provides:			
227	Calories	47 g	Carbohydrate
4 g	Protein	139 mg	Sodium
2 g	Total fat (0 g sat. fat)	1 mg	Cholesterol

Sweet Fruit and Nut Bread

Called panettone *in Italy, this sweet bread from Milan is traditionally made with yeast and baked in a large, high-sided pan. It is usually served at Christmas and often forms the basis for other desserts, either layered like a trifle with ricotta cheese and wine, or toasted and topped with hot fruit. I've taken a few liberties here, eliminating the butter and egg yolks, and turning it into a quick bread, and it's still a delicious treat.*

Makes 10 servings

1	cup all-purpose flour
1/2	cup whole wheat flour
1 1/2	teaspoons baking powder
1/2	teaspoon anise seeds, crushed slightly
1/8	teaspoon salt
1/4	cup raisins
1/4	cup chopped mixed dried fruit (such as apricots, dates, and prunes)
2	tablespoons chopped pecans
3/4	cup skim milk
2	egg whites
1/3	cup sugar
2	tablespoons vegetable oil
1 1/2	teaspoons vanilla extract
1	teaspoon brandy or rum extract
1/2	teaspoon grated fresh lemon peel

Preheat oven to 350°.

Lightly oil a 4 x 8-inch loaf pan or spray with a nonstick cooking spray.

In a large bowl, combine both types of flour, baking powder, anise seeds, and salt. Mix well. Stir in raisins, chopped fruit, and pecans.

In a medium bowl, combine remaining ingredients. Beat with a fork or wire whisk until blended. Add to flour mixture. Mix until all ingredients are moistened. Place in prepared pan.

Bake 40 to 45 minutes, until a toothpick inserted in the center of the bread comes out clean.

Cool in pan on a wire rack 5 minutes, then transfer bread to rack to finish cooling.

Each serving provides:			
163	Calories	27 g	Carbohydrate
4 g	Protein	123 mg	Sodium
4 g	Total fat (1 g sat. fat)	0 mg	Cholesterol

Berries with Apricot Creme

Any combination of fruit or berries will work in this heavenly dessert. I like it best with a mix of strawberries, raspberries, and blueberries. This is my low-fat version of a much higher-fat dessert.

Makes 6 servings

4   cups fresh strawberries, raspberries, or blueberries

Apricot Creme:
1   cup nonfat ricotta cheese (For a creamier texture, you can use part-skim ricotta cheese, but be aware that it has about 4 more grams of fat per 1/4-cup serving.)
1/4   cup fruit-only apricot jam
1/2   teaspoon vanilla extract
1/2   teaspoon grated fresh lemon peel
1/8   teaspoon almond extract

Garnish:
2   tablespoons chocolate chips (optional)

Wash and refrigerate berries.

Combine all *Apricot Creme* ingredients in a small bowl. Beat on low speed of an electric mixer until blended. Beat on high speed 2 minutes. Chill thoroughly.

To serve, divide berries evenly into six dessert bowls or tall-stemmed sherbet glasses. Spoon *Apricot Creme* over berries. Garnish with chocolate chips, if desired.

Each serving provides:

93	Calories	16 g	Carbohydrate
6 g	Protein	48 mg	Sodium
0 g	Total fat (0 g sat. fat)	0 mg	Cholesterol

Oranges in Amaretto

Simple and refreshing, this dish makes a perfect light ending to any Italian meal. You can also make a delicious shortcake-like dessert by spooning the oranges over slices of angel food cake that have been topped with vanilla non-fat yogurt.

Makes 4 servings

4   large oranges, peeled and sectioned (Discard white
     membranes.)
3   tablespoons amaretto or other almond-flavored liqueur
1   tablespoon confectioners sugar

Place orange sections in a single layer in a shallow 1-quart casserole. Drizzle with amaretto.

Chill several hours.

Just before serving, divide orange sections into individual serving bowls and sprinkle with confectioners sugar.

Each serving provides:

125	Calories	27 g	Carbohydrate
1 g	Protein	0 mg	Sodium
0 g	Total fat (0 g sat. fat)	0 mg	Cholesterol

Spiced Fruit and Nut Confection

This chewy, spicy confection originated in Siena, in the Tuscan region of Italy. It is called panforte *and is more like candy than cake. It is normally made with candied fruit, however, when I was unable to find any candied fruit without preservatives and artificial colors, I decided to use dried fruit instead. The result is wonderful, dense, chewy, and delicious.*

Makes 12 servings

1/2	cup coarsely chopped almonds, lightly toasted*
1	cup chopped, mixed dried fruit, cut into 1/4-inch pieces (A good combination is one of raisins, dates, figs, apricots, and prunes.)
1/2	cup all-purpose flour
1/4	cup cocoa, unsweetened
1	teaspoon ground cinnamon
1/4	teaspoon ground nutmeg
1/4	teaspoon ground cloves
1/2	cup sugar
1/2	cup honey
1	teaspoon grated fresh orange peel
1/2	teaspoon grated fresh lemon peel
1	tablespoon confectioners sugar

Preheat oven to 300°.

Lightly oil a 9-inch cake pan or spray with a nonstick cooking spray. Line the bottom of the pan with wax paper and spray again.

Place nuts and fruit in a large heatproof bowl. Combine flour, cocoa, and spices in a small bowl and add to fruit mixture. Mix well.

Place sugar, honey, orange peel, and lemon peel in a small saucepan. Bring to a boil over medium heat. Continue to boil 3 minutes, *no longer,* watching carefully and lowering the heat if necessary to keep mixture from boiling over.

Remove from heat and *immediately* spoon over fruit mixture. Working quickly, mix until all ingredients are moistened. (Mixture will be quite stiff.) Spoon into prepared pan. Spread evenly in pan using a knife dipped repeatedly in hot water.

Bake 25 minutes, until set.

*Place almonds in a single layer on an ungreased baking sheet. Place in a 300° oven until lightly toasted.

Cool 10 minutes in pan on a wire rack, then invert onto rack and peel off wax paper. Sprinkle with half of the confectioners sugar. Sprinkle with remaining sugar just before serving. Cut into wedges to serve.

Store at room temperature, tightly covered, for up to 2 weeks.

Each serving provides:			
168	Calories	35 g	Carbohydrate
2 g	Protein	4 mg	Sodium
4 g	Total fat (0 g sat. fat)	0 mg	Cholesterol

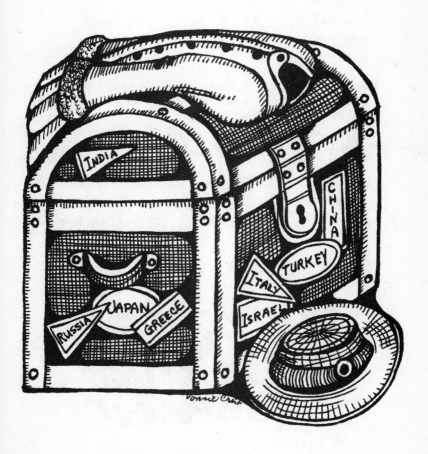

Orange-Burgundy Spiced Apples

These extraordinary apples baked in wine make a perfect, fruity ending to any Italian dinner. They have enough character to stand alone or serve them over a slice of cake, such as Almond Cornmeal Coffee Cake *(page 215).*

Makes 4 servings

4   small Golden Delicious apples, peeled, cored, and cut in half
         vertically
1   cup burgundy wine
1/2   cup orange juice
1/3   cup sugar
1   2¹/₂-inch cinnamon stick
2   whole cloves
1/2   teaspoon grated fresh orange peel

Preheat oven to 350°.

Place apples, cut-side down, in a 7 x 11-inch baking pan.

In a small bowl, combine remaining ingredients, mixing well. Pour over apples.

Bake uncovered, 40 to 60 minutes, until apples are just tender. Do not let them get mushy. The cooking time will depend on the ripeness and size of the apples.

Baste apples often during cooking time.

Cool slightly and serve warm or chilled.

Each serving provides:

141	Calories	36 g	Carbohydrate
0 g	Protein	4 mg	Sodium
0 g	Total fat (0 g sat. fat)	0 mg	Cholesterol

Flavors of the Middle East

When I began compiling recipes for this chapter, the first thing I did was to look at a map to decide which countries make up the Middle East. What I discovered was that while there are several countries that don't exactly fit the description *geographically*, they are typically Middle Eastern *gastronomically*. So, I have drawn my own boundaries and included the following countries: The countries that immediately come to mind when we think of this region, are Turkey, Syria, Lebanon, Iran, and Israel. (Israel is a relatively new country, but has its own culinary tastes and preferences.) Then there are the three North African countries of Egypt, Algeria, and Morocco, whose foods share many common themes with those of the countries listed above. Armenia and Greece also come to mind. While there are distinctive characteristics of Greek cuisine, its traditions are almost identical with those of Turkey, and with so many similarities to the other countries, I decided to include Greece.

In general, the climate in the Middle East yields an abundance of fruits and vegetables. Market stalls are filled with fresh fruits, including apricots, peaches, mangos, figs, bananas, grapes, lemons, melons, oranges, and pomegranates. Fresh fruits are served with almost every meal. Dried fruits are among the favorite snack foods in the region. These include dates, figs, raisins, apricots, and currants.

Vegetables are a significant part of Middle Eastern cuisine. Like fruits, most are purchased daily at open air markets. Vegetables include carrots, celery, cucumbers, lettuce, artichokes, eggplant, green and red bell peppers, leeks, parsley, onions, tomatoes, potatoes, sweet potatoes, and zucchini.

A large variety of spices and unique spice combinations are used in this region and spice shops are common, even in the smallest towns. Among the spices most commonly used are allspice, aniseed, basil, bay leaf, caraway seed, cumin, cloves, cinnamon, coriander, dill, fennel, ginger, mint, nutmeg, oregano, paprika, pepper, saffron, and turmeric. Many of the dishes in the Middle East also rely heavily on the use of lots and lots of garlic.

Most of the countries in the Middle East use some butter for cooking. However, the use of corn oil and olive oil predominates. Olives and olive oil are among the most important food staples in Greece.

Nuts and seeds are also used in large quantities. Pistachios, sesame seeds, walnuts, almonds, and pine nuts are among those most-commonly used, and they are often toasted before using to bring out their nutty flavor.

Yogurt is a very common ingredient, often combined with mint and garlic and served as a condiment with almost every meal. Cheese is another important cooking ingredient, especially in Greek cuisine in which feta and kasseri are used most often. Most of the regions feature their own varieties of homemade cheese, many made from goats' and sheep's milk.

The desserts of the region are very sweet. Cakes and pastries are among the favorites and they are often made with filo dough; a thin, flaky dough. Many of them are filled with nuts and topped with a sugary syrup after baking. Puddings are also popular, often made from farina (Cream of Wheat®) or rice. As in the West, sweets are eaten at the end of a meal and also on every possible festive occasion!

Adapting Middle Eastern cuisine to lowfat, meatless cuisine is relatively easy. In addition to fresh fruits and vegetables, grains and legumes are basic ingredients in the dishes of the region. Rice, couscous, barley, and bulgur are used in everything from salads to desserts. Beans such as lentils, chick peas, and split peas are even served for breakfast! I have greatly reduced the amount of oil and have chosen lowfat or nonfat dairy products, but the delicious spice combinations and the exotic blending of fruits, vegetables, and grains have remained the same.

Enjoy your culinary journey through the Middle East!

Flavors of the Middle East
Recipes

Suggested Menus

Lunch

Baba Ghannouj (231)
Pita Bread
Greek Pasta Salad (239)
on Bed of Lettuce
Fresh Fruit Cup

Vegetable Lentil Soup (233)
Tossed Salad
Spinach Turnovers (230)
Lemon Yogurt Cake (278)

Lentil Pockets with
Yogurt-Tahini Sauce (262)
Moroccan Carrot Salad (245)
Persian Apricot Pudding (282)

Dinner

Roasted Red Pepper and
Eggplant Salad (244)
on Bed of Lettuce with
Sliced Tomato
Moroccan Stew (249)
Brown Rice
Cobblestone Pudding (280)

Persian Carrot Soup (235)
Lentil-Stuffed Peppers (260)
Warm Rice Salad with
Fruits and Nuts (243)
Angel Food Cake
Spiced Orange and Berry
Compote (283)

Roasted Garlic and Butternut
Soup (237)
Spiced Vegetables over
Cinnamon Couscous (256)
Steamed Green Beans
Israeli Orange Pudding (281)

Artichoke Caviar (229)
Pita Bread
Tossed Salad
Olympic Stew (253)
Couscous
Clove-Spiced Apples (285)

Recipe page numbers appear in parentheses.

Greek Cheese Toast

I first tasted this savory, cheese-topped pita toast in a Greek restaurant and I came home determined to recreate it. It makes a perfect accompaniment to any Mediterranean meal and is also great served alongside a large Greek salad for a delightful light lunch.

Makes 4 servings

2	1-ounce whole wheat pita breads
	Nonstick cooking spray
1/4	cup plus 2 tablespoons crumbled feta cheese (2 ounces)
2	teaspoons grated Parmesan cheese
1/4	teaspoon dill weed

Preheat oven to 375°.

Separate each pita bread into two rounds by gently running a sharp knife around the edge. Place on an ungreased baking sheet with the smooth side up.

Lightly spray each piece with nonstick cooking spray.

Divide feta cheese and sprinkle evenly over bread, then divide Parmesan cheese and dill weed and sprinkle evenly over the feta cheese.

Bake 10 minutes, until cheese is melted and edges of bread just begin to brown.

Serve right away.

Each serving provides:

83	Calories	8 g	Carbohydrate
4 g	Protein	249 mg	Sodium
4 g	Total fat (2 g sat. fat)	13 mg	Cholesterol

Artichoke Caviar

This tart and tangy appetizer is made from finely chopped artichokes com-
bined with other tasty Greek favorites. It is usually served with crackers, but
is also good mounded on slices of crisp vegetable rounds, such as cucumbers
and zucchini. For a pretty presentation, garnish the bowl with sliced toma-
toes and olives.

Makes 18 servings
(2 tablespoons each serving)

1	1-pound can artichoke hearts, drained and coarsely chopped
1/4	cup crumbled feta cheese (1 1/2 ounces)
1	2-ounce jar chopped pimientos, drained
2	tablespoons chopped onion
2	cloves garlic, chopped
2	tablespoons lemon juice
2	teaspoons olive oil
1	teaspoon dried oregano
1/8	teaspoon salt
1/4	teaspoon pepper

Combine all ingredients in a food processor. Process with a steel blade until mixture is finely chopped. (Do not purée.)

Chill several hours or overnight. Serve cold.

(An alternative method is to finely chop everything by hand, but the result is not as smooth as with a food processor.)

Each serving provides:

17	Calories	2 g	Carbohydrate
1 g	Protein	41 mg	Sodium
1 g	Total fat (0 g sat. fat)	1 mg	Cholesterol

Spinach Turnovers

These turnovers are a delectable Lebanese snack. They are usually served at room temperature and are often made larger and eaten the same way that we would eat a sandwich.

Makes 10 turnovers

1	teaspoon olive oil
1	cup finely chopped onion
2	tablespoons pine nuts
2	tablespoons raisins or currants
1	10-ounce package frozen chopped spinach, thawed and drained well
1	teaspoon dill weed
2¹/2	teaspoons lemon juice
	Salt and pepper to taste
1	10-ounce container refrigerator biscuits

Heat oil in a small nonstick skillet over medium heat. Add onion and pine nuts. Cook, stirring frequently, 5 minutes, until onion begins to brown and pine nuts are lightly toasted. Remove from heat and stir in raisins, spinach, dill weed, lemon juice, salt, and pepper. Mix well. Taste and add additional lemon juice, salt, or pepper, if desired.

Preheat oven to 400°.

Have an ungreased baking sheet ready. Separate biscuits and place between two sheets of wax paper several inches apart. With a rolling pin, roll biscuits into 4- to 5-inch circles. Carefully remove the top sheet of wax paper.

Use a heaping tablespoonful of filling, placed slightly off-center on each circle. Fold carefully, making a half-circle and stretching the dough gently over the filling. Crimp the edges together with a fork. Place turnovers on baking sheet.

Bake 8 to 10 minutes, until golden.

Serve warm, at room temperature, or cold.

Each turnover provides:

112	Calories	16 g	Carbohydrate
3 g	Protein	322 mg	Sodium
5 g	Total fat (1 g sat. fat)	0 mg	Cholesterol

Baba Ghannouj

From Burgers 'n Fries 'n Cinnamon Buns, *this strange sounding dish is a wonderful, creamy, garlic and lemon eggplant dip*. In the Middle East it is often served with pita breads that have been cut into triangles, but it is also terrific on a toasted bagel topped with a slice of tomato.*

Makes 16 servings
(2 tablespoons per serving)

1	large eggplant (about 1¹/₂ pounds)
3¹/₂	tablespoons lemon juice (preferably fresh)
¹/₄	cup tahini (made from ground sesame seeds and available in health food stores and many large grocery stores)
3	large cloves garlic, crushed
1	tablespoon dried parsley flakes
¹/₂	teaspoon salt
¹/₈	teaspoon pepper

Preheat oven to 400°.

Cut off and discard the stem end of eggplant. Place eggplant on a baking sheet and bake 1 hour, until flesh is very soft and skin is slightly shriveled. Remove from oven and cool slightly.

Cut eggplant in half. Using a spoon, scoop the pulp into a large bowl. Discard the skin. Mash the pulp with a fork and add remaining ingredients, mixing well.

Place mixture in a blender container and blend just until mixture is smooth. (Do not let it blend until it is "soupy".)

Spoon into a bowl and chill several hours or overnight to blend flavors.

Each serving provides:

33	Calories	4 g	Carbohydrate
1 g	Protein	74 mg	Sodium
2 g	Total fat (0 g sat. fat)	0 mg	Cholesterol

---

*Burgers 'n Fries 'n Cinnamon Buns *is a delightful collection of lowfat, meatless versions of fast food favorites, written by Bobbie Hinman.*

Tofu-Tahini Spread

This wonderful spread was invented by my good friend, Ellie Ayscough. The mellow flavor of tahini, along with the spark of onions and garlic, will make this spread one of your favorites. Serve it on crackers or pile it into pita bread, with lettuce and tomatoes, and enjoy. (Thanks, Ellie!)

Makes 16 servings
(2 tablespoons each serving)

1	pound medium or firm tofu, drained slightly
1/3	cup tahini (made from ground sesame seeds and available in health food stores and many large grocery stores)
1 1/2	tablespoons reduced-sodium (or regular) soy sauce
1/4	cup chopped green onions (green part only)
1/16	teaspoon garlic powder

Place tofu in a large bowl and mash with a fork. Add remaining ingredients and mix well.

Chill several hours or overnight to blend flavors.

Serve in a pita bread or on toast or crackers.

Each serving provides:

52	Calories	2 g	Carbohydrate
3 g	Protein	64 mg	Sodium
4 g	Total fat (1 g sat. fat)	0 mg	Cholesterol

Vegetable Lentil Soup

Lentil soup, with its many variations, is a Middle Eastern favorite. The unusual combination of spices and vegetables in this version make a slightly tart, uniquely-flavored dish. Like most soups, this one tastes even better when made a day ahead and reheated.

Makes 6 servings
(1 1/3 cups each serving)

2	teaspoons vegetable oil
1	cup chopped carrots, 1/2-inch pieces
1	cup chopped onion
2	cloves garlic, crushed
1	teaspoon grated fresh ginger root
6	cups water
1	cup lentils, uncooked
1	10-ounce package frozen French-style green beans
1	10-ounce package frozen chopped spinach, undrained
1	1-pound can salt-free (or regular) tomatoes, chopped, undrained
2	tablespoons lemon juice
1 1/4	teaspoons *each* ground cumin and ground coriander
1	teaspoon turmeric
1/4	teaspoon pepper
	Salt and additional pepper to taste

Heat oil in a large soup pot over medium heat. Add carrots, onion, garlic, and ginger. Cook, stirring constantly, 3 minutes.

Add remaining ingredients, *except* salt and pepper. Bring mixture to a boil. Reduce heat to low, cover, and simmer 1 hour or until vegetables are tender.

Add salt and pepper to taste.

Each serving provides:

188	Calories	32 g	Carbohydrate
13 g	Protein	59 mg	Sodium
2 g	Total fat (0 g sat. fat)	0 mg	Cholesterol

White Bean and Tomato Soup
with Orange and Mint

This is actually a combination of two delicious soups, one from Syria and one from Greece. The flavors are so similar that I put them together and created my own version. The orange and mint work together to complement the tomatoes, and the beans add just the right amount of texture.

Makes 6 servings
(1¹/4 cups each serving)

2	teaspoons olive oil
1	cup chopped onion
4	cloves garlic, crushed
2	cups *Vegetable Broth*, or 2 cups of water plus 2 teaspoons *Vegetable Broth Mix* (See pages 26–27.)
2	1-pound cans salt-free (or regular) tomatoes, chopped, undrained
1	19-ounce can white beans (cannellini or Great Northern beans), rinsed and drained (or 2¹/4 cups of cooked beans)
3	1 x 3-inch strips of orange peel
1	teaspoon dried mint leaves
¹/2	teaspoon sugar
	Salt and pepper to taste

Heat oil in a large saucepan over medium heat. Add onion and garlic. Cook, stirring frequently, 3 minutes. Add remaining ingredients, *except* salt and pepper. Bring mixture to a boil, then reduce heat to medium-low, cover, and simmer 45 minutes.

Remove and discard orange peel before serving.

Add salt and pepper to taste.

Each serving provides:			
115	Calories	20 g	Carbohydrate
5 g	Protein	429 mg	Sodium
2 g	Total fat (0 g sat. fat)	0 mg	Cholesterol

Persian Carrot Soup

This is a smooth, mellow soup that can be served hot or cold. If you like, you can add cooked rice or noodles to the finished soup, or even leftover pilaf—nuts, raisins, and all.

Makes 6 servings
(1¹/₈ cups each serving)

1	teaspoon olive oil
1	large leek, chopped (white part only)
6	cloves garlic, crushed
5	cups *Vegetable Broth,* or 5 cups of water plus 5 teaspoons *Vegetable Broth Mix* (See pages 26–27.)
1	pound carrots, sliced crosswise into ¹/₄-inch slices
1	teaspoon ground cumin
1	bay leaf
2	tablespoons lemon juice (preferably fresh)
1	teaspoon sugar
	Salt and freshly ground pepper to taste

Heat oil in a large saucepan over medium heat. Add leek and garlic. Cook, stirring frequently, 3 minutes. Add small amounts of water if necessary, about a tablespoon at a time, to keep from sticking.

Add broth, carrots, cumin, and bay leaf. Bring mixture to a boil, then cover, reduce heat to medium-low, and simmer 45 minutes or until carrots are tender. Remove and discard bay leaf.

Working in small batches, purée soup in a blender, then return to saucepan. Stir in lemon juice, sugar, salt, and pepper.

Serve hot or refrigerate and serve cold.

Each serving provides:

75	Calories	16 g	Carbohydrate
2 g	Protein	123 mg	Sodium
1 g	Total fat (0 g sat. fat)	0 mg	Cholesterol

Red Lentil and Barley Soup

Lentils have played a dominant role in Middle Eastern cooking since ancient times. Red lentils, smaller than the brown ones, turn light in color when cooked and almost disintegrate, making a very thick soup similar to split pea soup. This one is thick and hearty enough to be called a stew. If you prefer a thinner soup, just add more water or broth. (Red lentils are available at most health food stores.)

Makes 6 servings
(1¹/4 cups each serving)

2	teaspoons olive oil
1	cup chopped onion
1	cup chopped carrots
¹/2	cup chopped celery
4	cloves garlic, crushed
6¹/2	cups water, or *Vegetable Broth* (See page 26.)
1	cup red lentils, uncooked
¹/2	cup barley, uncooked
1	tablespoon dried basil
1	tablespoon dill weed
¹/2	teaspoon salt
¹/4	teaspoon pepper
¹/4	teaspoon dried thyme
2	bay leaves

Heat oil in a large saucepan over medium heat. Add onion, carrots, celery, and garlic. Cook, stirring frequently, 5 minutes.

Add remaining ingredients to saucepan. Bring mixture to a boil, then reduce heat to medium-low, cover, and cook 1 hour.

Remove and discard bay leaves before serving.

Each serving provides:

203	Calories	36 g	Carbohydrate
12 g	Protein	205 mg	Sodium
2 g	Total fat (0 g sat. fat)	0 mg	Cholesterol

Roasted Garlic and Butternut Soup

Roasting garlic mellows its flavor and makes it a perfect accompaniment to the butternut squash in this smooth, rich Mediterranean soup. The flavor is based on a popular Greek pumpkin stew.

Makes 6 servings
(1 cup each serving)

1   medium butternut squash (2 pounds), unpeeled, washed and
         cut into large chunks
1   large bulb of garlic (2 to 2 1/2 ounces)
3 1/4   cups *Vegetable Broth*, or 3 1/4 cups of water plus 3 teaspoons
         Vegetable Broth Mix (See pages 26–27.)
1/8   teaspoon ground nutmeg
1 1/2   teaspoons lemon juice (preferably fresh)
         Salt and pepper to taste

Preheat oven to 375°.

In a shallow baking pan, place squash chunks, skin-side up in a single layer. Add water to a depth of 1/2 inch. Cover tightly and bake 1 hour or until squash is tender. Remove from oven and let stand uncovered until cool enough to handle.

While squash is cooking, cut the top off the garlic bulb removing just a tiny bit of each clove. Wrap garlic tightly in foil, twisting the ends of the foil to seal. Place in oven and bake 30 minutes or until soft. Unwrap and let stand until cool enough to handle. Then peel each clove and place them in a blender container.

Scoop out squash pulp, removing seeds. Place pulp in blender with garlic. Add 1/2 cup of the broth. Blend until smooth. Place in a medium saucepan and add remaining broth, along with nutmeg and lemon juice. Bring to a boil over medium heat, then reduce heat to medium-low, cover, and simmer 20 minutes.

Add salt and pepper to taste.

Each serving provides:			
81	Calories	20 g	Carbohydrate
2 g	Protein	66 mg	Sodium
0 g	Total fat (0 g sat. fat)	0 mg	Cholesterol

Favorite Greek Salad

Yes, this is my favorite version of this popular Greek salad. I've served it to friends and family and I've even made huge batches (multiplying all of the ingredients) for parties. It's always a success.

Makes 8 servings

2	tablespoons wine vinegar
2	tablespoons water
1¹/₂	tablespoons vegetable oil (or very light-tasting extra-virgin olive oil)
1	clove garlic, crushed
	Salt to taste
	Freshly ground pepper (lots!)
1	teaspoon dried oregano
1	medium head romaine lettuce, torn into bite-size pieces
4	plum tomatoes, cut lengthwise into sixths
1	large cucumber, peeled and sliced
1	small red onion, cut vertically into thin slivers
12	pitted black olives, cut in half (or use Greek olives and leave them whole)
¹/₂	cup feta cheese, crumbled (3 ounces)

In a small bowl or jar, combine vinegar, water, oil, garlic, salt, pepper, and oregano. Mix well. Chill until needed. (The dressing tastes best when made a day or two ahead.)

Place lettuce in a large salad bowl. Top with remaining ingredients. Just before serving, add dressing and toss.

Each serving provides:

85	Calories	6 g	Carbohydrate
3 g	Protein	180 mg	Sodium
6 g	Total fat (2 g sat. fat)	9 mg	Cholesterol

Greek Pasta Salad

Here are all the flavors of my favorite Greek salad, along with another Greek favorite—pasta. How can it go wrong?

Makes 12 servings

8	ounces elbow macaroni, uncooked
1/2	cup red onion, cut vertically into thin slivers
1/2	cup chopped green bell pepper
1	large cucumber, peeled, cut lengthwise into quarters, then thinly sliced
2	large tomatoes, chopped
12	pitted black olives, sliced
3/4	cup feta cheese, crumbled into small pieces (4 1/2 ounces)
2	tablespoons vegetable oil (or very light-tasting extra-virgin olive oil)
2	tablespoons water
2 1/2	tablespoons red wine vinegar
1/4	teaspoon garlic powder
2	teaspoons dried oregano
	Salt to taste
	Freshly ground pepper (lots!)

Cook macaroni according to package directions. Drain, rinse under cold water, and drain again.

Place cooked macaroni in a large bowl. Add onion, bell pepper, cucumber, tomatoes, olives, and feta cheese. Mix well.

In a small bowl, combine remaining ingredients. Pour over pasta and mix well.

Chill several hours or overnight to blend flavors. Stir occasionally. Serve cold.

Mix before serving.

Each serving provides:

133	Calories	18 g	Carbohydrate
4 g	Protein	144 mg	Sodium
5 g	Total fat (2 g sat. fat)	8 mg	Cholesterol

Potato Salad with Feta Cheese

If you thought potato salad was as American as apple pie, you may be surprised to learn that it's a very popular choice on Greek menus. The ingredients may vary, and unlike our version, Greek potato salads are often served warm or at room temperature. This one makes a nice lunch dish or light dinner when served with a variety of other salads and a basket of pita bread.

Makes 6 servings

1¹/₄	pounds red-skinned potatoes, quartered (Cut into halves if potatoes are very small.)
3	tablespoons red wine vinegar
1	tablespoon olive oil
2	cloves garlic, crushed
¹/₃	cup thinly sliced green onions (green part only)
¹/₃	cup crumbled feta cheese (2 ounces)
1	teaspoon dill weed
¹/₄	teaspoon salt
¹/₈	teaspoon pepper
¹/₂	cup plain nonfat yogurt

Place potatoes in 2 inches of boiling water in a medium saucepan. Cover and cook over medium heat, 15 minutes or until potatoes are tender. Do not let them get mushy. (Length of cooking time will depend on the age and size of the potatoes.)

While potatoes are cooking, combine vinegar, oil, and garlic in a small bowl or custard cup. Mix well and set aside

Drain potatoes and let them sit just until cool enough to handle. Leave skin on and cut potatoes into 1-inch chunks. (Using a serrated knife will allow you to cut through the skin without removing it.) Place potatoes in a large bowl. Add green onions and feta cheese. Sprinkle with dill weed, salt, and pepper. Mix well.

Drizzle vinegar mixture over potatoes and toss until mixed well. Stir in yogurt. Serve at room temperature. (Leftovers are also good cold.)

Each serving provides:

130	Calories	20 g	Carbohydrate
4 g	Protein	192 mg	Sodium
4 g	Total fat (1 g sat. fat)	7 mg	Cholesterol

Lebanese Carrot and Orange Salad

Oranges and onions are a popular combination in many Middle Eastern countries. In this easy Moroccan salad, the crunch and definitive flavor of the onions provide a delicious contrast to the sweetness of the carrots, oranges, and raisins.

Makes 6 servings

2	cups coarsely shredded carrots
2	large oranges, peeled and sectioned, then cut into 1-inch pieces (Discard white membranes.)
1/2	cup onion, cut vertically into thin slivers
1/3	cup raisins
1 1/2	tablespoons vegetable oil
1 1/2	tablespoons lemon juice
1	tablespoon water
1/4	teaspoon salt
1/8	teaspoon pepper

In a medium bowl, combine carrots, oranges, onion, and raisins. Toss to combine.

In a small bowl or custard cup, combine remaining ingredients. Spoon over carrot mixture. Mix well.

Chill several hours or overnight.

Mix before serving.

Each serving provides:

105	Calories	19 g	Carbohydrate
1 g	Protein	105 mg	Sodium
4 g	Total fat (0 g sat. fat)	0 mg	Cholesterol

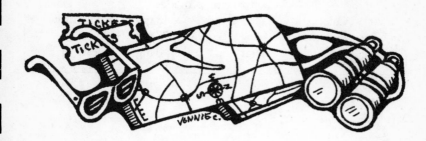

Garbanzo-Vegetable Salad

This Syrian favorite contains a myriad of flavors, textures, and colors. It can be served as a side dish or an entrée, and can even be stuffed inside pita bread for a delicious sandwich.

Makes 6 servings

1	1-pound can garbanzo beans (chick peas), rinsed and drained (or 2 cups of cooked beans)
1	cup chopped tomato
1/2	cup chopped cucumber (Peel cucumber if skin has been waxed.)
1/3	cup chopped green bell pepper
1/3	cup chopped red onion
1/4	cup thinly sliced black olives
1	tablespoon dried parsley flakes
1/2	teaspoon dried mint leaves
2	tablespoons olive oil
3	tablespoons vinegar
1	tablespoon water
1	tablespoon lemon juice (preferably fresh)
2	teaspoons sugar
1/2	teaspoon grated fresh lemon peel
3	cloves garlic, crushed
1/4	teaspoon *each* salt and pepper

In a large bowl, combine beans, tomato, cucumber, bell pepper, onion, and olives. Sprinkle with parsley flakes and mint. Mix well.

In a small bowl, combine remaining ingredients, mixing until blended. Pour over vegetables, mixing well.

Cover and chill several hours or overnight. Stir before serving.

Each serving provides:

120	Calories	13 g	Carbohydrate
3 g	Protein	227 mg	Sodium
6 g	Total fat (1 g sat. fat)	0 mg	Cholesterol

Warm Rice Salad with Fruits and Nuts

Rice is part of almost every Middle Eastern meal. This unusual warm salad combines a variety of colors, flavors, and textures.

Makes 6 servings

2¹/₂	cups water
1	cup brown rice, uncooked
¹/₄	cup *each* raisins and chopped dried apricots
2	tablespoons very finely chopped red bell pepper
2	tablespoons thinly sliced green onion (green and white parts)
2	tablespoons pine nuts, lightly toasted
2	tablespoons water
1	tablespoon *each* olive oil and lemon juice
1	teaspoon dried parsley flakes
¹/₂	teaspoon ground cumin
¹/₄	teaspoon ground coriander
¹/₈	teaspoon garlic powder
	Salt and pepper to taste

Bring water to a boil in a medium saucepan. Add rice. When water boils again, reduce heat to low, cover, and simmer 45 minutes, until rice is tender and most of the water has been absorbed. Remove from heat and let stand covered, 5 minutes. Then spoon rice into a large bowl. Add raisins, apricots, bell pepper, onion, and pine nuts. Toss to combine.

In a small bowl or custard cup, combine remaining ingredients. Add to rice and mix well. Serve right away. (Leftovers can be served cold.)

Each serving provides:

183	Calories	33 g	Carbohydrate
4 g	Protein	5 mg	Sodium
5 g	Total fat (1 g sat. fat)	0 mg	Cholesterol

Roasted Red Pepper and Eggplant Salad

This delectable salad from Israel has many versions and is served with almost every meal. It's as pretty as a picture and makes a wonderful party dish.

Makes 9 servings

3   large red bell peppers, cut in half vertically, stems removed
1   large eggplant, peeled and cut crosswise into $1/2$-inch slices
       (about $1\,1/2$ pounds)
3   tablespoons olive oil
$1/2$ teaspoon *each* dried oregano and dried basil
$1/4$ teaspoon *each* garlic powder, salt, and pepper

Preheat broiler.

Lightly oil a large baking sheet or spray with a nonstick cooking spray.

Place bell pepper halves cut-side down on prepared baking sheet. Broil until peppers are charred, about 5 minutes. Place peppers in a plastic bag and let stand at room temperature for 15 minutes. (This will allow the peppers to steam and make removal of the skin easy.)

While peppers are steaming in the bag, spray baking sheet again lightly. Place eggplant slices on baking sheet and broil about 10 minutes on each side or until eggplant is very brown, being careful not to let it burn.

Remove steamed peppers from bag and peel off skin. Cut peppers into $1/2$-inch strips and place in a shallow bowl.

Using a very sharp knife, cut broiled eggplant into $1/2$-inch strips. Add to peppers and toss gently.

In a small bowl or custard cup, combine olive oil and spices, mixing well. Pour over peppers and eggplant and gently toss to coat vegetables with spices.

Cover and chill overnight, mixing several times. Stir before serving.

Each serving provides:

70	Calories	6 g	Carbohydrate
1 g	Protein	63 mg	Sodium
5 g	Total fat (1 g sat. fat)	0 mg	Cholesterol

Moroccan Carrot Salad

As soon as I tasted this Moroccan salad I was hooked. I memorized the flavor, came home, and here it is. What a delicious salad!

Makes 6 servings

1	pound carrots, cut into 2- x $1/4$-inch strips
$1/4$	teaspoon salt
2	tablespoons lemon juice (preferably fresh)
2	tablespoons sugar
2	teaspoons vegetable oil
1	clove garlic, crushed
1	teaspoon paprika
1	teaspoon ground cumin
1	teaspoon dried parsley flakes
$1/8$	teaspoon ground cinnamon

Place a steamer rack in the bottom of a medium saucepan. Add enough water to come almost up to the bottom of the rack. Place saucepan over medium heat. When water boils, add carrots, cover saucepan, and cook 5 minutes or until carrots are tender-crisp. Drain. Place carrots in a medium bowl.

While carrots are cooking, combine remaining ingredients in a small bowl. Mix well. Spoon over hot carrots, tossing until carrots are well coated.

Chill several hours or overnight to blend flavors.

Mix before serving.

Each serving provides:

66	Calories	13 g	Carbohydrate
1 g	Protein	118 mg	Sodium
2 g	Total fat (0 g sat. fat)	0 mg	Cholesterol

Tomato-Orzo Salad

Macaroni products are almost as widely enjoyed by the Greeks as the Italians, with homemade pasta appearing in various sizes and shapes. I've used orzo, a very small rice-shaped pasta, in this dish because it cooks quickly and is a "manageable" size for salads. If you get everything ready while the orzo cooks, this tasty salad can be made very quickly.

Makes 6 servings

1	cup orzo, uncooked
1	1-pound can salt-free (or regular) stewed tomatoes
2	teaspoons dried parsley flakes
1	teaspoon dried basil
2	teaspoons lemon juice (preferably fresh)
1/4	teaspoon pepper
1/8	teaspoon garlic powder
1/4	cup feta cheese, crumbled (1 1/2 ounces)

Cook orzo according to package directions. Drain, rinse under cold water, and drain again. Place orzo in a large bowl.

While orzo is cooking, combine remaining ingredients, *except* feta cheese, in a small bowl. Mix well. Stir into orzo.

Sprinkle cheese evenly over the top.

Chill thoroughly. Stir when mixture is cold, mixing feta cheese into salad. (Mixing in the cheese after the salad has chilled keeps the cheese from melting.)

Each serving provides:

164	Calories	30 g	Carbohydrate
6 g	Protein	274 mg	Sodium
2 g	Total fat (1 g sat. fat)	6 mg	Cholesterol

Artichoke-Rice Salad

Artichokes are plentiful in Greece and they often appear in salads and appetizers. Marinated artichoke hearts add their wonderful, zesty flavor to this versatile salad that can also be served with an Italian dinner as part of an antipasto.

Makes 6 servings

2¹/₂   cups water
1   cup brown rice, uncooked
1   6-ounce jar marinated artichoke hearts, drained and thinly
        sliced (Liquid reserved.)
¹/₃   cup red onion, cut vertically into thin slivers
1   cup chopped tomato
1¹/₂   tablespoons reserved artichoke marinade
1¹/₂   tablespoons red wine vinegar
1¹/₂   tablespoons water
2   cloves garlic, crushed
1   teaspoon dried parsley flakes
        Salt and pepper to taste (lots of pepper!)

Bring water to a boil in a medium saucepan over medium heat. Add rice. When water boils again reduce heat to low, cover, and simmer 45 minutes, until rice is tender and most of the water has been absorbed. Remove from heat and let stand covered, 5 minutes. Spoon rice into a large bowl, cover the bowl with a dish towel, and let rice cool for 20 to 30 minutes.

Add artichoke hearts, onion, and tomato to rice. Toss to combine.

In a small bowl, combine remaining ingredients. Add to rice and mix well.

Serve warm or cold.

Each serving provides:

153	Calories	29 g	Carbohydrate
4 g	Protein	152 mg	Sodium
3 g	Total fat (0 g sat. fat)	0 mg	Cholesterol

Greek Peasant Beans

Aromatic herbs and vegetables make this down-to-earth dish popular throughout the Greek countryside, especially in the small villages. All it needs is a tossed salad and Cinnamon Couscous (page 256) and your delectable Grecian meal is complete.

Makes 6 servings

1	cup navy beans, uncooked
1	cup chopped onion
3	cloves garlic, crushed
1	cup chopped carrots
1/2	cup chopped celery
1	8-ounce can salt-free (or regular) tomato sauce
1	tablespoon parsley flakes
2	teaspoons dried basil
1	teaspoon dried oregano
1/2	teaspoon salt
1/4	teaspoon pepper
1	teaspoon olive oil

Rinse and drain beans. Place in a medium saucepan and add enough water to cover beans by 3 inches. Bring to a boil over medium heat. Boil 2 minutes, then cover, remove from heat and let stand 2 hours. (If you prefer, you can eliminate this step and soak the beans overnight instead. See page 13.)

Drain soaked beans and return them to saucepan. Add enough water to just cover the beans. Add remaining ingredients, mixing well. Bring to a boil over medium heat. Reduce heat to medium-low, cover, and cook 1 1/4 hours or until beans are tender. Stir beans once halfway through cooking. Add a little more water if liquid cooks out before beans are tender.

Each serving provides:

160	Calories	29 g	Carbohydrate
9 g	Protein	212 mg	Sodium
1 g	Total fat (0 g sat. fat)	0 mg	Cholesterol

Moroccan Stew

Lots of vegetables cooked with chick peas, raisins, and fragrant spices, and spooned over couscous make an authentic Moroccan meal.

Makes 6 servings

2	teaspoons vegetable oil
2	cups chopped onion
2	large cloves garlic, crushed
1	cup carrots, sliced crosswise 1/8-inch thick
1	large green bell pepper, cut into 1/4-inch strips
1	teaspoon ground cumin
1/2	teaspoon *each* ground allspice, ground ginger, and turmeric
1/4	teaspoon *each* salt and cayenne pepper
1/4	teaspoon ground cinnamon
3/4	cup water
1	medium eggplant, peeled and cut into 1/4-inch cubes (4 cups)
3	large, ripe tomatoes, chopped (3 cups)
1/2	cup raisins
1	1-pound can chick peas, rinsed and drained (or 2 cups of cooked chick peas)

Heat oil in a large saucepan over medium heat. Add onion and garlic. Cook, stirring occasionally, 3 minutes. Add carrots, bell pepper, spices, and 1/4 cup of the water. Cook, stirring occasionally, 5 minutes.

Add all remaining ingredients. Cover and simmer over medium-low heat, 30 minutes or until vegetables are tender. Stir several times during cooking. Serve over couscous, rice, or any cooked grain.

Each serving provides:

172	Calories	33 g	Carbohydrate
6 g	Protein	195 mg	Sodium
3 g	Total fat (0 g sat. fat)	0 mg	Cholesterol

Lentil and Potato Special

Combining favorite Middle Eastern flavors and cooking techniques, I came up with this delicious dish. Layers of lentils, onions, and mashed potatoes, topped with a crispy filo crust make this dish truly special. And it's easy too. I've used this dish as a meatless entrée for special occasions and it always gets rave reviews. Don't let the size scare you. Leftovers reheat beautifully.

Makes 12 servings

Potatoes:

5	large potatoes, 8 to 10 ounces each
1¹/₃	cups skim milk
1	tablespoon vegetable oil
¹/₂	teaspoon salt
¹/₄	teaspoon pepper
¹/₂	teaspoon garlic powder

Lentils:

4	cups water
1	cup lentils, uncooked
2	teaspoons vegetable oil
3	cups chopped onion
¹/₄	teaspoon salt
¹/₄	teaspoon pepper

Also:

18	sheets of filo dough (available in the freezer section of most large grocery stores)

Preheat oven to 350°.

Place potatoes in oven and bake for 1 hour or until tender. Cool slightly, then peel. Place potatoes in a large bowl and add milk, oil, salt, pepper, and garlic powder. Mash thoroughly, using a potato masher.

While potatoes are cooking, bring water to a boil in a medium saucepan. Add lentils, cover pot, reduce heat, and simmer 40 minutes, until lentils are tender. Drain.

Heat oil in a large nonstick skillet over medium heat. Add onion and cook, stirring frequently, until onion is nicely browned. (The best flavor is achieved when the onion is very brown and crisp, but be careful not to let it burn.) Remove from heat, stir in cooked lentils, salt, and pepper. Mix well.

To assemble: preheat oven to 375°.

Lightly oil a 9 x 13-inch baking pan or spray with a nonstick cooking spray.

Place filo sheets in a stack on the counter and top with wax paper or plastic wrap and then a damp towel to keep them from drying out.

Place 6 sheets of filo in the bottom of prepared pan, spraying every other sheet evenly with a nonstick cooking spray. Trim edges to fit pan. Cover remaining filo with the wax paper and damp towel. Spread *half* of the potatoes evenly over the filo. Top with all of the lentil-onion mixture.

Place 6 more sheets of filo over the lentils, spraying every other sheet, trimming edges to fit in pan, and covering remaining filo with the wax paper and damp towel. Top with remaining potatoes, spreading evenly. Top with 6 remaining sheets of filo, again spraying every other one. Be sure the top sheet is sprayed evenly.

Using a sharp knife, cut through the top filo layers, creating 12 servings. (If you try to cut through the filo after baking, it will crack.)

Bake uncovered, 45 minutes.

Cut into squares to serve.

Each serving provides:			
248	Calories	43 g	Carbohydrate
10 g	Protein	296 mg	Sodium
4 g	Total fat (1 g sat. fat)	1 mg	Cholesterol

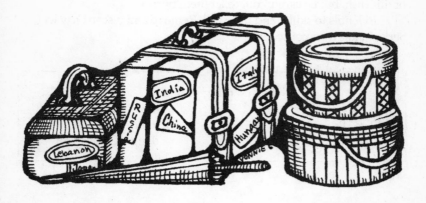

Lentils and Couscous

This superb North African favorite can only be described as heavenly, with the combination of aromatic spices and crisp, brown onion adding a real spark to the subtle flavors of the lentils and couscous.

Makes 6 servings

1	cup lentils, uncooked
4	cloves garlic, crushed
1	teaspoon ground cumin
1/2	teaspoon salt
1/8	teaspoon pepper
1/16	teaspoon ground cinnamon
1	bay leaf
3	cups water
2	teaspoons vegetable oil
2	cups onion, cut vertically into very thin slivers
1	cup water
1/2	cup couscous, uncooked

Place the lentils in a medium saucepan. Add garlic, spices, and 3 cups of water. Bring to a boil over medium heat, stirring occasionally. Reduce heat to low, cover, and simmer 40 minutes, stirring once halfway through cooking time.

While lentils are cooking, bring the 1 cup of water to a boil in a small saucepan. Remove from heat, stir in couscous, cover, and set aside for 15 minutes.

Heat oil in a large nonstick skillet over medium heat. Add onion and cook, stirring frequently, until onion is nicely browned, about 10 minutes. (Crisp, very brown onions are one of the secrets to the flavor of this dish, but be careful not to let them burn.)

Add lentils to skillet and mix well. Remove and discard bay leaf. Serve lentils over couscous.

Each serving provides:

198	Calories	34 g	Carbohydrate
12 g	Protein	189 mg	Sodium
2 g	Total fat (0 g sat. fat)	0 mg	Cholesterol

Olympic Stew

This savory stew features the versatile eggplant which is one of the staple foods of the Middle East. Serve it over brown rice or couscous, add a side serving of Favorite Greek Salad *(page 238) and a chunk of crusty bread and your delicious meal is complete.*

Makes 6 servings

1	tablespoon olive oil
1	medium eggplant, peeled and cut into 1/2-inch cubes (1 pound)
2	large leeks, sliced (white part only)
1	cup chopped green bell pepper
3	cloves garlic, crushed
3	cups sliced mushrooms
1	15-ounce can salt-free (or regular) tomato sauce
1	1-pound can white beans (cannellini), rinsed and drained (or 2 cups of cooked beans)
1/4	cup *each* water and sherry
1	teaspoon wine vinegar
1	teaspoon dried oregano
1/4	teaspoon dried thyme
1	bay leaf
	Salt and pepper to taste

Heat oil in a large nonstick skillet over medium heat. Add eggplant, leeks, bell pepper, and garlic. Cook, stirring frequently, 10 minutes. Add mushrooms. Continue to cook, stirring frequently, 5 minutes.

Add remaining ingredients, mixing well. When mixture boils, cover skillet, reduce heat to medium-low, and simmer 20 minutes. Remove and discard bay leaf before serving.

Each serving provides:

168	Calories	27 g	Carbohydrate
7 g	Protein	122 mg	Sodium
3 g	Total fat (0 g sat. fat)	0 mg	Cholesterol

Angel Hair Pasta with Feta and Broccoli

Pasta dishes are becoming increasingly popular throughout the Middle East. Often fresh vegetables are added, along with garlic and oil, producing light and colorful dishes.

Makes 4 servings

1	ounce sun-dried tomatoes, cut into 1/4-inch strips (1/3 cup) (Choose the ones that are dry and not packed in oil.)
8	ounces angel hair pasta, uncooked
2	cups broccoli, cut into very small flowerets
1	tablespoon olive oil
3	cloves garlic, crushed
1/3	cup dry white wine
2/3	cup water
1	teaspoon *Vegetable Broth Mix* (See page 27.)
2	teaspoons dried basil
1	teaspoon dried oregano
1/2	cup feta cheese, crumbled (3 ounces)
	Salt and pepper to taste

Place tomatoes in a small bowl. Cover with boiling water and set aside.

Cook pasta according to package directions. Before draining pasta, place broccoli in the colander. (The hot water and the hot pasta will lightly cook the broccoli.)

Heat oil in a large nonstick skillet over medium heat. Add garlic and cook 30 seconds. Combine wine, water, and broth mix and add to skillet along with spices. Cook 1 minute. Remove from heat and add pasta and broccoli. Drain tomatoes and add to pasta mixture. Mix well. Add feta cheese, salt, and pepper. Mix well and serve right away.

Each serving provides:

352	Calories	53 g	Carbohydrate
13 g	Protein	285 mg	Sodium
9 g	Total fat (4 g sat. fat)	19 mg	Cholesterol

Spiced Tofu

Stews were among the earliest recipes found in the Middle East. The idea for this dish of tofu cubes in a rich, spiced tomato sauce came from several meat-based Middle Eastern stews. It can be served over couscous, rice, or noodles and tastes even better when reheated.

Makes 4 servings

1	teaspoon olive oil
1	cup chopped onion
2	cloves garlic, finely minced
1	1-pound can salt-free (or regular) tomatoes, chopped, undrained
1	6-ounce can tomato paste
1/4	cup water
1/4	cup dry white wine
2	tablespoons lemon juice
1	teaspoon sugar
1/2	teaspoon *each* ground cinnamon and ground cloves
1/4	teaspoon salt
1/8	teaspoon pepper
1	pound firm tofu, drained slightly, cut into 1-inch cubes

Heat oil in a large nonstick skillet over medium heat. Add onion and garlic. Cook, stirring frequently, 3 minutes.

Add remaining ingredients, *except* tofu, to skillet. Mix well. Gently stir in tofu. Cover, reduce heat to medium-low, and cook 30 minutes. Stir once while cooking.

Serve over cooked couscous, rice, or noodles.

Each serving provides:

258	Calories	24 g	Carbohydrate
21 g	Protein	506 mg	Sodium
12 g	Total fat (2 g sat. fat)	0 mg	Cholesterol

Spiced Vegetables over Cinnamon Couscous

There's a delicate sweetness in this dish that's brought about by the carrots, parsnips, sweet potatoes, and dried fruit, and the cinnamon-laced couscous adds even more flavor. This is a popular North African dish, with as many variations as there are vegetables!

Makes 6 servings

2	teaspoons olive oil
1	cup chopped onion
1	cup chopped red bell pepper
1	large leek, chopped (white part only)
3	large cloves garlic, crushed
1	cup carrots, chopped into 1/4-inch pieces
1	small sweet potato, peeled and cut into 1/2-inch pieces (1 1/2 cups)
1	cup parsnips, chopped into 1/4-inch pieces
1	1-pound can salt-free (or regular) stewed tomatoes, undrained
1	cup *Vegetable Broth*, or 1 cup of water plus 1 teaspoon *Vegetable Broth Mix* (See pages 26–27.)
1	1-pound can kidney beans, rinsed and drained (or 2 cups of cooked beans)
1/2	cup chopped mixed dried fruit (peaches, apricots, prunes, raisins, etc.)
1	tablespoon honey
1/2	teaspoon *each* ground cinnamon and ground cumin
1/4	teaspoon ground allspice
1/4	teaspoon salt
1/8	teaspoon pepper

Couscous:

2 1/4	cups boiling water
1 1/2	cups couscous, uncooked
1 1/2	teaspoons ground cinnamon

Heat oil in a large nonstick skillet over medium heat. Add onion, bell pepper, leek, garlic, carrots, sweet potato, and parsnips. Cook, stirring frequently, 10 minutes. Add small amounts of water as necessary, about a tablespoon at a time, to prevent sticking.

Add remaining ingredients. When mixture boils, reduce heat to medium-low, cover, and cook 15 minutes or until vegetables are tender.

To prepare couscous: bring water to a boil in a small saucepan. Stir in couscous and cinnamon. Cover and remove from heat. Let stand 5 minutes. Fluff with a fork before serving.

Serve vegetables over couscous.

Each serving provides:

394	Calories	82 g	Carbohydrate
13 g	Protein	241 mg	Sodium
3 g	Total fat (0 g sat. fat)	0 mg	Cholesterol

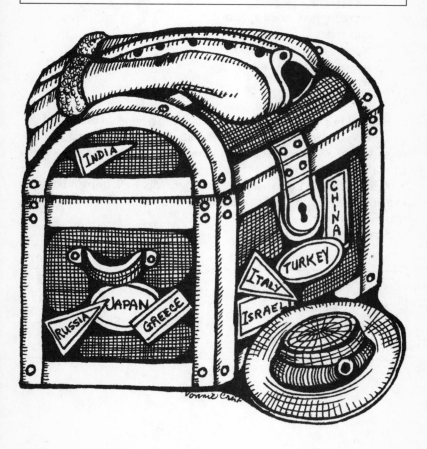

Apricot Chick Peas

The daughter of one of my dearest friends, Amy Grossblatt, brought this recipe home from Israel. It originated around Yemen and demonstrates the unique Middle Eastern taste for fruit and vegetable combinations. Serve it alongside rice or couscous and enjoy the leftovers hot or cold.

Makes 4 servings

1	teaspoon olive oil
1	cup chopped onion
3	cloves garlic, finely chopped
1	1-pound can salt-free (or regular) tomatoes, chopped, undrained
1	1-pound can chick peas, rinsed and drained (or 2 cups of cooked chick peas)
3/4	cup chopped, dried apricots
1/2	cup water
2	teaspoons dried oregano
1	teaspoon ground cumin
1/4	teaspoon salt
1/4	teaspoon pepper

Heat oil in a small saucepan over medium heat. Add onion and garlic. Cook, stirring frequently, until onion is tender, about 5 minutes. Add small amounts of water if necessary, about a tablespoon at a time, to prevent sticking.

Add remaining ingredients to saucepan. Mix well. Bring mixture to a boil, then reduce heat to medium-low, cover, and simmer 20 minutes.

Serve over couscous or rice.

Each serving provides:

191	Calories	36 g	Carbohydrate
7 g	Protein	280 mg	Sodium
4 g	Total fat (0 g sat. fat)	0 mg	Cholesterol

Yellow Split Peas with Leeks

When you read the ingredients in this recipe, you'll probably be surprised to discover that orange juice is used in cooking the split peas. I based the recipe on several dishes from Iran in which meats are cooked in fruit juices and then served over rice. Try it! You'll discover a very pleasant flavor combination.

Makes 6 servings

2	teaspoons olive oil
4	leeks, chopped (white part only) (3 cups)
3	cloves garlic, finely chopped
2	cups water
1	cup yellow split peas, uncooked
1	teaspoon dried basil
1/4	teaspoon salt
1/4	teaspoon pepper
1	cup orange juice

Heat oil in a medium saucepan over medium heat. Add leeks and garlic. Cook, stirring frequently, 3 minutes. Add small amounts of water if necessary, about a tablespoon at a time, to prevent sticking. Add remaining ingredients, *except* orange juice. Bring mixture to a boil stirring occasionally, then reduce heat to medium-low, cover, and cook 30 minutes.

Stir orange juice into saucepan. When mixture boils again, cover and continue to cook, 15 minutes more.

Serve over rice, couscous, or any other cooked grain.

Each serving provides:

179	Calories	32 g	Carbohydrate
9 g	Protein	106 mg	Sodium
2 g	Total fat (0 g sat. fat)	0 mg	Cholesterol

Lentil-Stuffed Peppers

In this festive party dish of the Middle East, green bell peppers are filled with a delectable mixture of lentils, apples, raisins, pine nuts, and aromatic spices.

Makes 6 servings

4	cups water
1	cup lentils, uncooked
6	large green bell peppers (about 6 ounces each)
1	teaspoon olive oil
1	cup chopped onion
2	cloves garlic, finely chopped
2	tablespoons pine nuts (or chopped almonds)
1	medium Golden Delicious apple, unpeeled, finely chopped
2	8-ounce cans salt-free (or regular) tomato sauce
8	small, stuffed green olives, chopped
1/3	cup raisins
1	teaspoon ground cumin
1/4	teaspoon ground cinnamon
1/4	teaspoon *each* salt and pepper

Bring the water to a boil in a medium saucepan. Add lentils. Reduce heat to medium-low, cover, and simmer 40 minutes or until lentils are tender. Drain.

Slice the tops off the bell peppers. Remove seeds and membranes. Fill a large saucepan with water and bring to a boil over medium heat. Add peppers. Boil 5 minutes, then remove peppers from water and place upside-down on towels to drain.

Heat oil in a large nonstick skillet over medium heat. Add onion, garlic, and pine nuts. Cook, stirring frequently, 5 minutes or until onion begins to brown and pine nuts are lightly toasted. Add apple and continue to cook, stirring frequently, 3 minutes more. Remove from heat and stir in lentils and remaining ingredients, mixing well.

Preheat oven to 350°.

Have a 7 x 11-inch baking pan ready.

Divide lentil mixture evenly and fill each pepper using about $3/4$ cup in each pepper. Place stuffed peppers in baking pan and fill bottom of pan with $1/4$-inch of water.

Cover tightly and bake 35 minutes.

Each serving provides:

250	Calories	46 g	Carbohydrate
13 g	Protein	208 mg	Sodium
4 g	Total fat (0 g sat. fat)	0 mg	Cholesterol

Lentil Pockets with Yogurt-Tahini Sauce

I patterned this easy sandwich after the popular Egyptian falafel, which is sold by street vendors throughout the Middle East. These are the Middle Eastern answer to tacos or sloppy joes.

Makes 6 servings
(1/2 cup lentils and 2 tablespoons sauce each serving)

Lentils:
2	cups water
1	cup lentils, uncooked
1/2	cup *each* finely chopped onion and chopped carrots
1	teaspoon *each* ground cumin and ground coriander
3/4	teaspoon garlic powder
1/4	teaspoon *each* salt and pepper

Yogurt-Tahini Sauce:
1/4	cup tahini
2	tablespoons lemon juice
1/4	teaspoon garlic powder
1/2	cup plain nonfat yogurt

Additional ingredients:
6	1-ounce whole wheat pita breads
	Shredded lettuce, chopped tomatoes, onion, olives, and peppers for topping

Bring water to a boil in a medium saucepan. Add lentils, onion, carrots, and spices. Mix well, cover, reduce heat to medium-low, and simmer 30 minutes, until water is absorbed. Remove from heat and keep covered.

In a small bowl, combine tahini, lemon juice, and garlic powder. Stir until blended. Add half the yogurt at a time, stirring until mixture is smooth.

Cut pitas in half crosswise and split each half open. Fill with lentils, then top with your choice of toppings. Top each half with sauce.

Each serving provides:			
267	Calories	40 g	Carbohydrate
15 g	Protein	275 mg	Sodium
7 g	Total fat (1 g sat. fat)	0 mg	Cholesterol

Artichoke and Mushroom Casserole

This Greek side dish shows a close resemblance to the foods of Italy. In fact, it can easily be served as a side dish with Italian entrées as well as with those of Greece and the Middle East.

Makes 6 servings

1	9-ounce package frozen artichoke hearts, or one 1-pound can of artichoke hearts
1	teaspoon olive oil
1/2	cup finely chopped onion
2	cloves garlic, finely chopped
3	cups sliced mushrooms
1	teaspoon dried basil
1/2	teaspoon dried oregano
	Salt and pepper to taste
1	tablespoon *each* lemon juice and dry white wine
1	tablespoon *each* Italian seasoned bread crumbs and grated Parmesan cheese

Preheat oven to 350°.

Lightly oil a 1-quart baking dish or spray with a nonstick cooking spray.

If using frozen artichoke hearts, place them in a steamer basket in a saucepan with 1 inch of boiling water, cover, and cook 6 minutes. Drain and place in pan. If using canned artichokes, drain them and place in pan.

Heat oil in a medium nonstick skillet over medium heat. Add onion and garlic. Cook, stirring frequently, 3 minutes. Add mushrooms. Sprinkle with spices. Add lemon juice and wine. Cook, stirring frequently, 3 minutes more. Remove from heat and stir in bread crumbs. Spoon mushroom mixture evenly over artichokes. Sprinkle with Parmesan cheese.

Bake uncovered, 30 minutes.

Each serving provides:

56	Calories	8 g	Carbohydrate
3 g	Protein	71 mg	Sodium
2 g	Total fat (0 g sat. fat)	1 mg	Cholesterol

Baked Sweet Potatoes with Apricots and Prunes

Sweet potatoes have been cultivated in Israel for many years. In this dish they are combined with dried fruit and cooked in a sweet honey and orange sauce.

Makes 6 servings

2	large sweet potatoes, peeled, cut in half lengthwise, then sliced into 1/2-inch slices (2 pounds total)
	Salt and pepper to taste
2/3	cup dried apricots, cut into quarters
2/3	cup pitted prunes, cut into quarters
	Boiling water
1/2	cup orange juice
1/4	cup honey
1	tablespoon lemon juice (preferably fresh)
1	teaspoon vegetable oil
1/2	teaspoon ground cinnamon
1/16	teaspoon ground cloves

Preheat oven to 400°.

Lightly oil an 8-inch square baking pan or spray with a nonstick cooking spray.

Place sweet potatoes in prepared pan and sprinkle with salt and pepper. Bake uncovered, until just tender, stirring several times, about 30 minutes.

While sweet potatoes are baking, place apricots and prunes in a small heatproof bowl and cover with boiling water. Let stand 30 minutes. Drain.

In a small saucepan, combine remaining ingredients. Bring to a boil over medium heat. Pour over sweet potatoes and add apricots and prunes. Mix well.

Return to oven and bake uncovered, stirring every 5 minutes, for 15 minutes.

Each serving provides:

259	Calories	61 g	Carbohydrate
3 g	Protein	18 mg	Sodium
2 g	Total fat (0 g sat. fat)	0 mg	Cholesterol

Greek Country Vegetables

This hearty side dish is so filling that I sometimes serve it as an entrée! It's colorful, tasty, and goes with just about anything. You can cook it as long as you like; the longer it cooks, the more stew-like it becomes. Sometimes green bell peppers are added too, giving it a flavor similar to the French ratatouille.

Makes 8 servings

2   medium potatoes, unpeeled, cut lengthwise into quarters, then cut crosswise into 1/2-inch slices (1 pound total)
1/2   pound green beans, cut in half crosswise, then cut in half lengthwise
1   cup chopped onion
1   cup *each* carrots and celery, sliced crosswise into 1/4-inch slices
4   cloves garlic, crushed
2   1-pound cans salt-free (or regular) tomatoes, chopped, undrained
2   tablespoons dried parsley flakes
1 1/2   tablespoons dill weed
2   teaspoons dried oregano
1/2   teaspoon salt
1/4   teaspoon pepper
2   medium zucchini, unpeeled, cut crosswise into 1/2-inch slices (3/4 pound total)

In a large saucepan, combine all ingredients, *except* zucchini. Mix well. Bring to a boil over medium heat, cover, and reduce heat to medium-low. Cook, stirring occasionally, 25 minutes. Add zucchini and mix well. Continue to cook, covered, 10 minutes or until vegetables are of desired tenderness.

Each serving provides:
100   Calories   22 g   Carbohydrate
4 g   Protein   179 mg   Sodium
1 g   Total fat (0 g sat. fat)   0 mg   Cholesterol

Yellow Squash Oreganato

In Greece, where squash is plentiful, simple, herbed dishes such as this one are very popular. This side dish complements not only Greek and Middle Eastern entrées, but most Italian entrées as well.

Makes 6 servings

2	teaspoons olive oil
2	cups chopped onion
3	to 4 cloves garlic, finely minced
4	cups yellow summer squash, unpeeled, sliced crosswise $1/2$ -inch thick
1	teaspoon dried oregano
$1/4$	teaspoon salt
$1/8$	teaspoon pepper

Heat oil in a large nonstick skillet over medium heat. Add onion and garlic. Cook, stirring frequently, until onion is lightly browned, 8 to 10 minutes.

Add squash. Sprinkle evenly with oregano, salt, and pepper.

Cover and cook until squash is lightly browned and tender-crisp, 5 to 7 minutes. Turn squash several times while cooking to brown both sides.

Each serving provides:

53	Calories	9 g	Carbohydrate
2 g	Protein	94 mg	Sodium
2 g	Total fat (0 g sat. fat)	0 mg	Cholesterol

Orange and Almond-Stuffed Onions

I combined several recipes from Turkey, Greece, and Armenia and came up with my own version of this picturesque side dish.

Makes 6 servings

4	slices whole wheat bread, cut into 1/4- to 1/2-inch cubes (1 1/2 cups of cubes)
6	medium onions, each about 4 inches in diameter
1/4	cup plus 2 tablespoons coarsely chopped almonds
1/4	cup raisins
1	teaspoon grated fresh orange peel
1/4	teaspoon *each* garlic powder and dried thyme
1/4	teaspoon *each* salt and pepper
1	tablespoon vegetable oil
1	cup apple juice

Preheat oven to 300°.

Place bread cubes in a single layer on an ungreased baking sheet. Bake 10 minutes, until lightly toasted.

Increase oven temperature to 375°.

Lightly oil a 7 x 11-inch baking pan or spray with a nonstick cooking spray.

Cut a very thin slice off the root end of each onion to keep it from tipping over while cooking. Cut a 1/4 -inch slice off the other end. Peel onions. Remove outer layer if it appears to be tough. Carefully scoop out the center of each onion using a melon ball scoop or a vegetable peeler. Leave a shell of two to three layers. (Reserve onion centers for another use, such as a salad or any recipe calling for chopped onions.)

In a small bowl, toss toasted bread cubes with almonds, raisins, orange peel, and spices. Drizzle with oil and mix well. Fill onion shells with stuffing, piling any remaining stuffing on top of onions. Place in prepared pan. Spoon 1 tablespoon of apple juice over the stuffing in each onion. Pour remaining apple juice around onions.

Cover tightly and bake 1 hour. Baste with pan juices before serving.

Each serving provides:

175	Calories	25 g	Carbohydrate
4 g	Protein	194 mg	Sodium
7 g	Total fat (1 g sat. fat)	0 mg	Cholesterol

Turkish Stuffed Eggplant

In this Turkish specialty the eggplant is sliced thick and then stuffed with a delicious mix of tomatoes, onions, and herbs.

Makes 4 servings

1	large eggplant (1 1/2 pounds)
3/4	cup chopped tomatoes
1/2	cup chopped onion
1	to 2 cloves garlic, crushed
1/4	teaspoon *each* dried oregano and dill weed
1/8	teaspoon *each* salt and pepper

Preheat oven to 375°.

Lightly oil a 9 x 13-inch baking dish or spray with a nonstick cooking spray.

Cut eggplant crosswise into slices 1 1/2 inches thick. (Do not peel). With a sharp knife, cut a slit several inches long in the side of each slice. Work the knife back and forth in the slit, creating a pocket. Be careful not to cut through the eggplant skin on the other side.

In a small bowl, combine remaining ingredients, mixing well.

Squeeze each eggplant slice from the sides, opening up the pocket. Fill with tomato mixture, packing it in firmly. Place eggplant in prepared pan. Sprinkle with additional oregano, dill weed, salt, and pepper.

Cover pan with aluminum foil and bake 45 minutes. Uncover and place under the broiler for a few minutes, until eggplant is lightly browned.

Each serving provides:			
71	Calories	14 g	Carbohydrate
2 g	Protein	80 mg	Sodium
1 g	Total fat (0 g sat. fat)	0 mg	Cholesterol

Baked Orzo

Noodles and pasta are among the favorite homemade specialties in Greek kitchens. For this easy casserole I've chosen orzo, a small, rice-shaped pasta that is actually Italian in origin. (Orzo in Italian means "barley".)

Makes 6 servings

2	teaspoons olive oil
1	cup finely chopped onion
3	cloves garlic, crushed
1	8-ounce can salt-free (or regular) tomato sauce
3	cups water
1	teaspoon dried basil
1/8	teaspoon pepper
1/16	teaspoon ground cinnamon
	Salt to taste
1	cup orzo, uncooked
	Grated Parmesan cheese (optional)

Preheat oven to 350°.

Lightly oil a 1 3/4-quart casserole or spray with a nonstick cooking spray.

Heat oil in a medium saucepan over medium heat. Add onion and garlic and cook 5 minutes or until onion starts to brown. Stir frequently while cooking.

Add remaining ingredients, *except* orzo and Parmesan cheese. Bring to a boil, then stir in orzo and remove from heat. Spoon into prepared casserole.

Bake uncovered, 45 minutes, stirring twice during cooking time.

Stir before serving. Sprinkle lightly with Parmesan cheese, if desired.

Each serving provides:

170	Calories	31 g	Carbohydrate
5 g	Protein	12 mg	Sodium
3 g	Total fat (0 g sat. fat)	0 mg	Cholesterol

Rice and Fruit in Filo

This is one version of a popular Middle Eastern dish that usually calls for meat. It makes a delicious and attractive side dish and it's easy to prepare. In fact, if you've never worked with filo, this is an ideal first dish to make. (Look for filo in the freezer section of most large grocery stores.)

Makes 8 servings

2¹/₂	cups water
1	cup brown rice, uncooked
1	tablespoon honey
1	teaspoon vegetable oil
¹/₂	cup raisins
¹/₃	cup dried apricots, cut into thin strips
	Boiling water
¹/₄	teaspoon pepper
2	teaspoons ground cinnamon
6	sheets of filo dough
	Nonstick cooking spray
1¹/₂	teaspoons confectioners sugar

Bring water to a boil in a medium saucepan. Add rice. When water boils again, reduce heat to low, cover, and simmer 45 minutes, until rice is tender and most of the liquid has been absorbed. Remove from heat and stir in honey and oil. Cover saucepan with a towel and set aside. (This will allow the rice to cool slightly without becoming dry.)

While rice is cooking, place raisins and apricot strips in a heatproof bowl. Cover with boiling water and let stand 15 minutes. Drain. Return to bowl and add the pepper and 1¹/₂ teaspoons of the cinnamon. Mix well.

Preheat oven to 350°.

Oil a 9-inch pie pan or spray with a nonstick cooking spray. (If possible, use a clear glass pan so you will be able to check the browning of the bottom crust.)

Place the filo sheets in a stack on the counter and top with wax paper or plastic wrap and then a damp towel to keep them from drying out.

Arrange 2 filo sheets across pan with the ends extending over the sides of the pan. Spray entire surface of dough lightly and evenly with nonstick cooking spray. Layer with 2 more sheets going in the opposite direction. Spray again with cooking spray.

Spoon *half* of the rice into the pan. Arrange fruit over the rice and top with remaining rice. Sprinkle with remaining 1/2 teaspoon of cinnamon.

Place last 2 sheets in a criss-cross pattern over the rice, spraying each sheet with cooking spray. Fold all of the leaves across the top to form a pie, pat them down, and spray the top with cooking spray.

Bake until nicely browned, 30 to 35 minutes.

Invert onto a serving plate and sprinkle with confectioners sugar. Cut into wedges and serve right away.

Each serving provides:			
190	Calories	39 g	Carbohydrate
3 g	Protein	72 mg	Sodium
3 g	Total fat (0 g sat. fat)	0 mg	Cholesterol

Lime-Scented Bulgur Pilaf
with Raisins and Pine Nuts

Bulgur wheat dishes are particularly popular in Turkey and Armenia, where delicately flavored pilafs are often served. Beautifully seasoned, this dish makes a wonderful accompaniment to any Middle Eastern entrée.

Makes 6 servings

1	teaspoon olive oil
1	cup finely chopped onion
2	cups water, or *Vegetable Broth* (See page 26.)
1	cup bulgur, uncooked
1/3	cup raisins
1	teaspoon grated fresh lime peel
1/2	teaspoon ground cinnamon
1/4	teaspoon dill weed
1/8	teaspoon salt
1/8	teaspoon dried thyme
2	tablespoons pine nuts, or coarsely chopped almonds, lightly toasted

Heat oil in a medium saucepan over medium heat. Add onion. Cook 5 minutes, stirring frequently and adding small amounts of water if necessary, about a tablespoon at a time, to prevent sticking.

Add water or broth and bring to a boil. Stir in remaining ingredients, *except* pine nuts, cover, reduce heat to low, and cook 10 minutes. Remove from heat and let stand covered, 5 minutes. Fluff bulgur with a fork and spoon into a shallow serving bowl. Top with toasted pine nuts.

Each serving provides:

137	Calories	27 g	Carbohydrate
4 g	Protein	52 mg	Sodium
3 g	Total fat (0 g sat. fat)	0 mg	Cholesterol

Fruit and Wheat

This sweet, fruity Lebanese dish is served as a side dish or a dessert. The orange juice and vanilla provide a perfect backdrop for the chewy texture of the dried fruit. (I love this dish for breakfast!) It's at its best when served fresh and warm.

Makes 6 servings

1¹/₂	cups water
¹/₂	cup orange juice
¹/₄	cup sugar
1	cup bulgur (cracked wheat), uncooked
2	teaspoons vanilla extract
1	teaspoon ground cinnamon
¹/₄	cup chopped dried figs
¹/₄	cup chopped dried apricots
¹/₄	cup raisins
2	tablespoons pine nuts (or chopped walnuts)

In a medium saucepan, combine water, orange juice, and sugar. Bring to a boil over medium heat. Add bulgur, reduce heat to medium-low, cover, and cook 15 minutes.

Remove saucepan from heat and stir in vanilla and cinnamon. Then add remaining ingredients, mixing well.

Serve right away for best flavor and texture.

Each serving provides:

195	Calories	43 g	Carbohydrate
4 g	Protein	7 mg	Sodium
2 g	Total fat (0 g sat. fat)	0 mg	Cholesterol

Date Squares

Dates in the Middle East are among the best in the world. They are popular throughout the region, where they are sold as snacks by the many street vendors. This recipe from Israel is just one that uses this prolific fruit. Sweet, rich, and moist, these cake squares are just loaded with luscious dates.

Makes 16 servings

Cake:

1/3	cup all-purpose flour
1/3	cup whole wheat flour
1/3	cup sugar
1/2	teaspoon baking soda
1/2	cup water
2	tablespoons vegetable oil
1	egg white
1	teaspoon vanilla extract
1/2	cup finely chopped pitted dates

Topping:

1/2	cup finely chopped pitted dates
3	tablespoons sugar
1/3	cup orange juice
1/2	teaspoon grated fresh orange peel
1	tablespoon chopped walnuts

Preheat oven to 350°.

Lightly oil an 8-inch square baking pan or spray with a nonstick cooking spray.

In a large bowl, combine both types of flour, sugar, and baking soda, mixing well. Add remaining cake ingredients. Beat on low speed of an electric mixer until blended. Increase speed to high and beat 3 minutes. Spread mixture in prepared pan.

Bake 20 to 25 minutes, until a toothpick inserted in the center of the cake comes out clean. Cool in pan on a wire rack.

When cake is cool, prepare topping: combine all topping ingredients, *except* walnuts, in a small saucepan. Bring to a boil over medium heat, stirring occasionally. Reduce heat slightly and simmer until thickened, about 15 minutes. Spoon over cooled cake. Sprinkle with nuts.

Cut into squares to serve.

Each serving provides:

98	Calories	19 g	Carbohydrate
1 g	Protein	43 mg	Sodium
2 g	Total fat (0 g sat. fat)	0 mg	Cholesterol

Brandied Spice Cake

My close friend and recipe tester, Betty Mihm, gave me her original recipe for this moist Greek spice cake and asked me to "de-fat" it. It was originally loaded with butter and topped with a heavy syrup. She and I (and all who tasted it) loved the results! It tastes great warm, but we also found that the flavor really develops after two to three days in the refrigerator.

Makes 12 servings

3/4	cup all-purpose flour
1/2	cup whole wheat flour
1/4	cup sugar
1/4	cup firmly-packed brown sugar
2	teaspoons ground cinnamon
1 1/2	teaspoons baking powder
1 1/2	teaspoons baking soda
1	cup skim milk
1	tablespoon lemon juice
3	tablespoons vegetable oil
2	teaspoons brandy extract
3	egg whites
3	tablespoons chopped walnuts

Topping:

2	tablespoons honey
1	tablespoon orange juice
1/2	teaspoon orange extract
1/8	teaspoon ground cloves
1/4	teaspoon brandy extract

Preheat oven to 350°.

Lightly oil an 8-inch square baking pan or spray with a nonstick cooking spray.

Into a large bowl, sift together both types of flour, both types of sugar, cinnamon, baking powder, and baking soda.

Place milk in a small bowl. Add lemon juice and let stand 1 minute. Add oil, brandy extract, and 1 of the egg whites. Beat with a fork or wire whisk until blended.

In another bowl, beat remaining 2 egg whites on high speed of an electric mixer until stiff.

Stir milk mixture into dry ingredients, along with chopped nuts. Mix until all ingredients are moistened. Fold in beaten egg whites, gently, but thoroughly. Place batter in prepared baking pan.

Bake 25 to 30 minutes, until a toothpick inserted in the center of the cake comes out clean.

While cake is baking, combine all topping ingredients in a small bowl or custard cup. Remove finished cake from oven, place it on a wire rack, and using a toothpick, punch holes in the cake about one inch apart. Drizzle topping evenly over hot cake spreading it with the back of a spoon.

Serve warm or cold. Refrigerate leftovers.

	Each serving provides:		
152	Calories	23 g	Carbohydrate
3 g	Protein	246 mg	Sodium
5 g	Total fat (1 g sat. fat)	0 mg	Cholesterol

Lemon Yogurt Cake

There are many variations of this delectable Greek cake, which is usually topped with lots of heavy syrup. My version gets its moistness and bright lemon flavor from lemon yogurt, and the heavy syrup has been replaced with a drizzle of honey.

Makes 12 servings

4	egg whites
3/4	cup Quick Cream of Wheat®, uncooked
1/2	cup sugar
3	tablespoons vegetable oil
1 1/2	teaspoons vanilla extract
1/2	teaspoon grated fresh lemon peel
1	cup lemon nonfat yogurt
1 1/2	teaspoons lemon juice (preferably fresh)
1/4	teaspoon baking soda
2	tablespoons honey

Preheat oven to 375°.

Lightly oil an 8-inch square baking pan or spray with a nonstick cooking spray.

In a large bowl, combine egg whites, Cream of Wheat®, sugar, oil, vanilla, and lemon peel. Mix on low speed of an electric mixer until blended. Increase speed to high and beat 1 minute. Reduce speed to low and gradually beat in yogurt.

Place lemon juice in a small bowl or custard cup. Stir in baking soda, then stir into cake batter right away.

Place mixture in prepared pan.

Bake 20 to 25 minutes until cake is set and top is lightly browned.

Place pan on a wire rack. Drizzle honey evenly over top of cake. Cover tightly with foil and let stand 1 hour.

This cake can be served either warm or cold. (Leftovers should be refrigerated.)

Each serving provides:			
141	Calories	24 g	Carbohydrate
3 g	Protein	86 mg	Sodium
4 g	Total fat (0 g sat. fat)	0 mg	Cholesterol

Vanilla Wheat Squares

These sweet, moist squares are a delectable way to end a spicy dinner.

Makes 16 servings

1/4	cup soft, tub-style margarine (not diet margarine)
1	cup Quick Cream of Wheat®, uncooked
1 1/2	cups skim milk
1	cup water
1/2	cup sugar
1 1/2	teaspoons vanilla extract
16	walnut halves (optional)
4	teaspoons fruit-only raspberry or strawberry jam (optional)
	Ground cinnamon

Lightly oil an 8-inch square baking pan or spray with a nonstick cooking spray.

Melt margarine in a large nonstick skillet over medium heat. Add Cream of Wheat®, reduce heat to medium-low, and cook, stirring frequently, 15 minutes.

While Cream of Wheat® is cooking, combine milk, water, and sugar in a small saucepan. Heat just to a simmer over medium heat, then remove from heat and stir in vanilla.

Gradually add hot milk mixture to Cream of Wheat®, stirring swiftly. Continue to cook for 5 minutes more, stirring constantly and pressing out any lumps in the Cream of Wheat® with the back of the spoon. Spread mixture in prepared pan, wetting the back of the spoon slightly to make spreading easier. If using walnuts, press them lightly into Cream of Wheat®, arranging them so that when mixture is cooled and cut into 16 squares there will be one walnut half on each square. Sprinkle lightly with cinnamon. (Or, if using jam, sprinkle with cinnamon first, and when cool, place 1/4 teaspoon of jam in the center of each square.)

Cover and set aside. Serve at room temperature, cutting into squares before serving. (Refrigerate leftovers.)

Each serving provides:			
102	Calories	16 g	Carbohydrate
2 g	Protein	82 mg	Sodium
3 g	Total fat (1 g sat. fat)	0 mg	Cholesterol

Cobblestone Pudding

Based on a traditional Syrian dish, this is a dessert that's fun for the kids to make. They love to "build" the cobblestones.

Makes 12 servings

3	cups miniature shredded-wheat biscuits, unsweetened (about 6 ounces)
1/2	cup sugar
1/4	teaspoon ground cinnamon
2²/3	cups skim milk
1	teaspoon vanilla extract
1	teaspoon almond extract
2¹/2	tablespoons finely chopped walnuts, almonds, *or* pistachio nuts

Lightly oil an 8-inch square baking pan or spray with a nonstick cooking spray.

Using half of the shredded-wheat biscuits, arrange them in the bottom of the pan in neat rows, covering the bottom of the pan. Top with remaining biscuits, making another layer of neat rows.

Place 2 teaspoons of the sugar in a small bowl or custard cup. Add the cinnamon and mix well. Set aside.

In a small bowl, combine milk, extracts, and remaining sugar. Stir until sugar is dissolved. Very gently, spoon over shredded wheat, being careful not to disturb the rows. Let stand 30 minutes, until milk is absorbed.

Preheat oven to 350°.

Sprinkle the top of the pudding evenly with the chopped nuts, followed by the reserved sugar and cinnamon mixture. Bake 30 minutes.

Serve slightly warm. Chill leftovers and serve them cold or reheat briefly in a microwave.

Each serving provides:

117	Calories	23 g	Carbohydrate
4 g	Protein	29 mg	Sodium
2 g	Total fat (0 g sat. fat)	1 mg	Cholesterol

Israeli Orange Pudding

Oranges are plentiful in Israel and many of the desserts take advantage of their sweetness and versatility. This pudding can be served warm or cold and is delicious by itself, or it can be "dressed up" by topping each serving with a dollop of vanilla nonfat yogurt and some fresh orange sections.

Makes 8 servings

1/2	cup sugar
2 2/3	cups water
1/3	cup frozen orange juice concentrate, thawed
3/4	cup Quick Cream of Wheat®, uncooked
1	tablespoon vanilla extract
1/2	cup cold skim milk
	Ground cinnamon

In a medium saucepan, combine sugar and 2 cups of the water. Bring to a boil over medium heat.

In a small bowl, combine orange juice concentrate, remaining water, and Cream of Wheat®, mixing well. Add to boiling water. Bring to a boil, stirring constantly. Continue to cook and stir 2 minutes, until mixture has thickened. Remove from heat.

Let mixture cool 5 minutes, then stir in vanilla and milk.

Spoon pudding into a large bowl. Beat on high speed of an electric mixer for 5 minutes. Sprinkle lightly with cinnamon.

Serve warm or cold.

Each serving provides:

138	Calories	31 g	Carbohydrate
2 g	Protein	10 mg	Sodium
0 g	Total fat (0 g sat. fat)	0 mg	Cholesterol

Persian Apricot Pudding

Rice is almost always on the table in Iran (formerly Persia) and rice pudding, with its many creative variations, is a popular dessert. Look closely. What seems like tapioca is really bits of rice in this unique dessert.

Makes 8 servings

1/4	cup brown rice, uncooked
3	tablespoons cornstarch
1/3	cup water
2	1-pound cans apricot halves (packed in juice), drained
2 1/2	cups skim milk (about)
1/3	cup sugar
1	tablespoon vanilla extract
1	teaspoon almond extract

Have a 1-quart shallow bowl ready.

Place rice in a blender container and blend until fine, about 1 minute. Place in a small bowl and add cornstarch and water. Stir to dissolve cornstarch.

Place drained apricots in blender container. Blend until smooth. Add enough milk to apricots to total 4 cups. (This will take about 2 1/2 cups of milk.) Pour into a small saucepan. Add sugar and rice mixture.

Cook over medium heat, stirring constantly, until mixture comes to a boil. Continue to cook and stir for 5 minutes. Remove from heat and stir in extracts.

Pour pudding into bowl. Let cool at room temperature for 30 minutes, then chill thoroughly.

Serve cold.

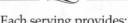

Each serving provides:

153	Calories	34 g	Carbohydrate
4 g	Protein	45 mg	Sodium
0 g	Total fat (0 g sat. fat)	2 mg	Cholesterol

Spiced Orange and Berry Compote

This is a cool, refreshing dish that often appears on the fabulous Israeli break-fast buffets. The delicious combination of fresh oranges and strawberries is delicately laced with spices. This compote is delicious plain or it can be spooned over angel food cake and topped with vanilla nonfat yogurt.

Makes 6 servings

1/2	cup orange juice
3	tablespoons honey
4	whole cloves
2	whole allspice
1	2 1/2 -inch cinnamon stick
2	3-inch strips of orange peel
3	large oranges, peeled and sectioned (Discard white membranes.)
2	cups sliced strawberries

In a small saucepan, combine orange juice, honey, spices, and orange peel. Bring to a boil over medium heat. Reduce heat to medium-low and simmer uncovered, 10 minutes.

While juice is cooking, combine orange sections and strawberries in a large bowl. When juice is finished cooking, remove and discard spices and orange peel. Pour juice over oranges and berries. Toss gently.

Chill several hours or overnight.

Mix before serving.

	Each serving provides:		
101	Calories	26 g	Carbohydrate
1 g	Protein	1 mg	Sodium
0 g	Total fat (0 g sat. fat)	0 mg	Cholesterol

Persian Grapes

Fruit in the Middle East is plentiful and varied. When fruits are in season they are often served at both lunch and dinner, and sometimes topped with thick cream, which gave me the idea for this recipe. This cool, refreshing dessert is just too easy for words!

Makes 6 servings

1¹/₂   cups seedless red grapes, cut in half (measure after cutting)
1   16-ounce container vanilla lowfat yogurt (Nonfat yogurt tends
        to get watery and does not work well here.)
¹/₄   cup plus 2 tablespoons firmly packed brown sugar

Divide grapes evenly into six custard cups or tall-stemmed sherbert or champagne glasses.

Divide yogurt evenly. Using ¹/₃ cup for each dessert, spoon over grapes smoothing the tops.

Using 1 tablespoon of brown sugar for each dessert, sprinkle evenly over yogurt, covering the yogurt as evenly as possible.

Chill for several hours until brown sugar has turned dark brown.

Note: If you prefer, in place of six individual glasses, this dessert can be made in a 1-quart shallow bowl.

Each serving provides:

149	Calories	37 g	Carbohydrate
4 g	Protein	59 mg	Sodium
1 g	Total fat (1 g sat. fat)	4 mg	Cholesterol

Clove-Spiced Apples

This popular Turkish fruit dessert is usually served warm and topped with cream, then sprinkled with toasted pine nuts or slivered almonds. My family actually prefers it cold and we top it with vanilla nonfat yogurt.

Makes 6 servings

4	large, sweet apples, peeled and cored, each cut vertically into 6 wedges
24	whole cloves
2/3	cup water
1/3	cup sugar
1	cup vanilla nonfat yogurt

Press one clove into each apple wedge.

In a large saucepan, combine water and sugar. Bring to a boil over medium heat. Add apples. Reduce heat to low, cover, and cook until apples are tender, about 3 to 5 minutes. (Length of cooking time will depend on the variety and ripeness of apples used.) Rearrange apples once during cooking time.

Serve warm or cold. (Be sure to remove cloves before serving.)

Top each serving with yogurt.

Each serving provides:

133	Calories	32 g	Carbohydrate
2 g	Protein	28 mg	Sodium
0 g	Total fat (0 g sat. fat)	1 mg	Cholesterol

Flavors of Eastern Europe

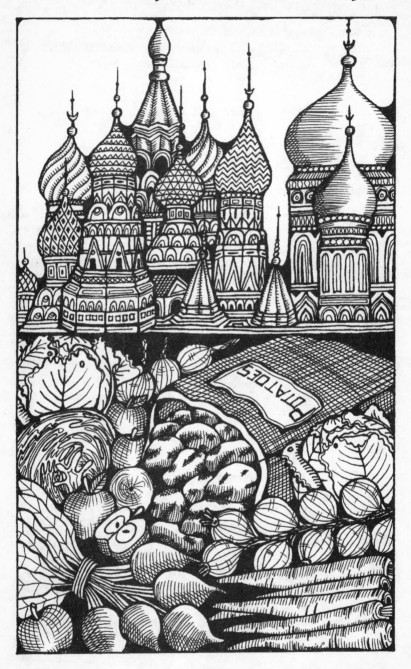

This chapter was inspired by my desire to recreate many of the unique specialties that I savored as a child. All of my grandparents came from Eastern Europe and it was through them that I came to appreciate the region's cuisine. I have included recipes from Russia, Hungary, Czechoslovakia, Poland, Romania, Bulgaria, and Yugoslavia. Even though boundaries and names change, the traditional foods of the region have been cherished for many decades.

A number of dishes seem to appear in all the European countries, although each country has its own way of preparing them. The difference in recipes may be as simple as a change in seasoning.

Because of severe winters, fresh fruits and vegetables are not always available in many parts of the region and what is available is often cooked and pickled and then packed in jars. Among the most commonly grown vegetables are onions, eggplant, green peppers, mushrooms, tomatoes, cucumbers, radishes, leeks, turnips, cabbage, carrots, beets, and potatoes. These vegetables form the basis of Eastern European cuisine, appearing abundantly in hearty soups and stews. The fruits, which are often dried or jarred, are plums, blueberries, cherries, cranberries, rhubarb (actually a vegetable, but thought of as a fruit by most people), apples, and currants.

Popular herbs and spices throughout the region include coriander, dill, mint, parsley, oregano, basil, cinnamon, cloves, nutmeg, cumin, saffron, paprika (especially in Hungarian cuisine), and pepper. Garlic plays an important role in seasoning, as do lemon juice and vinegar.

Dairy products such as milk, butter, and cottage cheese are frequently used and can be found at many meals. Sour cream seems to top everything!

Grains of the region include rye, wheat, oats, and barley. Buckwheat groats (kasha) have been a Russian staple for decades. In Romania a favorite grain dish is made with cornmeal that is boiled with water to make a porridge called *mamaliga*. This thick porridge is served as an entrée or side dish and is very similar to Italian *polenta*.

The basic cooking oils of the region are sunflower and olive. Butter is used freely, as are other animal fats, often making many of the traditional foods heavy and high in fat.

Components of Eastern European meals closely resemble those that we are accustomed to. Appetizers of vegetables and spreads, hearty soups, vegetable salads with oil and vinegar dressings, entrées, side dishes, and luscious desserts make up the fundamental parts of the meals, although not all elements are present at every meal. A simple, homey meal consisting of a hearty bowl of soup or a noodle casserole accompanied by a thick slab of crusty dark rye bread and a bowl of cooked fruit is most typical, with more elaborate fare reserved for Sundays and holidays. Since there is no living room per se in most Eastern European houses and apartments, often entire evenings are spent around the table, enjoying Russian tea and sweets.

Adapting the foods of this region to a lowfat, meatless lifestyle was an interesting challenge. Eliminating the butter and switching to lowfat or nonfat dairy products was easy, but replacing the large amounts of meat and fish was not. However, by replacing the meat with tofu, along with various beans and vegetables, I was able to meet the challenge. All of the flavors of my childhood are here without the fat.

Enjoy your journey through Eastern Europe!

Flavors of Eastern Europe
Recipes

Suggested Menus

Lunch

Cabbage and White Bean Soup (301)
Vegetable and Noodle Salad
with Dill Dressing (304)
Fresh Fruit Cup

Dilled White Bean Salad
and Tomatoes (306)
Lettuce and Sliced Cucumbers
Russian Oat and Rice Pudding (340)

Cucumber Boats (291)
Ukrainian Potato Salad (302)
Lettuce and Sliced Tomatoes
Bread or Rolls
Cranberry Fruit Pudding (342)

Dinner

Russian Vegetable Borscht (298)
Herbed Potato Stew (308)
Steamed Green Beans
Rye Bread
Apple Charlotte (336)

Mushroom Noodle Soup (299)
Tossed Salad
Hungarian Baked Potatoes (309)
Steamed Broccoli
Spiced Peaches and Dumplings (332)

Tossed Salad
Baked Tofu with Mushrooms
and Rosemary (315)
Lemon-Dijon Cauliflower (323)
Noodles
Creamy Rhubarb Pudding (341)

Tossed Salad
Mixed Bean Goulash (310)
Kasha with Onions and
Potatoes (331)
Steamed Green Beans
Mixed Berries Romanov (343)

Recipe page numbers appear in parentheses.

Cucumber Boats

Cucumbers are grown in abundance in Eastern Europe and are often combined with sour cream or cheese. This easy Yugoslavian recipe consists of cucumbers that are hollowed out and filled with tomatoes and feta cheese. It makes a perfect light appetizer or refreshing salad.

Makes 4 servings

2	medium, ripe tomatoes, chopped into 1/4-inch pieces (1 1/2 cups)
1 1/2	teaspoons olive oil
1	teaspoon vinegar
1/4	teaspoon dried oregano
	Salt and pepper to taste
	A pinch of sugar
4 1/2	tablespoons feta cheese, finely crumbled (1 1/2 ounces)
2	large cucumbers

In a small bowl, combine chopped tomatoes, oil, vinegar, oregano, salt, pepper, and sugar. Toss gently until well mixed. Chill until serving time (at least a few hours).

Just before serving, add feta cheese to tomatoes and mix well.

Peel cucumbers and cut them in half lengthwise. Using a melon ball scoop or a spoon, scoop out and discard seeds. Pile tomato mixture into cucumbers.

Serve right away.

Each serving provides:

73	Calories	7 g	Carbohydrate
3 g	Protein	131 mg	Sodium
4 g	Total fat (2 g sat. fat)	10 mg	Cholesterol

Herbed Cheese Spread

From Romania, this delicate herbed cheese spread is made with a variety of goat's milk or sheep's milk cheeses, depending on availability. It's wonderful spread on slices of crusty French bread, topped with a slice of tomato, and served as a party appetizer.

Makes 16 servings
(2 tablespoons per serving)

8	ounces feta cheese, crumbled (1 1/2 cups)
8	ounces fat-free cream cheese
1/2	teaspoon dried basil
1/2	teaspoon dried oregano
1/4	teaspoon garlic powder
1/4	teaspoon dill weed

Combine all ingredients in a large bowl. Beat on low speed of an electric mixer until combined. Increase speed to high and beat until smooth. (The feta cheese will not be completely smooth. Ignore the tiny lumps that remain.)

Spoon cheese into a serving bowl, cover, and chill several hours to blend flavors.

Note: For a pretty presentation, you can line the bowl with plastic wrap before filling it with the cheese. After chilling, invert bowl onto a serving dish and remove plastic wrap.

Each serving provides:

53	Calories	2 g	Carbohydrate
5 g	Protein	258 mg	Sodium
3 g	Total fat (2 g sat. fat)	15 mg	Cholesterol

Mushroom Caviar

A popular Russian appetizer, this delicious, nicely textured spread has the richness of sherry and the tang of lemon. It's usually served on small chunks of dark rye bread, but can also be spread on thin slices of dark party rye bread.

Makes 16 servings
(2 tablespoons each serving)

1	teaspoon vegetable oil
1	pound mushrooms, finely chopped (about 4 cups)
1	cup finely chopped onion
1	clove garlic, finely chopped
2	tablespoons lemon juice
2	tablespoons sherry
$1/4$	teaspoon dried thyme
$1/4$	teaspoon salt
$1/8$	teaspoon pepper
	Salt and pepper to taste

Heat oil in a large nonstick skillet over medium heat. Add mushrooms, onion, and garlic. Cook, stirring frequently, until vegetables are tender, about 5 minutes.

Place mushroom mixture in a blender container or in a food processor fitted with a steel blade. Blend or process, turning machine on and off, until mixture is very finely chopped, but not puréed. Spoon mixture into a bowl. Add remaining ingredients, mixing well.

Chill several hours or overnight.

Add additional salt and pepper to taste.

Each serving provides:

17	Calories	3 g	Carbohydrate
1 g	Protein	36 mg	Sodium
0 g	Total fat (0 g sat. fat)	0 mg	Cholesterol

Cheese-Filled Little Potatoes

Appetizers, or zakuski, *are one of the favorite parts of a Russian meal. Potatoes are often plentiful, and we see them used in all parts of the meal, including hors d'oeuvres. Here's a quick and easy appetizer that also makes a delicious side dish.*

Makes 8 servings

8	small, red skinned (new) potatoes, unpeeled (about 3 ounces each)
	Nonstick cooking spray
1/3	cup plain nonfat yogurt
3	tablespoons grated Parmesan cheese
2	large cloves garlic, crushed
	Pepper to taste

Preheat oven to 375°.

Lightly oil a baking sheet or spray with a nonstick cooking spray.

Cut each potato in half lengthwise. Using the small side of a melon ball scoop, cut a ball out of the center of each potato half. (You can bake these "holes" along with the potatoes and serve them with toothpicks.) Slice a very thin sliver off the bottom of each potato to keep them from rolling around in the pan. Place potatoes on baking sheet, skin-side down, and spray them lightly with cooking spray.

Bake uncovered, 30 to 35 minutes, until potatoes are tender. (If you are baking the potato "holes," they will only take 20 to 25 minutes.)

While potatoes are baking, combine remaining ingredients in a small bowl. Mix well and set aside.

When potatoes are tender, remove pan from oven and set the oven to broil. Fill the hole in each potato with yogurt mixture. Place potatoes under the broiler for a few minutes, until cheese is hot and begins to brown.

Serve warm.

Each serving provides:

92	Calories		16 g	Carbohydrate
3 g	Protein		49 mg	Sodium
2 g	Total fat (0 g sat. fat)		2 mg	Cholesterol

Cabbage-Filled Pastries

Filled pastries are popular all over Eastern Europe. Known as piroshki in Russia and pierogi in Poland, they hold a variety of fillings. These pastries make a great appetizer, snack, or side dish.

Makes 10 pastries

1	teaspoon vegetable oil
1	cup finely chopped onion
2	cups (packed) thinly sliced cabbage
1	tablespoon firmly packed brown sugar
1	teaspoon lemon juice
1	teaspoon dill weed
1/4	teaspoon salt
1/8	teaspoon pepper
1	10-ounce container refrigerator biscuits

Heat oil in a large nonstick skillet over medium heat. Add onion and cabbage. Sprinkle with brown sugar, lemon juice, dill weed, salt, and pepper. Cook, stirring frequently, about 8 minutes or until tender. Stir constantly toward the end of cooking time to keep vegetables from sticking. Remove from heat and let cool 5 to 10 minutes.

Preheat oven to 400°.

Have an ungreased baking sheet ready. Separate biscuits and place them between two sheets of wax paper several inches apart. With a rolling pin, roll biscuits into 4- to 5-inch circles. Carefully remove the top sheet of wax paper.

Using a heaping tablespoonful of filling, place slightly off-center on each circle. Carefully fold biscuits over, making a half-circle and stretching the dough gently over the filling. Crimp the edges together with a fork. Place pastries on baking sheet.

Bake 8 to 10 minutes, until golden. Serve hot or at room temperature.

Each pastry provides:

100	Calories	16 g	Carbohydrate
2 g	Protein	358 mg	Sodium
5 g	Total fat (1 g sat. fat)	0 mg	Cholesterol

Mushroom-Filled Pastries

This is a delicious variation of the popular turnover-style pastries. A splash of sherry intensifies the mushroom flavor and turns these easy pastries into a gourmet treat.

Makes 10 pastries

1	teaspoon vegetable oil
12	ounces mushrooms, finely chopped (about 3 cups)
1/2	cup very finely chopped onion
1 1/2	tablespoons all-purpose flour
1 1/2	tablespoons sherry
1/8	teaspoon *each* salt and pepper
1	10-ounce container refrigerator biscuits

Heat oil in a medium nonstick skillet over medium heat. Add mushrooms and onion. Cook, stirring frequently, until most of the mushroom juices have cooked out, about 4 minutes. Sprinkle with flour, stirring to mix well. Stir in sherry, salt, and pepper. Cook and stir until mixture is almost dry, about 2 minutes. Remove pan from heat and set aside to cool slightly.

Preheat oven to 400°.

Have an ungreased baking sheet ready. Separate biscuits and place them between two sheets of wax paper several inches apart. With a rolling pin, roll biscuits into 4- to 5-inch circles. Carefully remove the top sheet of wax paper.

Using a heaping tablespoonful of filling, place slightly off-center on each circle. Carefully fold biscuits over, making a half-circle and stretching the dough gently over the filling. Crimp the edges together with a fork. Place pastries on baking sheet.

Bake 8 to 10 minutes, until golden. Serve hot or at room temperature.

Each pastry provides:

103	Calories	15 g	Carbohydrate
3 g	Protein	329 mg	Sodium
5 g	Total fat (1 g sat. fat)	0 mg	Cholesterol

Potato and Barley Soup

Variations of this soup are served in most Eastern European countries, where potatoes and barley are abundant. It's smooth, hearty, and mildly spiced. Served with a salad and a chunk of crusty rye bread, this soup makes a nice, filling luncheon dish.

Makes 6 servings
(1 cup each serving)

2	teaspoons vegetable oil
1	cup chopped onion
1	clove garlic, finely chopped
6	cups water
1 1/2	pounds potatoes, peeled and cut into 1/2-inch cubes (3 medium potatoes)
1	cup thinly sliced carrots
1/2	cup barley, uncooked
5	teaspoons *Vegetable Broth Mix* (See page 27.)
2	bay leaves
1/2	teaspoon dill weed
	Salt and pepper to taste

Heat oil in a large saucepan over medium heat. Add onion and garlic. Cook, stirring frequently, until onion starts to brown, about 3 minutes.

Add remaining ingredients, *except* salt and pepper. Bring mixture to a boil, then cover, reduce heat to medium-low, and simmer 45 minutes or until vegetables are tender.

Remove and discard bay leaves.

Add salt and pepper to taste.

Each serving provides:

159	Calories	32 g	Carbohydrate
4 g	Protein	82 mg	Sodium
2 g	Total fat (0 g sat. fat)	0 mg	Cholesterol

Russian Vegetable Borscht

There are probably as many versions of this popular Russian soup as there are Russians! Here's my version of a fairly "typical" borscht.

Makes 8 servings
(1¹/₂ cups each serving)

2	teaspoons vegetable oil
1	cup *each* chopped onion and chopped green bell pepper
3	cloves garlic, crushed
4	cups thinly shredded cabbage
¹/₂	cup coarsely shredded carrots
2	medium potatoes, unpeeled, chopped into ¹/₂-inch pieces (1 pound total)
1	large beet, peeled and coarsely shredded (5 ounces)
8	cups water, or *Vegetable Broth* (See page 26.)
1	6-ounce can tomato paste
2	bay leaves
1	teaspoon *each* paprika and sugar
¹/₂	teaspoon dill weed
¹/₄	teaspoon salt
¹/₈	teaspoon pepper
1	tablespoon red wine vinegar

Heat oil in a large soup pot over medium heat. Add onion, bell pepper, and garlic. Cook, stirring frequently, 5 minutes.

Add remaining ingredients, *except* wine vinegar. Bring to a boil stirring occasionally. Reduce heat to medium-low, cover, and simmer 30 minutes or until vegetables are tender. Stir in wine vinegar.

Remove and discard bay leaves before serving. For best flavor, chill soup and reheat to serve.

Each serving provides:

106	Calories	22 g	Carbohydrate
3 g	Protein	258 mg	Sodium
2 g	Total fat (0 g sat. fat)	0 mg	Cholesterol

Mushroom Noodle Soup

This "homey" soup is served in slightly different variations all over Eastern Europe. Potatoes and mushrooms are the two vegetables most commonly used. This is a soup like the one that Mama used to make! (The ketchup is my own addition. I've used it in place of the thick, homemade tomato sauce that is often used.)

Makes 8 servings
(1¹/4 cups each serving)

2	teaspoons vegetable oil
2	cups sliced mushrooms
1	cup chopped onion
1	large leek, chopped (white part only) (1 cup)
1	cup finely chopped carrots
8	cups *Vegetable Broth,* or 8 cups of water plus 8 teaspoons *Vegetable Broth Mix* (See pages 26–27.)
1	large potato, unpeeled, cut into ¹/4- to ¹/2-inch pieces (9 ounces)
2	teaspoons dill weed
1	teaspoon paprika
¹/8	teaspoon pepper
2	cups medium (yolk-free) noodles, uncooked
¹/4	cup ketchup
	Salt and pepper to taste

Heat oil in a large saucepan over medium heat. Add mushrooms, onion, leek, and carrots. Cook, stirring frequently, 5 minutes.

Add broth, potato, dill weed, paprika, and pepper. Bring mixture to a boil. Reduce heat to medium-low, cover, and cook 40 minutes or until vegetables are tender.

Add noodles. Cook 10 minutes.

Stir in ketchup and add salt and pepper to taste.

Each serving provides:			
126	Calories	25 g	Carbohydrate
4 g	Protein	212 mg	Sodium
2 g	Total fat (0 g sat. fat)	9 mg	Cholesterol

Spiced Cherry Soup

*Sweet Hungarian fruit soups are often served as a prelude to a dairy meal,
such as one featuring a noodle pudding as the entrée. I substituted sweet
cherries for the sour ones that are used in most versions, eliminating the need
for a lot of sugar. (The white grape juice was also my own idea.) This soup is
usually served hot, although my family also enjoys it cold.*

*Makes 4 servings
(³/4 cup each serving)*

³/4	cup orange juice
1	tablespoon cornstarch
³/4	cup white grape juice
2	tablespoons honey
¹/2	large orange, unpeeled, sliced crosswise into ¹/4-inch slices, then each slice cut in half (Discard end slice.)
8	whole cloves
1	3-inch cinnamon stick
¹/2	teaspoon lemon juice
2	cups frozen, unsweetened pitted cherries (Fresh sweet pitted cherries will also work. If you can't find either, use canned cherries in light syrup and rinse them before using.)

Place ¹/4 cup of the orange juice in a small bowl or custard cup.
Add cornstarch and stir until dissolved. Set aside.

Combine remaining ingredients in a small saucepan. Bring to a boil
over medium heat. Reduce heat slightly, cover, and simmer 10 minutes. Stir cornstarch mixture and add to saucepan. Continue to cook
and stir 3 minutes more.

Remove and discard orange slices, cloves, and cinnamon stick.
Serve hot or cold.

Each serving provides:

154	Calories	39 g	Carbohydrate
2 g	Protein	6 mg	Sodium
1 g	Total fat (0 g sat. fat)	0 mg	Cholesterol

Cabbage and White Bean Soup

This superb soup demonstrates one of the Ukraine's delicious flavor principles; the blending of brown sugar and lemon juice to give foods a sweet and sour taste.

Makes 4 servings
(1¹/2 cups each serving)

2	teaspoons vegetable oil
1	cup *each* chopped onion and chopped carrots
1/2	cup chopped celery
2	cups (packed) thinly sliced cabbage
2	cups water
1	1-pound can salt-free (or regular) tomatoes, chopped, undrained
1	1-pound can white beans (cannellini or Great Northern beans), rinsed and drained (or 2 cups of cooked beans)
2	tablespoons lemon juice
2	tablespoons firmly packed brown sugar
1	teaspoon caraway seeds
1/4	teaspoon dried thyme
	Salt and pepper to taste

Heat oil in a large saucepan over medium heat. Add onion, carrots, and celery. Cook 5 minutes, stirring frequently and adding small amounts of water if necessary, about a tablespoon at a time, to prevent sticking.

Add remaining ingredients, *except* salt and pepper, mixing well. Bring to a boil, then reduce heat to medium-low, cover, and simmer 45 minutes or until vegetables are tender.

Add salt and pepper to taste. Add additional brown sugar or lemon juice, if desired.

Each serving provides:

192	Calories	34 g	Carbohydrate
8 g	Protein	192 mg	Sodium
3 g	Total fat (0 g sat. fat)	0 mg	Cholesterol

Ukrainian Potato Salad

This slightly tart potato salad is a typical Ukrainian dish, illustrating just one of their many uses for potatoes. Some people add chopped cooked beets, others add hard-boiled eggs, and still others add chopped dill pickles. Take your pick or enjoy it as is!

Makes 8 servings

2	pounds potatoes, unpeeled, cut into large chunks (4 medium potatoes)
1/3	cup thinly sliced green onions (green and white parts)
1	medium cucumber, peeled, seeded, and cut into 1/4-inch pieces (1 cup)
2	tablespoons vinegar
1 1/2	tablespoons vegetable oil
1 1/2	tablespoons water
1	tablespoon dried parsley flakes
1	teaspoon dill weed
1	teaspoon sugar
1/2	teaspoon salt
	Pepper to taste
1/2	cup plain nonfat yogurt

Place potatoes in 2 inches of boiling water in a medium saucepan. Cover and cook over medium heat, 15 to 20 minutes or until potatoes are tender. Do not let them get mushy. (Length of cooking time will depend on the variety of potatoes used.)

Drain potatoes and let them sit until cool enough to handle. Remove skin and cut potatoes into 1-inch chunks. Place in a large bowl. Add green onions and cucumber and mix well.

In a small bowl, combine remaining ingredients, *except* yogurt. Mix well and add to potatoes. Toss until potatoes are evenly coated, then stir in yogurt.

Chill several hours to blend flavors.

Each serving provides:

104	Calories	18 g	Carbohydrate
3 g	Protein	155 mg	Sodium
3 g	Total fat (0 g sat. fat)	0 mg	Cholesterol

Tomato Salad with Mustard-Basil Dressing

In Hungary tomatoes are often dressed up with sour cream and lots of cheese. I slimmed this salad down quite a bit and the result is still fresh, ripe tomatoes topped with a thick, creamy dressing.

Makes 4 servings

1/2	cup plain nonfat yogurt
1 1/2	teaspoons dried basil
1 1/2	teaspoons prepared horseradish
1	teaspoon olive oil
1	teaspoon grated Parmesan cheese
1/2	teaspoon red wine vinegar
1/4	teaspoon Dijon mustard
1/8	teaspoon sugar
1/8	teaspoon salt
1/8	teaspoon pepper
	Romaine lettuce leaves
2	large, ripe tomatoes, chopped just before serving (about 2 1/2 cups)

In a small bowl, combine all ingredients, *except* lettuce and tomato. Mix well. Chill several hours to blend flavors.

To serve, arrange lettuce leaves on four individual serving plates. Chop tomato and pile on lettuce. Spoon dressing over tomatoes, allowing 2 tablespoonfuls for each serving.

Serve right away.

Each serving provides:

47	Calories	6 g	Carbohydrate
3 g	Protein	116 mg	Sodium
2 g	Total fat (0 g sat. fat)	1 mg	Cholesterol

Vegetable and Noodle Salad with Dill Dressing

You'll love the many textures and flavors in this Hungarian noodle salad. When you make it, plan ahead so the dressing can chill for at least a few hours before adding it to the salad.

Makes 8 servings

Dill Dressing:

2/3	cup evaporated skim milk
3	tablespoons vinegar
1	tablespoon vegetable oil
1	teaspoon dill weed
1	teaspoon minced onion flakes
1/2	teaspoon dry mustard
1/2	teaspoon onion powder
1/4	teaspoon salt
1/8	teaspoon pepper

Salad:

6	ounces medium (yolk-free) noodles, uncooked (4 cups)
1	cup zucchini, unpeeled, cut into quarters lengthwise, then sliced crosswise into very thin slices
1	cup cucumber, cut into quarters lengthwise, then sliced crosswise into very thin slices (Peel cucumber if the skin has been waxed.)
1	cup chopped tomato
1	cup very thinly sliced radishes
1/2	cup coarsely shredded carrots
1/2	cup very finely minced onion
	Salt and pepper to taste

To prepare dressing: combine all dressing ingredients in a small bowl or jar. Mix well. Chill several hours or overnight.

To prepare salad: cook noodles according to package directions, using the minimum cooking time suggested. Drain noodles and rinse under cold water. Drain again.

In a large bowl, combine noodles with remaining salad ingredients. Toss to combine. Pour chilled dressing over salad and mix well.

Chill for several hours. Mix before serving.

Each serving provides:

126	Calories	22 g	Carbohydrate
5 g	Protein	106 mg	Sodium
2 g	Total fat (0 g sat. fat)	1 mg	Cholesterol

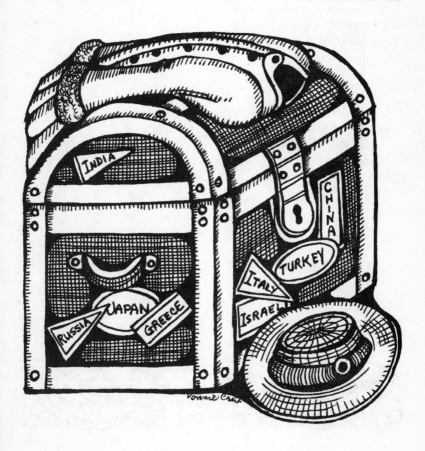

Dilled White Bean Salad and Tomatoes

From the republic of Georgia, where beans are often put to imaginative uses, comes this easy salad that can be put together quickly, refrigerated for up to two days, and assembled just before serving. It can be used to make six salad servings or four delicious, light entrées.

Makes 6 servings

1	19-ounce can white beans (cannellini), rinsed and drained (or 2¹/₄ cups of cooked beans)
2	tablespoons lemon juice
1	tablespoon olive oil
1	tablespoon water
2	tablespoons very finely minced onion
1¹/₂	teaspoons parsley flakes
1¹/₂	teaspoons dill weed
1	teaspoon dried mint leaves
¹/₄	teaspoon salt
¹/₈	teaspoon pepper
6	medium tomatoes

In a small bowl, combine all ingredients, *except* tomatoes. Mix well, cover, and chill several hours or up to two days.

Refrigerate tomatoes.

To serve, cut each tomato into six wedges, leaving the base intact. Divide bean salad evenly and pile into tomatoes.

Serve right away.

Each serving provides:			
112	Calories	17 g	Carbohydrate
6 g	Protein	214 mg	Sodium
3 g	Total fat (0 g sat. fat)	0 mg	Cholesterol

Russian Pickled Mushrooms

The Russians have a penchant for pickles, and most of the summer vegetables are pickled so they can be enjoyed throughout the long winters. I love these tart and tangy mushrooms served over a bed of fresh lettuce or spinach and garnished with tomato wedges. They can also be served with toothpicks as a delicious appetizer.

Makes 4 servings

1/4	cup dry white wine
1/4	cup red wine vinegar
3	tablespoons water
2	teaspoons olive oil
2	large cloves garlic, crushed
1	teaspoon sugar
1/2	teaspoon dried basil
1/2	teaspoon dried thyme
1/4	teaspoon salt
1/4	teaspoon pepper
12	ounces mushrooms, cut into quarters

In a small saucepan, combine all ingredients, *except* mushrooms. Bring to a boil over medium heat. Cook 3 minutes. Add mushrooms and when mixture boils again continue to cook and stir, 1 minute more.

Chill several hours or overnight to blend flavors.

Serve cold.

Each serving provides:			
62	Calories	7 g	Carbohydrate
2 g	Protein	140 mg	Sodium
3 g	Total fat (0 g sat. fat)	0 mg	Cholesterol

Herbed Potato Stew

Rosemary and sage give this delicious Bulgarian stew a mild, pleasant flavor that is enhanced by a sprinkling of Parmesan cheese.

Makes 4 servings

2	teaspoons olive oil
1	cup *each* chopped onion and chopped green bell pepper
3	cloves garlic, crushed
1	1-pound can salt-free (or regular) stewed tomatoes
1	large potato, unpeeled, cut into 1/2-inch pieces (9 ounces)
1	cup *Vegetable Broth,* or 1 cup of water plus 1 teaspoon *Vegetable Broth Mix* (See pages 26–27.)
1/4	teaspoon dried rosemary, crumbled
1/8	teaspoon dried sage
1	1-pound can white beans (cannellini), rinsed and drained (or 2 cups of cooked beans)
1/4	teaspoon salt
1/8	teaspoon pepper
	Parmesan cheese

Heat oil in a medium saucepan over medium heat. Add onion, bell pepper, and garlic. Cook, stirring frequently, until vegetables are tender, about 5 minutes. Add small amounts of water if necessary, about a tablespoon at a time, to prevent sticking.

Add stewed tomatoes, potato, broth, rosemary, and sage. Mix well. When mixture boils, reduce heat to medium-low, cover, and simmer 20 to 25 minutes, until potatoes are tender. Add beans, salt, and pepper. Simmer covered, 15 minutes more.

Spoon into serving bowls and top with a sprinkling of Parmesan cheese.

Each serving provides:

210	Calories	38 g	Carbohydrate
9 g	Protein	329 mg	Sodium
3 g	Total fat (0 g sat. fat)	0 mg	Cholesterol

Hungarian Baked Potatoes

This filling main-dish potato combines the flavors of Hungary with the favorite American baked potato.

Makes 4 servings

4	medium baking potatoes (about 8 ounces each)
2	teaspoons vegetable oil
1	cup finely chopped onion
2	cloves garlic, finely chopped
1/2	cup finely chopped green bell pepper (optional)
1	teaspoon *Vegetable Broth Mix* (See page 27.)
1/2	cup plain nonfat yogurt
1	teaspoon paprika
1/4	teaspoon *each* pepper and salt

Topping:
1/4 cup plain nonfat yogurt
     Paprika

Pierce potatoes several times and bake in a 375° oven for 1 hour or until tender.

Heat oil in a small nonstick skillet over medium heat. Add onion, garlic, and bell pepper. Sprinkle with broth mix. Cook, stirring frequently, 3 to 4 minutes or until vegetables are tender. Remove from heat.

Slice a thin vertical slice off the top of each potato. Using a teaspoon, scoop out the pulp leaving a 1/4-inch shell. Place potato pulp in a large bowl and add yogurt, paprika, and pepper. Mash with a fork or potato masher until smooth. Add additional yogurt (or a little skim milk) if potatoes are too dry. Add onion mixture to potatoes and mix well. Add salt.

Spoon potato mixture back into shells. Return potatoes to oven and heat 10 to 15 minutes. Just before serving, top each potato with 1 tablespoonful of yogurt and sprinkle with paprika.

Each serving provides:

230	Calories	46 g	Carbohydrate
7 g	Protein	66 mg	Sodium
3 g	Total fat (0 g sat. fat)	1 mg	Cholesterol

Mixed Bean Goulash

Based on a rich Hungarian stew, this dish is thick and delicious.

Makes 8 servings

2	teaspoons vegetable oil
2	large onions, thinly sliced (2 cups)
1	large green bell pepper, thinly sliced (1 cup)
2	cups *Vegetable Broth,* or 2 cups of water plus 2 teaspoons *Vegetable Broth Mix* (See pages 26–27.)
1	6-ounce can tomato paste
1	1-pound can kidney beans, rinsed and drained (or 2 cups of cooked beans)
1	1-pound can white beans (cannellini or Great Northern beans), rinsed and drained (or 2 cups of cooked beans)
1	1-pound can lima beans, rinsed and drained (or one 10-ounce package frozen limas)
2	medium potatoes, unpeeled, cut into 1/2-inch cubes (1 pound total)
2	tablespoons paprika
1	teaspoon dried basil
1/2	teaspoon *each* caraway seeds and salt
1/4	teaspoon pepper
1	cup plain nonfat yogurt

Heat oil in a large saucepan over medium heat. Add onions and bell pepper. Cook, stirring frequently, 5 minutes. Add small amounts of water as necessary, about a tablespoon at a time, to prevent sticking. Add remaining ingredients, *except* yogurt. Mix well. Bring mixture to a boil, then reduce heat to medium-low, cover, and simmer 45 minutes or until potatoes are tender. Stir several times while cooking. Serve over noodles or rice and top each serving with 2 tablespoonfuls of yogurt.

Each serving provides:

235	Calories	43 g	Carbohydrate
13 g	Protein	521 mg	Sodium
2 g	Total fat (0 g sat. fat)	1 mg	Cholesterol

Polish Sauerkraut Stew

Almost every Polish cookbook contains at least one recipe for a stew made with sauerkraut. I've created a "slimmed-down" version, substituting chick peas for the meat. I also replaced some of the sauerkraut with fresh cabbage, greatly reducing the sodium content of the dish.

Makes 8 servings

1	1-pound can sauerkraut, rinsed and drained
3	cups cabbage, thinly shredded
2	medium Granny Smith apples, unpeeled, chopped
2	large tomatoes, chopped
1	cup chopped onion
3	large cloves garlic, crushed
2	1-pound cans chick peas, rinsed and drained (or 4 cups of cooked chick peas)
2	tablespoons sugar
1¹/₂	tablespoons paprika
1	teaspoon dried marjoram
1	teaspoon dried basil
¹/₄	teaspoon pepper
1	6-ounce can tomato paste
3¹/₂	cups water
	Salt to taste

In a large soup pot, combine sauerkraut, cabbage, apples, tomatoes, onion, garlic, and chick peas. Add sugar, spices, tomato paste and water. Mix well.

Bring mixture to a boil over medium heat, stirring occasionally. Reduce heat to medium-low, cover, and simmer 45 to 55 minutes, until vegetables are tender. Stir once or twice while cooking. Add salt to taste.

Serve stew in bowls or over cooked brown rice.

Each serving provides:

161	Calories	31 g	Carbohydrate
6 g	Protein	430 mg	Sodium
2 g	Total fat (0 g sat. fat)	0 mg	Cholesterol

Bulgarian One-Pot

Bulgarian cuisine borrows flavors from both Greece and Turkey as you can see in this unique stew. Often dried fruits are combined with vegetables to make interesting one-pot meals. (The tofu was my own addition.)

Makes 6 servings

2	teaspoons vegetable oil
1	large onion, sliced and separated into rings
2	medium potatoes, unpeeled, cut into quarters lengthwise, then sliced crosswise into 1/4-inch slices (1 pound total)
2/3	cup pitted prunes, cut in half (about 10 prunes)
2	cups sliced mushrooms
1	15-ounce can salt-free (or regular) tomato sauce
1/2	cup orange juice
1/2	cup water
1	tablespoon red wine vinegar
1	teaspoon grated fresh orange peel
1/2	teaspoon ground cinnamon
1/2	teaspoon dried thyme
1/4	teaspoon ground allspice
1/4	teaspoon *each* salt and pepper
1	pound firm tofu, cut into 1-inch cubes, drained well between layers of towels

Heat oil in a large saucepan over medium heat. Add onion. Cook, stirring frequently, until onion is tender, about 5 minutes. Add small amounts of water if necessary, about a tablespoon at a time, to prevent sticking.

Add potatoes, prunes, and mushrooms. Mix well. Cook, stirring frequently, 5 minutes.

In a small bowl, combine tomato sauce with remaining ingredients, *except* tofu. Mix well. Pour over vegetables and mix until vegetables are evenly coated. When mixture boils, reduce heat to medium-low, cover, and simmer 45 minutes to 1 hour, until potatoes are tender. Stir

occasionally while cooking and add a little more water if sauce becomes too thick and vegetables start to stick to the pan.

Add tofu. Mix gently, being careful not to break the tofu.

Simmer covered, 10 minutes.

Serve in bowls or spoon over rice or noodles.

Each serving provides:

282	Calories	40 g	Carbohydrate
16 g	Protein	124 mg	Sodium
9 g	Total fat (1 g sat. fat)	0 mg	Cholesterol

Stuffed Cabbage and Potato Pie

This unique Hungarian main-dish pie is usually made with a layer of meat.
However, even without it, the dish is hearty enough to stand as an entrée.

Makes 8 servings

1	large head of cabbage (about 2¹/₄ pounds)
1	tablespoon vegetable oil
1	large onion, cut vertically into thin slivers (1 cup)
1	teaspoon dill weed
¹/₂	teaspoon dill seed
³/₄	teaspoon *each* garlic powder and salt
¹/₂	teaspoon pepper
2	pounds potatoes, unpeeled, finely shredded (4 medium potatoes)

Cut cabbage around the core and carefully remove 8 leaves. Place them in a large pot of boiling water, cover, and cook until tender, about 15 minutes. Drain, rinse with cold water, and drain again. Shred remaining cabbage to make 4 cups.

Heat oil in a large nonstick skillet over medium heat. Add shredded cabbage and onion. Sprinkle with spices. Cook, stirring frequently, 15 minutes or until cabbage is very tender. Add potatoes. Cook and stir, 5 minutes. Remove from heat.

Preheat oven to 375°.

Lightly oil a 9-inch pie pan or spray with a nonstick cooking spray.

Line pie pan with 5 of the cabbage leaves, placing the ribs in the center and letting the leaves overlap the sides of the pan. Place 1 more leaf in the center.

Fill with potato mixture, pressing gently with the back of a spoon, and smoothing the top. Fold the edges of the cabbage leaves over the filling and top with remaining 2 leaves.

Cover tightly with aluminum foil and bake 1 hour. Cut into wedges to serve.

Each serving provides:

144	Calories	28 g	Carbohydrate
4 g	Protein	232 mg	Sodium
3 g	Total fat (0 g sat. fat)	0 mg	Cholesterol

Baked Tofu with
Mushrooms and Rosemary

The flavor of rosemary abounds in this delicious adaptation of a Yugoslavian stew.

Makes 4 servings

1	pound firm tofu, cut into 1-inch cubes, drained well between towels
2	teaspoons olive oil
2	large onions, sliced and separated into rings
3	cloves garlic, crushed
8	ounces mushrooms, cut into quarters (about 3 cups)
1	1-pound can salt-free (or regular) tomatoes, chopped and drained (Liquid reserved.)
$1/2$	cup dry white wine
1	teaspoon *Vegetable Broth Mix* (See page 27.)
1	teaspoon dried rosemary, crumbled
$1/4$	teaspoon *each* salt and pepper
$1/4$	cup all-purpose flour
$1/4$	cup water

Preheat oven to 350°.

Lightly oil an 8-inch square baking pan or spray with a nonstick cooking spray.

Place tofu cubes in prepared pan. Set aside.

Heat oil in a large nonstick skillet over medium heat. Add onions and garlic. Cook, stirring frequently, 3 minutes. Add mushrooms. Cook, stirring frequently, 3 minutes more.

Reduce heat to medium-low. Add tomatoes, wine, broth mix, rosemary, salt, and pepper.

Place flour in a small bowl and gradually add water and reserved tomato liquid, stirring until smooth. Add to skillet. Increase heat to medium. Cook and stir until mixture boils. Remove from heat and pour over tofu. Cover tightly and bake 45 minutes.

Serve over brown rice or noodles.

Each serving provides:			
310	Calories	30 g	Carbohydrate
22 g	Protein	194 mg	Sodium
14 g	Total fat (2 g sat. fat)	0 mg	Cholesterol

Tofu Stroganoff

My version uses tofu and yogurt in place of beef and sour cream.

Makes 4 servings

1	pound firm tofu, cut into 2- x $1/2$- x $1/2$-inch strips, drained slightly on towels
1	teaspoon vegetable oil
2	cups sliced mushrooms
1	cup onion, sliced vertically into thin slivers
3	cloves garlic, finely chopped
3	tablespoons all-purpose flour
$1^1/2$	teaspoons dill weed
1	teaspoon dry mustard
$1/4$	teaspoon salt
$1/8$	teaspoon pepper
$1/16$	teaspoon ground nutmeg
1	cup *Vegetable Broth,* or 1 cup of water plus 1 teaspoon *Vegetable Broth Mix* (See pages 26–27.)
$1/4$	cup dry white wine
$1/2$	cup plain nonfat or lowfat yogurt (Lowfat yogurt makes a slightly creamier sauce.)

Heat a large nonstick skillet over medium heat. Add tofu strips and cook, turning tofu carefully, until brown on all sides. Remove tofu from skillet, place in a bowl, and cover to keep warm.

Add oil to skillet. Add mushrooms, onion, and garlic. Cook, stirring frequently, until onion is tender, about 4 minutes. Combine flour and spices and sprinkle over mushroom mixture. Add broth, a few tablespoons at a time, stirring constantly and mixing well after each addition. Stir in wine. When mixture is hot and bubbly, stir in tofu and yogurt. Heat through but do not boil. Serve over noodles.

Each serving provides:

257	Calories	19 g	Carbohydrate
22 g	Protein	204 mg	Sodium
12 g	Total fat (2 g sat. fat)	1 mg	Cholesterol

Hungarian Noodle Casserole

Unlike custard-based noodle dishes from other countries, this one is a loose medley of noodles with lots of green bell peppers and onions. It's a mellow and very tasty dish with a delicious, subtle flavor that is typical of Hungarian peasant dishes.

Makes 6 servings

6   ounces medium (yolk-free) noodles, uncooked (about 4 cups)
2   teaspoons olive oil
2   cups onion, cut vertically into thin slivers
2   cups green bell pepper, cut into thin strips
4   cloves garlic, finely chopped
1 1/2 cups lowfat (1%) cottage cheese
1   cup plain nonfat yogurt
2   teaspoons paprika
1/4   teaspoon *each* salt and pepper
1/2   teaspoon onion powder
       Paprika

Preheat oven to 375°.

Lightly oil a 7 x 11-inch baking pan or spray with a nonstick cooking spray.

Cook noodles according to package directions. Drain.

While noodles are cooking, heat oil in a large nonstick skillet over medium heat. Add onion, bell pepper, and garlic. Cook, stirring frequently, until onion begins to brown, about 10 minutes. Remove from heat.

In a large bowl, combine cottage cheese, yogurt, paprika, salt, pepper, and onion powder. Mix well. Add onion mixture and cooked noodles. Mix until well combined. Spoon mixture into prepared casserole. Press noodles down gently with the back of a spoon. Sprinkle with additional paprika.

Cover and bake 25 minutes. Uncover and bake 5 minutes more.

Each serving provides:

216	Calories	32 g	Carbohydrate
14 g	Protein	358 mg	Sodium
4 g	Total fat (1 g sat. fat)	3 mg	Cholesterol

Cabbage and Noodles

This Lithuanian recipe, shared with my Mom by a close friend, has definite similarities to both Russian and Hungarian recipes. The tender noodles, tossed with browned onions and cabbage make a hearty and tasty dish.

Makes 6 servings

8	ounces fine noodles (yolk-free), uncooked
2	teaspoons vegetable oil
2	cups onion, sliced vertically into thin slices
5	cups cabbage, thinly sliced
2	tablespoons water
2	teaspoons *Vegetable Broth Mix* (See page 27.)
1/8	teaspoon pepper
1/2	cup plain nonfat yogurt
1	teaspoon sugar
1/2	teaspoon caraway seeds
	Salt and pepper to taste
	Additional yogurt and paprika for topping

Cook noodles according to package directions. Drain.

While noodles are cooking, heat oil in a large nonstick skillet over medium heat. Add onion, cabbage, and water. Sprinkle with broth mix and pepper. Cook, stirring frequently, until onion and cabbage are nicely browned, about 20 minutes. Stir constantly during the end of cooking time to keep vegetables from burning.

Combine yogurt, sugar, and caraway seeds in a small bowl. When onion and cabbage have browned, reduce heat slightly and stir in yogurt mixture. Add noodles, mixing well. Cook and stir until mixture is well combined and heated through. Add salt and pepper to taste.

Top each serving with a dollop of yogurt and sprinkle with paprika.

Each serving provides:

195	Calories	37 g	Carbohydrate
8 g	Protein	62 mg	Sodium
3 g	Total fat (0 g sat. fat)	0 mg	Cholesterol

Mushroom and Bean Stew

This warm and friendly Georgian stew, which is usually made with a combination of meat and beans, is often served over cooked barley, kasha, or mamaliga (a cornmeal dish similar to Italian polenta). It makes a hearty rib-sticking dish.

Makes 6 servings

2	teaspoons vegetable oil
1	pound mushrooms, sliced (4 cups)
1	cup chopped onion
1	cup chopped red bell pepper
1/2	cup carrots, sliced crosswise into very thin slices (Use a vegetable peeler for thin, even slices.)
2	cloves garlic, crushed
1	1-pound can salt-free (or regular) tomatoes, chopped and drained slightly
1	1-pound can white kidney beans (cannellini), rinsed and drained (or 2 cups of cooked beans)
1	tablespoon lemon juice (preferably fresh)
1	teaspoon paprika
1/2	teaspoon fennel seeds, crushed slightly
1/4	teaspoon dried thyme
1/4	teaspoon *each* salt and pepper
1/2	cup dry white wine

Heat oil in a large nonstick skillet over medium heat. Add mushrooms, onion, bell pepper, carrots, and garlic. Cook, stirring frequently, 5 minutes.

Add remaining ingredients to skillet, mixing well. When mixture boils, reduce heat to medium-low, cover, and simmer 15 minutes.

Serve over any cooked grain.

Each serving provides:

137	Calories	21 g	Carbohydrate
7 g	Protein	203 mg	Sodium
3 g	Total fat (0 g sat. fat)	0 mg	Cholesterol

Bean-Stuffed Cabbage Rolls

Variations of this dish are made throughout Eastern Europe. Usually the filling consists of meat and rice, but in my version, based on a Polish recipe, the cabbage leaves are rolled around a filling of beans and rice, deliciously spiced with basil and oregano, then baked in an onion-filled tomato sauce. It can easily be made ahead and reheated, and actually tastes better that way.

Makes 6 servings

1	medium head of cabbage

Sauce:

1	12-ounce can salt-free (or regular) tomato sauce
1	6-ounce can tomato paste
1	cup finely chopped onion
2	cloves garlic, crushed
2	teaspoons sugar
1	teaspoon dried oregano
1/2	teaspoon dried basil
1/4	teaspoon pepper

Filling:

1	1-pound can white beans (cannellini or Great Northern beans), rinsed and drained (or 2 cups of cooked beans)
1	cup finely chopped onion
1	cup cooked brown rice
1	teaspoon dried oregano
1/2	teaspoon dried basil
1/4	teaspoon salt
1/4	teaspoon pepper

Carefully remove 12 large outside leaves from the cabbage. Place leaves in a large pot of boiling water and boil 5 minutes. Remove leaves from water, place in a colander, and run under cold water for a few minutes. Drain.

To prepare sauce: combine all sauce ingredients in a small saucepan. Bring to a boil over medium heat. Reduce heat to medium-low, cover, and simmer 15 minutes.

To prepare filling: place beans in a large bowl. Mash slightly with a fork or potato masher. Add remaining filling ingredients and mix well.

To assemble: preheat oven to 350°.

Lightly oil a 9 x 13-inch baking pan or spray with a nonstick cooking spray.

Divide filling evenly and place each portion near the base of a cabbage leaf. Roll leaves up tightly, folding in the sides as you roll. Place rolls seam-side down in prepared pan. Spoon sauce evenly over rolls.

Cover tightly and bake 1 hour.

Each serving provides:

197	Calories	38 g	Carbohydrate
9 g	Protein	444 mg	Sodium
2 g	Total fat (0 g sat. fat)	0 mg	Cholesterol

Lima Beans and Mixed Vegetables

This simplified version of a rich, Romanian peasant-style stew seems to have some Mediterranean characteristics, reminding us that world cuisine is truly a melting pot of flavors. You can serve it with any cooked grain or simply pile it into a bowl and serve with a chunk of crusty, dark rye bread.

Makes 6 servings

1	teaspoon vegetable oil
1	cup chopped onion
1	cup chopped green bell pepper
2	cloves garlic, finely chopped
3	cups eggplant, peeled, and cut into 1/2-inch cubes
1	cup coarsely chopped mushrooms
1	large potato, unpeeled, cut into 1/2-inch pieces (9 ounces)
1	10-ounce package frozen lima beans
1	1-pound can salt-free (or regular) tomatoes, chopped, undrained
1/4	cup ketchup
1	teaspoon cider vinegar
1	teaspoon paprika
1	teaspoon dried oregano
1/4	teaspoon salt
1/4	teaspoon pepper

Heat oil in a large saucepan over medium heat. Add onion, bell pepper, and garlic. Cook, stirring frequently, 3 minutes. Add eggplant and mushrooms. Continue to cook, stirring frequently, 3 minutes more.

Add remaining ingredients to saucepan. Bring to a boil, stirring occasionally. Cover, reduce heat to medium-low, and simmer 35 to 40 minutes, until potatoes and lima beans are tender. Stir several times during cooking.

Each serving provides:

149	Calories	30 g	Carbohydrate
6 g	Protein	253 mg	Sodium
1 g	Total fat (0 g sat. fat)	0 mg	Cholesterol

Lemon-Dijon Cauliflower

In Poland, whole cauliflower is often boiled in a large pot and then topped with lots of sour cream. This is my updated version of an old Polish recipe. I love to serve it to guests and I've prepared it in many cooking classes. It's easy to do, makes a beautiful presentation, and has a wonderful flavor.

Makes 6 servings

1	medium head cauliflower
1/2	cup plain nonfat yogurt
1	tablespoon Dijon mustard
1/2	tablespoon lemon juice
1/2	teaspoon grated fresh lemon peel
1	large clove garlic, crushed
2	teaspoons finely chopped fresh chives (or 1 teaspoon dried chives)
	Salt and freshly ground pepper to taste

Trim leaves from cauliflower and leave it whole. Place a steamer rack in the bottom of a saucepan just large enough to hold the cauliflower. Add enough water to come almost up to the bottom of the rack. Place saucepan over medium heat. When water boils, place cauliflower on rack, cover saucepan, and steam for 10 minutes or until cauliflower is just tender-crisp.

While cauliflower is cooking, combine yogurt, mustard, lemon juice, lemon peel, and garlic. Mix well.

Place cooked cauliflower in a large serving bowl, preferably one that is close to the size of the cauliflower. Spoon yogurt mixture over top of cauliflower. Sprinkle with chives, salt to taste, and lots of freshly ground pepper.

Each serving provides:

29	Calories	5 g	Carbohydrate
2 g	Protein	99 mg	Sodium
0 g	Total fat (0 g sat. fat)	0 mg	Cholesterol

Sherried Carrot Pudding

This is my adaptation of a delicious Czechoslovakian recipe that was shared with me by my close friend and fellow-cooking teacher, Pat Tabibian. The wonderful, mellow flavor is heightened by the richness of the sherry, and there's hardly an entrée that would not be enhanced by this delicious dish.

Makes 4 servings

1	pound carrots, sliced crosswise into 1/2-inch slices
2	teaspoons vegetable oil
1	cup finely chopped onion
1	tablespoon sugar
1	tablespoon water
1	tablespoon all-purpose flour
1	cup skim milk
1/4	teaspoon salt
1/16	teaspoon pepper
1/16	teaspoon ground nutmeg
2	tablespoons dry sherry
1	tablespoon dry bread crumbs
	Nonstick cooking spray

Place a steamer rack in the bottom of a medium saucepan. Add enough water to come almost up to the bottom of the rack. Place saucepan over medium heat. When water boils, add carrots, cover saucepan, and cook 12 minutes or until carrots are tender. Drain.

Preheat oven to 350°.

Lightly oil a 1-quart baking dish or spray with a nonstick cooking spray.

Place drained carrots in a food processor. Using the steel blade, process until carrots are puréed. Set aside.

Heat oil in a medium nonstick skillet over medium heat. Add onion. Cook, stirring frequently, until onion is golden, about 5 to 8 minutes. Stir in sugar and water, and then flour. Gradually stir in milk. Continue to cook, stirring constantly, until mixture has thickened slightly, about 5 minutes. Remove from heat.

Stir salt, pepper, nutmeg, and sherry into onion mixture. Add carrots and mix well. Spoon mixture into prepared pan and sprinkle with bread crumbs. Spray the top of the pudding lightly with cooking spray.

Bake uncovered, 35 minutes.

Serve hot.

Each serving provides:

155	Calories	25 g	Carbohydrate
4 g	Protein	223 mg	Sodium
4 g	Total fat (1 g sat. fat)	1 mg	Cholesterol

Apricot Noodle Kugel

One thing most kugels have in common is large amounts of high-fat ingredients. In this version I've replaced the "culprits" with orange juice, egg whites, and apricot jam.

Makes 9 servings

6	ounces fine noodles (yolk-free), uncooked (3 cups)
1/2	cup fruit-only apricot jam
1/2	cup orange juice
4	egg whites
1	teaspoon vanilla extract
1/2	teaspoon almond extract
1/3	cup raisins or chopped dried apricots

Topping:

2	teaspoons sugar
1/4	teaspoon ground cinnamon

Cook noodles according to package directions. Drain and let cool for about 10 minutes.

Preheat oven to 350°.

Lightly oil an 8-inch square baking pan or spray with a nonstick cooking spray.

In a large bowl, combine jam, orange juice, egg whites, and extracts. Beat with a fork or wire whisk until blended. Stir in raisins. Add noodles and mix well. Spoon mixture into prepared pan. Press the noodles down gently with the back of a spoon.

Combine sugar and cinnamon and sprinkle evenly over the top of the kugel.

Cover tightly and bake 15 minutes. Uncover and continue to bake 20 minutes more, until kugel is set.

Let stand for 20 minutes before serving. Cut into squares to serve.

Each serving provides:

144	Calories	30 g	Carbohydrate
4 g	Protein	29 mg	Sodium
1 g	Total fat (0 g sat. fat)	0 mg	Cholesterol

Mushrooms in Creamy Wine Sauce

This type of dish is popular all over Eastern Europe where mushrooms are one of the favorite vegetables. Sometimes it's served as a side dish and other-times it's spooned over a grain or even bits of torn bread and served as an en-trée. (My family loves it spooned over baked potatoes.)

Makes 6 servings

2	teaspoons vegetable oil
1	pound mushrooms, cut into quarters
1/2	cup thinly sliced green onions (green and white parts)
2	tablespoons all-purpose flour
1	teaspoon *Vegetable Broth Mix* (See page 27.)
1/8	teaspoon ground nutmeg
1/8	teaspoon pepper
	Salt to taste
3/4	cup skim milk
2	tablespoons dry white wine
	Paprika

Heat oil in a large nonstick skillet over medium heat. Add mushrooms and green onions. Cook, stirring frequently, 4 minutes. Sprinkle with flour, broth mix, nutmeg, pepper, and salt. Stir into mushrooms and onions.

Stir in milk and then wine. Continue to cook and stir for 2 minutes. Spoon into a serving dish and sprinkle with paprika.

Each serving provides:

60	Calories	8 g	Carbohydrate
3 g	Protein	34 mg	Sodium
2 g	Total fat (0 g sat. fat)	1 mg	Cholesterol

Potato and Carrot Pancakes *(Latkes)*

This is a variation of the traditional Russian potato pancakes, or latkes. *My version adds carrots, which give the pancakes an ever-so-delicate sweetness. The pancakes are usually topped with applesauce, and in most Russian households, are considered a special treat.*

Makes 4 servings
(3 pancakes each serving)

1¹/₂   cups finely shredded potatoes, unpeeled
1¹/₂   cups finely shredded carrots
3   tablespoons grated onion
¹/₄   cup plus ¹/₂ tablespoon whole wheat flour
¹/₂   teaspoon salt
¹/₈   to ¹/₄ teaspoon pepper

Place shredded potatoes in a large strainer and let them drain while you shred the carrots. Then press out any remaining potato liquid with the back of a spoon and place potatoes in a large bowl. Add carrots, along with remaining ingredients, mixing for several minutes to make sure that ingredients are thoroughly combined.

Preheat a large nonstick skillet or griddle over medium heat. Oil it lightly or spray with a nonstick cooking spray.

Using 3 tablespoonfuls of mixture for each pancake, shape into patties ¹/₄- to ¹/₂-inch thick. Place patties on griddle and cook, turning each one several times, until both sides are nicely browned. Spray the pancakes lightly with a nonstick spray if they begin to stick or get too dry.

Each serving provides:

180	Calories	34 g	Carbohydrate
4 g	Protein	225 mg	Sodium
4 g	Total fat (0 g sat. fat)	0 mg	Cholesterol

Root Vegetables with Lemon-Dill Glaze

This Romanian dish shows just how tasty the often-neglected root vegetables can be. The important thing to remember here is to cut the vegetables into uniform pieces so they will cook for the same amount of time.

Makes 6 servings

2   cups *each* carrots and parsnips, cut crosswise into 1/2-inch slices
2   cups turnips, peeled and cut into 1/2- to 1-inch pieces
1   medium onion, cut vertically into 6 wedges (Leave the root ends intact to keep onion wedges from falling apart.)
1/3   cup water
2   tablespoons honey
2   teaspoons cornstarch
1   teaspoon *each* grated fresh lemon peel and dill weed
1/4   teaspoon salt
1/8   teaspoon pepper

Place a steamer basket or rack in the bottom of a large saucepan and add enough water to come almost up to the bottom of the basket. Bring to a boil over medium heat. Add carrots, parsnips, turnips, and onion. Cover and cook 10 minutes or until vegetables are just tender.

Combine remaining ingredients in a small bowl. Mix until cornstarch is dissolved.

Remove vegetables, discard water, and return vegetables to saucepan (without steamer basket) over medium heat. Stir cornstarch mixture and pour over vegetables. Cook and stir until glaze has thickened and vegetables are coated, about 1 minute.

Each serving provides:

97	Calories	24 g	Carbohydrate
2 g	Protein	138 mg	Sodium
0 g	Total fat (0 g sat. fat)	0 mg	Cholesterol

Corn in Creamy Dill Sauce

The original version of this Russian dish was made with sour cream and topped with lots of cheese and butter. The only challenge I found with baking the corn in yogurt instead of sour cream, was that often the nonfat yogurt separates while cooking. That's why it's important to drain the corn well and to stir the mixture before adding the cheese. The flavor is superb.

Makes 4 servings

1/2	cup plain nonfat yogurt
1 1/2	teaspoons cornstarch
1	teaspoon dill weed
1/8	teaspoon salt
1/16	teaspoon pepper
1	12-ounce can salt-free (or regular) corn, or one 10-ounce package frozen corn, thawed and drained well (Spread the corn on a towel to drain.)
1/3	cup shredded reduced-fat Cheddar cheese (1 1/2 ounces)

Preheat oven to 375°.

Lightly oil a 1-quart baking dish or spray with a nonstick cooking spray.

In a small bowl, combine yogurt, cornstarch, dill weed, salt, and pepper. Mix well. Stir in corn. Place mixture in prepared pan.

Bake uncovered, 20 minutes or until hot and bubbly. Remove from oven and mix well, stirring until yogurt is smooth. Spread cheese evenly over corn.

Return to oven and bake 5 minutes more or until cheese is melted.

Each serving provides:

116	Calories	16 g	Carbohydrate
6 g	Protein	169 mg	Sodium
3 g	Total fat (1 g sat. fat)	8 mg	Cholesterol

Kasha with Onions and Potatoes

Besides borscht, *hardly any food is more Russian than* kasha *(buckwheat groats). It's a filling, high-fiber grain that really sticks to your ribs. Most people simmer kasha on the stovetop, however, the traditional Russian cooking method is baking. (Look for kasha in the grain section of most large grocery stores and if there are different sizes (granulation) available, choose medium.)*

Makes 8 servings

1	cup kasha, uncooked
1/2	teaspoon salt
1/4	teaspoon pepper
1	teaspoon vegetable oil
1 1/2	cups finely chopped onion
1	medium potato, baked or boiled, cut into 1/4- to 1/2-inch cubes (1 heaping cup)
3	cups boiling water

Preheat oven to 350°.

Lightly oil a 2-quart casserole or spray with a nonstick cooking spray.

Heat a large nonstick skillet over medium heat. Add kasha. Stir frequently, until kasha is lightly toasted and fragrant, about 5 minutes. Remove from heat and place kasha in prepared casserole. Stir in salt and pepper.

Return skillet to heat and add oil. Add onion and cook, stirring frequently, 3 minutes. Add potato. Cook, stirring frequently, until onion and potato are nicely browned, about 8 minutes. (The best flavor is achieved when the onion and potato are very brown and crisp, but be careful not to let them burn.)

Stir boiling water into kasha. Then add onion and potato. Mix well. Cover and bake 20 minutes.

Fluff with a fork before serving.

Each serving provides:			
132	Calories	27 g	Carbohydrate
4 g	Protein	141 mg	Sodium
2 g	Total fat (0 g sat. fat)	0 mg	Cholesterol

Spiced Peaches and Dumplings

My good friend and fellow food lover, Ema Robinson, gave me this delicious recipe. The tender, spiced dumplings are steamed on top of fresh fruit, rather than baking the dish the way it is usually done in our country. This dessert is just one illustration of the Eastern Europeans' love for dumplings. (Fresh nectarines will also work, and in a pinch, frozen, unsweetened fruit will do.)

Makes 8 servings

Topping:
2   teaspoons sugar
1/4   teaspoon ground cinnamon

Dumplings:
2/3   cup all-purpose flour
2/3   cup whole wheat flour
2   teaspoons baking powder
1/4   teaspoon ground cinnamon
1/4   teaspoon ground nutmeg
1/4   teaspoon ground ginger
1/8   teaspoon salt
2   tablespoons vegetable oil
3/4   cup skim milk
1/4   cup firmly packed brown sugar
1   teaspoon vanilla extract

Fruit:
6   large, ripe peaches, peeled and thinly sliced (6 cups)
1/4   cup water
1/4   cup firmly packed brown sugar
1 1/2   tablespoons lemon juice

To prepare topping: combine sugar and cinnamon in a small bowl or custard cup. Set aside.

To prepare dumplings: into a large bowl, sift both types of flour, baking powder, spices, and salt. Add oil. Mix with a fork or pastry blender until mixture resembles coarse crumbs. In a small bowl, combine remaining dumpling ingredients. Add to dry mixture, mixing just until all ingredients are moistened. Set aside.

To prepare fruit: choose either a saucepan that measures 9 or 10 inches across the top, or a 9- or 10-inch heavy skillet (not a shallow omelet skillet). Add all fruit ingredients. Bring to a boil over medium heat stirring frequently. Drop the dumpling batter by heaping table-spoonfuls onto peaches. Sprinkle evenly with topping. Cover, reduce heat to medium-low, and simmer 18 minutes or until the dumplings are firm.

Serve hot.

	Each serving provides:		
225	Calories	46 g	Carbohydrate
4 g	Protein	175 mg	Sodium
4 g	Total fat (1 g sat. fat)	0 mg	Cholesterol

Cranberry-Raisin Strudel

My Mom and I "reconstructed" this recipe based on her memories of a dessert her mother used to make. Of course we updated it a bit from the original Russian version, but the result is a truly elegant and delicious affair.

Makes 8 servings

1	cup whole-berry cranberry sauce
1/4	cup raisins
1	tablespoon *each* sugar and cornstarch
1/2	teaspoon almond extract
6	sheets of filo dough
	Nonstick cooking spray
3	tablespoons dry bread crumbs
	Ground cinnamon
1	teaspoon confectioners sugar

In a small saucepan, combine cranberry sauce, raisins, sugar, cornstarch, and almond extract. Bring to a boil over medium heat, stirring constantly. Continue to cook and stir for 1 minute. Remove from heat and let cool to room temperature.

Preheat oven to 375°.

Lightly oil a baking sheet or spray with nonstick cooking spray.

Place the filo sheets in a stack on the counter and top with wax paper or plastic wrap and then a damp towel to keep them from drying out.

Place 2 filo sheets on a kitchen towel. Spray them lightly and evenly with cooking spray. Place 2 more sheets on top and spray them. Repeat with remaining 2 sheets. Reserve 1 teaspoon of the bread crumbs and sprinkle remaining crumbs on filo, staying 2 inches away from all edges. Mound the cranberry mixture in a strip along one of the narrow edges, leaving a 2-inch border on all of the edges.

Starting from the narrow end, lift towel, using it to roll the dough over the filling jellyroll-style. After the first turn, when filling is covered, fold in long edges of filo. Spray strudel lightly after each turn. Spray top of strudel with cooking spray and sprinkle with reserved bread crumbs. Sprinkle lightly with cinnamon.

Place strudel on prepared baking sheet. Lightly score the top, marking 8 slices, only cutting through 1 or 2 layers and taking care not to cut through to the filling. (This will make the finished strudel easier to cut.)

Bake 20 minutes, until brown and crisp.

Remove strudel to a serving plate. Using a serrated knife, cut into 8 slices, but do not separate the slices. (It's important to cut the strudel right away as the crust will crumble if you wait until it cools.) Sprinkle the top with confectioners sugar and serve warm. (An easy way to sprinkle sugar evenly is to place it in a small strainer and shake it over the strudel.)

Each serving provides:

141	Calories	29 g	Carbohydrate
2 g	Protein	101 mg	Sodium
2 g	Total fat (0 g sat. fat)	0 mg	Cholesterol

Apple Charlotte

Baked Apple Charlotte is an old dessert with roots from many national cuisines. This version is similar to the one my grandmother used to make with leftover bread or coffee cake. It's a warm, homey dessert that's really a comfort food, yet it looks so elegant. The light yogurt topping can also be spooned over other desserts or fruits.

Makes 8 servings

Topping:
1	cup plain nonfat yogurt
3	tablespoons confectioners sugar
1	teaspoon vanilla extract
1/4	teaspoon almond extract

Apple Filling:
6	large, sweet apples (such as Golden Delicious), peeled and cut into 1/8-inch slices
1/3	cup sugar
1	tablespoon lemon juice
1	tablespoon water
1 1/2	teaspoons vanilla extract
1 1/2	teaspoons ground cinnamon
1	tablespoon cornstarch dissolved in 1/2 cup water

Crust:
6	slices whole wheat bread (preferably stale*)
1/2	cup skim milk
1/2	teaspoon vanilla extract
2 1/2	teaspoons sugar
1/4	teaspoon ground cinnamon

Preheat oven to 350°.

Lightly oil a 1 1/2-quart ovenproof bowl or spray with a nonstick cooking spray.

To prepare topping: combine all topping ingredients in a small bowl and mix well. Chill until needed.

To prepare apple filling: place apples in a large nonstick skillet. Add sugar, lemon juice, water, vanilla, and cinnamon. Cook over

---

* If bread is fresh, place on wire racks on the kitchen counter for a few hours before using or toast it lightly and let it cool to room temperature.

medium heat until apples start to sizzle. Cover, reduce heat to medium-low, and cook, stirring occasionally, 10 minutes or until apples are slightly tender. Combine water and cornstarch, stirring to dissolve cornstarch. Add to apples. Cook, stirring constantly, 2 to 3 minutes, until cornstarch has thickened. Remove from heat.

To prepare crust: cut each slice of bread into three strips. Combine milk and vanilla in a small bowl and quickly dip each slice of bread into the milk, just lightly touching each side of the bread to the milk. Place bread in a pan or on a piece of wax paper.

Combine sugar and cinnamon in a small bowl or custard cup. Mix well and sprinkle evenly on one side of the bread strips (about $1/8$ teaspoon on each strip).

To assemble: place two bread strips sugared side down in bottom of prepared bowl. Arrange remaining strips vertically, overlapping slightly around edge of bowl. Be sure the sugared sides are against the bowl.

Pile apples into crust, packing them down tightly. Pour any remaining liquid over the apples. Cover tightly with aluminum foil.

Bake 40 minutes.

Cool at least 1 hour, then invert onto a platter. Serve warm and pass the yogurt topping. (If you prefer to serve the Charlotte cold, it can be chilled in the bowl and inverted just before serving.)

Each serving provides:

201	Calories	43 g	Carbohydrate
4 g	Protein	142 mg	Sodium
2 g	Total fat (0 g sat. fat)	1 mg	Cholesterol

Honey Spice Cake

Patterned after an old Russian favorite, this egg-free cake was "updated" by my Mom.

Makes 8 servings

1	cup whole wheat flour
1/2	cup oat bran, uncooked
1	teaspoon *each* baking powder and baking soda
1/16	teaspoon salt
1/2	teaspoon ground nutmeg
1/4	teaspoon ground cloves
1/4	cup raisins
2	tablespoons chopped walnuts
1/2	cup honey
1/2	cup unsweetened applesauce
1/2	cup orange juice
1	tablespoon plus 1 teaspoon vegetable oil

Preheat oven to 350°.

Lightly oil a 5 x 9-inch loaf pan or spray with a nonstick cooking spray.

In a large bowl, combine flour, oat bran, baking powder, baking soda, salt, and spices. Mix well. Stir in raisins and walnuts.

In a small bowl, combine remaining ingredients. Beat with a fork or wire whisk until blended. Add to dry mixture, mixing just until all ingredients are moistened. Place mixture in prepared pan.

Bake 30 to 35 minutes. Cool in pan on a wire rack for 5 minutes, then turn out onto rack to finish cooling.

For best flavor, wrap cooled cake tightly and let it sit at room temperature overnight.

Each serving provides:

195	Calories	40 g	Carbohydrate
4 g	Protein	238 mg	Sodium
5 g	Total fat (1 g sat. fat)	0 mg	Cholesterol

Meringue-Topped Apples with Gingersnaps

Based on a Hungarian recipe, my easy version, served warm or cold, is truly an apple-lover's delight.

Makes 8 servings

6   medium, Golden Delicious apples, peeled and coarsely shredded
1/3   cup firmly packed brown sugar
1/3   cup raisins
1   tablespoon lemon juice
2   teaspoons grated fresh lemon peel
2   teaspoons *each* vanilla extract and ground cinnamon
1 1/4 cups broken gingersnap cookies, in small pieces (about 12 cookies)

Meringue Topping:
2   egg whites
1/4   teaspoon cream of tartar
3   tablespoons sugar
1/2   teaspoon vanilla extract

Preheat oven to 350°.

Have an ungreased 10-inch pie pan or 9-inch square pan ready.

In a large bowl, combine apples, brown sugar, raisins, lemon juice, lemon peel, vanilla, and cinnamon. Mix well.

Arrange cookies in bottom of pan. Spoon apple mixture over cookies. Press down lightly with the back of a spoon. Cover tightly with foil and bake 45 minutes. Remove from oven and uncover.

To prepare topping: place egg whites in a large, deep bowl and beat on medium speed of an electric mixer until frothy. Add cream of tartar and beat on high speed until egg whites are stiff. Gradually beat in sugar and then vanilla. Drop meringue by spoonfuls on top of apples and spread with a table knife. Be sure the meringue touches all edges of the pan, completely sealing in the apples.

Return pan to oven and bake 12 minutes, until meringue is golden brown. Let cool at least 30 minutes before serving.

Each serving provides:

180	Calories	42 g	Carbohydrate
2 g	Protein	87 mg	Sodium
1 g	Total fat (0 g sat. fat)	0 mg	Cholesterol

Russian Oat and Rice Pudding

My grandmother often made this sweet pudding when I was a child. I've made a few minor changes, but the flavor remains the same.

Makes 12 servings

Pudding:

2^1/$_2$ cups water
1^1/$_3$ cups rolled oats
2   cups cooked brown rice
1   cup skim milk
^{1}/$_2$ cup firmly packed brown sugar
^{1}/$_2$ cup raisins
1   tablespoon plus 1 teaspoon vanilla extract
^{1}/$_4$ teaspoon salt

Topping:

2   teaspoons sugar
^{1}/$_2$ teaspoon ground cinnamon

Preheat oven to 350°.

Lightly oil an 8-inch square baking pan or spray with a nonstick cooking spray.

Bring water to a boil in a medium saucepan over medium-high heat. Add oats. When oats start to boil reduce heat to medium-low and cook, stirring frequently, 5 minutes. Remove from heat.

Add remaining pudding ingredients and mix well. Spoon mixture into prepared pan.

Combine sugar and cinnamon in a small bowl. Mix well and sprinkle evenly over pudding.

Bake uncovered, 25 minutes. Let stand 10 minutes before serving.

Serve warm. Refrigerate leftovers and serve cold or reheat briefly in a microwave.

Each serving provides:

142	Calories	29 g	Carbohydrate
3 g	Protein	62 mg	Sodium
1 g	Total fat (0 g sat. fat)	0 mg	Cholesterol

Creamy Rhubarb Pudding

In Eastern European desserts, rhubarb is often mixed with whipped cream, which helps to mellow the taste, however I've used evaporated skim milk instead and the result is sweet and creamy.

Makes 9 servings

6	cups rhubarb, cut into 1-inch pieces, leaves discarded (about 2 pounds) (the leaves are toxic)
3/4	cup sugar
1/4	cup water
1	teaspoon grated fresh orange peel
1/2	teaspoon ground cinnamon
1	cup evaporated skim milk
2	tablespoons cornstarch
1	teaspoon vanilla extract
1/2	teaspoon almond extract
9	2 1/2-inch graham cracker squares
2	tablespoons graham cracker crumbs

Have an 8-inch square pan ready.

In a medium saucepan, combine rhubarb, sugar, water, orange peel, and cinnamon. Bring to a boil over medium heat, stirring occasionally. Cover and cook about 5 minutes, until rhubarb is just tender.

In a small bowl, combine evaporated milk, cornstarch, and extracts. Stir to dissolve cornstarch. When rhubarb is tender, gradually stir 1/2 cup of the hot rhubarb mixture into the milk, then stir it all back into the saucepan. Bring mixture to a boil and continue to cook, stirring constantly, 3 minutes. Remove from heat.

Arrange the graham crackers in a single layer in the bottom of the pan and top with pudding. Sprinkle evenly with the crumbs and chill. Serve cold.

Each serving provides:

150	Calories	32 g	Carbohydrate
3 g	Protein	89 mg	Sodium
1 g	Total fat (0 g sat. fat)	1 mg	Cholesterol

Cranberry Fruit Pudding

The Russian name for this pudding is kisel. *It's an old traditional dessert that can be made with a variety of puréed fruits and is usually on the tart side. To mellow the tartness, it's often served with cream on top, but I found that vanilla nonfat yogurt does the trick.*

Makes 6 servings

3	cups cranberries
1 1/2	cups water
2/3	cup sugar
2	tablespoons cornstarch
2	tablespoons orange juice
	Vanilla nonfat yogurt (optional)

Place cranberries and water in a medium saucepan. Bring to a boil over medium heat. Reduce heat to medium-low and simmer uncovered, 15 minutes.

Press cranberries through a strainer into a bowl. Discard skin and seeds. Return cranberry mixture to saucepan. Stir in sugar.

Combine cornstarch and orange juice in a small bowl or custard cup, stirring to dissolve cornstarch. Stir into cranberry mixture. Bring to a boil over medium heat, stirring constantly. Continue to cook and stir for 2 minutes.

Divide mixture evenly into six custard cups or small bowls. Chill.

Serve cold, by itself or topped with vanilla nonfat yogurt.

Each serving provides:			
126	Calories	32 g	Carbohydrate
0 g	Protein	1 mg	Sodium
0 g	Total fat (0 g sat. fat)	0 mg	Cholesterol

Mixed Berries Romanov

The traditional version of this simple, delectable Russian dish, is made by marinating fresh berries in a fruit-flavored liqueur (usually orange) for about an hour and then topping them with whipped cream. I've used orange juice for the marinating liquid and vanilla yogurt for the topping and guess what? It's still delectable!

Makes 4 servings

1¹/2 cups fresh strawberries, cut in half, or quartered if the berries are very large (Measure the berries *after* cutting them.)

1 cup blueberries (Blueberries may be fresh or frozen. If using frozen berries, thaw them first.)

2 tablespoons sugar (or more, depending on the sweetness of the berries)

2 tablespoons orange juice

1/8 teaspoon orange extract, *or* 1 tablespoon orange-flavored liqueur

1 cup vanilla nonfat yogurt

Place strawberries and blueberries in a medium bowl. Sprinkle with sugar and toss gently.

Combine orange juice and orange extract (or liqueur). Spoon over berries and toss again. Let berries sit at room temperature for 1 hour, mixing occasionally.

Divide berries and juice evenly into four individual serving bowls. Top each serving with 1/4 cup of yogurt.

Serve right away.

Each serving provides:

116	Calories	26 g	Carbohydrate
4 g	Protein	43 mg	Sodium
0 g	Total fat (0 g sat. fat)	2 mg	Cholesterol

Dried Fruit Compote

Dried fruit compotes are popular in almost all of Eastern Europe. In rural homes fresh summer fruits are often gathered and hung to dry in preparation for this cold-weather specialty. The compotes are made with whatever fruits are available, and often a few tablespoons of brandy are added to the finished dish.

Makes 6 servings

1/2	cup dried apricot halves
1/2	cup pitted prunes
1/2	cup raisins
3	cups water
1/4	cup sugar
1	2 1/2-inch cinnamon stick
1	tablespoon lemon juice
	A pinch of ground allspice
1/4	teaspoon orange extract

In a medium saucepan, combine all ingredients, *except* orange extract. Bring to a boil over medium heat. Reduce heat to medium-low and simmer uncovered, 20 minutes.

Remove and discard cinnamon stick.

Stir in orange extract.

Serve warm or cold.

Each serving provides:

128	Calories		33 g	Carbohydrate
1 g	Protein		4 mg	Sodium
0 g	Total fat (0 g sat. fat)		0 mg	Cholesterol

Flavors of India

The exotic cuisine of India has a culinary style that has evolved for several thousand years and is based on the many different racial, religious, and regional differences found throughout the country. Predominant in India, Hindus are for the most part, vegetarians. This vegetarianism has given rise to a wonderful variety of legume- and vegetable-based dishes that are at the heart of Indian cuisine.

Grains are a very important part of Indian meals. Wheat dishes, featuring cracked wheat, breads, and farina, are popular in the North of India, while rice dishes are more predominant in the South. In each region, these grains are usually prepared with butter, along with added meats, vegetables, dried beans, or eggs. Often rice is served as the center of the meal. It is either served plain or cooked with seasonings, vegetables, fruits, nuts, or beans. The rice is then surrounded by many other foods, such as a curry, a yogurt salad, chutney, pickles or salad, and perhaps some homemade cheese. (See *Cooking Rice—Indian Style* on page 347.)

While to many people Indian food is synonymous with curry, few people realize that there is not an actual spice called "curry." Rather, it is a blend of numerous spices. A typical curry blend might include cumin, coriander, cinnamon, cloves, cardamom, ginger, chili peppers, fenugreek, and pepper. Indian women use a mortar and pestle to grind their own spices daily, making their own blend, known as *garam masala*. Pronounced ga-RAHM ma-SAH-lah, this simply means a blend of spices. I have substituted commercial curry powder in my recipes, so it is important to buy a good brand, preferably an Indian curry powder. Other frequently used seasonings include garlic and ginger root. Green and red bell peppers, ranging from mild to hot, are added in one form or another to almost every dish. Fresh cilantro is also frequently used, often added at the end of cooking. If you like the delicious, almost musty flavor of cilantro, feel free to add it to most dishes.

Note: I found that in preparing Indian dishes, it is extremely important—actually necessary—to have all of the spices measured and ready *before* starting to cook. This saves a lot of frantic measuring when different spices need to be added quickly.

Dried peas and beans, known as *dal* (DAHL), are an important part of the Indian culinary tradition. Some form of bean dish is served at almost every meal, even those of nonvegetarians. The types of beans that are most commonly used are black-eyed peas, chick peas, kidney beans, lentils, mung beans, and split peas. There are also others such as aduki beans and kala chanas that are less familiar to us, but available in specialty stores.

Indian breads are very unique. Probably the most popular is *chapati*, a tortillalike flat bread that is often broken into pieces and used as we would use a fork or spoon. *Papadams* are another unusual bread. They are thin, spicy wafers that are made from lentil flour. Both breads are available in specialty stores and are well worth the trip.

No Indian meal is complete without sweets. Puddings are very common. Made from fruits, vegetables, nuts, and/or grains, they are often spiced with cinnamon, coriander, or saffron, and are often garnished with an edible, tissue-thin trim of silver leaf. Fresh fruits are also often used for dessert. Typical choices are mangos, lichees, bananas, pineapples, guavas, and melons.

Adapting Indian cuisine to lowfat, meatless meals was relatively easy due to the widespread use of fruits, vegetables, and beans. The real challenges were in eliminating the large quantities of butter often used and in creating spice blends that did not entail frequent visits to specialty stores. I also adapted the cooking methods for some of the recipes since many foods are deep-fried and ovens as we know them are not typically used in Indian households. Most cooking is done on a wood-burning or charcoal-burning stove that is similar to a small barbecue pit. Foods are typically fried or sautéed, and even breads are baked on pans on top of these stoves. Many Indian dishes are very highly spiced and in adapting the foods to American tastes I eliminated some of the "heat." If you like spicier foods, feel free to add a chopped jalapeño or some cayenne pepper to any dish. The popular curries and rice dishes are here, along with many other adapted versions of authentic Indian cuisine.

Enjoy your tour of India!

Cooking Rice—Indian Style

Rice has been a staple of Indian cuisine for thousands of years, especially in the southern and eastern regions where many varieties are cultivated. By far the rice of choice for Indian dishes is *basmati* rice. It has a special, nutty aroma and delicate flavor that is a perfect complement to spicy Indian foods. Basmati rice is readily available at health food stores, specialty stores, and many large grocery stores and is well worth the trip. If you wish to substitute any other type of rice, simply adjust the cooking times and amounts of water according to the type of rice used and follow the individual package directions. The spices can remain the same.

Two other varieties of aromatic rice that are becoming widely available are *Texmati,* which is a blend of basmati and white long grain rice, and *brown basmati* which is basmati rice that has not been milled to remove the nutritious bran. Like brown rice, brown basmati needs to cook longer, and while it does not taste exactly like white basmati, it is still aromatic and delicious. Neither of these varieties need to be washed or soaked as described below. (Most of the recipes in this section have been adapted for use with long grain brown rice, which is high in fiber and readily available in health food stores and grocery stores.)

Preparing Basmati Rice

This process will yield fluffy, tender rice:

Wash rice Place the uncooked rice in a bowl and cover with cold water. Swish the rice around and pour off the water. Repeat this process several times until the water runs clear. Drain rice. This process removes the surface starch that would make the cooked rice sticky.

Soak rice (optional)   Soak the washed rice in enough water to cover the rice by one inch for 15 to 30 minutes. This soaking process allows the rice to begin to absorb the water and to expand slightly. Drain rice, reserving the soaking water for cooking. (Indian cooks maintain that this step is essential to the quality of the finished dish, however, for the sake of time, I often eliminate it. I find the difference to be very small, so you may want to try it both ways and decide for yourself.)

Basic cooking directions In a saucepan, place a scant 2 cups of water (start with the soaking water, if you soaked the rice, and add to it if needed) and 1/4 teaspoon of vegetable oil for each cup of uncooked rice. (The oil helps to keep the grains separate.) Bring to a boil over medium heat. Stir in the soaked rice. When water boils again, reduce heat to medium-low, cover saucepan, and simmer gently for 15 to 20 minutes or until the water has been absorbed. Remove from heat.

Some basic rules
- Adjust the cooking heat so the rice is kept at a very low simmer.
- Do not remove the lid during cooking.
- If rice is ready before the rest of the meal, set it aside covered, for up to 25 minutes.
- Fluff rice with a fork just before serving.

Flavors of India
Recipes

Suggested Menus

Lunch

Split Pea and Vegetable Soup (359)   Melon Half
Vegetable Rice Fritters (356)   Samosas (354)
Spiced Tomato Chutney (370)   Curried Cole Slaw (363)
Sliced Tomatoes and Cucumbers   Orange Rice Salad (366)
Curry-Lime Fruit Salad (365)   Dried Fruit Candy Balls (401)

Tossed Salad
Mixed Bean Salad (364)
Bread or Rolls
Pineapple-Raisin Rice Pudding (397)

Dinner

Tossed Salad   Herbed Bombay Tomato Soup (358)
Spicy Yellow Dal (374)   Tandoori Tofu (378)
Cracked Wheat and   Bombay Rice and Peas (392)
Pumpkin Pilaf (389)   Steamed Green Beans
Steamed Green Beans   Fragrant Apples (400)
Curried Fruit Compote (399)

Golden Butternut Soup (357)   Marinated Melon Platter (351)
Sliced Tomatoes   Curried Chick Peas (373)
Cucumber and Tomato Raita (367)   Minted Rice (391)
Sweet Spiced Lentils   Steamed Cauliflower
and Tomatoes (375)   and Broccoli
Brown Rice   Cheese Pudding with
Carrot Cake with Pistachios (394)   Raisins and Almonds (396)

Recipe page numbers appear in parentheses.

Marinated Melon Platter

Alternate slices of cantaloupe and honeydew, marinated in fruit juices with subtle spices, make a beautiful display. The two melons end up with enticingly different flavors, adding interest to the dish. (You will need small plates for this dish. It's too "drippy" to be finger food.)

Makes 8 servings

1/2	medium, ripe honeydew melon, cut in half crosswise
1/2	medium, ripe cantaloupe (Try to choose melons that are fairly close to the same size.)
3	tablespoons honey
2 1/2	tablespoons lime juice
2 1/2	tablespoons orange juice
1/4	teaspoon ground cardamom
1/8	teaspoon ground ginger
1	teaspoon almond extract

Have a 14-inch round cake plate or platter with raised edges ready. (If you wish, you can use two 9-inch pie pans instead.)

Peel the melon halves and remove the seeds. Slice each half into slices 1/8-inch thick. Then cut each slice in half making half-circles. Arrange slices, alternating about 5 slices of cantaloupe, then 5 slices of honeydew, and so on, in a circular pattern around the platter. Fill in the center of the platter with additional slices or a garnish of greens with orange and lime slices.

In a small bowl, combine remaining ingredients. Mix until honey is incorporated into the liquid. Spoon evenly over fruit slices.

Cover and chill 4 to 6 hours before serving. (Longer may result in soggy fruit.)

Each serving provides:

53	Calories	13 g	Carbohydrate
1 g	Protein	7 mg	Sodium
0 g	Total fat (0 g sat. fat)	0 mg	Cholesterol

Savory Potato Patties

In India, patties such as these are traditionally shaped into balls and deep-fried. They appear either as an appetizer, a snack, or a side dish and are often served with a tomato-based chutney such as Spiced Tomato Chutney *(page 370). If you plan to serve them as a side dish, you may want to make them a little larger—just for ease.*

Makes 6 servings
(3 patties each serving)

1	pound potatoes, unpeeled, cut into large chunks (2 medium potatoes)
3	tablespoons skim milk
1	teaspoon vegetable oil
1	cup finely chopped onion
3	cloves garlic, crushed
1/2	teaspoon curry powder
1/4	teaspoon ground ginger
1/4	teaspoon turmeric
1/4	teaspoon ground coriander
3/4	teaspoon salt
1/8	to 1/4 teaspoon pepper
1	egg white
3	tablespoons water
3/4	cup wheat germ *or* dry bread crumbs

Place potatoes in 2 inches of boiling water in a medium saucepan. Cover and cook 15 to 20 minutes, until tender. Drain. When potatoes are cool enough to handle, remove skin and place potatoes in a large bowl. Add milk. Mash with a fork or potato masher until smooth.

While potatoes are cooking, heat oil in a small nonstick skillet over medium heat. Add onion and garlic. Sprinkle with spices and cook 5 minutes or until onion is tender. Add small amounts of water as necessary, about a tablespoon at a time, to prevent sticking. Remove from heat and add to potatoes. Mix well.

Whisk egg white and water together in a small bowl. Place wheat germ in another bowl.

Form potato mixture into 18 2-inch patties. Dip each one first in the egg white, and then in the wheat germ, coating all sides.

Heat a large nonstick skillet or griddle over medium heat. Oil it lightly or spray with a nonstick cooking spray. Cook patties until the bottoms are lightly browned. Spray the tops of the patties lightly with cooking spray, then turn and brown the other sides.

Each serving provides:

129	Calories	21 g	Carbohydrate
6 g	Protein	293 mg	Sodium
3 g	Total fat (0 g sat. fat)	0 mg	Cholesterol

Samosas

A very popular snack in India, these pastries are usually filled with meat or vegetables and then deep-fried. My version is baked and uses a quick pastry wrapper made from refrigerator biscuits. These make a wonderful appetizer or side dish.

Makes 10 servings
(2 samosas each serving)

1	medium potato (6 or 7 ounces)
1	teaspoon vegetable oil
$1/4$	cup finely chopped onion
1	teaspoon very finely minced fresh ginger root
$1/2$	teaspoon fennel seeds, slightly crushed
$1/2$	teaspoon ground coriander
$1/4$	teaspoon salt
$1/4$	teaspoon curry powder
$1/8$	teaspoon ground cumin
$1/8$	teaspoon turmeric
$1/16$	teaspoon cayenne pepper, or more to taste
$1/4$	cup frozen peas, or fresh peas
2	tablespoons water
1	10-ounce package refrigerator biscuits

Cut potato into large chunks and place in a small saucepan in 1 inch of boiling water. Cover and cook until tender (but not mushy), about 15 minutes. Drain. When potato is cool enough to handle, peel, discard skin, and cut into 1/4-inch cubes.

Heat oil in a small nonstick skillet over medium heat. Add onion and ginger. Cook, stirring frequently, 5 minutes. While onion is cooking, sprinkle with spices and continue to stir frequently.

Stir potato, peas, and water into onion mixture. Cover, reduce heat to low, and cook 5 minutes or until peas are just tender. Remove from heat and let cool 10 to 15 minutes.

Preheat oven to 400°.

Have an ungreased baking sheet ready.

Place biscuits on a lightly floured surface. Roll them into 4 1/2-inch circles. With a sharp knife, cut each circle in half. Place about 1 1/2 teaspoons of filling on the lower half of each semi-circle. Moisten the edges lightly with a finger dipped in water, fold the dough over the filling, and seal the edges. Crimp edges with a fork.

Place samosas on baking sheet.

Bake 8 to 10 minutes, until golden.

Serve hot.

Each serving provides:

103	Calories	16 g	Carbohydrate
3 g	Protein	359 mg	Sodium
4 g	Total fat (1 g sat. fat)	0 mg	Cholesterol

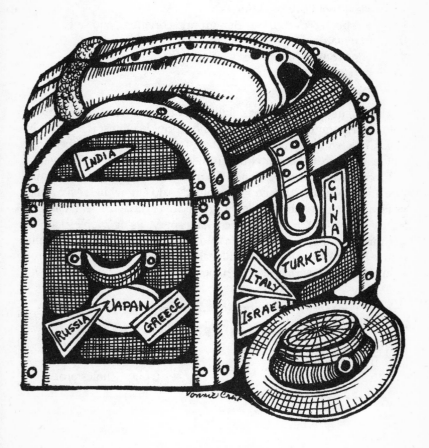

Vegetable Rice Fritters

Topped with chutney these fritters are unbeatable.

Makes 8 servings
(3 fritters each serving)

1	teaspoon vegetable oil
1	cup finely shredded carrots
1/2	cup finely chopped onion
3	cloves garlic, very finely chopped
1 1/2	teaspoons fresh ginger root, very finely chopped
1	jalapeño pepper (optional), finely chopped, seeds and inner membrane discarded
1 1/4	teaspoons ground cumin
3/4	teaspoon curry powder
1/2	teaspoon *each* chili powder, ground coriander, and salt
1/4	cup water
3	cups cooked brown rice
1/2	cup all-purpose flour
4	egg whites

Heat oil in a small nonstick skillet over medium heat. Add carrots, onion, garlic, ginger root, and jalapeño. Sprinkle with spices and mix well. Cook 8 minutes or until vegetables are tender, adding the water, a little at a time, to keep mixture from sticking. Remove from heat.

Place rice in a large bowl, add flour, and mix well. Add carrot mixture and mix until thoroughly combined. Add egg whites. Mix well.

Heat a large nonstick skillet or griddle over medium heat. Oil it lightly or spray with a nonstick cooking spray. Using 2 tablespoons of rice mixture for each fritter, form into patties 1/2-inch thick. Press mixture together firmly. Place in skillet and when bottoms of fritters are lightly browned, turn and brown the other side.

Each serving provides:

167	Calories	26 g	Carbohydrate
5 g	Protein	175 mg	Sodium
5 g	Total fat (1 g sat. fat)	0 mg	Cholesterol

Golden Butternut Soup

Yellow split peas and butternut squash lend their golden colors to this delectable curried soup that's hearty enough to be served as an entrée.

Makes 6 servings
(1¹/3 cups each serving)

2	teaspoons vegetable oil
1	cup chopped onion
¹/2	cup chopped celery
3	cloves garlic, finely chopped
1	tablespoon curry powder
¹/4	cup water
5¹/4	cups water
1	cup yellow split peas, uncooked
1	small butternut squash, peeled, seeded, and chopped into ¹/2-inch pieces (1 pound)
1	1-pound can salt-free (or regular) tomatoes, chopped, undrained
2	bay leaves
¹/4	teaspoon pepper (optional)
	Salt to taste and chopped fresh cilantro for garnish (optional)

Heat oil in a large saucepan over medium heat. Add onion, celery, and garlic. Sprinkle with curry powder and add 1 tablespoon of the water from the ¹/4 cup of water. Cook, stirring frequently, 5 minutes. Add the remainder of the ¹/4 cup of water, a little at a time, to keep onion from sticking.

Add remaining ingredients, *except* salt and cilantro. Bring to a boil, then cover, reduce heat to medium-low, and simmer 45 minutes or until squash and split peas are tender. Add salt to taste. Remove and discard bay leaves before serving. Garnish with cilantro, if desired.

Each serving provides:

188	Calories	34 g	Carbohydrate
10 g	Protein	28 mg	Sodium
2 g	Total fat (1 g sat. fat)	0 mg	Cholesterol

Herbed Bombay Tomato Soup

This soup is thick and rich! Filled with lots of sliced onions and dotted with sweet peas, it's visually appealing as well as delicious.

Makes 4 servings
(1¹/₂ cups each serving)

2	teaspoons vegetable oil
1	very large onion, thinly sliced
4	cloves garlic, crushed
2	teaspoons *each* ground coriander and ground cumin
¹/₂	teaspoon fennel seeds, slightly crushed
2	bay leaves
1	28-ounce can crushed tomatoes
1¹/₂	cups *Vegetable Broth,* or 1¹/₂ cups water plus 1¹/₂ teaspoons *Vegetable Broth Mix* (See pages 26–27.)
1	teaspoon sugar
1	cup frozen peas, or fresh peas
¹/₂	cup evaporated skim milk
1	tablespoon finely chopped fresh mint leaves or cilantro (optional)
	Freshly ground pepper to taste

Heat oil in a large saucepan over medium heat. Add onion, garlic, and then spices. Cook, stirring frequently, 5 minutes or until onion is tender. Add small amounts of water as necessary, about a tablespoon at a time, to prevent sticking. Add tomatoes, broth, and sugar. When mixture boils, reduce heat to medium-low, cover, and simmer 15 minutes. Stir in peas and cook covered, 10 minutes more. Stir in milk and remove from heat. Remove and discard bay leaves.

Spoon soup into bowls and garnish with mint leaves or cilantro, if desired. Sprinkle with freshly ground pepper.

Each serving provides:

168	Calories	29 g	Carbohydrate
8 g	Protein	786 mg	Sodium
4 g	Total fat (0 g sat. fat)	1 mg	Cholesterol

Split Pea and Vegetable Soup

Flavored with aromatic spices and loaded with carrots and potatoes, this is a delectable Indian version of a familiar homestyle soup.

Makes 6 servings
(1¹/₃cups each serving)

2	teaspoons vegetable oil
1	cup chopped onion
2	cups carrots, sliced ¹/₄-inch thick
1	teaspoon fresh ginger root, finely minced
2	teaspoons ground coriander
1	teaspoon curry powder
1	teaspoon ground cumin
¹/₂	teaspoon turmeric
1	cup green split peas, uncooked
1	1-pound can salt-free (or regular) tomatoes, chopped, undrained
5¹/₂	cups water
1	medium potato, peeled and cut into ¹/₄- to ¹/₂-inch cubes (about 8 ounces)
¹/₄	teaspoon salt
	Freshly ground pepper and salt to taste

Heat oil in a large saucepan over medium heat. Add onion, carrots, and ginger root. Cook, stirring frequently, 1 minute. Sprinkle with spices and continue to cook and stir 4 more minutes. Add small amounts of water as necessary, about a tablespoon at a time, to prevent sticking.

Stir in remaining ingredients, *except* pepper. When mixture boils, cover, reduce heat to medium-low, and simmer 45 to 60 minutes, until vegetables are tender.

Top each serving with freshly ground pepper and salt to taste.

Each serving provides:

192	Calories	35 g	Carbohydrate
10 g	Protein	121 mg	Sodium
2 g	Total fat (0 g sat. fat)	0 mg	Cholesterol

Creamy Cauliflower Soup

Both cauliflower and potatoes grow abundantly in India and appear in many dishes. The spices of the region greatly enhance the mild taste of cauliflower and potatoes. This is a vegetable and spice combination that is prevalent in the country's cuisine.

Makes 6 servings
(1¹/8 cups per serving)

2   teaspoons vegetable oil
1   cup chopped onion
4   cloves garlic, crushed
2   teaspoons curry powder
1   teaspoon ground coriander
¹/2   teaspoon ground cumin
¹/8   teaspoon pepper
¹/16   teaspoon ground nutmeg
4   cups *Vegetable Broth,* or 4 cups of water plus 4 teaspoons *Vegetable Broth Mix* (See pages 26–27.)
1   small cauliflower, cut into very small flowerets (4 cups)
1   large potato, peeled and cut into ¹/4-inch pieces (12 ounces)
1   cup evaporated skim milk
        Salt to taste
        Chopped fresh cilantro for garnish (optional)

Heat oil in a large saucepan over medium heat. Add onion and garlic. Cook, stirring frequently, 3 minutes, adding small amounts of water if necessary, about a tablespoon at a time, to prevent sticking. Reduce heat to medium-low and add spices. Again, add enough water just to keep mixture from sticking. Cook, stirring frequently, adding water as needed, 3 minutes more.

Add broth, cauliflower, and potato. Increase heat to medium once more and bring mixture to a boil. Cover, reduce heat to medium-low, and simmer 40 minutes or until vegetables are tender.

Set aside 2 cups of the cooked cauliflower and potatoes. Working in two or three batches, blend the remaining soup until smooth, using

a blender or food processor. Return soup to saucepan and add reserved vegetables.

Stir in milk and add salt to taste. Heat through, but do not boil.
Spoon into serving bowls and garnish with cilantro, if desired.

Each serving provides:

127	Calories	21 g	Carbohydrate
6 g	Protein	739 mg	Sodium
3 g	Total fat (1 g sat. fat)	2 mg	Cholesterol

Bombay Vegetable Salad

Vegetable salads are an important feature of Indian vegetarian meals, usually served as a first course before the rest of the meal. You'll love this interesting mix of vegetables and curry. It makes a salad that's pretty to look at, as well as delightful to eat.

Makes 8 servings

3	cups cauliflower, cut into flowerets
2	large turnips, peeled, quartered, and then sliced 1/4-inch thick (2 cups)
1	cup carrots, sliced crosswise 1/4-inch thick
1	large green bell pepper, cut into strips
1/3	cup vinegar
1/4	cup firmly packed brown sugar
1/4	cup water
1	tablespoon vegetable oil
2	teaspoons curry powder
1/8	teaspoon salt
1/8	teaspoon pepper, or more to taste

Combine vegetables in a large saucepan.

In a small bowl, combine remaining ingredients. Pour over vegetables and mix well. Bring mixture to a boil over medium heat. Reduce heat to medium-low, cover, and simmer 8 to 10 minutes or until vegetables are tender-crisp, stirring several times.

Cool slightly, then chill. Serve cold.

Each serving provides:

71	Calories	14 g	Carbohydrate
1 g	Protein	70 mg	Sodium
2 g	Total fat (0 g sat. fat)	0 mg	Cholesterol

Curried Cole Slaw

This is an Indian-inspired version of a classic American salad. The tangy flavor of curry highlights the sweetness of the pineapple and raisins in my unique version of an all-time favorite salad. (Mayonnaise is an American ingredient not usually found in Indian cuisine.)

Makes 8 servings

4	cups thinly shredded cabbage
1	cup canned crushed pineapple (packed in juice), drained slightly
1/3	cup raisins
2	tablespoons plain nonfat yogurt
2	tablespoons reduced-calorie mayonnaise
2	teaspoons sugar
1	teaspoon curry powder
1/2	teaspoon salt
1/8	teaspoon pepper, or more to taste

In a large bowl, combine cabbage, pineapple, and raisins.

In a small bowl, combine remaining ingredients. Mix well and add to cabbage mixture. Toss until cabbage is well coated. (It may seem like there is not enough mixture to coat cabbage, but just keep mixing and remember that chilling the salad will also add to the moisture of the salad.)

Chill several hours or overnight to blend flavors.

Each serving provides:

62	Calories	13 g	Carbohydrate
1 g	Protein	167 mg	Sodium
1 g	Total fat (0 g sat. fat)	1 mg	Cholesterol

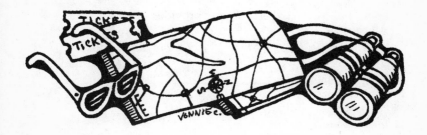

Mixed Bean Salad

This salad is often very highly spiced and can be made with any variety of beans. It's a great party dish and this recipe makes a lot. For a picture-pretty presentation, just before serving, pile the chilled salad on a bed of leafy greens and encircle the beans with alternating slices of cucumbers and tomatoes.

Makes 12 servings

1	1-pound can kidney beans, rinsed and drained (or 2 cups of cooked beans)
1	1-pound can black-eyed peas, rinsed and drained (or 2 cups of cooked black-eyes)
1	1-pound can chick peas, rinsed and drained (or 2 cups of cooked chick peas)
1/2	cup thinly sliced green onions (green and white parts)
1	jalapeño pepper (optional), finely minced, seeds and inner membrane discarded
2	teaspoons vegetable oil
1	teaspoon sesame oil
2	cloves garlic, crushed
2	tablespoons lemon juice (preferably fresh)
1	teaspoon ground cumin
1/2	teaspoon ground coriander
1/2	teaspoon salt
1/4	teaspoon pepper

In a large bowl, combine beans, onions, and jalapeño pepper. Toss gently.

In a small bowl or custard cup, combine remaining ingredients. Mix well. Pour over beans. Mix gently until dressing is evenly distributed. (This is not a juicy type of salad.)

Chill several hours or overnight to blend flavors.

Each serving provides:

87	Calories	12 g	Carbohydrate
5 g	Protein	242 mg	Sodium
2 g	Total fat (0 g sat. fat)	0 mg	Cholesterol

Curry-Lime Fruit Salad

Fruit salads are one of the most popular snacks in India, often consisting of tropical fruits and tangy spices. As a salad or a dessert, this refreshing dish adds a perfect "light" touch to any Indian meal. The fruits and dressing are chilled separately and combined just before serving, making it an easy do-ahead dish. The vanilla yogurt, which is not readily available in India, is my own "sweet" addition. Authentic recipes call for plain yogurt. (If you can't find a ripe papaya, you can substitute any fresh, ripe melon.)

Makes 6 servings

1	large, ripe banana, cut into 1-inch chunks (Choose one that is ripe, but not too soft.)
1	large orange, peeled and sectioned, each section cut into 1-inch pieces (Remove and discard white membrane.)
1	ripe papaya, peeled and cut into 1-inch pieces, seeds removed
1	8-ounce can pineapple chunks (packed in juice), drained
2	tablespoons coarsely chopped almonds, lightly toasted*
2/3	cup vanilla nonfat yogurt
2	teaspoons lime juice
1 1/2	teaspoons sugar
1/2	teaspoon curry powder
1/2	teaspoon grated fresh lime peel

Combine fruits and nuts in a large bowl. Mix gently. Chill up to several hours.

Combine remaining ingredients in a small bowl. Mix well. Chill. (This mixture may be prepared up to a day ahead.)

Just before serving, pour yogurt mixture over fruits. Toss gently.

*To toast almonds, place them on a baking sheet in a 350° oven or toaster oven for a few minutes, until lightly toasted.

Each serving provides:

120	Calories	26 g	Carbohydrate
3 g	Protein	21 mg	Sodium
2 g	Total fat (0 g sat. fat)	1 mg	Cholesterol

Orange Rice Salad

In this cool, light salad the sweetness of oranges mingles with the tang of lime and curry for a brilliant change of pace. In India this would be served as a "cooling" side dish, however, I have also found that it makes a great breakfast dish. In India, homemade yogurt would be used, rather than vanilla flavored yogurt. If you like, golden raisins make a delicious addition to this salad.

Makes 6 servings

2	cups cooked brown rice (If rice has just been cooked, let it cool almost to room temperature before using.)
2	large oranges, peeled and sectioned, each section cut into 1-inch pieces (Remove and discard white membranes.)
2/3	cup vanilla nonfat yogurt
1	tablespoon sugar
1	tablespoon lime juice
1/2	teaspoon curry powder
1/4	teaspoon grated fresh lime peel
1/4	teaspoon grated fresh orange peel

Toss rice and oranges together in a medium bowl. In a small bowl, combine remaining ingredients, mixing well. Pour over rice mixture. Mix well.

Chill. Serve cold.

Each serving provides:

133	Calories	29 g	Carbohydrate
4 g	Protein	22 mg	Sodium
1 g	Total fat (0 g sat. fat)	1 mg	Cholesterol

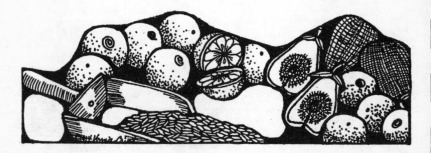

Cucumber and Tomato Raita

A raita (pronounced RAY-ta) is a salad made from a refreshing mixture of yogurt and fresh fruits or vegetables. Most Indian meals are served with a raita as an accompaniment, providing a cooling contrast to the usually spicy main dish. I've also served this one as a delicious—and unique—salad dressing. (Mint leaves are available in the produce section of most large grocery stores and can also be used to add a wonderful spark to iced tea.)

Makes 6 servings
(1/3 cup each serving)

1	cup plain nonfat yogurt
1	tablespoon finely chopped fresh mint leaves (or 1 teaspoon of dried mint leaves, but the fresh taste much better)
1/2	teaspoon ground cumin
1/4	teaspoon chili powder
1/4	teaspoon salt
1/8	teaspoon pepper
1	medium cucumber, peeled, seeded, and coarsely shredded (1/2 to 2/3 cup)
1	small tomato, chopped (1/2 cup)
1	tablespoon very finely chopped onion

In a small bowl, combine yogurt, mint leaves, and spices. Mix well. Add remaining ingredients. Mix until well blended.

Chill 1 hour before serving. (Raita will keep for several days in the refrigerator, but is best when made just 1 hour ahead.)

Stir before serving.

Each serving provides:

28	Calories	4 g	Carbohydrate
2 g	Protein	122 mg	Sodium
0 g	Total fat (0 g sat. fat)	1 mg	Cholesterol

Sweet Banana Raita

This sweet raita (pronounced RAY-ta), or yogurt salad, really adds a cool touch to a spicy meal. In addition to serving it as a side dish, I have used it as a light, refreshing dessert, with the leftovers adding a delicious spark to the next day's breakfast. (Many authentic recipes call for coconut, but I opted for coconut extract instead because it is fat-free as opposed to the coconut, which is high in saturated fat.)

Makes 4 servings
(1/2 cup each serving)

1	cup plain nonfat yogurt
2	tablespoons sugar
1/4	teaspoon ground cardamom
1/8	teaspoon coconut extract
1	tablespoon raisins
2	teaspoons slivered almonds
1	large, ripe banana, cut into 1/4-inch pieces

In a small bowl, combine yogurt, sugar, cardamom, and coconut extract. Mix well. Stir in raisins and almonds.

Add banana, mixing gently.

Chill 1 to 2 hours before serving. (This raita is best when made a few hours before serving. Leftovers will keep overnight in the refrigerator, but after that the bananas usually become mushy.)

Each serving provides:

101	Calories	20 g	Carbohydrate
4 g	Protein	44 mg	Sodium
1 g	Total fat (0 g sat. fat)	1 mg	Cholesterol

Apricot-Raisin Chutney

Chutney is a fruity sauce that is tart, hot, sweet, and savory—all at once. Most Indian meals include a small side dish of chutney served alongside the meal. (Typically, lemon juice, cider vinegar, or white vinegar are used in chutneys, but after trying it all different ways, I decided that I like the "slightly unauthentic" flavor of red wine vinegar best.) One of my favorite ways to serve chutney is to spread it on a chunk of fat-free cream cheese and serve it with crackers as an appetizer.

Makes 16 servings
(2 tablespoons each serving)

1	cup dried apricot halves, cut into quarters
2	cups boiling water
$1/2$	cup raisins
5	cloves garlic, crushed
1	teaspoon grated fresh ginger root
$1/2$	cup red wine vinegar
$3/4$	cup sugar
$1/8$	teaspoon salt
$1/16$	teaspoon cayenne pepper

Place apricots in a medium saucepan. Add boiling water and let stand 30 minutes.

Add remaining ingredients. Bring mixture to a boil over medium heat. Reduce heat slightly and simmer uncovered, 1 1/4 hours or until mixture is glazed and slightly thickened. Stir occasionally while cooking and reduce heat if necessary. Mixture should remain at a slow, bubbly simmer. Watch it carefully toward the end of cooking time to make sure it does not burn.

Cool slightly, then chill.

Serve cold. Chutney will keep for several weeks in the refrigerator.

Each serving provides:

72	Calories	19 g	Carbohydrate
0 g	Protein	19 mg	Sodium
0 g	Total fat (0 g sat. fat)	0 mg	Cholesterol

Spiced Tomato Chutney

Chutneys can be made from vegetables, as well as fruits. This sweet and tangy chutney is made from fresh tomatoes, and in addition to making a delicious meal accompaniment, it also makes a wonderful, quick appetizer. Just spread it on toasted bread, chapati *(crisp Indian flatbread available in specialty stores), or even melba toast. I've even used it to top grilled cheese sandwiches. (Looking for a delicious homemade holiday gift idea? Make a big batch and put it in pretty jars.)*

Makes 12 servings
(2 tablespoons each serving)

1¹/₄	pounds plum tomatoes, peeled and chopped* (12 to 14 tomatoes)
¹/₂	cup red wine vinegar
¹/₂	cup sugar
6	large cloves garlic, crushed (1 tablespoon)
1	tablespoon fresh ginger root, very finely minced
¹/₄	teaspoon salt
¹/₄	teaspoon ground cinnamon
¹/₈	teaspoon cayenne pepper
¹/₄	cup raisins

Combine all ingredients in a medium saucepan. Bring to a boil over medium heat. Reduce heat to medium-low and simmer uncovered, 2 to 2¹/₂ hours until thick. Stir occasionally while cooking and reduce heat if necessary to keep mixture at a slow simmer. Cool slightly, then chill.

Serve cold. Chutney will keep several weeks in the refrigerator.

*To peel tomatoes: With a sharp knife, cut an x in the skin at the stem end of each tomato. Place the tomatoes in a pot of boiling water for 1 minute, then place them immediately into a bowl of ice water. This will make them easy to peel.

Each serving provides:

53	Calories	13 g	Carbohydrate
1 g	Protein	50 mg	Sodium
0 g	Total fat (0 g sat. fat)	0 mg	Cholesterol

Delhi Potato and Bean Stew

This savory stew abounds with flavor. Don't let the long list of ingredients deter you. They all get "thrown together" in one pot!

Makes 6 servings

2	tablespoons tomato paste
2	tablespoons lemon juice
2	bay leaves
1	teaspoon *each* ground cumin and ground cinnamon
1/2	teaspoon ground coriander
1/4	teaspoon *each* ground cardamom and ground cloves
1/8	teaspoon cayenne pepper, or more to taste
2	cups water
2	teaspoons vegetable oil
3	cloves garlic, crushed
1	teaspoon grated fresh ginger root
2	1-pound cans kidney beans, rinsed and drained (or 4 cups of cooked beans)
1 1/2	pounds potatoes, unpeeled, cut into 1-inch cubes (3 medium potatoes)
	Salt to taste
1/2	cup plain nonfat yogurt

In a small bowl, combine tomato paste, lemon juice, spices, and water. Mix well.

Heat oil in a large saucepan over medium heat. Add garlic and ginger root and cook 1 minute. Stir in spice mixture, then add beans and potatoes. Mix well.

Bring to a boil, cover, reduce heat to medium-low, and simmer, stirring occasionally, 1 hour or until potatoes are tender. Remove and discard bay leaves. Add salt to taste.

Top each serving with a heaping tablespoonful of yogurt.

Each serving provides:

235	Calories	42 g	Carbohydrate
11 g	Protein	257 mg	Sodium
3 g	Total fat (0 g sat. fat)	0 mg	Cholesterol

Aromatic Lentil and Brown Rice Pilaf

Lentil and rice combinations are among the specialties from southern India. The delicate blend of spices and exotic aroma make this one of my family's favorite dishes. It makes the whole house smell good!

Makes 4 servings

2	teaspoons vegetable oil
1/2	cup chopped onion
2	cloves garlic, crushed
2	tablespoons slivered almonds
2 3/4	cups water
3/4	cup brown rice, uncooked
1/2	cup lentils, uncooked
1/4	cup raisins
2	teaspoons *Vegetable Broth Mix* (See page 27.)
1	teaspoon curry powder
1/4	teaspoon ground cumin
1/4	teaspoon ground ginger
1/8	teaspoon ground allspice
1/8	teaspoon *each* salt and pepper

Heat oil in a medium saucepan over medium heat. Add onion, garlic, and almonds. Cook and stir until onion is tender and almonds are lightly browned, about 5 minutes.

Add remaining ingredients and bring mixture to a boil. Reduce heat to low, cover, and simmer 40 to 45 minutes, until water has been absorbed.

Remove from heat and let stand covered, 5 minutes, then fluff with a fork and serve.

Each serving provides:			
297	Calories	52 g	Carbohydrate
11 g	Protein	538 mg	Sodium
6 g	Total fat (1 g sat. fat)	0 mg	Cholesterol

Curried Chick Peas

Almost every household in northern India has its own version of this popular, and very delicious, dish. This one was graciously shared with me by Sareena Mathew who teaches a wonderful Indian cooking class in Delaware. This dish is usually served alongside a rice dish and each serving is often topped with a dollop of yogurt.

Makes 6 servings

2	teaspoons vegetable oil
1	cup chopped onion
3	cloves garlic, very finely chopped
1	tablespoon very finely chopped fresh ginger root
2	teaspoons ground coriander
1/2	teaspoon turmeric
1/2	teaspoon ground cumin
1/4	teaspoon cayenne pepper, or more to taste
1/16	teaspoon *each* ground cinnamon and ground cloves
2	19-ounce cans chick peas, rinsed and drained (or 4 1/2 cups of cooked chick peas)
1	cup plus 2 tablespoons water
2	tablespoons lemon juice (preferably fresh)

Heat oil in a large nonstick skillet over medium heat. Add onion, garlic, and ginger root. Cook, stirring frequently, 5 minutes. Sprinkle with spices and add 2 tablespoons of the water. Continue to cook and stir for 1 minute.

Add chick peas and remaining water. Reduce heat to medium-low and simmer uncovered, stirring occasionally, 15 minutes.

Stir in lemon juice and cook 5 minutes more.

Each serving provides:

152	Calories	22 g	Carbohydrate
7 g	Protein	200 mg	Sodium
4 g	Total fat (0 g sat. fat)	0 mg	Cholesterol

Spicy Yellow Dal

This delicious dal (pronounced DAHL and meaning "bean dish") can be served with plain rice or a mild, herbed rice such as Minted Rice *on page 391. It can also be made into a soup simply by adding more water.*

Makes 6 servings

3	cups water
1	cup yellow split peas, uncooked
2	teaspoons vegetable oil
1	cup chopped onion
2	teaspoons curry powder
1/2	teaspoon *each* turmeric and chili powder
1/4	teaspoon ground cumin
3	cloves garlic, crushed
1	teaspoon finely minced fresh ginger root
1	cup chopped tomato
1/2	teaspoon salt
	A few tablespoons chopped fresh cilantro (optional)

Bring water to a boil in a medium saucepan over medium heat. Add split peas. Reduce heat to medium-low, cover, and simmer 45 minutes or until split peas are very tender. Drain.

Heat oil in a large nonstick skillet over medium heat. Add onion. Sprinkle with spices, *except* the garlic and ginger, and add about a tablespoon of water. Cook 3 minutes, stirring frequently and adding small amounts of water if necessary, about a tablespoon at a time, to prevent sticking. Add garlic and ginger. Cook and stir for 2 minutes. Add tomato. Cook and stir for 1 minute. Stir in split peas and salt, mixing well. Reduce heat to medium-low and cook, stirring frequently, 15 minutes or until mixture is thick. Top each serving with chopped fresh cilantro, if desired.

	Each serving provides:		
148	Calories	25 g	Carbohydrate
9 g	Protein	194 mg	Sodium
2 g	Total fat (0 g sat. fat)	0 mg	Cholesterol

Sweet Spiced Lentils and Tomatoes

Brown sugar gives this dish an unusual, sweet flavor. The authentic version relies on an unrefined cane sugar called jaggery (JUG-er-ee) for its sweetness. Available in some specialty stores, this type of sugar is usually sold in solid form that has to be grated first in order to be measured. This dish is a perfect match served with sweet Ginger-Apricot Rice with Peanuts (page 393).

Makes 4 servings

2	teaspoons vegetable oil
1	cup chopped onion
1/2	cup chopped celery
3	cloves garlic, finely chopped
2	teaspoons grated or very finely minced, fresh ginger root
1	teaspoon *each* ground cumin and ground coriander
1/8	teaspoon cayenne pepper
1	1-pound can salt-free (or regular) tomatoes, chopped, undrained
1 1/2	cups *Vegetable Broth,* or 1 1/2 cups of water plus 1 1/2 teaspoons *Vegetable Broth Mix* (See pages 26–27.)
1/2	cup lentils, uncooked
1	tablespoon firmly packed brown sugar
1/4	teaspoon salt

Heat oil in a large nonstick skillet over medium heat. Add onion, celery, garlic, and ginger root. Sprinkle with cumin, coriander, and cayenne pepper. Cook, stirring frequently, 3 minutes.

Add remaining ingredients, mixing well. When mixture boils, reduce heat to medium-low, cover, and simmer 40 minutes or until the lentils are tender.

Each serving provides:

169	Calories	28 g	Carbohydrate
9 g	Protein	549 mg	Sodium
3 g	Total fat (0 g sat. fat)	0 mg	Cholesterol

Curried Kidney Beans

This dish from northern India is flavored with garlic, ginger, and a variety of aromatic spices. Often a lot more ginger is added, making it quite spicy. This dish is quick and easy and can be served with any of the rice or wheat side dishes in this chapter. It also freezes and reheats well.

Makes 4 servings

1	teaspoon vegetable oil
1	cup chopped onion
1	tablespoon very finely minced fresh ginger root
4	cloves garlic, very finely minced
2	teaspoons ground coriander
1	teaspoon ground cumin
1	teaspoon curry powder
2	large tomatoes, chopped (2 cups)
1	1-pound can kidney beans, rinsed and drained (or 2 cups of cooked beans)
1/4	teaspoon salt
1/8	teaspoon cayenne pepper, or more to taste

Heat oil in a large nonstick skillet over medium heat. Add onion, ginger root, and garlic. Cook, stirring frequently, until onion starts to brown, about 5 minutes. Add small amounts of water if necessary, about a tablespoon at a time, to prevent sticking.

Add coriander, cumin, and curry powder. Cook, stirring constantly, 1 minute.

Add remaining ingredients, mixing well. Cook, stirring frequently, 5 minutes.

Each serving provides:

134	Calories	22 g	Carbohydrate
7 g	Protein	288 mg	Sodium
2 g	Total fat (0 g sat. fat)	0 mg	Cholesterol

Pumpkin and Red Lentil Stew

This hearty stew has a mellow flavor that can only be described as "warm and friendly." Generally a dish like this, which works equally well for lunch or supper, is served with bread, a yogurt salad, and a refreshing fruit dessert.

Makes 8 servings
(1¹/₄ cups each serving)

2	teaspoons vegetable oil
2	cups chopped onion
2	cups carrots, sliced ¹/₄-inch thick
5	cloves garlic, crushed
2	teaspoons *each* ground cumin and ground coriander
1	teaspoon *each* curry powder and turmeric
1	cup red lentils, uncooked
1	28-ounce can salt-free (or regular) tomatoes, chopped, undrained
2	cups *Vegetable Broth,* or 2 cups of water plus 2 teaspoons *Vegetable Broth Mix* (See pages 26–27.)
2	pounds pumpkin, peeled and cut into 1-inch cubes (about 5¹/₂ cups)
	Salt and pepper

Heat oil in a large saucepan over medium heat. Add onion, carrots, and garlic. Sprinkle with spices, add about a tablespoon of water, and cook, stirring frequently, 5 minutes.

Add small amounts of water as necessary, about a tablespoon at a time, to prevent sticking. Add lentils, tomatoes, and broth. Bring mixture to a boil, then reduce heat to medium-low, cover, and simmer 10 minutes.

Add pumpkin and increase heat to medium until mixture boils. Reduce heat to medium-low, cover, and simmer 30 minutes, until lentils and pumpkin are tender. Add salt and pepper to taste.

Each serving provides:			
171	Calories	31 g	Carbohydrate
9 g	Protein	282 mg	Sodium
2 g	Total fat (0 g sat. fat)	0 mg	Cholesterol

Tandoori Tofu

The spices are fragrant, the flavor is wonderful, and the preparation is easy. (In India dishes like this are often made in a special clay oven called a tandoor). You can mix it up the night before, place it in the refrigerator, and broil when ready. For an authentic Indian meal, serve it with a flavored rice dish and add a side dish of chutney.

Makes 4 servings

1	pound firm tofu, drained slightly on layers of towels
1¹/₃	cups plain nonfat yogurt
2	tablespoons tomato paste
1	teaspoon grated fresh ginger root
2	cloves garlic, crushed
1	tablespoon lemon juice
¹/₂	teaspoon grated lemon peel
¹/₂	teaspoon ground cumin
¹/₄	teaspoon ground turmeric
¹/₄	teaspoon pepper
¹/₄	teaspoon ground coriander
¹/₈	teaspoon chili powder
	Salt to taste

Cut tofu crosswise into ¹/₄-inch slices. Cut slices into strips about ³/₄-inch wide. Place in a shallow bowl or baking pan.

In a small bowl, combine remaining ingredients, mixing well. Spread over tofu. Cover and chill overnight.

To cook: place tofu (along with marinade) on a broiler pan that has been oiled lightly or sprayed with a nonstick cooking spray.

Broil about 12 minutes or until edges of tofu begin to crisp, turning tofu once to brown both sides.

Each serving provides:

219	Calories	13 g	Carbohydrate
23 g	Protein	140 mg	Sodium
10 g	Total fat (2 g sat. fat)	2 mg	Cholesterol

Curried Chick Peas and Mixed Vegetables

Chick peas, cultivated mainly in the northern regions of India, are often combined with a mixture of vegetables, creating interesting dishes. Simple and basic, this dish has many variations, often determined by the availability of the different vegetables. This colorful combination offers a nice medley of flavors and textures. Spoon it over any hot, cooked grain such as rice, millet, or bulgur.

Makes 6 servings

2	teaspoons vegetable oil
1	cup chopped onion
3	cloves garlic, finely chopped
2¹/₂	teaspoons curry powder
1	teaspoon ground cumin
¹/₈	teaspoon cayenne pepper, or more to taste
1	small head cauliflower, cut into small flowerets (4 cups)
¹/₂	cup water
1	1-pound can salt-free (or regular) stewed tomatoes
1	1-pound can chick peas, rinsed and drained (or 2 cups of cooked chick peas)
1	cup frozen peas (or fresh peas)
¹/₄	teaspoon salt

Heat oil in a large nonstick skillet over medium heat. Add onion and garlic. Sprinkle with curry powder, cumin, and cayenne. Cook 3 minutes, stirring frequently and adding small amounts of water as necessary, about a tablespoon at a time, to prevent sticking.

Add cauliflower and water to skillet. When water boils, reduce heat to medium-low, cover skillet, and simmer, 5 minutes or until cauliflower is tender-crisp.

Add remaining ingredients, mixing well. Cover and simmer 15 minutes.

Each serving provides:

136	Calories	22 g	Carbohydrate
7 g	Protein	226 mg	Sodium
3 g	Total fat (0 g sat. fat)	0 mg	Cholesterol

Curried Vegetable Pie
Topped with Chick Pea Pastry

It takes a little time to chop all the veggies, but this "Americanized" main-dish pie is definitely worth the effort! A cooling side dish, such as Cucumber and Tomato Raita *(page 367) would make a nice accompaniment.*

Makes 6 servings

2	teaspoons vegetable oil
3	cloves garlic, crushed
1	teaspoon finely minced fresh ginger root
1	cup carrots, cut into 1/4-inch pieces
1/2	cup celery, cut into 1/4-inch pieces
4	medium leeks (white part only), cut into 1/4-inch pieces (2 cups)
2	medium, red bell peppers, cut into 1/4-inch pieces (11/2 cups)
4	teaspoons curry powder
1	teaspoon ground cumin
1/2	teaspoon salt
	Pepper to taste
11/2	cups chopped broccoli flowerets
2	medium tomatoes, chopped (2 cups)
1/2	cup water
1	tablespoon cornstarch dissolved in 1 tablespoon water

Chick Pea Pastry:

3/4	cup whole wheat flour
3/4	cup all-purpose flour
1	teaspoon baking powder
1/2	teaspoon ground coriander
1/4	teaspoon salt
1	cup canned chick peas, rinsed and drained (or cooked chick peas)
1/4	cup skim milk
2	tablespoons vegetable oil
1/4	cup plus 3 tablespoons water

Heat oil in a large nonstick skillet over medium heat. Add garlic and ginger root. Cook until they just begin to brown. Add carrots, celery, leeks, and bell peppers. Sprinkle with curry powder, cumin, salt, and pepper. Cook, stirring frequently, 6 minutes.

Add broccoli. Cook, stirring frequently, 2 minutes.

Add tomatoes and water. Cover, reduce heat to medium-low, and cook 15 minutes. Uncover and stir in cornstarch mixture. Increase heat to medium. Cook and stir, 1 minute. Remove from heat.

Preheat oven to 375°.

Lightly oil a 9-inch pie pan or spray with a nonstick cooking spray.

To prepare pastry: in a large bowl, combine both types of flour, baking powder, coriander, and salt. Mix well. Purée chick peas and milk in a blender. Add to flour mixture. Mix with a fork or pastry blender until mixture resembles coarse crumbs.

Add oil and continue to mix until crumbly. Add water and mix until all ingredients are moistened.

With your hands, work dough into a ball. Add a small amount of flour if dough is sticky or a small amount of water if dough is too dry to hold together. Place dough on a lightly floured surface and roll into an 11-inch circle.

To assemble: spoon vegetable mixture into prepared pan. Carefully place crust over pan. Crimp edges of dough to seal. Prick top of pie about 10 times with a fork to let the steam escape.

Bake 30 minutes or until pastry is lightly browned.

Let stand 5 minutes before serving.

	Each serving provides:		
278	Calories	44 g	Carbohydrate
9 g	Protein	451 mg	Sodium
9 g	Total fat (1 g sat. fat)	0 mg	Cholesterol

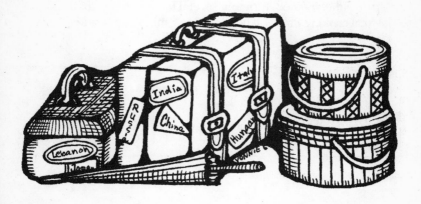

Grilled Spiced Tofu Triangles

Soybeans are an important crop in India and tofu, which is made from soybeans, can be used to replace both meat and cheese in Indian dishes. In this dish, tofu is cut into triangles and marinated in a delicious, spicy yogurt sauce. Then it is grilled or broiled until crisp and served with a side dish of rice or wheat. If you wish, you can press or freeze the tofu before using, giving it a different texture. (See What Is Tofu *on page 17.)*

Makes 4 servings

1/2	cup plain nonfat yogurt
2	cloves garlic, crushed
2	tablespoons grated onion
1	tablespoon very finely minced fresh ginger root
1/2	teaspoon ground cumin
1/2	teaspoon curry powder
1/4	teaspoon turmeric
1/4	teaspoon salt
	Pepper to taste
1	pound firm tofu, cut into 1-inch slices, then cut diagonally to form triangles, and drained slightly between layers of towels

In a medium bowl, combine all ingredients, *except* tofu. Mix well. Add tofu. Mix gently, coating each piece of tofu with marinade. Be careful not to break the tofu.

Cover and marinate in the refrigerator for 5 to 6 hours.

To cook, preheat grill or broiler.

If grilling, place tofu pieces directly on the grill and cook until lightly browned and crisp. If broiling, place tofu and marinade in a shallow pan. Place under broiler until tofu is lightly browned and crisp. In either method, turn tofu several times to brown both sides. The total cooking time will be about 5 to 7 minutes per side.

Each serving provides:

188	Calories		9 g	Carbohydrate
20 g	Protein		174 mg	Sodium
10 g	Total fat (1 g sat. fat)		1 mg	Cholesterol

Potatoes Calcutta

A simple recipe from eastern India, these fragrant potatoes are a perfect ac-companiment to any entrée in this chapter or in the Middle East chapter.Try them with Tandoori Tofu *(page 378) along with some steamed broccoli and* Apricot-Raisin Chutney *(page 369).*

Makes 6 servings

1	teaspoon ground cumin
1/2	teaspoon turmeric
1/2	teaspoon dry mustard
1/2	teaspoon ground cardamom
1/4	teaspoon ground ginger
1/4	teaspoon ground cloves
1/4	teaspoon ground cinnamon
1/4	teaspoon pepper, or more to taste
2	teaspoons vegetable oil
2	cups chopped onion
4	cloves garlic, crushed
2	pounds potatoes, unpeeled, cut into 1-inch cubes (4 medium potatoes)
1 1/4	cups water
	Salt to taste

Combine spices, *except* salt, in a small bowl. Mix well. Set aside.

Heat oil in a large nonstick skillet over medium heat. Add onion and garlic. Cook, stirring frequently, until onion is lightly browned, about 5 minutes.

Add potatoes to skillet. Sprinkle with spice mixture. Cook, stirring frequently, 10 minutes. Add water. Cover, reduce heat to medium-low, and cook, stirring occasionally, 30 minutes or until potatoes are tender and water has been absorbed.

Before serving, add salt to taste.

Each serving provides:

163	Calories	33 g	Carbohydrate
4 g	Protein	15 mg	Sodium
2 g	Total fat (1 g sat. fat)	0 mg	Cholesterol

Cauliflower Curry

This is really a cross-cultural dish, combining the flavors of soy sauce and sherry with some of the basic flavors of India. The result is superb.

Makes 6 servings

2	tablespoons reduced-sodium (or regular) soy sauce
2	tablespoons sherry
1	tablespoon vegetable oil
2	teaspoons cornstarch
2	tablespoons water
4	cups cauliflower, cut into small flowerets
1	cup chopped onion
1	cup chopped red bell pepper
3	cloves garlic, crushed
1/2	teaspoon grated fresh ginger root
1	teaspoon ground cumin
1/2	teaspoon ground coriander

In a small bowl, combine soy sauce, sherry, and oil. Place 2 tablespoons of the mixture in a large nonstick skillet and set remaining soy mixture aside.

In a small bowl or custard cup, combine cornstarch and water. Set aside.

Heat the skillet over medium heat. Add cauliflower, onion, bell pepper, garlic, ginger root, and spices. Cook, stirring constantly, 3 minutes.

Add remaining soy mixture and continue to cook and stir, 2 minutes more.

Stir cornstarch mixture and pour over vegetables. Cook and stir, 1 minute.

Each serving provides:

69	Calories	9 g	Carbohydrate
2 g	Protein	213 mg	Sodium
3 g	Total fat (0 g sat. fat)	0 mg	Cholesterol

Stewed Eggplant and Peppers

Every region in India seems to have its favorite eggplant recipe. This one, from northern India, is often made with lots of chopped green chilies making it a very spicy dish. This delicious vegetable combo can be served over rice or as a wonderful (although non-traditional) topper for mashed or baked potatoes.

Makes 6 servings

1	teaspoon vegetable oil
2	large green bell peppers, cut vertically into 1/4-inch slices
1	teaspoon finely chopped fresh ginger root
1	jalapeño pepper (optional), finely chopped, seeds and inner membrane discarded
1	medium eggplant (1 pound), peeled and cut into 1/2-inch cubes (4 cups)
2	teaspoons ground cumin
1	teaspoon ground coriander
1/2	teaspoon fennel seeds, crushed slightly
1/4	teaspoon ground cinnamon
1/4	teaspoon salt
1/8	teaspoon pepper
1/16	teaspoon ground cloves
3	large tomatoes, chopped (3 cups)

Heat oil in a large nonstick skillet over medium heat. Add bell peppers, ginger root, and jalapeño. Cook, stirring frequently, 5 minutes.

Add eggplant to skillet. Sprinkle with spices. Cook, stirring frequently, 3 minutes.

Add tomatoes. Cover skillet, reduce heat to medium-low, and simmer 15 to 20 minutes, until eggplant is tender. Then uncover skillet, return heat to medium, and cook, stirring frequently, 10 minutes or until most of the liquid has cooked out.

Spoon over rice or any cooked grain.

Each serving provides:

54	Calories	11 g	Carbohydrate
2 g	Protein	103 mg	Sodium
1 g	Total fat (0 g sat. fat)	0 mg	Cholesterol

Bombay Green Beans and Tomatoes

Thanks to my dear friend Pat Tabibian for sharing one of her favorite Indian recipes with me. She takes an ordinary package of green beans and turns it into an easy, elegant, side dish that will complement not only Indian entrées, but those of the Middle East as well.

Makes 4 servings

1	10-ounce package frozen, French-style green beans
2	teaspoons cornstarch
1	tablespoon water
1	teaspoon vegetable oil
1/2	cup finely chopped onion
1	large clove garlic, finely minced
1	teaspoon ground cumin
1	1-pound can salt-free (or regular) tomatoes, chopped and drained (Liquid reserved.)
	Salt and pepper to taste

Cook green beans according to package directions. Drain.

Dissolve cornstarch in water in a small bowl. Set aside.

Heat oil in a large nonstick skillet over medium heat. Add onion and garlic. Cook, stirring frequently, 3 minutes or until onion is tender. Sprinkle with cumin. Cook and stir, 1 minute. Reduce heat to medium-low.

Stir cornstarch mixture and add to skillet along with reserved tomato liquid. Cook and stir, until mixture is thick and bubbly. Then add tomatoes and green beans. Continue to cook and stir until mixture is heated through.

Add salt and pepper to taste.

Each serving provides:

72	Calories	14 g	Carbohydrate
3 g	Protein	189 mg	Sodium
2 g	Total fat (0 g sat. fat)	0 mg	Cholesterol

Curried Carrots and Pineapple

In the southern regions of India vegetable salads are often made with finely chopped or shredded vegetables. Many of the salads often contain hot peppers, which really add a spark when coupled with the mild flavor of the vegetables. In this easy side dish, shredded carrots, with a sweetness and texture all their own, mingle nicely with the "bite" of the curry powder. (Try the leftovers cold for a delicious salad!)

Makes 6 servings

1	1-pound can pineapple tidbits (packed in juice)
2¹/₂	tablespoons firmly packed brown sugar
¹/₂	cup reserved pineapple juice
¹/₂	teaspoon curry powder
¹/₈	teaspoon salt
3	cups finely shredded carrots (about 1 pound)

Drain pineapple, reserving ¹/₂ cup of the juice.

In a large nonstick skillet, combine brown sugar, reserved pineapple juice, curry powder, and salt. Heat over medium heat, stirring until brown sugar is dissolved. Add pineapple tidbits and carrots. Mix well, making sure the spices are evenly distributed.

Reduce heat to medium-low, cover skillet, and cook 15 minutes. Stir once halfway through cooking time.

Serve hot. Refrigerate leftovers.

Each serving provides:

100	Calories	25 g	Carbohydrate
1 g	Protein	76 mg	Sodium
0 g	Total fat (0 g sat. fat)	0 mg	Cholesterol

Vegetable Medley with Farina

When I first heard of serving farina as a side dish, I thought it rather strange. In this country farina is only served as a breakfast cereal. But after trying this dish from Northern India I was really very pleasantly surprised. The mild taste of the wheat acts as a perfect backdrop for the vegetables and spices. I especially like it with Curried Chick Peas *(page 373) or* Curried Kidney Beans *(page 376).*

Makes 6 servings

1	teaspoon vegetable oil
1/2	cup finely chopped onion
2	cloves garlic, sliced into paper-thin slices
2	nickel-size slices of fresh ginger root
1	3-inch strip fresh lemon peel
1	cup farina (or Quick Cream of Wheat®), uncooked
1	large tomato, chopped (1 cup)
1/2	cup finely shredded carrots
1/2	cup thinly sliced green onions (green part only)
3	cups water
2	tablespoons lemon juice (preferably fresh)
1/2	teaspoon salt
1/8	teaspoon pepper, or more to taste

Heat oil in a large nonstick skillet over medium heat. Add onion. Cook, stirring frequently, until onion begins to brown, about 3 minutes. Add garlic, ginger root, and lemon peel. Cook and stir, 1 minute.

Add farina, mixing well. Stir in tomato, carrots, and green onions. Gradually add water, stirring constantly. Then add lemon juice, salt, and pepper. Mix well, reduce heat to low, cover, and cook 10 minutes.

Stir before serving. Remove and discard ginger root and lemon peel.

Each serving provides:			
135	Calories	27 g	Carbohydrate
4 g	Protein	191 mg	Sodium
1 g	Total fat (0 g sat. fat)	0 mg	Cholesterol

Cracked Wheat and Pumpkin Pilaf

Wheat is as much a staple in Northern India as rice is in Southern India. This easy northern-style pilaf has a mild, subtle flavor that makes it suitable, not only as a "go with everything" side dish, but also as a filling and nutritious breakfast.

Makes 6 servings

2	teaspoons vegetable oil
1	cup finely chopped onion
2	cups pumpkin, peeled, seeded, and cut into 1/4-inch pieces
7	whole cloves
2	2 1/2-inch cinnamon sticks
2	bay leaves
1	teaspoon curry powder
1	cup cracked wheat (bulgur), uncooked
2	cups *Vegetable Broth,* or 1 cup of water plus 1 teaspoon *Vegetable Broth Mix* (See pages 26–27.)
1/4	teaspoon salt
1/8	teaspoon pepper

Heat oil in a medium saucepan over medium heat. Add onion, pumpkin, and spices. Cook, stirring frequently, until onion is tender, about 5 minutes. Add small amounts of water if necessary, about a tablespoon at a time, to prevent sticking.

Add cracked wheat. Cook and stir, 2 minutes. Stir in broth, salt, and pepper. When mixture boils, cover saucepan, reduce heat to low, and cook 15 minutes, until the liquid has been absorbed.

Fluff pilaf with a fork before serving.

Remove and discard cloves, cinnamon sticks, and bay leaves.

Each serving provides:

128	Calories	25 g	Carbohydrate
4 g	Protein	433 mg	Sodium
2 g	Total fat (0 g sat. fat)	0 mg	Cholesterol

Lemon-Scented Rice with Pistachios

Lemons and limes are often used to flavor rice and wheat dishes in India. Here the tang of lemon is coupled with exquisitely-flavored pistachios, creating a subtle, yet flavorful dish. Dotted with plump raisins, this attractive dish makes a nice accompaniment to any entrée.

Makes 4 servings

1	cup basmati rice (or other long grain rice)
2	cups water (2^1/2 cups if using brown rice)
^{1}/3	cup raisins
2	teaspoons grated fresh lemon peel
3	tablespoons coarsely chopped pistachio nuts

Wash the rice (and soak, if desired) as described on page 348. If you are using a rice other than basmati, skip these steps.

Bring water to a boil in a medium saucepan. If you are using soaked basmati rice, start with the rice soaking water and add enough tap water to equal the 2 cups (Use 2^1/2 cups if using brown rice.) Stir in rice, raisins, and lemon peel. When water boils again, reduce heat to medium-low, cover saucepan, and simmer 20 minutes (45 minutes for brown rice), until liquid has been absorbed.

Remove from heat and let stand covered, 5 minutes. Fluff rice with a fork, spoon into a serving bowl, and sprinkle with pistachios.

Each serving provides:

226	Calories	47 g	Carbohydrate
7 g	Protein	22 mg	Sodium
4 g	Total fat (0 g sat. fat)	0 mg	Cholesterol

Minted Rice

Whole spices and fresh mint leaves are used in this dish, giving the rice a wonderful herbed flavor and aroma. Fresh mint leaves (available in the produce section of most large grocery stores) are used frequently in Indian cuisine adding a sparkling, fresh flavor. (Leftover mint leaves make a wonderful addition to iced tea.)

Makes 4 servings

1	cup basmati rice (or other long grain rice)
2	teaspoons vegetable oil
2	whole cloves
2	nickel-size slices of fresh ginger root
1	2^1/$_2$-inch cinnamon stick
1	bay leaf
2	cups water
1	tablespoon finely chopped fresh mint leaves

Wash the rice (and if desired soak the rice) as described on page 348. If you are using a rice other than basmati, skip these steps.

Heat oil in a medium saucepan over medium heat. Add cloves, ginger root, cinnamon stick, and bay leaf. Cook, stirring constantly, 2 minutes.

Add water, starting with the rice soaking water if you are using soaked basmati rice, and adding enough tap water to equal the 2 cups. (Use 2^1/$_2$ cups of water if using brown rice.) Bring to a boil, then stir in rice. When water boils again, stir, reduce heat to medium-low, cover the saucepan, and simmer gently for 20 minutes (45 minutes for brown rice), until liquid has been absorbed. Remove from heat and stir in mint. Then cover and let stand 5 minutes.

Fluff rice with a fork before serving.

Remove and discard cloves, ginger root, cinnamon stick, and bay leaf.

Each serving provides:

177	Calories	36 g	Carbohydrate
5 g	Protein	21 mg	Sodium
3 g	Total fat (0 g sat. fat)	0 mg	Cholesterol

Bombay Rice and Peas

I've substituted brown rice for the more-typically used basmati rice in this classic dish from southwestern India. This picturesque arrangement boasts a delightful blend of brilliant colors and flavors. A sprinkling of fresh cilantro adds even more appeal.

Makes 6 servings

2	teaspoons vegetable oil
1/2	cup chopped onion
1	clove garlic, crushed
1	teaspoon ground coriander
1/2	teaspoon ground cumin
1/8	teaspoon ground cloves
1/8	teaspoon ground cinnamon
1	jalapeño pepper (optional), finely chopped, seeds and inner membrane discarded
1	10-ounce package frozen green peas
1	large, ripe tomato, coarsely chopped
1/2	teaspoon salt
1/4	teaspoon pepper
3	cups cooked brown rice
	A few tablespoons chopped fresh cilantro (optional)

Heat oil in a large nonstick skillet over medium heat. Add onion and garlic. Sprinkle with coriander, cumin, cloves, cinnamon, and jalapeño. Cook, stirring frequently, 5 minutes.

Add peas, tomatoes, salt, and pepper. Mix well so that spices are evenly distributed. Cover and cook 5 minutes.

Add rice. Cook, stirring constantly, until mixture is well blended and rice is hot.

Top each serving with chopped fresh cilantro, if desired.

Each serving provides:

171	Calories	32 g	Carbohydrate
5 g	Protein	244 mg	Sodium
3 g	Total fat (0 g sat. fat)	0 mg	Cholesterol

Ginger-Apricot Rice with Peanuts

This slightly sweet rice makes a delicious accompaniment to any Indian entrée.

Makes 4 servings

1	cup basmati rice (or other long grain rice)
1¹/₂	teaspoons vegetable oil
¹/₂	cup *each* chopped onion and chopped celery
1	teaspoon very finely minced fresh ginger root
¹/₄	cup chopped dried apricots
1	teaspoon curry powder
¹/₂	teaspoon turmeric
¹/₈	teaspoon ground cinnamon
¹/₁₆	teaspoon ground cloves
2	cups water
¹/₄	teaspoon salt
2	tablespoons coarsely chopped dry roasted peanuts (unsalted)

Wash the rice (and soak, if desired) as described on page 348. If you are using a rice other than basmati, skip these steps.

Heat oil in a medium saucepan over medium heat. Add onion and celery. Cook, stirring frequently, 1 minute. Add ginger root. Continue to cook 2 minutes more. Add apricots and spices, along with about a tablespoon of water. Continue to cook for 2 minutes, stirring constantly and adding small amounts of water as necessary, about a tablespoon at a time, to prevent sticking.

Add the water starting with the rice soaking water if you are using soaked basmati rice, and adding enough tap water to equal the 2 cups. (Use 2¹/₂ cups of water if using brown rice.) Add salt. Bring to a boil, then stir in rice. When water boils again, stir, reduce heat to medium-low, cover the saucepan, and simmer gently for 20 minutes (45 minutes for brown rice), until liquid has been absorbed. Remove from heat and let stand covered, for 5 minutes.

Fluff rice with a fork, spoon into a serving bowl, and top with peanuts.

Each serving provides:

229	Calories	45 g	Carbohydrate
7 g	Protein	171 mg	Sodium
5 g	Total fat (1 g sat. fat)	0 mg	Cholesterol

Carrot Cake with Pistachios

This tender and moist carrot cake is slightly different from the type most of us are used to. It's loaded with carrots, laced with cardamom, and has the delicious and colorful addition of pistachios and raisins. (This modern-day Indian dish relies on the use of an oven which is not found in all Indian homes.)

Makes 12 servings

$1/2$	cup whole wheat flour
$1/2$	cup all-purpose flour
1	teaspoon baking soda
$1/2$	teaspoon baking powder
$1/2$	teaspoon ground cardamom
$1/4$	cup raisins
3	tablespoons chopped pistachios
4	egg whites
$2/3$	cup sugar
2	tablespoons vegetable oil
2	tablespoons skim milk
2	teaspoons vanilla extract
$1^1/2$	cups finely shredded carrots (firmly packed)

Topping:
1　　　　tablespoon confectioners sugar

Preheat oven to 350°.

Lightly oil a 9-inch cake pan or spray with a nonstick cooking spray. Line the pan with wax paper and oil or spray again.

In a large bowl, combine both types of flour, baking soda, baking powder, and cardamom. Mix well. Stir in raisins and pistachios.

In another bowl, combine egg whites, sugar, oil, milk, and vanilla. Beat with a fork or wire whisk until blended. Stir in carrots. Add to the dry mixture, mixing until all ingredients are moistened. Spoon into prepared pan. Smooth the top with the back of a spoon.

Bake 35 minutes, until a toothpick inserted in the center of the cake comes out clean.

Cool 5 minutes in pan on a wire rack, then turn out onto rack and gently remove wax paper.

When cake is completely cool, dust the top with confectioners sugar. (For a pretty effect, place a lace doily over the cooled cake, dust with sugar, then remove the doily. You can even make your own doily by cutting snowflake designs out of a piece of paper.) If you are not serving the cake right away, cover the cooled cake and top with the confectioners sugar just before serving.

Each serving provides:

141	Calories	24 g	Carbohydrate
3 g	Protein	151 mg	Sodium
4 g	Total fat (0 g sat. fat)	0 mg	Cholesterol

Cheese Pudding with Raisins and Almonds

This popular pudding from the northeastern region of India is usually made with chenna (a local cheese) and flavored with fragrant rose water. With a few substitutions, I came up with this version that's rich and satisfying and made from readily available ingredients. It can be served warm or cold, but my vote is definitely for warm.

Makes 8 servings

3	cups lowfat (1%) cottage cheese (one 24-ounce container)
1/4	cup cornstarch
1/2	cup sugar
2	tablespoons orange juice
3/4	teaspoon ground cardamom
1	tablespoon vanilla extract
1	teaspoon almond extract
1/2	cup raisins
2	tablespoons coarsely chopped almonds

Preheat oven to 325°.

Lightly oil a 1-quart baking dish or spray with a nonstick cooking spray.

In a blender container, combine all ingredients, *except* raisins and almonds. Blend until smooth. Stir in raisins and almonds. Pour into prepared baking dish.

Bake uncovered, 1 hour or until pudding is set and edges are lightly browned.

Let cool 30 minutes to 1 hour before serving.

	Each serving provides:		
179	Calories	27 g	Carbohydrate
11 g	Protein	347 mg	Sodium
3 g	Total fat (1 g sat. fat)	3 mg	Cholesterol

Pineapple-Raisin Rice Pudding

Traditional Indian rice puddings are made with milk and cooked for a very long time until the milk has thickened. I created an instant version using silken tofu and the result is a thick, creamy, delightful dish that requires no cooking at all. (Silken tofu is available in health food stores and most large grocery stores. It is usually found in the produce department in aseptic packages under the brand name of Mori-Nu®). If you can't find silken tofu, soft tofu will do.

Makes 6 servings

1	10-ounce package silken tofu
1/4	cup firmly packed brown sugar
2	teaspoons vanilla extract
1 1/2	teaspoons lime juice
1/8	teaspoon ground cinnamon
1/8	teaspoon ground cardamom
1/16	teaspoon ground cloves
1	8-ounce can crushed pineapple (packed in juice), drained
1/4	cup raisins
1/2	cup cooked brown rice
2	tablespoons coarsely chopped pistachios (or almonds)

Place tofu in a blender container and blend until smooth. Spoon into a medium bowl. Add brown sugar, vanilla, lime juice, and spices. Mix well. Stir in pineapple, raisins, and rice, mixing well. Spoon pudding into a shallow serving bowl and sprinkle with nuts.

Chill several hours or overnight.

Each serving provides:			
140	Calories	26 g	Carbohydrate
4 g	Protein	9 mg	Sodium
3 g	Total fat (0 g sat. fat)	0 mg	Cholesterol

Apricot-Honey Wheat Pudding

A specialty of the northwestern region of India, where wheat is a staple, this sweet dish is served as a dessert or a delicious breakfast treat. If apricots are not available, it can be made with any type of chopped, dried fruit. The leftovers can be served cold or reheated in a microwave.

Makes 6 servings

1¹/₃	cups water
²/₃	cup bulgur (cracked wheat), uncooked
1¹/₂	cups skim milk
¹/₂	cup honey
¹/₃	cup chopped, dried apricots
¹/₄	teaspoon ground cinnamon
¹/₄	teaspoon ground cardamom
1	teaspoon vanilla extract
¹/₄	teaspoon almond extract
1	tablespoon coarsely chopped almonds or pistachios

Bring water to a boil in a small saucepan. Stir in bulgur, cover, and cook over medium-low heat, 15 minutes. Add milk, honey, apricots, cinnamon, and cardamom. Increase heat to medium and, stirring occasionally, bring mixture to a boil. Then reduce heat to medium-low and cook, stirring frequently, 20 minutes or until mixture is thick. Stir constantly near the end of cooking time to keep mixture from sticking. Remove saucepan from heat and stir in vanilla and almond extracts.

Spoon pudding into a 1-quart shallow serving bowl and smooth the top. Sprinkle with chopped nuts.

This dessert can be served hot, warm, or at room temperature.

Each serving provides:

189	Calories	43 g	Carbohydrate
5 g	Protein	37 mg	Sodium
1 g	Total fat (0 g sat. fat)	1 mg	Cholesterol

Curried Fruit Compote

One of the specialties of the southern region of India is cooked fruit mixed with yogurt. (In Indian homes that do not have an oven, this compote is simmered slowly rather than baked.) This versatile dish can be served as an appetizer, a dessert, or a side dish, and although it is usually served warm, it is also quite good cold. The sweetness of fruit and brown sugar and the tang of curry really add pizzazz to this warm and homey compote.

Makes 12 servings

1	1-pound can pineapple chunks (packed in juice)
1	large, ripe pear, unpeeled, halved lengthwise, cored, and then sliced $1/8$-inch thick
1	large, sweet apple, unpeeled, quartered, cored, and then sliced $1/8$-inch thick
12	dried apricot halves, cut in half
12	pitted prunes, cut in half
$1/4$	cup firmly packed brown sugar
2	teaspoons curry powder
	Vanilla nonfat yogurt (optional)

Preheat oven to 350°.

Have a 2-quart covered casserole ready.

Drain pineapple, reserving juice.

Combine pineapple and remaining fresh and dried fruit in a large bowl.

In a small bowl, combine reserved pineapple juice with brown sugar and curry powder. Mix well and pour over fruit. Mix until fruit is evenly coated.

Place in prepared casserole. Bake covered, 1 hour.

Serve warm or cold. Top with yogurt, if desired.

Each serving provides:

86	Calories	22 g	Carbohydrate
1 g	Protein	3 mg	Sodium
0 g	Total fat (0 g sat. fat)	0 mg	Cholesterol

Fragrant Apples

These warm apples, cooked with raisins in a delicate orange cream sauce, make a cool, smooth ending to any spicy meal. For an elegant presentation, spoon the apples into tall-stemmed sherbet glasses and garnish with fresh orange slices.

Makes 6 servings

4	medium Golden Delicious apples, peeled, cored, and cut into 1/4-inch pieces (4 cups)
1/3	cup raisins
2/3	cup orange juice
2	teaspoons cornstarch
1/3	cup evaporated skim milk
2	tablespoons honey
1/2	teaspoon grated fresh orange peel
1/2	teaspoon ground cardamom
1/4	teaspoon ground nutmeg
	Vanilla nonfat yogurt
	Chopped or slivered almonds (optional)

Place apples and raisins in a medium saucepan.

Place 1 tablespoon of the orange juice in a small bowl or custard cup and add cornstarch. Mix to dissolve cornstarch. Set aside.

Add remaining orange juice to saucepan. Add milk, honey, orange peel, and spices. Bring to a boil over medium heat. Reduce heat slightly and cook, stirring frequently, until apples are tender, about 8 to 10 minutes. Stir cornstarch mixture and add to saucepan. Continue to cook and stir, 1 to 2 minutes, until mixture has thickened slightly.

Remove from heat and cool slightly.

Serve warm, topped with yogurt and a few pieces of almonds, if desired.

	Each serving provides:		
115	Calories	29 g	Carbohydrate
2 g	Protein	18 mg	Sodium
0 g	Total fat (0 g sat. fat)	1 mg	Cholesterol

Dried Fruit Candy Balls

India is a nation that loves little sweets and "nibblers." While many such snacks are either deep fried or contain large amounts of butter and coconut, this one offers the sweetness of dried fruit. Sometimes the finished candies are rolled in powdered sugar, however, they're pretty sweet without it. They're easy to make and keep well in the refrigerator for several weeks.

Makes 36 candies

2/3	cup raisins
2/3	cup chopped dried apricots
2/3	cup chopped, pitted dates
1	teaspoon grated fresh lemon peel
1	teaspoon grated fresh orange peel
1	cup almonds, whole or chopped
1/4	teaspoon ground cardamom
1/4	teaspoon ground cinnamon
1/16	teaspoon ground cloves

Combine all ingredients in a food processor. With a steel blade, process until mixture is uniformly ground and holds together.

Form mixture into 1-inch balls, wetting your hands slightly to prevent sticking. Place candies on a plate in a single layer, wrap tightly, and chill several hours to blend flavors. Store in the refrigerator. (They can be stacked in a container when they are cold and will keep well for several weeks if covered tightly.)

Each candy provides:

44	Calories	7 g	Carbohydrate
1 g	Protein	1 mg	Sodium
2 g	Total fat (0 g sat. fat)	0 mg	Cholesterol

Flavors of the Orient

This chapter provides a delicious overview of the foods of the Orient. Most of the recipes in this section are from China and Japan, however, there is also a sampling of dishes from Thailand, Indonesia, Korea, Vietnam, and the Philippines. Although these countries have different and distinctive cuisines, there is a definite similarity in cooking styles and flavors.

Noodles and rice are staples of Chinese cooking, often flavored with soy sauce, garlic, sherry, and ginger root, and usually cooked in peanut oil. Other popular flavorings are cinnamon and anise. Among the most commonly used ingredients are bamboo shoots, bean sprouts, tofu, water chestnuts, mushrooms, cabbage, scallions, onions, celery, pineapple, and lychees.

Since China is a vast country with a great range of climate and customs, its cuisine has evolved into regional styles. Peking in the north, has sweet and sour sauces and wheat noodles, and Shanghai in the east, has wheat noodles, rice, and light, delicate dishes. Canton in southeastern China, has the mild foods, which are the ones most commonly found in Chinese restaurants in America. Finally there are the Hunan and Szechuan regions in southwestern China, known for robust, hot, and spicy dishes. The popular cooking techniques in all four regions include braising, steaming, roasting, deep-frying, and of course the most popular, uniquely Chinese method of stir-frying.

In Japanese cuisine, rice is vitally important. Noodles are consumed in large quantities, in both hot and cold dishes. Because Japan is an island, seafood plays a dominant role in the cuisine. Soy sauce, sake (rice wine), and ginger are often used together to flavor foods, along with a wide variety of sea vegetables. Among the familiar vegetables in Japanese cooking are carrots, eggplant, onions, scallions, bamboo shoots, mushrooms, snow peas, and cabbage. There are also a number of not-so-familiar vegetables, such as burdock root and daikon radishes. Strawberries and mandarin oranges (tangerines) are among the most prized fruits in Japan. As in Chinese cuisine, tofu is a widely used ingredient, along with miso, a fermented soybean paste that is often used to thicken and season soups and sauces. (The Japanese often contribute their good health and longevity to the use of miso.) There are also sesame seeds, sesame oil, and a host of unfamiliar (to us) sauces and pickled vegetables.

The cuisine of Korea lies somewhere between that of China and Japan. Food preparation is more complex than that of Japan, yet not as sophisticated as that of China. Hot chili peppers and garlic are favorite ingredients in the foods, which tend to be rather spicy. The daily Korean diet is centered around rice, bean sprouts, cabbage, sesame seeds, nuts, and seafood. Other vegetables include turnips, cucumbers, and green onions, which are often pickled, along with cabbage to make a spicy salad called *kim-chee* that is served with almost every Korean meal.

Thailand is perhaps one of the most exotic countries of the Orient. Its food is light, yet quite spicy and relies largely on the use of rice, noodles, vegetables, spiced barbecued dishes, and pungent curries. The flavors of mint and lime lace many dishes, as do cardamom, cilantro, ginger, garlic, soy sauce, and lemon grass. There seems to be an Indian influence on Thai food, seen in the curries, and a Middle Eastern influence, seen in some of the cumin-based sauces. Local markets are filled with fresh fruits such as coconuts, mangos, melons, pineapples, bananas, oranges, lychees, and guavas, and fresh vegetables such as broccoli, carrots, celery, cucumbers, tomatoes, green onions, radishes, along with a variety of hot and spicy chilies. Peanuts also appear frequently in everything from soups to desserts. As in Chinese cooking, stir-frying is the dominant Thai cooking method.

The cuisine of Indonesia consists of a tremendous variety of delicious preparations. The main course of all meals is rice, with most meals consisting of a bowl of boiled rice that is surrounded by many different platters of spicy foods. Although the foods are generally very hot and spicy, they are meant to be mixed with the rice, which tends to "soften the blow." Noodles, vegetables (many pickled), fresh fruits, and coconut are also eaten every day. Grilled foods, served with *sa-tay* (dipping sauces) are popular, often featuring the flavors of chilies, peanuts, lime juice, ginger root, and various other spices.

In the Philippines, seafood dominates the cuisine, with soups and stews being the most common method of preparation. All of these one-pot meals are served with rice, however, rice does not play as dominant a role here as it does in other Asian countries. Garlic, vinegar and bay leaves help to create the often sour flavor that is typical of Philippine foods.

In the cuisine of Vietnam there are unmistakable Chinese influences, such as the use of chopsticks and the addition of rice to every meal. The diet in the South consists of a lot more fruits and vegetables, and much spicier foods than in the North, however, both regions share many tastes. Instead of stir-frying, in both regions foods are boiled often in combinations that seem strange to us, and usually cooked on an open hearth. A very salty fish sauce is used as a condiment and added to almost every type of dish. This sauce contains chilies, sugar, vinegar, garlic, and either lemon or lime juice. Coconut milk and lemon grass are also used extensively.

If we were to look for similarities in Oriental cuisine in general, one thing that stands out is the necessity for the cutting and chopping of ingredients. While the majority of dishes take very little actual cooking time, it is vitally important to have all the ingredients chopped before you start so the dishes can be assembled quickly. In most Oriental countries, foods are not baked in an oven in the Western sense. Typically they are fried, steamed, grilled, or boiled. Perhaps one of the major differences between their cuisine and ours is that dairy products are rarely used. Coconut milk is often used in sauces and desserts, however, milk, cream, and cheeses are practically unheard of. Another characteristic that sets the food apart from that of the rest of the world is that meat is used mostly for flavoring, with the bulk of most dishes being comprised of noodles, rice, and vegetables.

In most Oriental meals the appetizer is served first, followed by a variety of dishes, with no one dish being the "entrée" as we know it. Fresh fruits, puddings, and custards are the most common desserts. The emphasis in most Asian countries is on the arrangement and appearance of the food, which is definitely regarded as an esthetic experience. This is especially true in Japan where food is meticulously prepared and there is a serious dedication to visual appeal and harmony.

Adapting Oriental foods to a lowfat, meatless lifestyle is a relatively easy task. Seafood can easily be replaced with tofu, vegetable broth can be used to replace meat broth, and with the use of a nonstick skillet, large amounts of oil can be greatly reduced. Perhaps the biggest challenge is in finding readily available ingredients to replace the foreign ingredients and sauces. In keeping with today's busy lifestyle, I had to sacrifice authenticity for ease, however, I learned that this can be done without sacrificing flavor.

This is an exciting region of the world. Enjoy your tour of the Orient!

Flavors of the Orient
Recipes

Suggested Menus

Lunch

Sesame Asparagus Salad (426)
Honey Sweet Noodles (455)
Oranges in Cinnamon Syrup (464)

Lychee Fruit Salad (459)
Tofu Salad with
Peanuts and Ginger (424)
Szechuan Cold Noodles (457)

Indonesian Cabbage Salad with
Pineapple and Peanuts (423)
Stir-Fried Noodles with
Mushrooms and Garlic (454)
Hot Orange Dessert Soup (460)

Dinner

Chinese Egg Rolls (408)
Dipping Sauces (410)
Sweet and Pungent Tofu (430)
Steamed Broccoli with
Hoisin Sauce (442)
Brown Rice
Anise Pears (461)

Miso Onion Soup (417)
Japanese Tofu with Broccoli
and Mushrooms (436)
Grilled Eggplant with
Sesame-Soy Marinade (443)
Brown Rice
Philippine Citrus Custards (462)

Sweet Carrot Salad with
Fruits and Nuts (425)
Tofu Kabobs with
Peanut Sauce (434)
Pineapple Fried Rice (448)
Steamed Green Beans
Thai Fried Bananas (463)

Velvet Corn Soup (418)
Chinese Bean Cakes with
Garlic and Ginger (412)
Stir-Fried Vegetables (438)
Brown Rice
Chinese Almond Cream (458)

Recipe page numbers appear in parentheses.

Chinese Egg Rolls

Making these Chinese favorites is easier than you think! This easy egg roll recipe, from Burgers 'n Fries 'n Cinnamon Buns* *has all of the flavor of the authentic egg rolls, with almost none of the fat.*

Makes 8 egg rolls

2	teaspoons reduced-sodium (or regular) soy sauce
2	tablespoons water
2	teaspoons cornstarch
1	teaspoon *each* vegetable oil and sesame oil
1¹/2	cups finely shredded cabbage
1¹/2	cups finely shredded Chinese cabbage
¹/2	cup shredded carrots
¹/2	cup canned bamboo shoots, cut into matchstick-size pieces
2	green onions, thinly sliced (green and white parts)
1	package egg roll wrappers (available in Oriental markets and many large grocery stores)
1	teaspoon all-purpose flour
1	tablespoon water

In a small bowl, combine soy sauce, water, and cornstarch. Stir to dissolve cornstarch. Set aside.

Heat both oils in a large nonstick skillet over medium heat. Add both types of cabbage, carrots, bamboo shoots, and green onions. Cook, stirring constantly, until vegetables are tender, about 3 minutes. Stir soy sauce mixture and drizzle over cabbage. Cook and stir, 1 minute. Remove skillet from heat.

To assemble egg rolls, place 2 tablespoons of vegetable mixture diagonally across one wrapper, keeping remaining wrappers covered with a damp towel to prevent drying. Fold bottom corner over filling, then fold over left and right corners. Roll up egg roll to enclose filling. Combine flour and water in a small bowl or custard cup. With your finger, spread a little on the last corner to seal the edges. (Most packages of wrappers have handy diagrams to demonstrate the rolling process.)

Reheat the skillet over medium heat. Oil it lightly or spray with a nonstick cooking spray. With your finger, "paint" a small amount of

Burgers 'n Fries 'n Cinnamon Buns is a delightful collection of lowfat, meatless versions of fast food favorites, written by Bobbie Hinman.

oil on each egg roll. Place egg rolls in skillet and, turning frequently, cook until brown on all sides. (If you make the egg rolls cylindrical, rather than flat, they will brown more evenly.)

Serve with *Mustard Sauce* or *Sweet and Sour Sauce*. (Recipes follow.)

	Each egg roll provides:		
129	Calories	22 g	Carbohydrate
4 g	Protein	240 mg	Sodium
3 g	Total fat (0 g sat. fat)	3 mg	Cholesterol

Dipping Sauces

Mustard Sauce

This tangy sauce is often served in Chinese restaurants and can be used as a condiment for any Asian dish. Be careful though, it's hot! A little goes a long way!

Makes 3 tablespoons

2　　tablespoons dry mustard
2　　tablespoons water

Place mustard in a small bowl or custard cup. Add water, 1 teaspoon at a time, stirring until smooth. Add more water if a thinner sauce is desired.

Store in the refrigerator.

Each tablespoon provides:

6	Calories	0 g	Carbohydrate
0 g	Protein	0 mg	Sodium
0 g	Total fat (0 g sat. fat)	0 mg	Cholesterol

Note: This recipe is from *Burgers 'n Fries 'n Cinnamon Buns*. A delightful collection of lowfat, meatless versions of fast food favorites, written by Bobbie Hinman.

Sweet and Sour Sauce

This is similar to the "duck sauce" that is served in most Chinese restaurants. It's slightly sweet and slightly sour and is great for dipping. It makes a tasty sauce to serve with any of the appetizers in this chapter.

Makes 1/3 cup

1/4	cup fruit-only peach or apricot jam
1/2	teaspoon dry mustard
1	teaspoon reduced-sodium (or regular) soy sauce
1	teaspoon white vinegar
1	teaspoon water

In a small bowl or custard cup, combine all ingredients, mixing well. Add more water if a thinner sauce is desired.

Store in the refrigerator.

Each tablespoon provides:

35	Calories	9 g	Carbohydrate
0 g	Protein	40 mg	Sodium
0 g	Total fat (0 g sat. fat)	0 mg	Cholesterol

Note: This recipe is from *Burgers 'n Fries 'n Cinnamon Buns*. A delightful collection of lowfat, meatless versions of fast food favorites, written by Bobbie Hinman.

Chinese Bean Cakes
with Garlic and Ginger

This easy Chinese appetizer can be made with any type of cooked beans.

Makes 4 servings
(4 bean cakes each serving)

1	1-pound can kidney beans, rinsed and drained (or 2 cups of cooked beans)
1	teaspoon reduced-sodium (or regular) soy sauce
1/2	teaspoon sesame oil
1	teaspoon grated fresh ginger root
1	teaspoon finely minced garlic
1/8	teaspoon pepper
1/4	cup all-purpose flour
1	egg white
2	tablespoons water
1/2	cup dry bread crumbs

Place beans in a large bowl and mash with a fork or potato masher.

Heat soy sauce and oil in a small nonstick skillet over medium heat. Add ginger and garlic, cooking until ginger and garlic start to stick together. Remove from heat and add to bean mixture, along with pepper. Mix well.

Place flour in a small bowl. Whisk egg white and water together in a second bowl. Place bread crumbs in a third bowl. Form mixture into 2-inch patties about 1/2-inch thick. Dip each patty in flour, coating all sides. Dip in egg white and then in bread crumbs, coating all sides.

Heat a large nonstick skillet over medium heat. Oil it lightly or spray with a nonstick cooking spray. Place bean cakes in skillet and cook until lightly browned on both sides. Spray them lightly when you turn them so both sides will be moistened.

Serve hot with hoisin sauce or *Sweet and Sour Sauce* (page 411).

Each serving provides:

194	Calories	29 g	Carbohydrate
9 g	Protein	321 mg	Sodium
4 g	Total fat (1 g sat. fat)	0 mg	Cholesterol

Lentil Wontons

I replaced the meat filling with lentils and added the spark of ginger and onion, with impressive results.

Makes 8 servings
(4 wontons each serving)

1/3   cup lentils, uncooked
2   cups water
2   teaspoons reduced-sodium (or regular) soy sauce
1   green onion (green and white part), finely chopped
1/2   teaspoon grated fresh ginger root
32   wonton wrappers (available in most grocery stores)
        Boiling water

Place lentils and water in a small saucepan. Bring to a boil over medium heat. Cover, reduce heat to medium-low, and simmer 45 minutes, until lentils are tender. Drain.

Place lentils in a small bowl and mash with a fork or potato masher. Add soy sauce, onion, and ginger root. Mix well.

Place one teaspoonful of lentil mixture in the center of each wonton wrapper. Fold each one in half to form a triangle. Dip your finger in water and "paint" the edges of the wrapper, then press them together to seal. Bring the opposite corners together, forming the wonton into a ring shape, overlap the corners and seal with a dab of water.

Place wontons in a large saucepan of boiling water and simmer 3 to 4 minutes, until tender. Carefully remove them from the water with a slotted spoon.

Serve with *Sweet and Sour Sauce* (page 411) or serve in hot vegetable broth.

For crisp wontons, drain cooked wontons well and place on a baking sheet that has been sprayed with a nonstick cooking spray. Spray the wontons lightly and bake them in a 400° oven until crisp, 10 to 15 minutes.

Each serving provides:

121	Calories	23 g	Carbohydrate
5 g	Protein	234 mg	Sodium
1 g	Total fat (0 g sat. fat)	3 mg	Cholesterol

Indonesian Corn Fritters
with Peanut Dipping Sauce

These delicious little pancakes are served as an appetizer or snack in Indonesia. They combine the interesting flavors of garlic, coriander, and cumin, and along with the delicious peanut sauce, really make a terrific dish. This recipe doubles easily, so you can make enough for a crowd.

Makes 4 servings
(4 fritters and 2 tablespoons sauce each serving)

Corn Fritters:

1	11-ounce can salt-free (or regular) corn, drained (Choose vacuum packed corn.)
$1/4$	cup water
2	large cloves garlic, crushed
$1/3$	cup all-purpose flour
2	egg whites
$3/4$	teaspoon ground coriander
$1/4$	teaspoon ground cumin
$1/4$	teaspoon salt
$1/4$	teaspoon pepper
$1/3$	cup thinly sliced green onions (green and white parts)

Peanut Sauce:

2	tablespoons creamy-style peanut butter (Choose one without added sugar or fat.)
$1/3$	cup skim milk
2	tablespoons very finely minced onions
$1/2$	tablespoon reduced-sodium (or regular) soy sauce
$1/2$	tablespoon lemon juice
$1/2$	teaspoon coconut extract
$1/16$	teaspoon cayenne pepper
1	teaspoon cornstarch

In a blender container, combine corn, water, and garlic. Blend for a few seconds, until the mixture is blended but not completely puréed. Spoon into a bowl and add remaining fritter ingredients. Mix well.

Preheat a large nonstick skillet or griddle over medium heat. Oil it lightly or spray with a nonstick cooking spray. Using a tablespoonful for each fritter, drop the corn mixture onto the griddle. Turn when edges appear dry and bottoms are lightly browned. Cook until golden brown on both sides.

Peanut sauce: (This can be made before fritters and kept warm or you can make the fritters first and keep them warm in a 200° oven while making the sauce.)

Place peanut butter in a small saucepan. Gradually stir in milk, then add remaining ingredients. Stir to dissolve cornstarch. Bring mixture to a boil over medium heat, stirring constantly. Continue to cook and stir, 1 to 2 minutes more. Serve with fritters, allowing about 1/2 tablespoon of sauce for each fritter.

Each serving provides:

164	Calories	25 g	Carbohydrate
7 g	Protein	284 mg	Sodium
4 g	Total fat (0 g sat. fat)	0 mg	Cholesterol

Shiitake Mushroom and Tofu Patties

The idea for this recipe came from a delicious (but deep-fried) patty that I tasted in a Japanese restaurant. If you love the "woodsy" taste of shiitake mushrooms, this dish is for you.

Makes 8 servings
(4 patties each serving)

1	teaspoon vegetable oil
4	ounces shiitake mushrooms, stems discarded, and caps finely chopped (1 cup)
3	cloves garlic, finely chopped (Mushrooms and garlic can be chopped together in a food processor.)
1	pound medium or firm tofu, thinly sliced and drained well between layers of towels
2	tablespoons reduced-sodium (or regular) soy sauce
1/8	teaspoon pepper

Heat oil in a small nonstick skillet over medium heat. Add mushrooms and garlic. Cook, stirring frequently, until mushrooms are tender and fragrant, about 5 minutes.

While mushrooms are cooking, place drained tofu in a large bowl. Mash with a fork or potato masher. Add soy sauce and pepper and mash again.

Add cooked mushrooms to tofu. Mix well. Divide mixture evenly and shape into 32 small patties, pressing mixture together firmly.

Heat a large nonstick griddle or skillet over medium heat. Oil it lightly or spray with a nonstick cooking spray. Place patties on griddle and cook until the bottoms are nicely browned. Turn patties several times, until nicely browned on both sides. (They will be easier to turn and will hold together better if you let the bottoms brown before turning them.) Serve with your favorite dipping sauce.

Each serving provides:

64	Calories	2 g	Carbohydrate
5 g	Protein	154 mg	Sodium
4 g	Total fat (1 g sat. fat)	0 mg	Cholesterol

Miso Onion Soup

Miso is made from fermented soybeans and is used in Japan to thicken and season soups and sauces. The Japanese favor miso as a promoter of good health and many eat it daily. (Miso comes in a variety of flavors and colors, from light to dark. I prefer the rich flavor of a medium to dark miso.) If you haven't tried miso, it's definitely worth a trip to a health food store.

Makes 6 servings
(1 cup each serving)

2   tablespoons vegetable oil
1 1/2   pounds yellow onions, thinly sliced (about 5 medium onions)
1/2   teaspoon sugar
1/4   cup miso
4 1/4   cups water
1 1/2   teaspoons reduced-sodium (or regular) soy sauce

Heat oil in a large saucepan over low heat. Add onions, stirring to coat them with the oil. Cover and cook until onions are tender, about 15 minutes. Add small amounts of water as necessary, about a table-spoon at a time, to prevent sticking.

Uncover saucepan, increase heat to medium, and sprinkle sugar over onions. Cook, stirring frequently, until onions are golden, about 15 minutes.

Place miso in a small bowl. Add 1/4 cup of the water, stirring until mixture is smooth. Add to onions, along with remaining water and soy sauce.

Heat through, but do not boil.

Variation: To make a French version of this soup, after cooking, divide soup into six ovenproof bowls, reserving about 1/3 cup of the broth. Place a toasted slice of french bread over the soup in each bowl. Top with a small amount of shredded part-skim Mozzarella cheese or reduced-fat Swiss cheese and spoon reserved broth over the cheese. Place in a preheated 350° oven until the cheese melts.

Each serving provides:

109	Calories	13 g	Carbohydrate
3 g	Protein	471 mg	Sodium
5 g	Total fat (1 g sat. fat)	0 mg	Cholesterol

Velvet Corn Soup

Many Americans are familiar with this soup because versions of it appear on the menus of many Cantonese restaurants. In this flavorful variation of the classic, the broth is laced with sherry and sparked with lots of pepper, creating a memorable combination of flavors.

Makes 4 servings
(1¹/4 cups each serving)

3	cups *Vegetable Broth,* or 3 cups of water plus 3 teaspoons *Vegetable Broth Mix* (See pages 26–27.)
1	1-pound can salt-free (or regular) cream-style corn
3	tablespoons sherry
2	tablespoons reduced-sodium (or regular) soy sauce
2	tablespoons cornstarch
3	tablespoons water
¹/3	cup thinly sliced green onion (green part only)
	Pepper or bottled hot sauce to taste

In a medium saucepan, combine broth, corn, sherry, and soy sauce. Bring mixture to a boil over medium heat.

Combine cornstarch and water in a small bowl and mix until cornstarch is dissolved. Stir into boiling soup, along with green onions. When soup boils again, continue to cook and stir, for 2 minutes.

Remove from heat and add lots of pepper.

Each serving provides:

135	Calories	30 g	Carbohydrate
3 g	Protein	708 mg	Sodium
1 g	Total fat (0 g sat. fat)	0 mg	Cholesterol

Indonesian Peanut Soup

This soup has a very interesting, almost complex flavor. It combines the sweetness of molasses, the saltiness of soy sauce, the smoothness of peanut butter, and the tartness of lemon. Add to that sliced green onions and chopped peanuts, and you have a unique and delicious broth.

Makes 6 servings
(3/4 cup each serving)

4	cups *Vegetable Broth* or 4 cups of water plus 4 teaspoons *Vegetable Broth Mix* (See pages 26–27.)
1 1/2	tablespoons molasses
1	tablespoon reduced-sodium (or regular) soy sauce
1	tablespoon freshly squeezed lemon juice
2	large cloves garlic, crushed
2	tablespoons creamy-style peanut butter (Choose one without added sugar or fat.)
1/3	cup thinly sliced green onions (green and white parts)
2	tablespoons chopped dry roasted peanuts (unsalted)

In a medium saucepan, combine broth, molasses, soy sauce, lemon juice, and garlic.

Place peanut butter in a small bowl and stir in some broth mixture, a few teaspoons at a time, until mixture is thin and smooth, then stir it into the saucepan. Bring mixture to a boil over medium heat, then reduce heat to medium-low, cover, and simmer 15 minutes.

Stir soup and spoon into serving bowls. Top each serving with some of the sliced green onions and chopped peanuts.

Each serving provides:

81	Calories	9 g	Carbohydrate
3 g	Protein	201 mg	Sodium
4 g	Total fat (1 g sat. fat)	0 mg	Cholesterol

Tomato Ginger Soup

From the coastal region of China where clear soups are popular, comes this clear, aromatic broth. The original version was made with fresh tomatoes (and you can still use them), but when good fresh tomatoes weren't available, I tried it with canned. Much to my delight, it works quite well. Often cooked rice or noodles are placed in each serving bowl and then the soup is spooned in.

Makes 4 servings
(1¹/₄ cups each serving)

4	cups *Vegetable Broth*, or 4 cups of water plus 4 teaspoons *Vegetable Broth Mix* (See pages 26–27.)
1	1-pound can salt-free (or regular) tomatoes, chopped and drained (or 1¹/₂ cups ripe, peeled tomatoes, chopped and drained)
2	tablespoons reduced-sodium (or regular) soy sauce
2	teaspoons grated fresh ginger root
2	teaspoons sugar

Combine all ingredients in a small saucepan. Bring to a boil over medium heat.

Reduce heat to medium-low, cover, and simmer 20 minutes.

Serve with rice or noodles, if desired.

Each serving provides:			
54	Calories	12 g	Carbohydrate
2 g	Protein	424 mg	Sodium
0 g	Total fat (0 g sat. fat)	0 mg	Cholesterol

Hot and Sour Soup

My daughter Traci, whose cooking makes me very proud, came up with this easy recipe for one of the most popular Chinese soups. It will definitely clear your sinuses!

Makes 4 servings
(1 cup each serving)

1/4	cup water
2	tablespoons cornstarch
4	cups *Vegetable Broth,* or 4 cups of water plus 4 teaspoons *Vegetable Broth Mix* (See pages 26–27.)
1	large carrot, coarsely shredded
1/2	cup sliced water chestnuts, cut into thin strips
1	tablespoon sherry
4	ounces firm tofu, thinly sliced, then cut into small rectangles
8	snow peas, cut diagonally into 1/4-inch strips
2	tablespoons red wine vinegar
1 1/2	tablespoons reduced-sodium (or regular) soy sauce
1	teaspoon sesame oil
1/2	teaspoon pepper
2	green onions, thinly sliced (green and white parts)

In a small bowl, combine water and cornstarch. Stir to dissolve cornstarch. Set aside.

In a medium saucepan, combine broth, carrot, water chestnuts, and sherry. Bring to a boil over medium heat. Reduce heat to medium-low, cover, and simmer 5 minutes.

Add tofu, snow peas, vinegar, and soy sauce. Increase heat to medium and when mixture boils again, cook uncovered, 3 minutes. Stir cornstarch mixture and add to saucepan. Continue to cook and stir, for 2 minutes more. Remove from heat and stir in sesame oil and pepper. Stir in green onions.

Each serving provides:			
128	Calories	18 g	Carbohydrate
6 g	Protein	351 mg	Sodium
4 g	Total fat (1 g sat. fat)	0 mg	Cholesterol

Gingered Cabbage and Vegetables

In Japan this medley of colorful vegetables in a tangy ginger dressing is usually served as a side dish, along with several entrées and vegetable dishes. (I've served it as a summer barbecue salad and received rave reviews.)

Makes 12 servings

5	cups cabbage, shredded 1 1/4-inch thick
1	teaspoon salt
	Boiling water
1	cup thinly sliced radishes
1	cup thinly sliced green onions (green and white parts)
1	cup thinly sliced cucumber (Peel cucumber if the skin has been waxed.)
1	cup green bell pepper, cut into matchstick-size pieces
1	cup turnip, peeled and cut into matchstick-size pieces
1	cup coarsely shredded carrots

Ginger Dressing:

1	teaspoon grated fresh ginger root
1	cup white vinegar
1/3	cup sugar
1/4	teaspoon plus 1/8 teaspoon pepper

Place sliced cabbage in a medium saucepan and sprinkle with salt. Pour enough boiling water in saucepan to cover cabbage. Let stand 10 minutes, then drain, rinse cabbage well under cold water, and drain again.

Place cabbage in a large bowl and add remaining vegetables. Mix well.

In a small bowl, combine all dressing ingredients, mixing for a few minutes until most of the sugar is dissolved. Pour over salad and mix well.

Chill thoroughly. Mix before serving.

Each serving provides:

45	Calories	11 g	Carbohydrate
1 g	Protein	65 mg	Sodium
0 g	Total fat (0 g sat. fat)	0 mg	Cholesterol

Indonesian Cabbage Salad
with Pineapple and Peanuts

The inventive nature of the people of Indonesia has created a tremendous variety of delicious preparations, among them some very interesting salads. The peanuts and vegetables give this one lots of crunch, while the pineapple and molasses add a delicious, sweet flavor. Most of the authentic versions are loaded with hot peppers, which I eliminated, however, you can easily add a chopped jalapeño or some red pepper flakes if you'd like.

Makes 6 servings

3	cups (packed) finely shredded cabbage
2	medium carrots, sliced lengthwise into thin strips, using a vegetable peeler
1/2	medium green bell pepper, cut lengthwise into very thin strips
1	8-ounce can pineapple tidbits or chunks (packed in juice), drained, (Juice reserved.)
1/4	cup dry roasted peanuts (unsalted), finely chopped
1/4	cup reserved pineapple juice
1	tablespoon molasses
1	tablespoon reduced-sodium (or regular) soy sauce
1 1/2	teaspoons lemon juice
2	cloves garlic, very finely minced
	Salt and pepper to taste

In a medium bowl, combine cabbage, carrot, bell pepper, pineapple, and peanuts.

In a small bowl, combine remaining ingredients. Pour over cabbage mixture. Mix well.

Chill several hours or overnight to blend flavors. Mix before serving.

Each serving provides:

95	Calories	16 g	Carbohydrate
3 g	Protein	120 mg	Sodium
3 g	Total fat (0 g sat. fat)	0 mg	Cholesterol

Tofu Salad with Peanuts and Ginger

In Asian countries, tofu even shows up in salads! In this marinated medley, the flavors of Thailand and China intermingle with wonderful results. A pretty way to serve this tangy salad is on a bed of fresh spinach, garnished with sliced tomatoes and cucumbers. It makes a delectable salad for six or light entrée for four.

Makes 6 servings

1	pound medium or firm tofu, cut into 1/4-inch cubes, drained well between towels
1/3	cup thinly sliced green onions (green and white parts)
1/2	cup finely shredded carrots
2	tablespoons reduced-sodium (or regular) soy sauce
2	tablespoons sherry
1	teaspoon sesame oil
1	teaspoon grated fresh ginger root
1/2	teaspoon sugar
	A few drops bottled hot sauce, or to taste
2	tablespoons finely chopped dry roasted peanuts (unsalted)
	Fresh spinach leaves, sliced tomato, and sliced cucumber (optional)

Place tofu in a medium bowl. Add green onions and carrots. Toss gently.

In a small bowl, combine remaining salad ingredients, *except* peanuts and optional ingredients. Mix well and pour over tofu. Mix gently but thoroughly.

Chill several hours or overnight.

Mix before serving. Sprinkle each serving with chopped peanuts.

Arrange salad on a bed of fresh spinach and garnish with tomatoes and cucumbers, if desired.

Each serving provides:

100	Calories	5 g	Carbohydrate
7 g	Protein	211 mg	Sodium
6 g	Total fat (1 g sat. fat)	0 mg	Cholesterol

Sweet Carrot Salad with Fruits and Nuts

Dates are a popular fruit in China, most often used in sweets, and occasionally showing up in salads. This sweet and crunchy dish is laced with the delectable flavors of orange and almond. The unmistakable texture of the carrots, along with the chewy sweetness of the raisins and dates, makes a truly superb dish.

Makes 4 servings

1	cup coarsely shredded carrots
1/2	cup crushed pineapple (packed in juice), drained slightly
1/4	cup raisins
1/4	cup chopped, pitted dates
2	tablespoons coarsely chopped almonds
1/3	cup orange juice
1	teaspoon sugar
1/8	teaspoon almond extract

In a small bowl, combine carrots, pineapple, raisins, dates, and almonds. Mix well.

Combine orange juice, sugar, and almond extract in a small bowl or custard cup. Stir to dissolve sugar. Add to carrot mixture and mix well.

Chill several hours or overnight.

Mix again before serving.

Each serving provides:

126	Calories	27 g	Carbohydrate
2 g	Protein	12 mg	Sodium
2 g	Total fat (0 g sat. fat)	0 mg	Cholesterol

Sesame Asparagus Salad

In this salad I combined ideas and ingredients from a few Asian cultures and created my own delicious dish. Although its origins may be "generic," the dark, rich flavor is really wonderful. Try to find young, very thin asparagus stalks, as they are usually more tender and absorb more of the marinade.

Makes 6 servings

1	pound fresh asparagus, trimmed and cut diagonally into 1¹/₂- to 2-inch lengths
3	tablespoons cider vinegar
3	tablespoons reduced-sodium (or regular) soy sauce
1¹/₂	tablespoons sugar
2	teaspoons sesame oil
	Pepper or bottled hot sauce to taste
1	tablespoon sesame seeds, lightly toasted (optional)

Place a steamer rack in the bottom of a medium saucepan. Add enough water to come almost up to the bottom of the rack. Place saucepan over medium heat. When water boils, add asparagus, cover saucepan, and cook 3 to 5 minutes or until asparagus is just tender-crisp. Drain, then rinse asparagus under cold water and drain again. Place asparagus in a shallow bowl.

Combine remaining ingredients, *except* sesame seeds, in a small bowl. Mix well and pour over asparagus. Chill several hours, or preferably overnight, mixing several times.

Mix before serving and sprinkle with sesame seeds, if desired.

Each serving provides:

40	Calories	6 g	Carbohydrate
2 g	Protein	301 mg	Sodium
2 g	Total fat (0 g sat. fat)	0 mg	Cholesterol

Chinese Cucumber Pickles

Chinese-style pickled vegetables can be served as crisp appetizers or as a side dish with any meal. In this salad from Northern China, the light sesame vinaigrette provides a delightful, piquant contrast to the fresh cucumbers. These delicious pickles go well with Chinese or Western meals and they're ideal for picnics.

Makes 4 servings

1	large cucumber, unpeeled, sliced crosswise into diagonal slices 1/4-inch thick (Peel the cucumber if the skin has been waxed.)
1	teaspoon salt
1	teaspoon dried, crushed hot peppers (optional)
1	teaspoon sugar
2	teaspoons white vinegar
1	teaspoon sesame oil

Arrange cucumbers on a plate in a single layer. Sprinkle with salt and let stand 10 minutes. Then drain off any liquid and place cucumber slices in a small bowl. If using chili peppers, add them to the cucumbers and mix well. Cover cucumbers and chill several hours.

About 10 minutes before serving, sprinkle cucumbers with the sugar and vinegar and mix well. Add oil and mix again. Let stand 10 minutes, then serve.

These pickles are at their best when served fresh, however the leftovers will keep in the refrigerator for four to five days.

Each serving provides:

24	Calories	3 g	Carbohydrate
0 g	Protein	275 mg	Sodium
1 g	Total fat (0 g sat. fat)	0 mg	Cholesterol

Oriental Pickled Beets

Many years ago my cousin brought this recipe back from a trip through Asia. She gave it to my mother who made a few slight alterations and came up with this delightful version. It's sweet, yet tangy, and can be served alone or used (American style) to top a tossed salad.

Makes 8 servings

2	1-pound cans sliced beets, drained (Reserve 2/3 cup liquid.)
1 1/2	tablespoons cornstarch
1/3	cup vinegar
1/3	cup sugar
1	tablespoon ketchup
1/2	teaspoon vanilla extract
1/8	teaspoon ground cloves
1/16	teaspoon salt

In a small saucepan, combine beet liquid and cornstarch. Mix until cornstarch is dissolved. Stir in remaining ingredients, adding beets last.

Bring mixture to a boil over medium heat, stirring frequently. Continue to cook and stir, for 2 to 3 minutes.

Cool slightly, then spoon into a bowl and chill.

Serve cold.

Each serving provides:			
71	Calories	18 g	Carbohydrate
1 g	Protein	281 mg	Sodium
0 g	Total fat (0 g sat. fat)	0 mg	Cholesterol

Shanghai Tofu and Nectarines

The cuisine of Shanghai is just like this dish—subtle, yet complex. Served over rice, this dish is sure to become a favorite.

Makes 4 servings

1/2	cup water
3	tablespoons reduced-sodium (or regular) soy sauce
1	teaspoon *Vegetable Broth Mix* (See page 27.)
1	tablespoon sherry
1	tablespoon cornstarch
3	teaspoons vegetable oil
1	pound firm tofu, sliced 1/4-inch thick, then cut into 1/4-inch strips and drained between layers of towels
2	cups onion, cut vertically into thin slivers
5	large cloves garlic, crushed
2	cups thinly sliced mushrooms
2	large, ripe nectarines, unpeeled, sliced 1/8- to 1/4-inch thick (2 cups)

In a small bowl, combine water, soy sauce, broth mix, sherry, and cornstarch. Stir to dissolve cornstarch. Set aside.

Heat 2 teaspoons of the oil in a large nonstick skillet or wok over medium-high heat. Add tofu. Cook, stirring gently, 5 minutes or until tofu is lightly browned. Place tofu in a bowl and cover with foil to keep warm.

Return skillet to heat and add remaining oil. When oil is hot, add onion and garlic. Cook and stir constantly, 2 minutes. Add mushrooms. Cook, stirring, 2 minutes.

Stir soy sauce mixture and add to skillet along with nectarines and tofu. Cook and stir, 1 to 2 minutes, until sauce has thickened and mixture is glazed.

Serve over brown rice.

Each serving provides:

297	Calories	27 g	Carbohydrate
21 g	Protein	491 mg	Sodium
14 g	Total fat (2 g sat. fat)	0 mg	Cholesterol

Sweet and Pungent Tofu

"Sweet and pungent" is a familiar theme in Chinese cooking, varying slightly from region to region. This is a popular Cantonese version, one that is popular in Chinese restaurants in America. If you know any Chinese food connoisseurs, you must make this dish for them! It really tastes like it came from the finest Chinese restaurant!

Makes 4 servings

1	pound firm tofu, sliced 1/2-inch thick, then cut into 1- x 2-inch rectangles
1	tablespoon reduced-sodium (or regular) soy sauce
1	tablespoon sherry
1/2	teaspoon vegetable oil

Sauce:

1	cup pineapple juice
1/2	cup sugar
1/4	cup plus 2 tablespoons water
3	tablespoons vinegar
1	tablespoon soy sauce
3	tablespoons cornstarch
1	teaspoon vegetable oil

Additional Ingredients:

1	8-ounce can pineapple chunks (packed in juice), drained
1	cup green bell pepper, cut into 1-inch squares
1/3	cup carrots, sliced crosswise into 1/8-inch slices
12	snow peas, cut into 1-inch pieces

Drain tofu well between layers of towels. Place tofu in a plastic bag and set the bag in a large bowl. Combine soy sauce and sherry and pour over tofu. Marinate at least 30 minutes (and up to several hours), turning bag over several times.

Heat the 1/2 teaspoon of oil in a large nonstick skillet or wok over medium-high heat. Add tofu and marinade. Cook, stirring frequently, until tofu is nicely browned on both sides. Remove tofu from skillet, place in a bowl, and cover with foil to keep warm.

Combine sauce ingredients in a small bowl. Stir to dissolve cornstarch. Set aside.

Add remaining teaspoon of oil to the skillet and heat over medium-high heat. Add pineapple, bell pepper, and carrots. Cook and stir, 2 minutes. Add snow peas and continue to cook and stir, 1 minute more.

Stir sauce and add to skillet along with tofu. Cook, stirring constantly, until sauce has thickened and is hot and bubbly, about 1 to 2 minutes.

Serve over rice.

Each serving provides:

392	Calories	57 g	Carbohydrate
19 g	Protein	322 mg	Sodium
12 g	Total fat (2 g sat. fat)	0 mg	Cholesterol

Kung Pao Tofu

This is my easy version of a very popular Szechuan dish that's made with chicken in most Chinese restaurants. It's normally quite hot and spicy, and if you prefer it that way, just add a few whole dried chili peppers or a teaspoon of crushed red pepper flakes. In addition to the wonderful flavor, you'll love the crunch of the peanuts.

Makes 4 servings

1	pound firm tofu, cut into 1/2-inch cubes and drained between layers of towels
3	tablespoons reduced-sodium (or regular) soy sauce
2	tablespoons sherry
1	tablespoon vinegar
2	teaspoons sugar
1/8	teaspoon pepper
1	cup *Vegetable Broth,* or 1 cup of water plus 1 teaspoon *Vegetable Broth Mix* (See pages 26–27.)
1	tablespoon cornstarch
2	teaspoons sesame oil
3	large cloves garlic, finely chopped
1	teaspoon finely chopped fresh ginger root
1	cup chopped onion
1	cup chopped green bell pepper
1/2	cup dry roasted peanuts (unsalted)

Place drained tofu in a small bowl. Combine 1 tablespoon of soy sauce and 1 tablespoon of sherry and spoon over tofu. Mix gently and set aside to marinate for about 10 minutes.

In a small bowl, combine remaining soy sauce and sherry, vinegar, sugar, pepper, broth, and cornstarch. Stir to dissolve cornstarch. Set aside.

Heat 1 teaspoon of sesame oil in a large nonstick skillet or wok over medium-high heat. Add tofu. Cook, stirring frequently, until tofu cubes are lightly browned on all sides, about 5 minutes. Remove tofu from skillet, place in a bowl, and cover to keep warm.

Return skillet to heat and add remaining sesame oil. Add garlic and ginger root and cook for 10 seconds or until sizzling. Add onion, bell pepper, and peanuts. Cook and stir, for a few minutes, until vegetables are tender-crisp. Return tofu to skillet. Stir sauce and pour over tofu and vegetables. Cook, stirring constantly, 1 to 2 minutes, until sauce has thickened.

Serve with rice.

Each serving provides:			
358	Calories	22 g	Carbohydrate
24 g	Protein	497 mg	Sodium
21 g	Total fat (3 g sat. fat)	0 mg	Cholesterol

Tofu Kabobs with Peanut Sauce

Barbecuing foods on skewers is commonplace in Thailand where this recipe originated.

Makes 4 servings

1	pound firm tofu, cut into 1-inch cubes, drained between towels
2	large cloves garlic, coarsely chopped
1/2	cup chopped onion
2	tablespoons *each* lime juice and water
1	tablespoon reduced-sodium (or regular) soy sauce
1	tablespoon firmly packed brown sugar

Peanut Sauce:

2/3	cup skim milk
1/4	cup very finely chopped onion
1/4	cup creamy-style peanut butter (Choose one without added sugar or fat.)
1	tablespoon reduced-sodium (or regular) soy sauce
1	tablespoon lemon juice
1	teaspoon coconut extract
1/8	teaspoon cayenne pepper

Place tofu in a plastic bag and set bag in a large bowl. In a blender container, combine remaining ingredients, *except* those for sauce. Blend until smooth. Pour over tofu in bag. Marinate in the refrigerator 5 to 6 hours or longer, turning bag over several times. Remove tofu from refrigerator and let stand at room temperature 30 minutes.

In a small saucepan, combine sauce ingredients. Mix well.

Preheat broiler or grill. Thread tofu onto four skewers. Place on a broiler pan or grill rack that has been oiled lightly or sprayed with a nonstick cooking spray. Broil until edges of tofu are crisp, turning several times and basting with marinade.

While tofu is broiling, bring sauce to a boil over medium heat. Spoon sauce into individual little serving bowls and use for dipping.

Each serving provides:			
315	Calories	18 g	Carbohydrate
24 g	Protein	404 mg	Sodium
18 g	Total fat (2 g sat. fat)	1 mg	Cholesterol

Chinese Tofu and Peppers

This is an excellent version of a well-known dish from Canton, where food is generally simple and basic with lots of taste appeal.

Makes 4 servings

2   teaspoons vegetable oil
1   pound firm tofu, cut into 1/2-inch cubes and drained between
       layers of towels
1/2   cup chopped onion
3   cloves garlic, finely minced
2   cups *Vegetable Broth,* or 2 cups of water plus 2 teaspoons
       Vegetable Broth Mix (See pages 26–27.)
2   cups chopped green bell pepper, in 1/2-inch pieces
3   large, ripe tomatoes, each cored and cut into 8 wedges
1/4   cup water
2   tablespoons reduced-sodium (or regular) soy sauce
1 1/2 tablespoons cornstarch
1/8   teaspoon pepper

Heat oil in a large nonstick skillet or wok over medium-high heat. Add tofu, onion, and garlic. Cook, stirring frequently, 3 to 4 minutes, until onion and tofu begin to brown.

Add 1 1/4 cups of the broth to skillet, along with bell pepper. Reduce heat to medium, cover skillet, and simmer, stirring occasionally, 15 minutes. Add tomatoes and remaining broth mixture. Cover and cook 5 minutes.

Combine water, soy sauce, cornstarch, and pepper in a small bowl, stirring to dissolve cornstarch. Add to skillet. Reduce heat to medium-low and cook, stirring constantly, 3 minutes or until mixture has thickened slightly and is hot and bubbly.

Serve with rice.

Each serving provides:

252	Calories	20 g	Carbohydrate
20 g	Protein	389 mg	Sodium
13 g	Total fat (2 g sat. fat)	0 mg	Cholesterol

Japanese Tofu with Broccoli and Mushrooms

One of the mainstays of Japanese cooking are tender and moist, vegetable medleys.

Makes 4 servings

1	pound firm tofu, cut into 2- x ¹/2- x ¹/2-inch strips and drained on towels
3	tablespoons reduced-sodium (or regular) soy sauce
3	tablespoons sherry
2	tablespoons water
3	cloves garlic, crushed
1	teaspoon sesame oil
3	cups broccoli, cut into flowerets
8	ounces mushrooms, sliced
1	tablespoon sesame seeds, lightly toasted (optional)

Place tofu in a single layer in a 7x11-inch baking pan.

Place 2 tablespoons of the soy sauce in a small bowl. Add sherry, water, and garlic and mix well. Pour over tofu. Marinate in the refrigerator for 4 to 5 hours. Turn tofu occasionally while marinating.

When ready to cook, heat oil in a large nonstick skillet over medium-high heat. Remove tofu from marinade, reserving marinade, and place in skillet. Cook, turning tofu carefully, until it is browned on all sides, about 8 minutes.

Move browned tofu to the edges of the pan and add broccoli and mushrooms to the center of the pan. Pour reserved marinade over vegetables, along with remaining soy sauce. Gently stir tofu into vegetables. Cook, stirring gently and frequently, until vegetables are tender-crisp and most of the liquid has cooked out, about 5 minutes.

Serve with rice or noodles. Sprinkle each serving with sesame seeds, if desired.

Each serving provides:

235	Calories	14 g	Carbohydrate
22 g	Protein	487 mg	Sodium
12 g	Total fat (2 g sat. fat)	0 mg	Cholesterol

Tofu in Ginger Sauce

Based on a variety of Asian flavors, small pieces of tofu are stir-fried with lots of ginger and then glazed with a sweet and sour tomato sauce. Like most stir-fried dishes, this one is delicious over rice or noodles. (Be sure to buy a good brand of canned tomatoes for this dish so you can be sure of getting a lot of tomatoes in the can.)

Makes 4 servings

2   teaspoons cornstarch
2   tablespoons reduced-sodium (or regular) soy sauce
1   tablespoon red wine vinegar
1   teaspoon sugar
1   1-pound can salt-free (or regular) tomatoes, chopped, and drained slightly
2   teaspoons vegetable oil
1   pound firm tofu, cut into 1/4-inch cubes, and drained well between towels
1   tablespoon grated fresh ginger root

In a medium bowl, combine cornstarch and soy sauce, stirring to dissolve cornstarch. Add vinegar, sugar, and tomatoes. Mix well. Set aside.

Heat oil in a large nonstick skillet or wok over medium-high heat. Add tofu and ginger. Cook and stir, until tofu pieces are lightly browned on all sides, about 3 to 5 minutes. Stir tomato mixture and add to skillet. Continue to cook and stir, for 1 minute or until sauce has thickened slightly and mixture is hot and bubbly.

Serve over rice or noodles.

Each serving provides:

223	Calories	13 g	Carbohydrate
19 g	Protein	331 mg	Sodium
12 g	Total fat (2 g sat. fat)	0 mg	Cholesterol

Stir-Fried Vegetables

Stir-frying is probably the best-known technique of Chinese cooking. Fresh vegetables, with their bright colors and crisp textures, can be cooked to perfection in a matter of minutes. Be sure to add the vegetables that require the longest cooking time first and the ones that require the shortest cooking time last. Also, have the vegetables that are to be added together in similar-size pieces so they will cook in the same amount of time. The vegetables in this recipe are merely a suggestion. Feel free to add or substitute any others that you wish. (Other suggested vegetables: asparagus, bamboo shoots, bean sprouts, carrots, celery, cucumbers, eggplant, green beans, peas, spinach, tomatoes, water chestnuts, zucchini.)

Before you begin, remember the most important rule of stir-frying: Always have the vegetables chopped and the sauces mixed before you start. (You can easily turn this into a complete meal by adding tofu to the stir-fry and serving over brown rice.)

Makes 4 servings

Sauce:

2	tablespoons reduced-sodium (or regular) soy sauce
2	tablespoons sherry
2	tablespoons water

Cornstarch Mixture:

1	teaspoon cornstarch
1	tablespoon water

Vegetables:

2	teaspoons vegetable oil
3	cloves garlic, finely chopped
1	teaspoon finely chopped fresh ginger root
1 1/2	cups cauliflower, cut into flowerets
1 1/2	cups broccoli, cut into flowerets
1	large onion, sliced vertically
1	cup sliced red or green bell pepper
1	cup thinly sliced mushrooms
12	snow peas
3	cups coarsely shredded Chinese cabbage

In a small bowl or custard cup, combine sauce ingredients. In another bowl, combine cornstarch and water, stirring to dissolve cornstarch. Add 1 tablespoon of the sauce to the cornstarch mixture.

Heat oil in a large nonstick skillet or wok over medium-high heat. Add garlic and ginger root and cook 10 seconds.

Add cauliflower and broccoli, along with about a third of the sauce. Cook, stirring constantly with a tossing motion, 2 minutes.

Add onion and bell pepper, along with another third of the sauce. Continue to cook and stir, 2 minutes more.

Add mushrooms and snow peas with remaining sauce. Cook and stir, 1 minute.

Add cabbage. Cook and stir, 1 minute.

Stir cornstarch mixture and add to vegetables. Cook, stirring until vegetables are glazed, about 30 seconds.

Each serving provides:

106	Calories	16 g	Carbohydrate
4 g	Protein	324 mg	Sodium
3 g	Total fat (2 g sat. fat)	0 mg	Cholesterol

Hot and Sour Cauliflower and Carrots

The fiery Hunan flavors of garlic, ginger, and peppers sparkle under a sweet and sour glaze in this colorful and tasty dish.

Makes 4 servings

Sauce:

1/2   cup *Vegetable Broth,* or 1/2 cup of water plus 1/2 teaspoon *Vegetable Broth Mix* (See pages 26–27.)

2   tablespoons each vinegar and reduced-sodium (or regular) soy sauce

1/4   teaspoon sugar

Cornstarch Mixture:

2   teaspoons cornstarch dissolved in 2 tablespoons water

Vegetables:

2   teaspoons vegetable oil

1   tablespoon finely chopped fresh ginger root

5   large cloves garlic, finely chopped

1/2   teaspoon crushed red pepper flakes

4   cups cauliflower, cut into small flowerets

2   cups carrots, sliced crosswise into diagonal slices 1/8-inch thick

12   snow peas

In a small bowl, combine sauce ingredients. In another bowl, combine cornstarch and water, stirring to dissolve cornstarch.

Heat oil in a large nonstick skillet or wok over medium-high heat. Add ginger root, garlic, and red pepper flakes. Cook 10 seconds. Add cauliflower and carrots, along with about a third of the sauce. Cook, stirring constantly, 3 to 4 minutes, until vegetables are tender-crisp. Add snow peas and another third of the sauce. Cook and stir, 1 minute.

Stir remaining sauce into cornstarch mixture. Add to skillet. Cook and stir, until vegetables are glazed, about 30 seconds.

Each serving provides:

95	Calories	16 g	Carbohydrate
4 g	Protein	349 mg	Sodium
3 g	Total fat (0 g sat. fat)	0 mg	Cholesterol

Gingered Asparagus and Tomatoes

The Japanese emphasis on the appearance of food is evident in this colorful dish. And the flavor of the fresh vegetables, sparkling under a glaze of ginger, soy sauce, and sherry, is truly unbeatable.

Makes 4 servings

1	tablespoon sherry
1	tablespoon reduced-sodium (or regular) soy sauce
1	teaspoon water
1	teaspoon cornstarch
2	teaspoons vegetable oil
1	teaspoon finely chopped fresh ginger root
1	pound fresh asparagus, cut diagonally into 1 1/2-inch lengths (Discard woody ends.)
4	green onions, cut into 1-inch lengths (green and white parts)
1 1/2	cups sliced mushrooms
2	medium, ripe (yet firm) tomatoes, cut vertically into small wedges

In a small bowl or custard cup, combine sherry, soy sauce, water, and cornstarch. Stir to dissolve cornstarch. Set aside.

Heat oil in a large nonstick skillet or wok over medium-high heat. Add ginger. Cook for 10 seconds.

Add asparagus and green onions to skillet and cook, stirring constantly, for 3 to 4 minutes, until asparagus is tender-crisp. Add mushrooms. Cook and stir, 1 minute.

Stir soy mixture and add to skillet along with tomatoes. Cook and stir for about 30 seconds, until vegetables are glazed.

Serve right away.

Each serving provides:

69	Calories	9 g	Carbohydrate
3 g	Protein	161 mg	Sodium
3 g	Total fat (0 g sat. fat)	0 mg	Cholesterol

Steamed Broccoli with Hoisin Sauce

Steaming is one of the most popular ways to cook food in the Asian countries. Often a sauce such as hoisin is used as a condiment to add the touch of spice that the Chinese feel helps to bring out the subtler flavors of vegetables. (Look for hoisin sauce in Oriental grocery stores and in the imported foods section of many large grocery stores. I haven't found a vegetable yet that it doesn't excite.)

Makes 4 servings

1/4	cup hoisin sauce
1 1/2	tablespoons honey
1	tablespoon lemon juice (preferably fresh)
1/4	teaspoon ground ginger
1/4	teaspoon garlic powder
4	cups broccoli, cut into flowerets

In a small bowl, combine hoisin sauce, honey, lemon juice, ginger, and garlic powder. Mix well and set aside.

Place a steamer rack in the bottom of a medium saucepan. Add enough water to come almost up to the bottom of the rack. Place saucepan over medium heat. When water boils, add broccoli, cover saucepan, and cook 8 minutes or until broccoli is just tender-crisp.

Arrange broccoli on a serving platter. Spoon sauce over broccoli and serve right away.

Each serving provides:

73	Calories	16 g	Carbohydrate
3 g	Protein	535 mg	Sodium
0 g	Total fat (0 g sat. fat)	0 mg	Cholesterol

VONNIE

Grilled Eggplant with Sesame-Soy Marinade

The long, thin Chinese or Japanese eggplants that are about the size of a zucchini are ideal for this Japanese dish. If they are not available, use small, tender eggplants, rather than very large ones, which are often bitter and full of seeds. You can broil the eggplant, but grilling over hot coals intensifies the delicious flavor of the marinade.

Makes 4 servings

1 1/2	tablespoons reduced-sodium (or regular) soy sauce
1 1/2	tablespoons sherry
1	teaspoon sesame oil
1/2	teaspoon sugar
3	cloves garlic, crushed
1 1/4	pounds eggplant, unpeeled, sliced crosswise into 3/4-inch slices

In a small bowl or custard cup, combine soy sauce, sherry, sesame oil, sugar, and garlic. Let stand for a half hour.

Arrange the eggplant slices in a single layer on a tray or piece of wax paper. Using half the marinade, baste the tops of the slices. Let stand 10 minutes.

Oil the grill rack lightly or spray with a nonstick cooking spray. Place on grill over hot coals. Place eggplant on rack, marinade-side down. Cook about 3 to 5 minutes on each side or until eggplant is browned and edges are crisp, turning the slices once and basting with remaining marinade.

If broiling, oil the broiler rack lightly or spray with a nonstick cooking spray. Place eggplant on the rack, marinade-side up. Basting with marinade, broil 3 to 5 minutes on each side, until eggplant is browned and edges are crisp.

Each serving provides:

66	Calories	11 g	Carbohydrate
2 g	Protein	232 mg	Sodium
2 g	Total fat (0 g sat. fat)	0 mg	Cholesterol

Sweet Potatoes with Ginger and Peanuts

Sweet potatoes are a popular ingredient in the daily Vietnamese diet, where vegetables are the basic food of the country people. This easy recipe has a delicate flavor, topped off with the delightful crunch of peanuts. In its homeland, it is often served for breakfast.

Makes 4 servings

2	cups water
1/4	cup sugar
1	teaspoon grated fresh ginger root
2	large sweet potatoes, peeled and cut into 1-inch chunks (1 1/4 pounds total)
	Salt and pepper to taste
3	tablespoons coarsely chopped dry roasted peanuts (unsalted)

Place water, sugar, and ginger root in a large saucepan. Bring to a boil over medium heat. Add sweet potatoes. Cover and cook 10 to 15 minutes, until sweet potatoes are tender, but not mushy.

Drain sweet potatoes in a colander and place in a serving bowl. Sprinkle with salt, pepper, and chopped peanuts.

Serve right away.

Each serving provides:

172	Calories	33 g	Carbohydrate
3 g	Protein	14 mg	Sodium
4 g	Total fat (1 g sat. fat)	0 mg	Cholesterol

Spicy Turnip and Carrot Medley

This sizzling medley of two favorite Chinese root vegetables has lots of garlic and ginger, giving it a wonderful spicy flavor. The hoisin sauce (available in Asian grocery stores and many large supermarkets) also adds a bit of zip.

Makes 4 servings

3	tablespoons hoisin sauce
2	teaspoons sugar
1	cup water
2	teaspoons vegetable oil
2	large cloves garlic, sliced lengthwise into paper-thin slices
2	teaspoons grated fresh ginger root
2	cups carrots, cut in half lengthwise, then cut crosswise into 1-inch pieces
2	cups turnips, peeled and cut into 1-inch cubes

Combine hoisin sauce and sugar in a small bowl. Gradually stir in 2/3 cup of the water, mixing until blended. Set aside.

Heat oil in a large nonstick skillet over medium-high heat. Add garlic and ginger and cook for 10 seconds. Add carrots and hoisin mixture. Mix well, then cover and cook 5 minutes.

Uncover and add turnips and remaining 1/3 cup of water. Cook, stirring frequently, 3 to 5 minutes, until vegetables are tender-crisp and glazed with the sauce. (There will be very little sauce left in the pan.)

Each serving provides:

90	Calories	16 g	Carbohydrate
2 g	Protein	446 mg	Sodium
3 g	Total fat (0 g sat. fat)	0 mg	Cholesterol

Stir-Fried Garlic Green Beans

Based on a delicious Szechuan dish, green beans and garlic are cooked until just tender-crisp and glazed with soy sauce.

Makes 4 servings

Soy Mixture:
1/4	cup water
2	tablespoons *each* sherry and reduced-sodium (or regular) soy sauce
1/2	teaspoon sugar

Cornstarch Mixture:
1	tablespoon water
1	teaspoon *each* cornstarch and reduced-sodium (or regular) soy sauce

Green Beans:
1	teaspoon sesame oil
1	pound green beans, ends trimmed and strings removed
5	cloves garlic, finely chopped

In a small bowl, combine all ingredients for soy mixture. Set aside.
In another small bowl, combine all ingredients for cornstarch mixture. Stir to dissolve cornstarch. Set aside.

Heat oil in a large nonstick skillet or wok over medium-high heat. Add green beans and garlic. Cook, stirring constantly, 3 minutes or until garlic is lightly browned. Reduce heat to medium, add soy mixture, cover skillet right away and cook for 1 minute. Add about 3 tablespoons of water, replace cover, and cook for 4 minutes or until beans are just tender-crisp. (Stir beans occasionally and add small amounts of water, about a tablespoon at a time, to keep beans and garlic from sticking.)

Uncover skillet. Stir cornstarch mixture and pour over beans. Cook, stirring constantly, until beans are glazed, about 1 minute.

Each serving provides:

68	Calories	11 g	Carbohydrate
3 g	Protein	357 mg	Sodium
1 g	Total fat (0 g sat. fat)	0 mg	Cholesterol

Indonesian Fried Rice

*Fried rice (*nasi goreng*) is a great favorite in Indonesia. It has a wonderful, fragrant combination of flavors. I substituted brown rice for white rice and eliminated the fried egg that often adorns the top of the finished dish. If you like, you can stir-fry strips of tofu along with the onions and turn this side dish for six into a filling entrée for four.*

Makes 6 servings

2	tablespoons reduced-sodium (or regular) soy sauce
1 1/2	tablespoons molasses
1 1/2	teaspoons curry powder
1/2	teaspoon ground coriander
1/4	teaspoon ground cumin
2	teaspoons vegetable oil
1	cup chopped onion
2	cloves garlic, crushed
1	teaspoon grated fresh ginger root
1/2	teaspoon crushed red pepper flakes (optional)
3	cups cooked brown rice (preferably cold)
3	green onions, thinly sliced (green and white parts)
3	tablespoons dry roasted peanuts (unsalted), chopped

In a small bowl or custard cup, combine soy sauce, molasses, curry powder, coriander, and cumin. Mix well and set aside.

Heat oil in a large nonstick skillet over medium heat. Add onion, garlic, ginger root, and red pepper flakes. Cook, stirring frequently, 3 minutes.

Add rice and soy sauce mixture. Cook, stirring constantly, 2 minutes or until rice is hot and sizzling and soy sauce is evenly distributed. Remove from heat and stir in green onions. Spoon into a serving bowl and sprinkle with peanuts.

Each serving provides:

182	Calories	31 g	Carbohydrate
4 g	Protein	210 mg	Sodium
5 g	Total fat (1 g sat. fat)	0 mg	Cholesterol

Pineapple Fried Rice

This is my easy version of a popular Thai dish that is often served in hollowed out pineapple shells, doubling as a tasty dish as well as an attractive centerpiece. It makes a perfect accompaniment to almost any Asian entrée.

Makes 6 servings

2 1/2	tablespoons reduced sodium (or regular) soy sauce
1/4	teaspoon garlic powder
1/4	teaspoon ground ginger
2	teaspoons vegetable oil
1/2	cup chopped onion
1	cup canned crushed pineapple (packed in juice), drained well
4	cups cooked brown rice

In a small bowl or custard cup, combine soy sauce, garlic powder, and ginger. Set aside.

Heat oil in a large nonstick skillet over medium-high heat. Add onion. Cook and stir, 2 minutes. Add pineapple and continue to cook and stir 2 more minutes.

Add rice and soy sauce mixture. Cook, stirring with a tossing motion, until rice is heated through and starts to sizzle.

Each serving provides:

192	Calories	38 g	Carbohydrate
4 g	Protein	257 mg	Sodium
3 g	Total fat (0 g sat. fat)	0 mg	Cholesterol

Rice with Almonds and Pine Nuts

This tasty dish comes from Korea, where nuts and seeds play a fairly large role in the country's cuisine. Sweet dishes such as this are often served with highly spiced foods.

Makes 6 servings

2 1/2   cups water
1   cup brown rice, uncooked
1/4   cup coarsely chopped almonds
3   tablespoons pine nuts
3   tablespoons honey
1 1/2   tablespoons reduced-sodium (or regular) soy sauce

Bring water to a boil in a medium saucepan. Add rice. When water boils again, reduce heat to low, cover, and simmer 45 minutes, until rice is tender and most of the liquid has cooked out. Remove from heat and let stand covered, 5 minutes.

While rice is cooking, heat a small nonstick skillet over medium-high heat. Spray with a nonstick cooking spray. Place almonds and pine nuts in skillet and cook, stirring constantly, just until nuts are lightly toasted. (Watch them carefully as they burn quickly.)

Spoon hot rice into a serving bowl and add nuts, along with honey and soy sauce. Mix well.

Serve hot.

Each serving provides:

205	Calories	35 g	Carbohydrate
5 g	Protein	153 mg	Sodium
6 g	Total fat (1 g sat. fat)	0 mg	Cholesterol

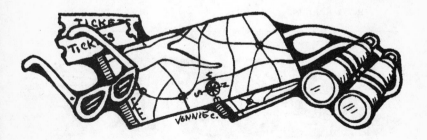

Coconut Rice with Corn and Peanuts

This Vietnamese recipe is typical of the native rice dishes. I've replaced the original coconut milk with a combination of skim milk and coconut extract, and greatly decreased the amount of peanuts used in some of the more authentic versions. The result is still an unusual and very pleasing combination of flavors and textures. Served with any of the tofu dishes in this chapter, you'll have a wonderful international dinner.

Makes 6 servings

2 1/2	cups water
1	cup brown rice, uncooked
1	cup skim milk
1	teaspoon coconut extract
1/4	teaspoon salt
1	tablespoon sugar
1	cup salt-free (or regular) canned corn, drained
	Salt and pepper to taste
3	tablespoons coarsely chopped dry roasted peanuts (unsalted)

Bring water to a boil in a medium saucepan. Add rice. When water boils again, reduce heat to low, cover, and simmer 40 to 45 minutes, until water has been absorbed.

Combine milk, coconut extract, salt, and sugar, and stir into rice along with corn. Cover and keep on low heat for 5 to 10 minutes.

Spoon rice into a shallow serving bowl. Sprinkle lightly with salt and liberally with pepper. Top with peanuts.

Serve right away.

	Each serving provides:		
191	Calories	35 g	Carbohydrate
6 g	Protein	115 mg	Sodium
4 g	Total fat (1 g sat. fat)	1 mg	Cholesterol

Exotic Rice Salad

Based on the flavors of several Asian cuisines, this salad is a delicious combination of color, flavor, and texture.

Makes 8 servings

1	cup brown rice, uncooked
2 1/2	cups water
1/4	cup orange juice
2	teaspoons vegetable oil
1	teaspoon sesame oil
2	tablespoons reduced-sodium (or regular) soy sauce
1	teaspoon *each* honey and cider vinegar
2	cloves garlic, crushed
	A few drops bottled hot sauce, or more to taste
1/2	cup crushed pineapple (packed in juice), drained slightly
1/2	cup sliced water chestnuts, each slice cut into quarters
1/2	cup finely chopped red bell pepper
1/4	cup *each* finely chopped onion and celery
1/4	cup raisins
1	tablespoon sesame seeds

Bring water to a boil in a medium saucepan over medium heat. Add rice. When water boils again, reduce heat to low, cover, and simmer 45 minutes. Remove from heat and let stand covered, 5 minutes.

In a small bowl, combine orange juice, both oils, soy sauce, honey, vinegar, garlic, and hot sauce. Add to rice and mix well. Add remaining ingredients. Mix well, cover, and chill several hours or overnight.

Mix again before serving.

Serve cold.

Each serving provides:

152	Calories	29 g	Carbohydrate
3 g	Protein	158 mg	Sodium
3 g	Total fat (0 g sat. fat)	0 mg	Cholesterol

Stir-Fried Noodles in Ginger-Orange Sauce

Noodles are one of the staples of Chinese cooking, often stir-fried with vegetables and spices and served as just one of several main dishes. (Whole wheat noodles (somen) are available at Oriental grocery stores, health food stores, and many large grocery stores.) Very thin spaghetti can be substituted in a pinch, but the flavor and texture are just not the same.

Makes 4 servings

8   ounces Oriental whole wheat noodles, uncooked

Sauce:
1/2   cup water
1/2   cup orange juice
3   tablespoons reduced-sodium (or regular) soy sauce
1 1/2 tablespoons vinegar
1   tablespoon sugar
2   teaspoons cornstarch

Vegetables:
2   teaspoons vegetable oil
1   tablespoon finely chopped fresh ginger root
1 1/2 teaspoons grated fresh orange peel
1   teaspoon crushed red pepper flakes (optional)
1   cup thinly sliced onion, sliced vertically
1   cup thinly sliced red bell pepper
3   green onions (green and white parts), cut into 1-inch lengths
2   cups thinly sliced Chinese cabbage

Cook noodles according to package directions. Drain.

In a small bowl, combine all sauce ingredients, stirring to dissolve cornstarch. Set aside.

Heat oil in a large nonstick skillet over medium-high heat. Add ginger root, orange peel, and red pepper flakes. Cook 10 seconds.

Add onion and bell pepper. Cook, stirring constantly, 2 minutes. Add green onions and cabbage. Cook and stir, 1 minute. Add drained noodles. Cook and stir, 1 minute.

Stir sauce mixture and add to skillet. Cook and stir, until sauce has thickened and noodles are glazed, about 30 seconds.

Serve right away.

Each serving provides:

294	Calories	59 g	Carbohydrate
9 g	Protein	1501 mg	Sodium
3 g	Total fat (0 g sat. fat)	0 mg	Cholesterol

Stir-Fried Noodles with Mushrooms and Garlic

This delicious noodle dish can be made with "regular" mushrooms or a combination of different varieties. Many large grocery stores now carry packages containing a mixed variety of fresh mushrooms and they work quite well, each type of mushroom adding its own delicate flavor. (As with other noodle dishes, very thin spaghetti will work, but the flavor is so much better with the Oriental noodles.)

Makes 4 servings

8   ounces Oriental whole wheat noodles, uncooked

Sauce:
1   cup *Vegetable Broth,* or 1 cup of water plus 1 teaspoon
     Vegetable Broth Mix (See pages 26–27.)
3   tablespoons reduced-sodium (or regular) soy sauce
2   teaspoons cornstarch

Mushrooms:
2   teaspoons vegetable oil
6   large cloves garlic, sliced lengthwise into paper-thin slices
3   cups sliced mushrooms
5   green onions, cut into 1-inch lengths (green and white parts)

Cook noodles according to package directions. Drain.

In a small bowl, combine all sauce ingredients, stirring to dissolve cornstarch. Set aside.

Heat oil in a large nonstick skillet or wok over medium-high heat. Add garlic. Cook 10 seconds. Add mushrooms and green onions. Cook, stirring constantly, 2 minutes. Add noodles to skillet. Cook and stir, 1 minute.

Stir sauce mixture and add to skillet. Cook adn stir, until sauce has thickened and noodles are glazed, about 30 seconds.

Serve right away.

Each serving provides:

267	Calories	51 g	Carbohydrate
9 g	Protein	1527 mg	Sodium
3 g	Total fat (0 g sat. fat)	0 mg	Cholesterol

Honey Sweet Noodles

My brother Richard created this very easy noodle dish, inspired by his travels to Indonesia and Thailand. It makes a perfect accompaniment to almost any Asian entrée and its mild, sweet flavor enhances, rather than competes with, other foods.

Makes 6 servings

1	8-ounce package thin Oriental whole wheat noodles (or linguine)
2	tablespoons creamy-style peanut butter (Choose one without added sugar or fat.)
2	tablespoons reduced-sodium (or regular) soy sauce
2	tablespoons honey
1	tablespoon very finely chopped dry roasted peanuts, unsalted (optional)

Cook noodles according to package directions. Drain.

While noodles are cooking, place peanut butter in a small bowl. Gradually stir in soy sauce and then honey, stirring until mixture is smooth.

Place drained noodles in a serving bowl. Drizzle sauce over noodles and mix well. Sprinkle with chopped peanuts, if desired.

Serve right away.

Each serving provides:

193	Calories	35 g	Carbohydrate
6 g	Protein	917 mg	Sodium
3 g	Total fat (0 g sat. fat)	0 mg	Cholesterol

Asparagus Noodle Salad
with Orange-Soy Vinaigrette

In the warm climate of Hunan province in southwestern China, cold noodle dishes are extremely popular. This one features some of the more prominent seasonings of Chinese cuisine and is always a crowd pleaser.

Makes 6 servings

1	8-ounce package thin Oriental whole wheat noodles (or linguine)
3/4	pound asparagus, cut diagonally into 1 1/2 inch pieces (Discard woody ends.)
1/2	cup orange juice
2	tablespoons reduced-sodium (or regular) soy sauce
1	tablespoon sesame oil
2	teaspoons vinegar
2	cloves garlic, crushed
1	teaspoon grated fresh ginger root
1	teaspoon grated fresh orange peel
1/4	teaspoon sugar
	Dash hot pepper sauce, or to taste
1/2	cup sliced green onions (green part only)

Prepare noodles according to package directions.

Place asparagus pieces in a colander. To drain the noodles, pour them into the colander over the asparagus. (The hot water and noodles will lightly steam the asparagus.) Leave noodles in the colander on top of asparagus for 10 minutes.

In a large bowl, combine remaining ingredients, mixing well. Add noodles and asparagus. Mix gently, until well combined.

Chill several hours or overnight, mixing several times.

Mix again just before serving.

Serve cold.

Each serving provides:

179	Calories	33 g	Carbohydrate
6 g	Protein	898 mg	Sodium
3 g	Total fat (0 g sat. fat)	0 mg	Cholesterol

Szechuan Cold Noodles

*In most Asian countries, where people tend to waste very little, leftover noo-
dles are often made into salads and served cold. In this dish the flavors of the
Szechuan province of China combine to make a salad that has the crunch of
fresh vegetables, the mellow flavor of peanut butter, and the fire of hot sauce.*

Makes 4 servings

1	8-ounce package thin Oriental whole wheat noodles (or linguine)
2	cups fresh bean sprouts
1	cup red bell pepper, cut into matchstick-size pieces
1	cup snow peas, cut into 1-inch pieces
1/4	cup thinly sliced green onions (green and white parts)
2	tablespoons water
2	tablespoons creamy-style peanut butter (Choose one without added sugar or fat.)
3	tablespoons reduced-sodium (or regular) soy sauce
1	tablespoon red wine vinegar
2	teaspoons sesame oil
2	teaspoons honey
3	large cloves garlic, crushed
1/2	teaspoon grated fresh ginger root
	A few drops bottled hot sauce, to taste

Cook noodles according to package directions. Drain.

In a large bowl, combine cooked noodles, bean sprouts, bell pepper, snow peas, and green onions. Toss to combine.

In a small bowl, gradually stir water into peanut butter, stirring
until smooth. Add remaining ingredients. Mix with a fork or wire
whisk until well blended. Spoon over noodle mixture. Toss until noodles are evenly coated.

Chill several hours or overnight to blend flavors.

Mix well before serving. Serve cold.

Each serving provides:

334	Calories	56 g	Carbohydrate
12 g	Protein	1531 mg	Sodium
7 g	Total fat (1 g sat. fat)	0 mg	Cholesterol

Chinese Almond Cream

I first tasted this Chinese specialty many years ago. As an almond lover, it's been a favorite of mine ever since. The original version was topped with kumquats in syrup, but I have found that the pineapple-apricot combination enhances the almond flavor. For a special touch, you can also top it with a small sprinkling of slivered almonds.

Makes 12 servings

3	cups skim milk
1/4	cup plus 1 tablespoon cornstarch
1/4	cup sugar
1	teaspoon almond extract

Topping:

1	cup canned crushed pineapple (packed in juice), drained slightly
2	tablespoons fruit-only apricot spread
1/8	teaspoon almond extract

Lightly oil an 8-inch square baking pan or spray with a nonstick cooking spray.

In a small saucepan, combine milk, cornstarch, and sugar. Mix well, stirring until cornstarch is dissolved.

Bring mixture to a boil over medium-low heat, stirring constantly. Continue to cook and stir for 2 to 3 minutes more. Remove from heat and stir in almond extract. Pour into prepared pan. Cool slightly, then cover and chill thoroughly.

In a small bowl, combine topping ingredients. Mix well, cover, and chill.

To serve, cut almond cream into squares or diamonds, place each one in an individual serving bowl and top with 1 1/2 tablespoons of topping.

Each serving provides:

74	Calories	15 g	Carbohydrate
2 g	Protein	32 mg	Sodium
0 g	Total fat (0 g sat. fat)	1 mg	Cholesterol

Lychee Fruit Salad

Lychees, the fruits of a Chinese tree, have a sweet, perfumy flavor all their own. They come packed in cans and jars and are sold in Oriental markets and many large grocery stores. (I have never found lychees packed in water or light syrup, so I buy the ones in heavy syrup and rinse and drain them several times.) In this dish, the lychees are stuffed with pieces of pineapple and marinated in orange juice and sherry, making a very cool, refreshing way to end an Oriental meal.

Makes 6 servings

1	1-pound can lychees, rinsed and drained
1	8-ounce can pineapple tidbits (packed in juice), drained
1	large orange, peeled and sectioned (Discard white membrane.)
1/4	cup orange juice
3	tablespoons sherry
3	tablespoons honey
2	teaspoons lemon juice

Place a piece of pineapple inside each lychee. Place lychees in a large bowl and add the remaining pineapple. Cut each orange section into thirds and add to lychees.

In a small bowl, combine remaining ingredients. Mix until honey is completely incorporated into the juices. Pour over lychees.

Cover and chill several hours or overnight. Stir several times while chilling.

Each serving provides:

126	Calories	31 g	Carbohydrate
1 g	Protein	21 mg	Sodium
0 g	Total fat (0 g sat. fat)	0 mg	Cholesterol

Hot Orange Dessert Soup

In China this soothing, hot dessert soup is served in small bowls and garnished with assorted fruits, such as cherries and thin slices of papaya. It's usually made with tapioca flour, however, I used cornstarch because of its availability. (You can chill the leftover soup and eat it like pudding.)

Makes 4 servings

2	cups orange juice
1/4	cup sugar
2	tablespoons cornstarch
2	large oranges, peeled and sectioned, each section cut into three or four pieces (Discard white membranes.)
1/4	teaspoon orange extract
1/16	teaspoon vanilla extract

In a small saucepan, combine orange juice, sugar, and cornstarch. Mix well, stirring until cornstarch is completely dissolved.

Bring mixture to a boil over medium heat, stirring constantly. Continue to cook and stir, 1 to 2 minutes. Remove from heat and add orange pieces and extracts. Mix well, spoon into small bowls and serve right away.

Each serving provides:

165	Calories	40 g	Carbohydrate
2 g	Protein	2 mg	Sodium
0 g	Total fat (0 g sat. fat)	0 mg	Cholesterol

Anise Pears

Aniseed is used widely in Chinese cooking, both in entrées and in desserts, adding a sweet, licorice-like flavor to foods. Any variety of firm, ripe pears can be used in this refreshing dish, but you may have to adjust the cooking time according to the texture and ripeness of the pears.

Makes 4 servings

1/2	cup water
1/4	cup sugar
1	teaspoon lemon juice
1/4	teaspoon aniseed, crushed
3	large pears (or 4 medium ones), peeled, cored, and cut into quarters (1 pound total)

In a small saucepan, combine water, sugar, lemon juice, and aniseed. Bring to a boil over medium heat, stirring occasionally. Add pears.

When water returns to a boil, reduce heat slightly, cover saucepan, and simmer until pears are just tender, about 6 to 10 minutes.

Cool slightly, then place in a shallow bowl and chill.

Each serving provides:

111	Calories	28 g	Carbohydrate
0 g	Protein	0 mg	Sodium
0 g	Total fat (0 g sat. fat)	0 mg	Cholesterol

Philippine Citrus Custards

This dessert from the Philippine Islands combines the zests (peels) of lemon, lime, and orange for a delightful citrus flavor. I made a few changes from the original version, substituting egg whites and evaporated skim milk for the eggs and cream, and creating my own version of the usual caramelized sugar topping. The results, are light and refreshing.

Makes 4 servings

1	12-ounce can evaporated skim milk (1 1/2 cups)
4	egg whites
1/3	cup sugar
2	teaspoons (total) grated fresh lemon, lime, and orange peel (Try to mix equal amounts of all three peels.)
1	teaspoon vanilla extract

Topping:

4	teaspoons maple syrup
1/4	teaspoon lemon extract

Preheat oven to 325°.

Lightly oil four six-ounce custard cups or spray with a nonstick cooking spray.

In a small bowl, combine all custard ingredients. Beat thouroughly with a fork or wire whisk for several minutes. Pour mixture into prepared custard cups. Place cups in a baking pan and pour enough hot water into the larger pan to come halfway up the sides of the cups.

Bake 50 minutes or until custard is set.

Remove cups to a rack to cool slightly, then chill.

To serve, run a sharp knife around the sides of the custard and invert onto four individual serving plates. Combine maple syrup and lemon extract and spoon onto the top of each custard. Serve right away.

Each serving provides:			
189	Calories	33 g	Carbohydrate
11 g	Protein	166 mg	Sodium
1 g	Total fat (0 g sat. fat)	4 mg	Cholesterol

Thai Fried Bananas

In Thai meals the dessert rarely steals the show. A simple fruit dessert provides a refreshing touch after a meal of many flavors. These "fried" bananas are worth the last minute preparation and they are always in keeping with the spirit of a Thai meal.

Makes 2 servings

1/4	cup orange juice
2	tablespoons firmly packed brown sugar
1	teaspoon coconut extract
2	medium, ripe (yet firm) bananas, cut in half crosswise, then each piece cut in half lengthwise
1	teaspoon lime juice, freshly squeezed

In a medium nonstick skillet, combine orange juice, brown sugar, and coconut extract. Heat over medium heat, stirring occasionally, until mixture is hot and bubbly. Add bananas to pan and cook 1 minute, then turn bananas and cook 1 minute more. Place bananas in serving bowls, top with pan juices, and drizzle with lime juice.

Serve right away.

	Each serving provides:		
174	Calories	44 g	Carbohydrate
1 g	Protein	7 mg	Sodium
1 g	Total fat (0 g sat. fat)	0 mg	Cholesterol

Oranges in Cinnamon Syrup

Boiling the syrup really intensifies the sweet cinnamon flavor of this cool, fresh dessert that comes from Korea. It's often made with tangerines, however I really prefer the unbeatable sweetness of navel oranges. It's a perfect way to end a spicy meal. (It's also fantastic over vanilla ice milk!)

Makes 6 servings

1	cup orange juice
1	cup water
$1/2$	cup sugar
$1/2$	teaspoon ground cinnamon
6	medium oranges, peeled and sectioned (Discard white membranes.)

In a small saucepan, combine orange juice, water, sugar, and cinnamon. Bring to a boil over medium heat. Reduce heat slightly and cook 40 to 45 minutes, or until you have about half the amount of syrup you started with. Remove from heat and let syrup cool for about 10 minutes.

Place orange sections in a medium bowl. Add syrup and mix gently.

Chill.

Each serving provides:

153	Calories	39 g	Carbohydrate
1 g	Protein	1 mg	Sodium
0 g	Total fat (0 g sat. fat)	0 mg	Cholesterol

Pineapple-Lemon Rice

This truly delectable dish is based on a dessert from Vietnam. The rice is simmered in pineapple juice and laced with lemon and brown sugar. It's at its best when served warm and makes a great (although non-traditional) accompaniment to a scoop of vanilla ice milk.

Makes 6 servings

1	20-ounce can crushed pineapple (packed in juice), drained (Juice reserved.)
1	teaspoon grated fresh lemon peel
3/4	cup brown rice, uncooked
1 1/2	teaspoons vanilla extract
2 1/2	tablespoons firmly packed brown sugar

Add water to pineapple juice to equal 1 3/4 cups and place in a medium saucepan. Add lemon peel. Bring to a boil over medium heat.

Stir rice into saucepan. When juice returns to a boil, cover, reduce heat to medium-low, and simmer 40 minutes, until most of the liquid has cooked out.

Stir in pineapple, vanilla extract, and brown sugar. Mix well, cover and continue to cook 10 minutes more. Let stand, covered, until serving time.

Serve warm.

Each serving provides:

168	Calories	39 g	Carbohydrate
2 g	Protein	5 mg	Sodium
1 g	Total fat (0 g sat. fat)	0 mg	Cholesterol

Honey-Sesame Biscuits

In the Peking region of China, sesame biscuits are made by folding dough over and over to create layers, then the dough is cut into biscuits, deep-fried, rolled in honey, and sprinkled with sesame seeds. Although not quite authentic, I've come up with a shortcut using refrigerator biscuits that are baked with honey and sesame seeds. Served hot or lukewarm, for breakfast or dessert, they're really a treat.

Makes 10 biscuits

1	10-ounce package refrigerator biscuits
1/3	cup honey
1 1/2	tablespoons sesame seeds

Preheat oven to 400°.

Line a baking sheet with aluminum foil. Oil it lightly or spray with a nonstick cooking spray. (The foil will make cleanup easier. These biscuits get very sticky.)

Place the honey in a small saucepan and heat over low heat until warm. Leave on heat to keep warm.

Place biscuits on prepared baking sheet. Baste them with honey and sprinkle them with sesame seeds, using about one fourth each of the honey and the seeds. Place in oven. Every 3 minutes, remove pan from oven, baste biscuits with honey, and sprinkle with seeds. (Use up all of the honey and seeds.)

Bake until biscuits are nicely browned, a total of about 15 minutes.

Remove biscuits from baking sheet right away and place on a serving plate that has been lightly sprayed with nonstick spray.

Serve hot or lukewarm.

Each serving provides:

126	Calories	22 g	Carbohydrate
2 g	Protein	301 mg	Sodium
5 g	Total fat (1 g sat. fat)	0 mg	Cholesterol

Index

International Conversion Chart

These are not exact equivalents: they have been slightly rounded
to make measuring easier.

LIQUID MEASUREMENTS

American	Imperial	Metric	Australian
2 tablespoons (1 oz.)	1 fl. oz.	30 ml	1 tablespoon
1/4 cup (2 oz.)	2 fl. oz.	60 ml	2 tablespoons
1/3 cup (3 oz.)	3 fl. oz.	80 ml	1/4 cup
1/2 cup (4 oz.)	4 fl. oz.	125 ml	1/3 cup
2/3 cup (5 oz.)	5 fl. oz.	165 ml	1/2 cup
3/4 cup (6 oz.)	6 fl. oz.	185 ml	2/3 cup
1 cup (8 oz.)	8 fl. oz.	250 ml	3/4 cup

SPOON MEASUREMENTS

American	Metric
1/4 teaspoon	1 ml
1/2 teaspoon	2 ml
1 teaspoon	5 ml
1 tablespoon	15 ml

WEIGHTS

US/UK	Metric
1 oz.	30 grams (g)
2 oz.	60 g
4 oz. (1/4 lb)	125 g
5 oz. (1/3 lb)	155 g
6 oz.	185 g
7 oz.	220 g
8 oz. (1/2 lb)	250 g
10 oz.	315 g
12 oz. (3/4 lb)	375 g
14 oz.	440 g
16 oz. (1 lb)	500 g
2 lbs	1 kg

OVEN TEMPERATURES

Farenheit	Centigrade	Gas
250	120	1/2
300	150	2
325	160	3
350	180	4
375	190	5
400	200	6
450	230	8